THE CAMBRIDGE COMPANION TO
RELIGION AND ARTIFICIAL INTELLIGENCE

Religion and artificial intelligence are now deeply enmeshed in humanity's collective imagination, narratives, institutions and aspirations. Their growing entanglement also runs counter to several dominant narratives that engage with long-standing historical discussions regarding the relationship between the 'sacred' and the 'secular' – technology and science. This Cambridge Companion explores the fields of religion and AI comprehensively and provides an authoritative guide to their symbiotic relationship. It examines established topics, such as transhumanism, together with new and emerging fields, notably, computer simulations of religion. Specific chapters are devoted to Judaism, Christianity, Islam, Hinduism and Buddhism, while others demonstrate that entanglements between religion and AI are not always encapsulated through such a paradigm. Collectively, the volume addresses issues that AI raises for religions and contributions that AI has made to religious studies, especially the conceptual and philosophical issues inherent in the concept of an intelligent machine, and social-cultural work on attitudes to AI and its impact on contemporary life. The diverse perspectives in this Companion demonstrate how all religions are now interacting with AI.

Beth Singler is Assistant Professor in Digital Religion(s) at the University of Zurich. Her first book, *Indigo Children: New Age Experimentation with Self and Science*, is the first ethnography of a New Age group who define their identity and spirituality in relation to their view of science. She is also the author of *Religion and AI: An Introduction*. She is a fellow of the International Society for Science and Religion, an associate fellow of Homerton College, University of Cambridge, an associate professor at the Digital Society Initiative, the University of Zurich, and a member of the Human Augmentation Research Network.

Fraser Watts is a former senior scientist at the UK Medical Research Council's Applied Psychology Unit in Cambridge and has served as President of the British Psychological Society. Until retirement he was Reader in Theology and Science in the University of Cambridge, Director of the Psychology and Religion Research Group and a fellow of Queens' College. He has also been President of the International Society for Science and Religion, of which he is now Executive Secretary. He is currently Visiting Professor in Psychology of Religion at the University of Lincoln.

CAMBRIDGE COMPANIONS TO RELIGION

This is a series of companions to major topics and key figures in theology and religious studies. Each volume contains specially commissioned chapters by international scholars, which provide an accessible and stimulating introduction to the subject for new readers and nonspecialists.

Other Titles in the Series

APOSTOLIC FATHERS Edited by Michael F. Bird and Scott Harrower

AMERICAN CATHOLICISM Edited by Margaret M. McGuinness and Thomas F. Rzeznik

AMERICAN ISLAM Edited by Juliane Hammer and Omid Safi

AMERICAN JUDAISM Edited by Dana Evan Kaplan

AMERICAN METHODISM Edited by Jason E. Vickers

AMERICAN PROTESTANTISM Edited by Jason E. Vickers and Jennifer Woodruff Tait

ANCIENT MEDITERRANEAN RELIGIONS Edited by Barbette Stanley Spaeth

APOCALYPTIC LITERATURE Edited by Colin McAllister

AUGUSTINE'S CITY OF GOD Edited by David Vincent Meconi

AUGUSTINE'S "CONFESSIONS" Edited by Tarmo Toom

KARL BARTH Edited by John Webster

THE BIBLE, 2nd edition Edited by Bruce Chilton

THE BIBLE AND LITERATURE Edited by Calum Carmichael

BIBLICAL INTERPRETATION Edited by John Barton

BLACK THEOLOGY Edited by Dwight N. Hopkins and Edward P. Antonio

DIETRICH BONHOEFFER Edited by John de Gruchy

JOHN CALVIN Edited by Donald K. McKim

CHRISTIAN DOCTRINE Edited by Colin Gunton

CHRISTIAN ETHICS Edited by Robin Gill

CHRISTIAN MYSTICISM Edited by Amy Hollywood and Patricia Z. Beckman

CHRISTIAN PHILOSOPHICAL THEOLOGY Edited by Charles Taliaferro and Chad V. Meister

CHRISTIAN POLITICAL THEOLOGY Edited by Craig Hovey and Elizabeth Phillips

CHRISTIANITY AND THE ENVIRONMENT Edited by Alexander J. B. Hampton and Douglas Hedley

THE CISTERCIAN ORDER Edited by Mette Birkedal Bruun

CLASSICAL ISLAMIC THEOLOGY Edited by Tim Winter

THE COUNCIL OF NICAEA Edited by Young Richard Kim

JONATHAN EDWARDS Edited by Stephen J. Stein

EVANGELICAL THEOLOGY Edited by Timothy Larsen and Daniel J. Treier

FEMINIST THEOLOGY Edited by Susan Frank Parsons

(continued after index)

THE CAMBRIDGE COMPANION TO
RELIGION AND ARTIFICIAL INTELLIGENCE

Edited by

Beth Singler
University of Zurich

Fraser Watts
University of Lincoln

Shaftesbury Road, Cambridge CB2 8EA, United Kingdom

One Liberty Plaza, 20th Floor, New York, NY 10006, USA

477 Williamstown Road, Port Melbourne, VIC 3207, Australia

314–321, 3rd Floor, Plot 3, Splendor Forum, Jasola District Centre, New Delhi – 110025, India

103 Penang Road, #05–06/07, Visioncrest Commercial, Singapore 238467

Cambridge University Press is part of Cambridge University Press & Assessment, a department of the University of Cambridge.

We share the University's mission to contribute to society through the pursuit of education, learning and research at the highest international levels of excellence.

www.cambridge.org
Information on this title: www.cambridge.org/9781316516034

DOI: 10.1017/9781009031721

© Cambridge University Press & Assessment 2024

This publication is in copyright. Subject to statutory exception and to the provisions of relevant collective licensing agreements, no reproduction of any part may take place without the written permission of Cambridge University Press & Assessment.

When citing this work, please include a reference to the
DOI 10.1017/9781009031721

First published 2024

A catalogue record for this publication is available from the British Library

Library of Congress Cataloging-in-Publication Data
NAMES: Singler, Beth, editor. | Watts, Fraser, editor.
TITLE: The Cambridge companion to religion and artificial intelligence / edited by Beth Singler, University of Zurich; Fraser Watts, University of Lincoln.
DESCRIPTION: 1. | Cambridge, United Kingdom : Cambridge University Press, 2024. | Series: Cambridge companions to religion | Includes bibliographical references and index.
IDENTIFIERS: LCCN 2023057155 | ISBN 9781316516034 (hardback) | ISBN 9781009031721 (ebook)
SUBJECTS: LCSH: Cyberspace – Religious aspects. | Computers – Religious aspects. | Transhumanism – Religious aspects. | Artificial intelligence.
CLASSIFICATION: LCC BL255.5 .C36 2024 | DDC 200.285/63–dc23/ eng/20240412
LC record available at https://lccn.loc.gov/2023057155

ISBN 978-1-316-51603-4 Hardback
ISBN 978-1-009-01365-9 Paperback

Cambridge University Press & Assessment has no responsibility for the persistence or accuracy of URLs for external or third-party internet websites referred to in this publication and does not guarantee that any content on such websites is, or will remain, accurate or appropriate.

Contents

	List of Contributors	*page* vii
	Acknowledgements	xi
1	Introduction	1
	BETH SINGLER AND FRASER WATTS	
2	Steps towards Android Intelligence	15
	WILLIAM CLOCKSIN	

Part I *Religions and AI*

3	Hinduism and Artificial Intelligence	33
	ROBERT M. GERACI AND STEPHEN KAPLAN	
4	The Buddha in AI/Robotics	50
	HANNAH GOULD AND KEIKO NISHIMURA	
5	Artificial Intelligence and Jewish Thought	69
	DAVID ZVI KALMAN	
6	Artificial Intelligence and Christianity: Friends or Foes?	88
	MARIUS DOROBANTU	
7	Islam and Artificial Intelligence	109
	YAQUB CHAUDHARY	

Part II *Social and Moral Issues*

8	Transhumanism and Transcendence	131
	ILIA DELIO	
9	The Eschatological Future of Artificial Intelligence: Saviour or Apocalypse?	148
	NOREEN HERZFELD	
10	AI Ethics and Ethical AI	165
	PAULA BODDINGTON	
11	Black Theology × Artificial Intelligence	182
	PHILIP BUTLER	

vi CONTENTS

| 12 | Imag(in)ing Human–Robot Relationships | 201 |
| | SCOTT MIDSON | |

Part III **_Religious Studies_**

13	The Anthropology and Sociology of Religion and AI	223
	BETH SINGLER	
14	Simulating Religion	241
	F. LERON SHULTS AND WESLEY J. WILDMAN	
15	Cognitive Modelling of Spiritual Practices	257
	FRASER WATTS	
16	Artificial Companions and Spiritual Enhancement	275
	YORICK WILKS	

| | *Bibliography* | 293 |
| | *Index* | 312 |

Contributors

Paula Boddington is Associate Professor of Philosophy and Healthcare in the Geller Institute of Aging and Memory at the University of West London. Much of her work has concerned applied topics in medicine, science and technology, with a particular focus on ethical and philosophical issues arising from artificial intelligence. She is the author of *Towards a Code of Ethics for Artificial Intelligence*. She holds degrees in philosophy, psychology and medical law. She has held academic posts at the University of Bristol, the University of Oxford and the Australian National University.

Philip Butler is an international scholar whose work primarily focuses on the intersections of neuroscience, technology, spirituality and Blackness. He uses the wisdom of these spaces to engage in critical and constructive analysis on Black posthumanism, artificial intelligence and pluriversal future realities. Dr Butler is Partner Director of Iliff's AI Institute where he leads the 8020 project, where the institute works to change how computers see people, relate to culturally iterative languages and build the bones for a data ownership model that hopefully creates a relational framework for the way AI is made around the globe. He is also the founder of the Seekr Project, a distinctly Black conversational artificial intelligence with mental health capacities. He is the author of *Black Transhuman Liberation Theology: Spirituality and Technology* and most recently the editor of *Critical Black Futures: Speculative Theories and Explorations*. He is currently working on his second monograph, *Still Black Posthuman: A Theory of Uncertainty and Disorder.*

Yaqub Chaudhary is a philosopher and scientist with research interests in the use of artificial intelligence and machine learning in and for science, and the use of AI in the mind and brain sciences. He specialises in the epistemology of AI and computational methods in science, as well as Islam and AI, and Islam and science more broadly. He completed his doctoral studies in physics at Imperial College London, followed by post-doctoral research in the field of plastic electronics. He then undertook a fellowship at Cambridge Muslim College where he began philosophical, theological and metaphysical inquiries into the nature of AI and digital technologies. He has written scholarly articles on Islam and AI, the use of AI in the ecological sciences and climate change research, the metaphysics of AI and emerging technologies such as the philosophy of augmented reality. He is currently an independent scholar and technologist working with general purpose AI and machine-learning technologies as part of his research interests in the epistemological limits of AI.

vii

LIST OF CONTRIBUTORS

William Clocksin is Emeritus Professor of Computer Science at the University of Hertfordshire, where he was Dean of the School of Computer Science. He previously held a research professorship at Oxford Brookes University and a lectureship at the University of Cambridge. His area of work is artificial intelligence, and he has developed software for analysis of Syriac manuscripts, automated inspection of ceramic tiles and problem solving using logical theorem proving. He is a priest in the Church of England and is currently serving in the Diocese of Cyprus and the Gulf.

Ilia Delio holds the Josephine C. Connelly Endowed Chair in Theology at Villanova University. Her area of research is systematic-constructive theology. She holds a doctorate in pharmacology from Rutgers University, Graduate School of Biomedical Sciences and a doctorate in historical theology from Fordham University. She is the author of twenty-four books, including *The Hours of the Universe: Reflections on God, Science and the Human Journey*, which won the 2022 Gold Nautilus Book Award, *Making All Things New: Catholicity, Cosmology and Consciousness*, a finalist for the 2019 Michael Ramsey Prize and *The Unbearable Wholeness of Being: God, Evolution and the Power of Love*, which won a 2014 Silver Nautilus Book Award and a 2014 Catholic Press Association Book Award. She is founder and Director of the Center for Christogenesis, an online spiritual and educational resource for the integration of science, religion and culture.

Marius Dorobantu is a researcher and lecturer at the Faculty of Religion and Theology, the Free University of Amsterdam, and a fellow of the International Society for Science and Religion. His award-winning doctoral dissertation, written at the University of Strasbourg, explored the potential theological implications of human-level artificial intelligence for the notions of human distinctiveness and the image of God. His first book, *Artificial Intelligence and the Image of God: Are We More than Intelligent Machines?*, is in press with Cambridge University Press.

Robert M. Geraci is the Knight Distinguished Chair for the Study of Religion and Culture at Knox College. He is the author of *Apocalyptic AI: Visions of Heaven in Robotics, Artificial Intelligence, and Robotics, Virtually Sacred: Myth and Meaning in World of Warcraft and Second Life, Temples of Modernity: Nationalism, Hinduism, and Transhumanism in South Indian Science*, and *Futures of Artificial Intelligence: Perspectives from India and the United States*. His research has been funded by the US National Science Foundation, the Republic of Korea National Research Foundation, the American Academy of Religion and twice by Fulbright-Nehru Professional Excellence (Research) Awards. He is a fellow of the International Society for Science and Religion.

Hannah Gould is a cultural anthropologist studying religion, materiality, death and discarding, with a regional focus in North-East Asia and Australia. She is the Melbourne Postdoctoral Fellow in Arts with the School of Social and Political Sciences and a member of the DeathTech Research Team at the University of Melbourne. She is currently President of the Australian Death Studies Society. Gould is the author of *When Death Falls Apart* and co-editor of *Aromas of Asia*.

LIST OF CONTRIBUTORS

Noreen Herzfeld is the Nicholas and Bernice Reuter Professor of Science and Religion at St. John's University and the College of St. Benedict. She holds degrees in computer science and mathematics from Pennsylvania State University and a PhD in theology from the Graduate Theological Union, Berkeley. Herzfeld is the author of *The Artifice of Intelligence: Human and Divine Relationship in a Robotic World, In Our Image: Artificial Intelligence and the Human Spirit, Technology and Religion: Remaining Human in a Co-Created World,* and *The Limits of Perfection in Technology, Religion, and Science,* and editor of *Religion and the New Technologies.* Herzfeld is a research associate at the Institute for Philosophical and Religious Studies, Koper, Slovenia. She is also co-founder and writer for the Avon Hills Salon

Stephen Kaplan is Professor Emeritus of Religious Studies, Manhattan College, and the author of two books (*Hermeneutics, Holography and Indian Idealism* and *Different Paths, Different Summits: A Model for Religious Pluralism*). He has also written numerous journal articles focusing on Hindu and Buddhist theories of mind in relationship to neuroscientific perspectives on the brain, the mind and perception. He is a fellow of the International Society for Science and Religion. Kaplan is the founder of the Veterans at Ease Program at Manhattan College, which integrates academic study, stress reduction techniques and bonding opportunities for student veterans in order to ease their transition from military to civilian-academic life.

Scott Midson is Director of Liberal Arts at the University of Manchester. With a background in interdisciplinary and constructive theology, he researches and teaches on human–technology interactions at the interface of posthumanism and theological anthropology. This work includes asking questions about what it is to be human and humane, specifically in a world of anthropomorphic and anthropocentric technologies such as robots and AI. Scott has previously published on our hopes and fears of staying human or becoming something more or less than human through the figure of the cyborg (*Cyborg Theology: Humans, Technology and God*). More recently, he has been exploring the notion of 'love' as a way of characterising and critiquing our relationships with and through machines (*Love, Technology and Theology*).

Keiko Nishimura received her PhD in communication (cultural studies) from the University of North Carolina at Chapel Hill, and was a recipient of Japan Foundation Doctoral Fellowship for 2017–2018. Her research and teaching focus on media and technology with a particular interest in the socio-cultural history of postwar and contemporary Japan. Nishimura's recent publications include "Semi-autonomous Fan Fiction: Japanese Character Bots and Nonhuman Affect," published in the edited volume *Socialbots and Their Friends: Digital Media and the Automation of Sociality* and "Surechigai Sociality: Location-Aware Technology on the Yamanote Line," published in *Japan Forum.*

F. LeRon Shults is a professor at the Institute for Global Development and Planning at the University of Agder in Kristiansand, Norway. He has led several international research projects utilising social simulation and published on topics such as social simulation, philosophical ethics, philosophy of science, intergroup conflict and the scientific study of religion.

LIST OF CONTRIBUTORS

Beth Singler is Assistant Professor in Digital Religion(s) at the University of Zurich. Prior to this she was the Junior Research Fellow in Artificial Intelligence at Homerton College, University of Cambridge. Her first book, *Indigo Children: New Age Experimentation with Self and Science,* was the first ethnography of a New Age group who define their identity and spirituality in relation to their view of science. She has published peer reviewed articles in *Zygon: Journal of Religion and Science, AI and Society* and *Nova Religio: the Journal of Alternative and Emergent Religions,* among others, and has had book chapters on artificial intelligence in volumes on religion and science, religion and film, religion and literature, AI narratives, new religious movements, and in the forthcoming *Oxford Compendium on Hope.* She co-edited the *Cambridge Companion to Religion and AI* with Fraser Watts and also has a forthcoming sole author book, *Religion and AI: An Introduction.*

Fraser Watts is a former senior scientist at the UK Medical Research Council's Applied Psychology Unit in Cambridge and has served as President of the British Psychological Society. Until retirement he was Reader in Theology and Science in the University of Cambridge, Director of the Psychology and Religion Research Group and a Fellow of Queens' College. He has also been President of the International Society for Science and Religion, of which he is now Executive Secretary. He is also Visiting Professor in Psychology of Religion at the University of Lincoln.

Wesley J. Wildman is Professor of Philosophy, Theology, and Ethics, and of Computing and Data Sciences at Boston University. He is also Executive Director of the Center for Mind and Culture in Boston. His primary research and teaching interests are in philosophical theology, philosophy of religion, philosophical ethics, religion and science, the scientific study of religion, computational humanities, computational social sciences and the ethics of emerging technologies.

Yorick Wilks (1939–2023) was a leading figure in AI, a brilliant intellectual and a larger-than-life personality. He had a lifelong interest in the interface between information, science and religion, and shortly before his death completed a book on AI and God. Sadly, he passed away during the final stages of the publication of this volume. His obituary in the *Guardian* (9 June 2023) stated: 'The artificial intelligence tools we use today, including Siri, Google Translate or ChatGPT, would not exist if pioneers such as the computer scientist Yorick Wilks had not helped to establish the field of natural language processing: teaching computers to interpret, generate and translate human language.'

David Zvi Kalman is a research fellow at the Shalom Hartman Institute. His work covers Jewish history, the history of technology, material culture and technological ethics, with a particular focus on artificial intelligence. He is a founding member of AI & Faith and is currently working on a book about religious responses to the novel moral problems of the twenty-first century. His popular work has been published in many places, including *Slate,* the *LA Review of Books* and the *Forward.*

Acknowledgements

Beth Singler and Fraser Watts would like to thank all of the contributors for their hard work and diligence on the various drafts of their chapters. Without their expertise and effort this volume would not have been possible.

They would also like to thank Gaia Di Salvo, Professor Singler's research assistant at the University of Zurich, who provided help with proofing and indexing of the volume.

Beth Singler thanks Homerton College, University of Cambridge for their support through her appointment as the Junior Research Fellow in Artificial Intelligence (2018–2022) and the University Research Priority Program in Digital Religion(s) and the Faculty of Theology and Religious Studies at the University of Zurich for their welcome since her arrival as the new Assistant Professor in Digital Religion(s) in October 2022.

Fraser Watts thanks the Templeton World Charity Foundation for supporting his own involvement in this volume, and also the chapters by William Clocksin, Marius Dorobantu and Yorick Wilks, through grant TWCF0542 on Understanding Spiritual Intelligence.

1 Introduction

BETH SINGLER AND FRASER WATTS

"WORDS MATTER"

In March 2022, the Center on Privacy and Technology at Georgetown Law, in the USA, announced that it would no longer be using the term "artificial intelligence" (AI). "Words matter" began the explanation written by the executive director, Emily Tucker. The post on the online publishing platform Medium explained that: "Whatever the merit of the scientific aspirations originally endorsed by the term 'Artificial Intelligence', it's a phrase that now functions in the vernacular primarily to obfuscate, alienate, and glamorize."[1]

Instead, the Privacy Center declared that it would, from now on: "(1) be as specific as possible about what the technology is and how it works, (2) identify any obstacles to our own understanding of technology that result from failures of corporate or government transparency, (3) name the corporations responsible for creating and spreading the technological product, and (4) attribute agency to the human actors building and using the technology, never to the technology itself."

All of this was in recognition that Turing's 1950 prediction in his 1950 paper "Computing Machinery and Intelligence" had happened, just not in the way in that it is often understood:

> The original question, "Can machines think?" I believe to be too meaningless to deserve discussion. Nevertheless I believe that at the end of the [twentieth] century the use of the words and general educated opinion will have altered so much that one will be able to speak of machines thinking without expecting to be contradicted.[2]

Instead, the centre argued that "Turing's large prediction has nevertheless been fulfilled [...] The terms 'artificial intelligence', 'AI', and 'machine

---

[1] Centre on Privacy and Technology, 2022, "Artifice and Intelligence," https://medium .com/center-on-privacy-technology/artifice-and-intelligence%C2%B9-fooda128d3cd.

[2] A. M. Turing, 1950, "Computing Machinery and Intelligence," *Mind*, 59(236), 433–460.

learning' placehold everywhere for the scrupulous descriptions that would make the technologies transparent to the average person." The centre's ambition is admirable, especially as it comes in conjunction with a desire to make explicit, as the centre claims to, the "marketing campaigns, and market control of tech companies."[3]

However, while high-level think tanks and research institutes might push back against the obfuscating legacies of language, 'AI' as an object and term remains enmeshed in our imaginaries, narratives, institutions and aspirations. AI has that in common with the other object of discussion in this Cambridge Companion: 'religion'. But beyond such similarities in form and reception, we can also speak to how enmeshed these two objects have been, and are yet still becoming, with each other. This growing entanglement also runs counter to several dominant narratives that partake of longstanding historical discussions of the relationship between anything deemed 'sacred' (i.e., religion) and anything deemed 'secular' (i.e., technology and science).

However, a problem arises in recognising the difficulties of definition with two such fluid, yet enmeshed, objects. Our academic habitus suggests that books should begin with 'introductions' to their subject through definitions and potted histories that set the scene for the larger discussions of the volume. However, both 'AI' and 'religion' are resistant to such clarifying efforts. The technologists of both AI and religion have offered attempts at encompassing definitions, appearing online and in textbooks. But these definitions are temporally and culturally contextual. Both our key terms have made their way into the world of popular discourse to be understood and shaped anew by various modes of interpretation and influences. In the case of AI, we should identify the role played by the charismatic authorities and voices in the AI story, anthropomorphism (and its counter, robomorphisation – the tendency to see the human as machine-like), utopianism and dystopianism, commercial hype and fake or faux bots that encourage us to view the technology as more advanced than it is, science fiction narratives and even religious narratives.

Also, on those occasions when we are given potted histories of AI, they are often retrospectively shaped in such a way as to give us a singular 'creation' moment, rather than recognising the historical context and previous fields that informed what came to be called 'artificial intelligence'. Thus, such histories commonly begin with the Dartmouth

---

[3] Centre on Privacy and Technology, "Artifice and Intelligence."

INTRODUCTION 3

Summer Research Project of 1956 that brought together the 'founding fathers' of this new field, such as Marvin Minsky, John McCarthy and Herbert A. Simon. This near fabled moment is described as giving the field its name while also defining its aspirations.

However, the term did not really dominate discourse until later when research funding for AI escalated around the late 1950s. At that time elite research institutes welcomed AI into the fold, creating spaces such as the Artificial Intelligence Project, which was part of both the Research Laboratory for Electronics in Building 26 and the Computation Center at the Massachusetts Institute of Technology. It is at that time that we begin to see the scare quotes around Minsky's notions of machine 'learning' disappearing in his work, leading to a stronger assertion of the limits, or lack of them, of the field, according to historian of AI Jonnie Penn.[4]

Instead of uncritically retelling this 'creation story' of AI, we must instead, as Penn argues, "situate early AI efforts in relation to a set of conceptually adjacent modes of analysis that practitioners and commentators retrospectively annexed into 'artificial intelligence' after the late 1950s. These include complex information processing, heuristic programming and machine learning."[5] Other methodological and societal influences include: "Management science, operations research, Hayekian economics, instrumentalist statistics, automatic coding techniques and pedagogy, cybernetics" and the "broadscale mobilisation of Cold War–era civilian-led military science."[6]

With regard to cybernetics in particular, an interesting point to note from the perspective of this Companion is that there was a good deal of interest in spirituality among cyberneticians,[7] whereas, as we discuss, the relationship between religion and AI has often been one of mutual suspicion and detraction. Why was there such interest in religion and spirituality, especially Eastern spirituality, among the early cyberneticians? Pickering suggests several factors. One was that cybernetics naturally led to curiosity about the brain and its capacity for altered states of consciousness, developing a relational understanding of the brain and how it responded to various contexts and technologies of the self.

---

[4] J. Penn, 2022, "Inventing Intelligence: On the History of Complex Information Processing and Artificial Intelligence in the United States in the mid-Twentieth Century," unpublished PhD thesis, Cambridge University. www.repository.cam.ac.uk/handle/1810/315976.

[5] Penn, "Inventing Intelligence," 12.

[6] Penn, "Inventing Intelligence," 3.

[7] A. Pickering, 2010, *The Cybernetic Brain*, University of Chicago Press.

Further, the cybernetic focus on adaptation eroded the modern view of the bounded individual and took a more contextual approach to the human person, which could include the transcendent. AI, in contrast, has generally tended to see intelligence as a property of a particular device. However, that is not a necessary feature of AI, and it is arguable that if AI is to simulate human intelligence it needs to find ways to take a more relational approach.

Further, as the next section shows, religious narratives and tropes have a role to play in the formation of the field of AI, in its discursive modes. Subsequent chapters also draw attention to the role of religious beliefs in the approaches of those founding fathers and other significant voices in the early field of AI. In short, AI as an object of discussion has emerged out of its specific context and history, including religious influences, while rewriting both retrospectively for a 'creation' story that reminds us of other such myths and stories of the creation of intelligence.

'Religion' also emerges from society even as it shapes society. Contemporary critical religious studies scholars encourage us to recognise that "some societies organise themselves by using the category of 'religion' and they have multiple means by which classifying something as religious is stabilised and made effective."[8] Religion is similarly shaped by societal forces and ideological concerns, and the diffuse religious activities, texts and ideas that we label with recognisable names are equally contextual and historically bound.

How then to introduce these two objects and then expand on their relationship? First, we propose not to hide such complexities but to consider AI and religion in their 'entanglements' with each other and with society. That is, we draw on anthropologist Courtney Bender who in turn drew on the philosopher John Dewey in her considerations of contemporary spirituality:

> I begin thus with the view that spirituality, whatever it is and however it is defined, is entangled in social life, with history, and in our academic and non-academic imaginations [...] spiritual forms have thrived and been shaped by entanglements with the secular, including its powerful engagements with science and progress.[9]

---

[8] T. Taira, 2022, *Taking 'Religion' Seriously: Essays on the Discursive Study of Religion*, from Supplements to *Method & Theory in the Study of Religion*, vol. 18, Brill, 2. https://brill.com/display/title/61969.

[9] C. Bender, 2010, *The New Metaphysics: Spirituality and the American Religious Imagination*, University of Chicago Press, 5–6.

INTRODUCTION 5

Begin with things in their complex entanglements [rather than] with simplifications made for the purpose of effective judgement and action; whether the purpose is economy, or dialectical aesthetic, or moral.[10]

However, this desire to push back against essentialism in the conversation around religion and spirituality – and further, in the discussion of religion and AI – runs afoul of its very own entanglements. Even after revealing these intricacies and essentialisms, such a conversation must take place among the institutional habits and linguistic limitations that require bounded objects for such conversations to begin and to be shared. Hence, while the Center on Privacy and Technology might hope to do away with 'AI', it is unlikely that most contemporary societies and cultures will. And likewise, in our discussion of AI and religion in this volume we must also make use of bounded categories such as 'AI', as well as indicate towards specific religions in which we might find individual experts in their fields able to write on such topics.

How then to proceed? We need both an introduction and a volume that recognises these terms both as constructions and as familiar ones that are employed for reasons and to specific ends. To demonstrate how this specificity can be valuable for the wider conversation on religion and AI, we now examine the history of AI and religion through the language and perspectives of some of the AI technologists and philosophers who have employed the term 'religion' in their discussions of the technology itself. This helps to set the scene for the larger conversation on religion and AI of this volume by demonstrating some of the tensions and lacunae that the following chapters address in greater detail.

RELIGION AND AI WORDS: HERESY, IDOLATRY, SIN AND MORE

It is not unusual, in our experience as researchers in this field, to come across the perspective that AI and religion have little to do with each other – if not, in fact, being antagonistic to each other. Partly this view comes from how AI can be framed as a project of post-Enlightenment teleological rationalism, a point recognised by some philosophers and historians of AI. Hubert L. Dreyfus, for instance, acknowledges AI's conceptual debt to "four hundred years of rationalist philosophy and the individual men who championed it."[11]

[10] J. Dewey, 1925, *Experience and Nature*, Open Court, 33.
[11] Penn, "Inventing Intelligence," 40.

Ethnographically speaking, the view that religion is irrational and AI rational – and never the twain shall meet – is borne out in one of this volume's co-editor's research into overtly secular rationalist transhumanist groups who deride the 'religionists' and 'goddists' who are described as being wedded to naïve supernaturalisms such as 'sky-gods' or 'magic'.[12] However, as Singler has also noted, religious narratives and tropes persist even among such communities online being put to work for specific cultural and ideological reasons. And in the academic discussion of AI, religion as an object was also put to work in the discourse of some of the earliest thinkers on AI, although of course this is 'religion' of a very specific type: WEIRD (Western, educated, industrialised, rich and democratic) monotheistic Protestant Christianity.

For instance, we can see religion being put to work in Anatol Rapaport's 1964 review of *Computers and Thought* by Edward Feigenbaum, Julian Feldman and Mike Sharples. Rapaport's description of the conflict between the 'vitalists' (those who assert that machines can think) and the 'negativists' (those who "at all costs" deny this claim) is couched in language that evokes historical religious conflict and heresy, as well as stereotypical views of religion as non-rational:

> It appears, then, that the only possible defensible ground on which the negativists could make a stand is the admittedly non-rational (i.e., religious) commitment against idolatry. If one fears that 'thinking' gives the computer a claim on human empathy and if one fears that the extension of empathy to computers may jeopardize the extension of empathy to men (or to living beings, or to God, as the believers would have it), then attributing thought to computers can indeed be viewed as idolatry.[13]

We can also see this negative language in his criticism that once the "cyberneticians showed that the distinction between teleological and mechanistic laws was an artificial one, the vitalists retreated to theological positions,"[14] 'retreating' being a pejorative way to frame any such intellectual move. Words such as 'dogma', 'sin', 'idolatry' and 'theology' also appear elsewhere in his review, which are all familiar from a Christian cultural context but employed with similar negative overtones.

---

[12] B. Singler, 2018, "Roko's Basilisk or Pascal's? Thinking of Singularity Thought Experiments as Implicit Religion," *The Journal of Implicit Religion*, 20(3), 279–297.

[13] A. Rapaport, 1964, "Review: Computers and Thought by Edward Feigenbaum and Julian Feldman," *Management Science*, 11(1), Series A, Sciences, 210.

[14] Rapaport, "Review", 203.

INTRODUCTION 7

In 1972, the British philosopher Guy Robinson wrote an article for the journal *Mind* on the subject of "How to Tell Your Friends from Machines." A discussion of responses to the possibility of machine intelligence, Robinson's article notes how the word idolatry has been employed:

> Other extra-philosophic analyses have recently been offered. [Peter] Geach has turned to the notion of religious deviance in characterizing the belief in machine intelligence as 'idolatry'. It is not clear whether he intends this characterization as a contribution to our understanding of the attraction the notion seems to have for some people or whether it is meant simply as a piece of what might be called 'dissuasive description' – or, more baldly, 'name calling'.[15]

Geach approached machine learning from a theological perspective in his 1969 book *God and the Soul*, which is also indicative of the long history of religion's entanglements with AI as a field. In this instance religion, and its subordinate objects and concepts such as 'idolatry', have their place in the conversation as indicators of particular irrationalities or as a black mark to be made next to a specific AI thinker's approach.

Robinson himself is also sure that there is a distinction to be made between scientific and non-scientific cultures and how they respond to the idea of minds in non-human spaces – and he leaves religion and its attendant beliefs very much in the 'primitive' category:

> Sincere, non-imaginative confusion between animate and inanimate in what we should call 'central' cases can be excused only in a primitive from a non-scientific culture where the distinction is not yet drawn in the way we draw it nor things seen and understood in the way we see and understand them. He may well seek to propitiate the spirit of some machine he has only recently encountered for the first time, but if our next-door neighbour is found sacrificing a guinea-pig because his car has been giving him trouble, we take steps. And our society's reaction to behaviour that manifests a genuine belief in the intelligence of machines is quick and extreme.[16]

The much more recent 2022 case of the AI engineer Blake Lemoine is also illustrative of these kinds of uses of the term 'religion'. Lemoine made claims about the sentience of the LaMDA (Language Model for

---

[15] G. Robinson, 1972, "How to Tell Your Friends from Machines," *Mind*, New Series, 81(324), 504.

[16] Robinson, "How to Tell Your Friends from Machines," 505.

Dialogue Applications) AI chatbot he was working on for Google. In the reaction to Lemoine's declarations we can see both this view of religion as 'primitive' and Robinson's assertion that society would be censorious in the face of such claims. In the online discussions of Lemoine's claim, observed by Singler and other researchers, members of the public were excited, thrilled or even scared by the claim of LaMDA's sentience. However, among AI technologists there was widespread mockery that only seemed to grow as Lemoine's own religious beliefs were subsequently revealed.

One of his biographies, in a piece from the *Washington Post*, describes his spiritual journey as follows: "He grew up in a conservative Christian family on a small farm in Louisiana, became ordained as a mystic Christian priest, and served in the Army before studying the occult."[17] Elsewhere he is described as having been a Pagan priest, and in interviews he describes his Zen meditation practices. Lemoine's specific religiosity is hard to pin down, and perhaps need not be, in parallel to our wider discussion of the fluidity of the modern concept of religion itself. The response to his religiosity seemed to suggest that this new context reassured onlookers that even with his secular credibility as a Google engineer and person of respectable science, he was really a 'true believer' and therefore a 'crank' through and through: "This is not a story about AI becoming sentient or Google shirking its ethical duties. It's about a guy who wants to believe in fairy tales and could probably use a break."[18]

The idea of there being 'true believers' in AI appeared earlier than Lemoine in 2022 and was more explicitly phrased in some responses to the machine minds debate. On 25 October 1971, at Anaheim, California, the Foundation of Cybernetics Committee of the Institute of Electrical and Electronics Engineers 'Systems, Man, and Cybernetics' Society organised, in conjunction with the Joint National Conference on Major Systems, a workshop on "Possibilities and Limitations of Artificial Intelligence." Three years later, a report on the conference focused again on the debate on the philosophical question of the limitations of machine intelligence – recognising as Rapaport did that there were clear factions. Balakrishnan Chandrasekaran and Larry H. Reeker called these factions the 'True Believers' and the 'Infidels' and wrote out

[17] Washington Post, 2022, "The Google Engineer Who Thinks the Company's AI Has Come To Life," www.washingtonpost.com/technology/2022/06/11/google-ai-lamda-blake-lemoine/.

[18] Tweet from Bloomberg writer Ashley Vance, 12 June 2022, https://twitter.com/ashleevance/status/1535766165846253568.

a philosophical dialogue for them in the Platonic style and introduced the more ideal character of the 'Agnostic'. They also drew parallels with theological debates on the existence, or not, of a god:

> The juxtaposition: Is there a God? Is the mind a machine? is interesting for another reason – a sort of empirical semidecidability that they share. The question about God could presumably be answered in the affirmative by any given individual to whom He chose to provide sufficient evidence. Likewise, a person's doubts about robots would probably vanish if his best friend, about whom no suspicion had crossed his brow, turned out to be a clever artifact [...] The prospects for evidence are not very good in either case at this time.[19]

Further, Chandrasekaran and Reeker outlined the Agnostic position on the topic of the mind as machine. Agnostics would inevitably counter the True Believer's logic by refuting some of the clauses that make up their claim:

> The True Believer holds that man 'as a behaving system' cannot be so complex as to be practically beyond design. Given the True Believer's syllogism: 'The mind is a machine; all machines can be designed; therefore, we can design mind-like machines,' the Agnostic takes exception to the minor premise as unproven, asserting the mind may be 'simply' a machine, but it is not a simple machine.[20]

It is worth noting that these conversations about the possibilities of the mind as machine came just as AI hype was beginning to decline – resulting in what is seen as the first 'AI winter' of 1974–1980. But there were similar, religiously flavoured conversations at the end of that period of decline. Thus, in 1980 we have Searle's influential article, "Minds, Brains and Programs," which gave us his famous 'Chinese Room' thought experiment. The article was published along with open peer review commentary that drew out these religious parallels, again sometimes with the same negativity that we have already seen Guy Robinson call 'dissuasive description' (or 'name calling'). For instance, Douglas R. Hofstadter's response was blunt: "This religious diatribe against AI, masquerading as a serious scientific argument, is one of

---

[19] B. Chandrasekaran and L. H. Reeker, 1974, "Report on Workshop on Possibilities and Limitations of Artificial Intelligence," *IEEE Transactions on Systems, Man, and Cybernetics*, SMC-4(1), 89.

[20] Chandrasekaran and Reeker, "Report on Workshop," 92.

the wrongest, most infuriating articles I have ever read in my life."[21] He goes on to argue that Searle's term 'intentionality' is just his name for the soul and that his Chinese Room thought experiment is based on his own faith positions:

> Searle is representative of a class of people who have an instinctive horror of any 'explaining away' of the soul. I don't know why certain people have this horror while others, like me, find in reductionism the ultimate religion [...] I know that this journal is not the place for philosophical and religious commentary, yet it seems to me that what Searle and I have is, at the deepest level, a religious disagreement, and I doubt that anything I say could ever change his mind.[22]

In this section, we have explored examples from the early decades of discourse around AI and its potential to be a machine-mind, and how religion as an object appeared in that, oftentimes fractious, conversation. It is worth summarising the aspects of this discourse we have noted. First, being a 'believer' is often used to indicate a retreat from rationality, placing religion in a pejorative class as a 'vestige' left over from more primitive times. Second, this pejorative language is employed in marking divisions between factions of thought about AI. Third, the language is primarily from a Western Christian perspective: terms such as 'idolatry', 'sin', etc. are culturally specific, although there are more abstract, if weighted, terms as well, such as 'True Believer'. What is most relevant to the rest of this Companion is the way in which AI has been viewed through specific religious frames at different times. Religion and AI were entangled in this way because of the existing assumptions about religion that some commentators on AI had, and continue to have, as in the contemporary example of Blake Lemoine and LaMDA.

Thus, words matter. But of course, the entanglements of AI and religion are not limited to interactions in discourse. The following chapters describe many more examples of when AI and religion in their many forms have been in interaction and resulted in specific outcomes and changes. In preparation for these examples in our chapters, it is perhaps valuable to revisit an article from one of our co-editors, which originally laid out the possible interactions of AI and religion and their consequences.

---

[21] D. Hofstadter, 1980, "Reductionism and Religion," in *The Behavioral and Brain Sciences*, ed. J. Searle, Cambridge University Press, 3, 433.

[22] Hofstadter, "Reductionism and Religion," 434.

THE FOUR ENTANGLEMENTS OF RELIGION AND AI: FURTHER DISCUSSION

In Singler's other 2018 article, "An Introduction to Religion and AI for the Religious Studies Scholar," she outlined what she saw as the three areas in which the entanglements of AI and religion might be observed by the religious studies scholar. These are also areas in which theologians and people of faith would have interest and direct involvement, but the methodological approach of Singler's work was to make anthropologically grounded descriptions of phenomena and to demonstrate possible areas of further research rather than normativity. These three entanglements were later joined by a fourth, and the full list is by no means exhaustive.

The first entanglement recognised that AI is disruptive for society, and consequently religion, and that established religions would necessarily engage with and seek to ameliorate the negative societal changes brought about by epistemic and physical automation. The second entanglement suggested that AI as an aim will result in new religious movements inspired by the utopian and dystopian aspirations embedded in the discourse around AI. Existing religious tropes and images from within the cultural context of the observers and storytellers of AI are also being drawn upon to develop our accounts of AI. Third, the framing of AI as a potential new sentience will spark interest in the longstanding debates about personhood from within and without established religions and drive internal discussion on this topic within religions themselves. Finally, there will be a clear relationship between AI and atheist narratives, explored in publications after this 2018 introductory religious studies article.[23]

We might even try to identify a meta-entanglement for the religious studies scholar or theologian: that each of these individual entanglements reflects the overarching concern of what it means for religions to exist (and perhaps flourish) in an age of AI. But we could also put this question the other way around and not cede the age to AI and instead push back against the secularisation narrative that has been used to tell us that we no longer live in an age of religion and religious

---

[23] For instance, see B. Singler, 2022, "Origin and the End: Artificial Intelligence, Atheism, and Imaginaries of the Future of Religion," in *Emerging Voices in Science and Theology: Contributions from Young Women*, ed. B. Sollereder and A. McGrath. Routledge and B. Singler, 2022b, "Left Behind? Religion as a Vestige in 'The Rapture of the Nerds' and Other AI Singularity Literature," in *Science and Religion in Western Literature: Critical and Theological Studies*, ed. M. Fuller, Routledge.

importance. So, instead, we might also ask what it means to develop a technology through which some intend to replicate the human mind in an age of religious belief. Lemoine's case can be understood through both these framings: his claim that the chatbot was sentient raises deep questions for those of religious belief while, from the other perspective, his pre-existing religious beliefs have shaped his response to the technology. Writ large in society, the same dialectic appears, worked out in individual case after individual case. The following chapters of this Companion provide further examples, but we must also hold the opposing framing in our minds as we read from our contributors how religions have responded to AI – rejecting it, using it or adapting to it – and how AI has been shaped by existing and developing religious concerns and narratives.

While this Companion is a significant contribution to the 'field' of AI and religion, that field, as with the field of AI itself, should not be given a 'creation story' that ignores the predecessors and influences that have been brought together and summarised by that one term. There has been valuable work for decades under the umbrellas of 'digital religion' or 'digital theology', or under even broader categories such as 'religion and technology' and in numerous on and offline ethnographies of religion in the contemporary world. In this Companion we have also included a set of chapters about particular faith traditions, each of which has engaged with AI in somewhat distinctive ways. Such engagements often involve commentary on the AI project from the perspective of a particular faith tradition. However, there is also potential for AI to contribute constructively to religious thought, bringing clarification to theological discussion. For example, to discuss whether or not a computer could 'sin' is valuable, not only for what it says about AI but for the precision it brings to the concept of 'sin'.

We can also draw on the work of scholars from the history of technology, science and technology studies, communication studies, gender studies, Black history and new religious studies, as well as scholars who have specialised in the study of specific religions, wherever they determine the boundaries for that focus. There is also potential, as Chapters 14 and 15 in this Companion illustrate, for AI to make a constructive contribution to the study of religion. Computational theorising has begun to make a valuable contribution in many areas of the human sciences but so far has not been much applied in the study of religion. We are pleased to be able to include chapters that explore what might be possible.

INTRODUCTION 13

What is significant – and what is also shaping how the field of religion and AI is welcomed within institutions and by scholars – is the perception that there is an urgency in the need to answer those two meta-entanglement questions: 'what does it mean to be a religion in an age of AI?' and 'what does it mean to create AI in an age of religion?' There might be a responsibility to address these questions, because – for established religions at least – there is the sense that crisis might follow a lack of their consideration. There are some, especially among atheist commentators, who suggest that there is a danger in AI being developed in an age of religious belief. For instance, the hyperbolic view of a 'religious AI' expressed by some transhumanists, such as Zoltan Istvan, who wrote a short story about the apocalyptic outcome of an AI reading the Bible called "The Jesus Singularity" in 2016.

Overall, we would claim that the impact of religion on AI is underconsidered, while the impact of AI on religion is of concern primarily to academics of religion and to established religions who have already seen significant changes wrought on their membership by the Network Society in which "[s]ystemic digitization has reconfigured the entire realm of human activities and organizations."[24] Arguably, every technological revolution before the computer and Web 2.0 social media also had a disruptive effect, but that only means that institutions such as religions are perhaps more familiar with the destabilising effect of such changes. Such disruptions might be exponential when caused by a technology that doesn't just act as a medium but also increasingly as an interactive agent and user interface to the world. This Cambridge Companion therefore seeks to unpack these entanglements through discussions and examples, drawing on the expertise of religious studies scholars, theologians, sociologists, historians and anthropologists.

BIBLIOGRAPHY

Bender, C. 2010. *The New Metaphysicals: Spirituality and the American Religious Imagination.* University of Chicago Press.

Castells, M. 2022. "The Network Society Revisited." *American Behavioral Scientist* 67(7), 940–946.

Chandrasekaran, B. and Reeker. L. H. 1974. "Report on Workshop on Possibilities and Limitations of Artificial Intelligence." In *IEEE Transactions on Systems, Man, and Cybernetics* SMC-4(1), 8

Dewey, J. 1925. *Experience and Nature.* Open Court.

---

[24] M. Castells, 2022, "The Network Society Revisited," *American Behavioral Scientist* 67(7), 2.

Hofstadter, D. 1980. "Reductionism and Religion." In *The Behavioral and Brain Sciences*, ed. J. Searle. Cambridge University Press.

Penn, J. 2022. "Inventing Intelligence: On the History of Complex Information Processing and Artificial Intelligence in the United States in the Mid-Twentieth Century." Unpublished PhD Thesis, Cambridge University. www.repository.cam.ac.uk/handle/1810/315976.

Rapaport, A. 1964. "Review: Computers and Thought by Edward Feigenbaum and Julian Feldman." *Management Science* 11(1), Series A, Sciences, 535.

Robinson, G. 1972. "How to Tell Your Friends from Machines." *Mind, New Series* 81(324), 504–518.

Singler, B. 2018a. "Roko's Basilisk or Pascal's? Thinking of Singularity Thought Experiments as Implicit Religion." *Implicit Religion* 20(3), 279–297.

2018b. "An Introduction to Artificial Intelligence and Religion for the Religious Studies Scholar." *Implicit Religion* 20(3), 215–231.

2022a. "Origin and the End: Artificial Intelligence, Atheism, and Imaginaries of the Future of Religion." In *Emerging Voices in Science and Theology: Contributions from Young Women*, ed. B. Sollereder and A. McGrath. Routledge.

2022b. "Left Behind? Religion as a Vestige in 'The Rapture of the Nerds' and Other AI Singularity Literature." In *Science and Religion in Western Literature: Critical and Theological Studies*, ed. M. Fuller. Routledge.

Taira, T. 2022. "Introduction." In *Taking "Religion" Seriously: Essays on the Discursive Study of Religion*, ed. T. Taira. Supplements to Method and Theory in the Study of Religion, vol. 18. Brill.

Tucker, E. 2022. "Artifice and Intelligence." Center on Privacy and Technology. https://medium.com/center-on-privacy-technology/artifice-and-intelligence%C2%B9-fooda128d3cd.

Turing, A. M. 1950. "Computing Machinery and Intelligence." *Mind* 59(236), 433–460.

2 Steps towards Android Intelligence

WILLIAM CLOCKSIN

Artificial intelligence (AI) is the study of computer models of intelligent behaviour. AI has been an active area of research since the 1950s when electronic computers became sufficiently powerful to execute programs to solve simple problems requiring logical reasoning, pattern matching and searching for solutions to puzzles. For the last nearly seventy years, the researchers in AI have continued to explore the idea of intelligence as problem solving. This research has resulted in computer programs that can perform tasks such as translating human speech into written words, translating documents from one language to another, planning complicated travel routes and playing the games of chess and go at world-beating level. Only relatively recently have some AI researchers taken seriously the idea that intelligence may be based on principles other than a capacity to solve abstract problems through the basic operations of symbolic reasoning, pattern matching and search.

The pioneers of AI research considered AI as an entirely distinct subject from human intelligence. From the late 1990s, the term artificial general intelligence (AGI) has been used to describe the hypothetical ability of a computer to understand or learn any intellectual task that a human can. AGI research has become extremely diverse, ranging from brain research to techniques for learning how to solve problems that are specified more generally, for example, a program that can learn how to play any game by observing examples of gameplay. AGI research also considers philosophical and ethical issues such as whether fully intelligent and conscious machines could pose an existential threat to human existence.

This chapter is motivated by the goal to work towards computational models of human intelligence in the form of an android: a human-like robot that people would accept as equal to humans in how they perform and behave in society. An android as considered here is not designed to imitate a human, nor is its purpose to deceive humans into believing that the android is a human. Instead, the android self-identifies as a non-human with its own integrity as a person.

To make progress on android intelligence, AI research will need to focus on developing computer models of how people engage in relationships, how people explain their experience in terms of stories and how people reason about the things in life that are most significant and meaningful to them: their affinities, beliefs, values, needs and desires. These topics have long been studied in psychology, sociology, philosophy and theology, but studies have not always yielded theories specific enough to be specified in computational form. Therefore, one aim of research in android intelligence is to develop a computational model of reasoning about relationships and stories about relationships and connecting these with the needs and desires that facilitate the android's engagement with society.

Through known history, religion has been one tool that people have used to understand and evaluate their situation in the world and their relationships with each other, their relationships with other creatures, objects and artefacts, and their relationships with others considered as sacred and supernatural. Therefore, for the intelligent android who, in order to operate fluently, needs to understand its role in the world and its relationship with other humans and things whether tangible or intangible, the importance of having a functional capacity for religious reasoning cannot be overlooked. Religious reasoning is taken here not to mean matters of specific confessional faith and belief according to established doctrines but about computational models of the cognitive processes involved in negotiating significant values and relationships. Religious reasoning also is not restricted to abstract problem solving but makes broader use of the human cognitive repertoire. It engages the abilities to tell and understand stories, to be affected by emotions in oneself and others, and to negotiate relationships. Religious reasoning is one way for intelligent entities – whether human or android – to process what Emmons calls ultimate concerns: attitudes and goals that are highly valued, meaningful and significant.[1]

Religious reasoning has also been associated with moral reasoning, in that humans are able to do wrong, to be wronged and to be considered responsible for wrongdoing. There are several ways to consider artificial moral agents. One way asks about what kind of 'mind' or brain states androids need to have in order to count as moral agents. Another way

---

[1]   R. A. Emmons, 2003, *The Psychology of Ultimate Concerns: Motivation and Spirituality in Personality*, Guilford Press.

would be to ask what good or harm an android could do to humans, and another way would be to ask what value an android could have in society. Behdadi and Munthe point out that literature on artificial moral agents has focused mainly upon issues in philosophy of mind and action, metaphysics and epistemology.[2] They propose that a more straightforward, normative approach would instead consider questions of how and to what extent artificial entities should be involved in human practices where we normally assume moral agency and responsibility. A normative approach would be consistent with our definition of the android as performing and behaving in society in ways considered to be equal to humans.

This chapter looks at new proposals for making progress in AI research based on considering the requirements for android intelligence and its connection with religious reasoning. The field of android science[3] studies the interaction of people with robots that have been built to resemble people. While the many important insights from this field will contribute to progress in android intelligence, this chapter confines itself to the computational modelling of android intelligence and makes no direct contribution to the aspects of android science to do with physical resemblance to people.

ARTIFICIAL INTELLIGENCE

The term 'artificial intelligence' was coined at a workshop in 1956, where pioneers of the subject formed an agenda of work that would take us to the present day. As problem solving was to them the most conspicuous manifestation of human intelligence, the idea was set that intelligence is based on a capability to solve problems expressed in a symbolic form. In addition, representations of objects and events in the world would need to be represented in symbolic form within the computational model. This assumption became known as the physical symbol system hypothesis[4] and was applied to domains of AI including proving logical theorems, planning, learning, processing human languages, visual perception and robotics. A paper by one of the AI pioneers

---

[2] D. Behdadi and C. Munthe, 2020, "A Normative Approach to Artificial Moral Agency," *Minds and Machines* 30, 195–218.

[3] For example, K. F. MacDorman and H. Ishiguro, 2006, "The Uncanny Advantage of Using Androids in Social and Cognitive Science Research," *Interaction Studies* 7(3), 297–337.

[4] A. Newell and H. A. Simon, 1976, "Computer Science as Empirical Inquiry: Symbols and search," *Communications of the ACM* 19(3), 113–126.

or 'founding fathers', Minsky, also anticipated and explored two of the key ideas that are at the root of the most up-to-date AI systems today: Bayesian reasoning and reinforcement learning.[5]

For about thirty years, the physical symbol system hypothesis was the main driver for AI research, and it soon supplanted other research currents from the 1950s including cybernetics and the earliest work on artificial neural networks. Because of its engineering and technological focus, it also neglected the foundational role in human intelligence of social, emotional and narrative behaviours. From the 1980s, researchers began to ask why progress in AI research based on solving abstract problems according to the physical symbol system hypothesis seemed to stall. According to Brooks, the AI system needs to be closely coupled, through perception and action, to the real world.[6] The world is considered to be its own best model, so an internal symbolic representation is not always necessary, and the AI system must be embodied to sense and act in the world. Brooks developed the subsumption architecture, which organises behaviour into a hierarchy of computational layers spanning the range from perception to action. Robot perception involves simple sensors such as touch, ultrasonic and visual sensors; and robot action involves actuators such as motors for locomotion and grippers for grasping objects. Each layer in the hierarchy is coupled to the next through signals that can be compared to reflexes. The work of Brooks and colleagues demonstrated that many seemingly lifelike behaviours are exhibited by simple robots that use layers of direct mappings from sensors to actuators without the need for any symbolic computation.

It is possible to see the physical-grounding hypothesis as a direct conceptual descendant of cybernetics with its main principle of the perception–action cycle. The perception–action cycle is the circular flow of information that takes place within the robot in the course of a sequence of actions towards a goal. Each action by the system causes changes in the environment that are sensed and processed to form a decision, which is then sent to the actuators to produce another action. These actions cause new changes in the environment that are processed and lead to new actions, continuing the cycle. The work of Brooks and colleagues inspired new currents in AI research including situatedness (the robot should react to the environment within a human time frame),

---

[5] M. Minsky, 1961, "Steps toward Artificial Intelligence," *Proceedings of the IRE* 49(1), 8–30.

[6] R. Brooks, 1990, "Elephants Don't Play Chess," *Robotics and Autonomous Systems* 6(1–2), 3–15.

embodiment (the robot consists of sensors and actuators that operate within the world) and emergence (the idea that intelligence emerges as a result of the complexity needed to interact with the environment). It also encouraged the idea that perception–action skills are a necessary foundation for the development of human-like intelligence. Clark has provided a general integration of these strands of thought and has defined the research area known as 'embodied AI'.[7]

The renewed development of artificial neural networks from the 1980s onwards arose from new methods for implementing trainable classifiers that overcame the limitations that artificial neural networks were previously thought to have. While this has led to the new field of machine learning and delivered remarkable results, its connection with intelligence seems to remain within the thought world of early AI. Machine-learning techniques have been used successfully to solve problems based on improving the classification and prediction power of functions through experience of input and output data. A significant contribution of machine-learning research has been to show how complex problems may be implemented in the form of trainable classifiers. Systems based on machine learning have brought much higher levels of performance to perception and problem-solving tasks such as optical character recognition, speech recognition, coordination of robot sensors and effectors, and game playing. However, despite being inspired by biological neural networks, and being one of the inspirations for AGI research, it is not yet clear how machine-learning methods might fit into a model of android intelligence other than as a technique for implementing trainable classifiers.

PERSONS, EMOTIONS AND RELATIONSHIPS

From the 1990s, some AI researchers have considered that for AI to make progress in achieving human levels of intelligence in the form of android intelligence, study should focus on distinctive characteristics of human intelligence. The characteristics considered thus far have included emotions, the ability to tell and understand stories, and engaging in long-term relationships. These characteristics go beyond intelligence as abstract problem solving and are part of what it means to be a person. Therefore, a new computational framework for AI that moves towards android intelligence needs to consider not only problem solving but personhood.

[7]   A. Clark, 1997, *Being There: Putting Brain, Body, and World Together Again*, MIT Press.

One challenge to early thinking in AI was the development of 'affective computing': the idea that understanding and reasoning about emotions has an important part to play in human–computer interaction. Picard was one of the first to argue that AI research should take seriously the role and purpose of human emotions or 'affect' when designing intelligent machines.[8] Emotion is a diverse and complicated concept that is richly contested by psychologists and spans many scientific categories. AI researchers tend to remain agnostic about the biological and psychological definitions of emotions and consider emotions in terms of their social performance for two different but related reasons. The first reason is to improve communication between humans and computer-controlled devices such as vending machines and vehicles. Machines that understand human emotions could potentially achieve a higher-quality interaction with people and improve the user's experience of interacting with computers. If AI research can arrive at a computationally effective model of how people use emotion to understand each other's mental states and intentions, devices could in principle be programmed to both perform a kind of emotional display to a user and to understand emotions that are displayed by users. The aim would be to improve the perceived usability of the device. Currently, working implementations of this are primitive, and there is scope for further development. The second reason is to raise questions about whether computers can have the potential to have emotional experiences themselves. This suggests a longer-term goal: to be able to model human emotion so well that an intelligent android could be programmed to 'have' emotions and use them in a way that people would accept as equal to humans in how the android performs and behaves in society.

AI researchers working within the pioneering problem-solving paradigm tended to think of emotions as undesirable impediments that can lead to error, or at best optional extras to improve performance in certain situations such as reacting quickly to a threat. And yet, emotion must have a fundamental role to play in human cognition, because it is clear that people are able to express meaning not only in propositional form but also as the experience of "feelings as felt meanings."[9] One challenge to the traditional AI approach proposes that emotions should take a foundational role in AI models as an underlying substrate

[8] R. Picard, 1997, *Affective Computing*, MIT Press.
[9] P. J. Barnard and J. D. Teasdale, 1991, "Interacting Cognitive Subsystems: A Systemic Approach to Cognitive-Affective Interaction and Change," *Cognition and Emotion* 5(1), 1–39.

in the cognitive architecture.[10] This foundational role includes mediating the bonding process when relationships are formed through need, desire and affinity, and being involved with connecting valuations to sensations within the body. For the purposes of the present chapter, we suggest that for android intelligence to engage with religious reasoning, emotions should be modelled in such a way that they are assumed to be not simply physiological changes, or perceptions of those changes, or simply social constructions, but as episodes that unify physiological, cognitive, perceptual and social elements.[11]

MacDorman and Cowley have explored what they call benchmarks for robot personhood, taking as a starting point that people are socially embedded selves with narrated beliefs and desires that take the intentional stance towards themselves.[12] They surveyed and critiqued over a dozen psychological benchmarks from the human–robot interaction literature, including autonomy, cooperation, moral accountability reciprocity and self-awareness, and found that although most of the benchmarks could be useful for appraising personhood depending on how they were applied, none of them fundamentally confronts what it means to be a person. They conclude that an ability to form and maintain long-term relationships is emblematic of personhood. They stress that contingency is inherent in what makes human relationships more than just fixed transactional behaviour. People develop mutual expectations in a relationship that are specific to the individuals involved. People develop intertwined 'biographies' that exhibit mutual expectations and ways of interacting that are unique to particular relationships. Successful relationships are underpinned by trust and authenticity, which are maintained by consistency with a real past history. A robot without the ability to develop its identity and beliefs in tandem with evolving social relationships is a robot that is merely stuck in a moment in time. These observations by MacDorman and Cowley point towards the primary requirement for android intelligence: the ability of the android to develop personhood by fluent negotiation of long-term relationships.

[10] W. F. Clocksin, 2005, "Memory and Emotion in Cognitive Architecture," in *Visions of Mind: Architectures for Cognition and Affect*, ed. D. N. Davis, Idea Group.
[11] J. A. Russell and L. F. Barrett, 2015, *The Psychological Construction of Emotion*, Guilford Press.
[12] K. F. MacDorman and S. J. Cowley, 2006, "Long-Term Relationships as a Benchmark for Robot Personhood," in *Proceedings of the 15th IEEE International Symposium on Robot and Human Interactive Communication*, 6–9 September, University of Hertfordshire, Hatfield, UK.

NARRATIVES

While some trained humans are able to solve mathematical problems and play an expert game of chess, the intelligent capabilities of people in general are connected with developing social relationships and gaining an understanding of themselves and others by listening to stories, telling stories and engaging in conversations. The idea that humans are storytelling animals, and that the telling and understanding of stories is a mark of human intelligence, has been long recognised. People make sense of their experience through narratives about their own lives and the lives of others. People seek meaning through narratives, and they form bonds with others who share that narrative. Narratives can provide people with a sense of identity, community and purpose. Narratives are not restricted to written texts, although stories can be good examples of narratives. Narratives not only influence the meaning that people give to experience, they also provide for the development of personhood. We have previously set out some implications of narrative in a framework for AI.[13] Furthermore, the religious reasoning implications of narrative in the intelligent android is obvious. For millennia, religious reasoning has been based upon the telling of stories. If the intelligent android is to understand – and possibly engage with – religious practice, it will require a capacity for understanding narrative.

A narrative can be generally considered computationally as a sequence of information-bearing states extended in time. A 'state' is a data point that represents an action or event. Computer scientists and AI researchers have long been interested in computational models of understanding sequences of states and how sequences can be created, compared and, more recently, learned from data. This research can be traced back to finite-state machines, Markov chains and dynamic programming from the 1950s, and more recently reinforcement learning and latent variable Markov models. Reinforcement learning in particular has been used to implement the remarkable breakthrough in programs that demonstrate superhuman performance in go and chess.[14] More generally, reinforcement learning is the currently accepted way

---

[13] W. F. Clocksin, 1998, "Artificial Intelligence and Human Identity," in *Consciousness and Human Identity*, ed. J. Cornwell, Cambridge University Press; W. F. Clocksin, 2003, "Artificial Intelligence and the Future," *Philosophical Transactions of the Royal Society A* 361, 1721–1748, reprinted in M. Winston and R. Edelbach, eds, *Society, Ethics, and Technology*, 4th ed., Wadsworth.

[14] D. Silver et al. 2018. "A General Reinforcement Learning Algorithm that Masters Chess, Shogi, and Go through Self-Play," *Science*, 362(6419), 1140–1144.

to solve the credit assignment problem, one of the ideas anticipated in Minsky's pioneering paper.5

There is a link between the computational processing of information-bearing sequences and the processing of narratives or stories. Most generally, we can define a narrative or story as having two aspects: (1) an information-bearing sequence of states, and (2) a performance of that sequence. Narratives or stories are not restricted to written or spoken form but can also take the form of a dance, a musical performance, playing a game, an algorithm or a culinary recipe, for example. The story can occupy a duration of time during which it is performed, or it can also be considered a monad or 'object' to be stored and processed computationally. Humans in relationships have the ability to organise mutual experience into narratives or stories. Narratives provide meaning, and people can form bonds with others who share that narrative.

Researchers in AI have explored story understanding since at least the 1970s. One of the topics of conventional AI research is understanding natural language. AI research in story understanding has been motivated mainly by the ability people have to summarise a long story into a shorter story. This can have practical applications in summarising a long document and in automatically generating a readable and informative story according to a given set of facts the story must explain. The work of Roger Schank and his colleagues was probably the first to use stories – represented as sequences of actions and events – to represent meaning in computer programs for performing certain natural language–processing tasks.[15] Schank later argued for a crucial link between narrative and intelligence, with narratives guiding learning, structuring memory and supporting generalisation in intelligent systems.[16] Clocksin proposed a framework for AI in which the capacity to process narratives plays a crucial role as the mechanism through which intelligent systems make sense of their experience.[17] This capacity serves to engage the intelligent system with the contingencies of its identity and relationships with others and involves the production and performance of a 'self' that takes up roles or positions within narratives.

[15] R. Schank, and C. K. Riesbeck, 1981, *Inside Computer Understanding*, Psychology Press.
[16] R. Schank, 1990, *Tell Me a Story*, Macmillan.
[17] Clocksin, "Artificial Intelligence and Human Identity"; Clocksin, "Artificial Intelligence and the Future."

Riedl has applied what he describes as "computational narrative intelligence" to computer game development.[18] Following Bruner, as many writers on narrative and intelligence have done,[19] Riedl also notes that stories are an effective means of conveying complex tacit and experiential knowledge that implicitly encodes social and cultural values. Riedl suggests that narrative intelligence may be a crucial step in machine enculturation, allowing AI systems to acquire human social norms and values. We consider that a capacity for what Riedl calls narrative intelligence would be an important enabler of religious reasoning in the intelligent android.

In a wide-ranging study that takes for granted a strong commitment to the intentional stance, Winfield has conducted experiments with small mobile robots linking robot navigation, the theory of mind and storytelling.[20] The main idea is based around the need for a theory of mind: a robot would have a theory of mind if it can ascribe mental states to other individuals, whether robot or human, and use its understanding of those states to explain and predict the actions of those other individuals. Using a robot navigation problem in which two robots attempt to pass each other in a corridor safely, Winfield has implemented a simulation-based internal model called a consequence engine (CE) and compared its performance with a purely reactive model. In the experiment, each CE-programmed robot knows the position of the other, and it tries to anticipate how the other might behave by internally simulating the other's behaviour, planning its own actions accordingly. Performance is generally improved over robots that have been programmed simply with a reactive obstacle-avoidance strategy. The connection with storytelling is twofold. First, the simulation-based internal model allows the robot to explore alternative sequences of actions and their consequences. Winfield suggests that a representation of action–consequence pairs generated during simulation could be represented as a story constructed from a sequence of 'what if' questions. Second, the storytelling models could provide a mechanism for the robot to generate explanations for actual or possible actions in a form intelligible to people as well as other robots.

---

[18] M. O. Riedl, 2016, "Computational Narrative Intelligence: A Human-Centred Goal for Artificial Intelligence" in *CHI'16 Workshop on Human-Centered Machine Learning*, 8 May 2016, San Jose, California, USA, www.cc.gatech.edu/~riedl/pubs/chi-hcml16.pdf.

[19] J. Bruner, 1991, "The Narrative Construction of Reality," *Critical Inquiry* 18(1), 1–21.

[20] A. F. T. Winfield, 2018, "Experiments in Artificial Theory of Mind: From Safety to Story-Telling," *Frontiers in Robotics and AI* 5(75), 1–13.

While the experimental work of Winfield and his colleagues has demonstrated that simulation-based internal modelling can form the basis for a computational theory of mind that also has an intriguing connection with narratives and the representation of counterfactual conditionals, it is fair to point out that the need for a theory of mind and the intentional stance is contested. Bermúdez argues that much social understanding and social coordination are subserved by mechanisms that do not need the machinery of intentional psychology.[21] According to Bermúdez, much social interaction is enabled by a suite of relatively simple mechanisms that exploit purely behavioural regularities, without needing to attribute propositional attitudes to others. It is also possible that some type of meta-representational cognition characteristic of intentional psychology may be necessary in complex situations when the standard mechanisms of social understanding and negotiation of relationships break down. It is still a valid question whether the intentional stance is a necessary given, as it is in Winfield's work, or if the intentional stance is an explanation we give because we value our ability to predict the actions of others. It is also relevant to point out that interacting cognitive subsystems (ICS), a sophisticated cognitive model mentioned earlier, has no particular commitment to a theory of mind, and that ICS may be a better fit to basing functionality on exploiting behavioural regularities.

In recent work on narratives and intelligence, Winston has advocated the strong story hypothesis, in which storytelling and understanding have a central role in human intelligence, and went on to propose an artificial system, called 'Genesis', for story processing with some human-like capabilities.[22] Despite other work on storytelling during the previous twenty-five years that established the idea that processing stories is fundamental to intelligence, Winston and Holmes considered the idea behind Genesis – that story understanding provides the substrate for problem solving – to be "taking artificial intelligence to another level," "controversial" and a "departure from the mainstream."[23] In the implementation of Genesis there is a clear line of

[21] J. L. Bermúdez, 2005, *Philosophy of Psychology: A Contemporary Introduction*, Routledge.

[22] P. Winston, 2011, "The Strong Story Hypothesis and the Directed Perception Hypothesis," AAAI Fall Symposium Series, https://dspace.mit.edu/handle/1721.1/67693.

[23] P. Winston, and D. Holmes, 2018, "The Genesis Enterprise: Taking Artificial Intelligence to Another Level via a Computational Account of Human Story Understanding," https://dspace.mit.edu/handle/1721.1/119668.

ideas going back to the work of Schank and Riesbeck;[24] however, the Genesis project has developed the area in several new and interesting ways. Stories normally involve multiple characters, and story understanding involves recognising characters and modelling their beliefs. Nosshas built a Perspectives Expert for Genesis, which analyses a story to form detailed models of the characters in a story.[25] The analysis involves tracking which character does what with other characters and establishing the continuity of characters as they leave scenes and return to scenes. Equipped with the Perspectives Expert, Genesis can retell stories from different characters' perspectives, answer some reading-comprehension questions involving characters, and detect and explain opposing viewpoints.

For the intelligent android, a narrative is more than just a story in the sense of Winston, and the characters in the story are more than just a way to track consistency of the actors in a story. As an information-bearing sequence, the narrative is the basic representation used in memory, meaning and identity. Characters in the narrative are understood as persons, just as the leading character in one's own life story is understood to be a person. This suggests that the same computational principle can be the basis both for understanding others and for understanding the self.

Furthermore, fluent engagement in relationships requires not only understanding stories but engaging in conversations. We do not understand each other simply by understanding stories that we put to each other. We develop shared understandings through negotiation with each other over a period of time in the course of a conversation. Stories and conversations are located within a complex web of culturally defined relationships and conventions that exist because participants experience emotions and have feelings for one another. Fluent understanding of stories and taking part in a conversation both call for the coordination of the participants' goals with their understanding of other people. Stories and conversations thereby have a 'moral order', in which every culture and relationship develops expectations for our behaviours as participants in a society. When understanding a story, we place ourselves in the story and imagine how we might react and how particular episodes or characters would make us feel if we encountered them

---

[24] Schank and Riesbeck, *Inside Computer Understanding*.

[25] J. Noss, 2017, "Who Knows What? Perspective-Enabled Story Understanding," MEng thesis, Massachusetts Institute of Technology, https://dspace.mit.edu/handle/1721.1/113174.

in our lives. Finding meaning in stories and conversations therefore requires the understanding of interlocutors as persons and not simply as a representation of facts about actors.

ANDROID INTELLIGENCE AND PERSONS

Following the idea of MacDorman and Cowley[26] that long-term relationships are markers of the human person, the next question is what kinds of relationship? The distinct identity of the human as a person is given by the relationships in which it is engaged, whether biological, social or political. These engagements include relationships with family and friends, the natural environment, affinities, beliefs and possessions. Some of these relationships are tangible and associated with people, places and physical objects. Some are intangible but no less real, such as spiritual relationships, beliefs and attitudes. They may be judged as good or bad, healthy or unhealthy, but taken together this complex of relationships confers personhood to the human. Through relationships over time, the human assembles a long-term existence that develops meaning and purpose. The future prospects for android intelligence depend upon the ability to substitute 'android' for 'human' in the preceding sentences without loss of generality.

For over two millennia, some people have attempted to understand human identity as being made in the image of their God (e.g., Genesis 1:27). This continues to be a fruitful path for Christian theologians to explore in connection with AI.[27] People have also attempted to understand their relationships as being mediated by God. For example, 1 John 4 may be summarised as: "God is love, and those who live in love also live in God, and God lives in them." If the intelligent android can understand itself through tangible relationships with other humans and androids, then it may also understand itself through intangible relationships with 'spiritual' others. The key claim here is that the same computational principles would need to hold for the negotiation of relationships, whether these relationships are tangible or intangible.

---

[26] MacDorman and Cowley, "Long-Term Relationships as a Benchmark for Robot Personhood."

[27] N. Herzfeld, 2003, "Creating in Our Own Image: Artificial Intelligence and the Image of God," *Zygon: Journal of Religion & Science* 37(2), 303–316; M. Dorobantu, 2020, "Will Robots Too Be in the Image of God? Artificial Consciousness and Imago Dei in Westworld," in *Theology and Westworld*, ed. J. Gittinger and S. Sheinfeld, Lexington Books.

One undeniable feature of society is that it involves more than one person. The traditional AI concern has been to focus on modelling the computational mechanisms of the single intelligent agent. This approach has been reinforced by situated AI with its emphasis on the perception–action cycle. Within the cycle, any actions by other agents in the environment are sensed only insofar as they cause disturbances of the environment. And yet, when the android is defined through its relationships with others, it is likely there is a processing burden, or at least specialised processing, involved in distinguishing agents from other disturbances in the environment. Such processing involves reasoning about the self and about other persons in relationship and is independent of whether the relationships are with tangible or intangible persons.

Of all the relationships to consider in connection with the design of the intelligent android, one significant relationship is the giving and receiving of care. Caregiving is not a distinctively human property, as it is known that other animals show behaviours we would associate with caregiving. But humans have developed an understanding of caregiving that has biological, psychological and religious dimensions. Caregiving engages humans emotionally with reciprocities of need and desire. Humans need care, give care and need to give care. The development of human personhood depends upon the care that it has received and the ability it has to give care. The prospects for androids that people would accept as equal to humans in how they perform and behave in society will depend upon the android's fluency in giving and receiving care. In humans, the most manifest example of caregiving and receiving is in reproduction. While it is not expected that androids would reproduce biologically, androids could be placed in roles that involve caregiving to humans and to other androids. Fluency in caregiving can be related to the care that has been received in the past, and therefore the most fluent of caregiving androids is one that has experienced the receiving of care in such a way that caregiving has emerged as an ability. This suggests a requirement for the android to undergo a 'childhood' during which crucial aspects of human personhood would be developed. We intend no implication that such development would take place only at a specific stage in the operational timescale of the android. Yet in this case it is during human infancy and childhood that receiving care is crucial and that elements of caregiving are learned. Instead of learning caregiving/receiving by programming or rote instruction, the android as a person will come to understand needs and vulnerability in others by itself being vulnerable and in need at times during its operation. This area of thought is discussed further in Chapter 12.

CONCLUSIONS

The historical focus for AI research has been on building algorithms that solve abstract problems in a mathematical domain of symbolic or numerical processing. This focus has been carried through to the present day, even with the development of new technology such as deep reinforcement learning that has led to remarkable levels of performance in game playing and other practical applications. A few AI researchers have recognised that other factors are involved in intelligence, such as Weizenbaum's observation that intelligence manifests itself only relative to specific social and cultural contexts.[28] Others have called for a re-examination of the rationalistic tradition and its influence on AI research,[29] and others have posed alternatives to the physical symbol system hypothesis. However, these challenges have had little effect so far. More significantly, mainstream AI research has tended to overlook the kinds of intelligence that are involved in religion and morality. There remains a possibility that intelligence may be based upon fundamental principles, which can be formalised computationally, that mediate the development of personhood and long-term relationships. A community of persons – including human and android – would seek meaning and understanding of themselves and each other through the experience of relationships with each other and with intangible others. Abstract problem solving might then be seen as a later development in human society, a practice of a community driven by the inchoate needs and desires of its members, but which comes to value consistency and accountability in its discourse and goals.

We have considered here a wider goal of AI research, to work towards emulating human intelligence in the form of an android: a human-like robot that people would accept as equal to humans in how they perform and behave in society. We have discussed a number of capabilities needed by the intelligent android and showed a connection between the requirements of the intelligent android and a capacity for religious reasoning. The key concepts are based on personhood and include emotions as a substrate for the development of relationships and narrative intelligence as the way that communities of individuals make sense of experience, construct identities and produce meaning in the world as conversants and story users. Implications for the design of android

[28]   J. Weizenbaum, 1976, *Computer Power and Human Reason*, Penguin.
[29]   T. Winograd and F. Flores, 1985, *Understanding Computers and Cognition: A New Foundation for Design*, Addison-Wesley; H. L. Dreyfus and S. E. Dreyfus, 1986, *Mind over Machine*, Macmillan.

intelligence include the claims that the same computational principles are the basis for the negotiation of relationships with tangible others as for intangible others, and that the same computational principles are the basis both for understanding others and for understanding the self.

BIBLIOGRAPHY

Barnard, P. J. and Teasdale, J. D. 1991. "Interacting Cognitive Subsystems: A Systemic Approach to Cognitive-Affective Interaction and Change." *Cognition and Emotion* 5(1), 1–39.

Bermúdez, J. L. 2005. *Philosophy of Psychology: A Contemporary Introduction.* Routledge.

Brooks, R. 1990. "Elephants Don't Play Chess." *Robotics and Autonomous Systems* 6(1–2), 3–15.

Clark, A. 1997. *Being There: Putting Brain, Body, and World Together Again.* MIT Press.

Clocksin, W. F. 2005. "Memory and Emotion in Cognitive Architecture." In *Visions of Mind: Architectures for Cognition and Affect,* ed. D. N. Davis. Idea Group Pub.

Dreyfus, H. L. and Dreyfus, S. E. 1986. *Mind over Machine.* Macmillan.

Emmons, R. A. 2003. *The Psychology of Ultimate Concerns: Motivation and Spirituality in Personality.* Guilford Press.

Minsky, M. 1961. "Steps toward Artificial Intelligence." *Proceedings of the IRE* 49(1), 8–30.

Noss, J. 2017. "Who Knows What? Perspective-Enabled Story Understanding." MEng thesis, Massachusetts Institute of Technology. https://dspace.mit .edu/handle/1721.1/113174.

Picard, R. 1997. *Affective Computing.* MIT Press.

Riedl, M. O. 2016. "Computational Narrative Intelligence: A Human-Centred Goal for Artificial Intelligence," in *CHI'16 Workshop on Human-Centered Machine Learning,* 8 May 2016, San Jose, California, USA. www.cc.gatech .edu/~riedl/pubs/chi-hcml16.pdf.

Schank, R. 1990. *Tell Me a Story.* Macmillan.

Weizenbaum, J. 1976. *Computer Power and Human Reason.* Penguin

Winfield, A. F. T. 2018. "Experiments in Artificial Theory of Mind: From Safety to Story-Telling." *Frontiers in Robotics and AI* 5(75), 1–13.

Winograd, T. and Flores, F. 1985. *Understanding Computers and Cognition: A New Foundation for Design.* Addison-Wesley.

Part I
Religions and AI

3 Hinduism and Artificial Intelligence

ROBERT M. GERACI AND STEPHEN KAPLAN

INTRODUCTION

The term 'Hinduism' refers to a wide range of practices, texts and traditions originating in South Asia and now found throughout the world. While there exists no single Hindu tradition or authorised institution, it is possible to see intriguing intersections of religion and artificial intelligence (AI) in the wide range of historical and contemporary Hindu thought and practice. Hindu beliefs about the world and, in particular, about human beings raise different questions about the role of AI than those of other religious traditions. These differences are most notable with regard to Hindu approaches to mind, body and consciousness. The differences suggest that Hindus may reject the possibility of conscious machines while still accepting that machines can be intelligent. Concomitantly, enthusiasm for incorporating advanced technologies means that Hindus will take advantage of advancing AI technologies in a variety of religious practices. Whether intelligent and/or conscious robots could exist remains hypothetical, so the obvious limits of machines and their philosophical potential mean that AI can assist in Hindu practice but there are significant theological challenges to them replacing human beings in it.

THE HINDU CONTEXT FOR TECHNOLOGICAL
DEVELOPMENT AND AI

Rapid uptake of technology has long been part of the Hindu religious experience, and it includes strong interest in mechanical forms of life. The integration of religion and technology often generates an experience of wonder in Hindu religious practice;[1] simultaneously, the

---

[1] Tulasi Srinivas, 2018, *The Cow in the Elevator: An Anthropology of Wonder*, Duke University Press, 138–71.

religious adoption of technology indigenises it. In India, religious and cultural practices often serve as a mechanism for adopting technologies and transforming social networks: people enlarge "the domain of beliefs we hold about technology in order to enable us to deal with it in a manner suited to us."[2] Such integrations also allow, as they do in non-Hindu contexts, for "traditional customs and religious beliefs" to appear "in a new, modern look."[3] Often, this entails significant changes to the culture and practice of religious ritual.[4] Perhaps surprisingly, even *sādhus* – ascetic renunciants – are receptive to change and see the divine as "manifest in the technological."[5] We should look, therefore, at how AI is both indigenised through its integration into Hinduism and also at what changes are incurred to both the technology and the religion. From medieval automata to twenty-first-century animatronic robots, Hindus have incorporated machines into their worldview in a way that builds towards contemporary and future usages of AI.

Medieval portrayals of Indian automata prefigure possible intersections of Hinduism and AI in contemporary life and reveal a long history of interest in artificial life. In the *Śṛṅgāramañjarīkathā* (eleventh or twelfth century), Bhoja imagines moving mechanical dolls in the form of human beings and animals providing amusement in a king's palace garden.[6] The author claims that at least one of these could speak.[7] Another text credited to Bhoja refers to guardian automata that could kill thieves.[8] Contemporaneously, in Somadeva's

[2] Sundar Sarukkai, 2008, "Culture of Technology and ICTs," in *ICTs and Indian Social Change: Diffusion, Poverty, Governance*, ed. Ashwani Saith, M. Vijayabaskar and V. Gayathri, Sage, 47, emphasis removed.

[3] Brigitte Luchesi, 2018, "Modern Technology and Its Impact on Religious Performances in Rural Himachal Pradesh: Personal Remembrances and Observations," in *Religion and Technology in India: Spaces, Practices and Authorities*, ed. Knut A. Jacobsen and Kristina Myrvold, Routledge, 125.

[4] For example, see Knut Jacobsen, 2018, "Pilgrimage Rituals and Technological Change: Alterations in the *Shraddha* Ritual at Kapilashramin in the Town of Siddhpur," in *Religion and Technology in India: Spaces, Practices and Authorities*, ed. Knut A. Jacobsen and Kristina Myrvold, Routledge.

[5] Antoinette DeNapoli, 2017, "'*Dharm* Is Technology': The Theologizing of Technology in the Experimental Hinduism of Renouncers in Contemporary North India," *International Journal of Dharma Studies* 5(18), 2, 19.

[6] Bhojadeva, *Śṛṅgāramañjarīkathā*, in Kumari Kalpalata K. Munshi, ed. and trans., 1959, *Śṛṅgāramañjarīkathā Paramāmara King Bhojadeva of Dhārā*, Bharatiya Vidya Bhavan, 8–11 (note the pagination restarts when the translation of the text begins; this page reference is to the English translation). Description of the provenance of the text happens on 2–3 of the earlier section of the manuscript.

[7] Bhojadeva, *Śṛṅgāramañjarīkathā*, 11.

[8] V. Raghavan, 1952, *Yantras or Mechanical Contrivances in Ancient Culture*, Indian Institute of Culture, 24.

Kathāsaritsāgara, various dolls are alleged to move, dance and gossip.[9] While the most advanced automata described in medieval manuscripts could not have existed, European contemporaries certainly believed in them. E. R. Truitt notes that Latin Christians believed Indians "had access to the kind of esoteric knowledge required to build automata" and cites *De Universo* by William of Auvergne as an example of such attribution.[10] To European Christians, India was a land of marvels; they thus happily credited Indians with esoteric and mechanical genius. The inclusion of such automata within pleasure gardens indicates that, like Europeans, medieval Indians saw automata as a sign of power and prestige. Although the fantastical promises of garden automata cannot be taken as historical fact, Hindus long benefited from advanced technology and surely more modest automata existed.

After an enforced interregnum in Indian technological capabilities under colonial rule, the pursuit of technological innovation occupied twentieth-century India, and this impacted the practice of Hinduism. In the latter decades of the twentieth century, artisans strove to produce increasingly dynamic animatronic deities for temples, commercial locations and individual clients.[11] For example, in 1998 the International Society for Krishna Consciousness (ISKCON, popularly known as the Hare Krishnas) built a temple in Delhi with an animatronic theatre featuring Krishna and Arjuna performing from the *Bhagavad Gītā*, and another of Swami Prabhupada (the movement's founder).[12] Shortly after, an animatronic goddess arrived in Bangalore. Although the 'robot' was limited in its ability, each time the goddess thrust her trident into the buffalo demon Mahishāsura, "devotees gasped audibly in sheer delight; children burst into scattered applause and laughter."[13] Within a decade of the ISKCON and Bangalore robots, the international Swaminarayan Akshardham community also established animatronic shows at their

---

[9] Raghavan, *Yantras or Mechanical Contrivances in Ancient Culture*, 17.

[10] E. R. Truitt, 2015, *Medieval Robots: Mechanism, Magic, Nature, and Art*, University of Pennsylvania Press, 16, 18. Suzanne Akbari describes 'the Orient' as an "inexhaustible storehouse of curiosities" to Europeans; Suzanne Akbari, 2009, *Idols in the East: European Representations of Islam and the Orient, 1100–1450*, Cornell University Press, 106.

[11] Emmanuel Grimaud, 2011, *Gods and Robots*, trans. Matthew Cunningham, Grandmother India

[12] Kenneth J. Cooper and *The Washington Post*, 1998, "High-Tech, Talking Robots to Spread Krishna Gospel: Robots Representing Hindu Gods Dramatize Ancient Epic in a Modern Theatre," *The Ottawa Citizen*, 21 April, A16.

[13] Srinivas, *The Cow in the Elevator*, 139.

temples in Gandhinagar and Delhi.[14] These examples challenge the false impression that religious groups are stuck in the past and unable to change with the times. Hindus, like other religious practitioners, cheerfully use digital technology to provide new forms of ritual and spiritual experience.

The comfortable collusion between mechanical marvels and Indian culture persists in contemporary Hindu visions of AI. Ethnographic work indicates that some north Indian *sādhus* align technology – and the interdependent relationship of human beings with it – with Kalki, the divine redeemer. In Hinduism, Kalki is the forthcoming tenth avatar of the god Vishnu, destined to arrive on Earth and end the degenerate age of *Kali Yuga*. To some *sādhus*, Kalki is a "redemptive transhuman metaphor for (and a symbol of) the relationships that humans, nature, and technology create together every day."[15] Consonant with this, Holly Walters cites a *sādhu* in Nepal who predicts that Kalki will arrive on Earth as a robot because that is what the times call for.[16] As one might expect, similar perspectives appear outside the renunciant community: for example, the question arose during the question and response period after an academic lecture about AI in Bangalore, with one Hindu student reflecting on AI by asking: "What is god right now? … About Kalki, the day of Kalki: so my suspicion is AI is Kalki. I mean a truly artificial intelligent being is Kalki, maybe."[17] For him, the future avatar of Vishnu might actually come to inaugurate a better world and do so in the form of AI. These isolated examples show the way Hindus elaborate upon traditional beliefs using AI technology and also how AI technologies are integrated into Hindu culture.

Although formal studies are rare, preliminary evidence indicates that Hindus will accept robots as assistants in a wide range of secular services, perhaps coinciding with growing religious interest in robotics and AI. In a comparative study, individuals from 'Southeast Asia' indicate much greater comfort with humanoid robots in hospitals and

---

[14] See Jonathan Allen, 2006, "The Disney Touch at a Hindu Temple," *New York Times*, 8 June, www.nytimes.com/2006/06/08/travel/08letter.html; Bochasanwasi Shri Akshar Purushottam Swaminarayan Sanstha, "First Time Ever in India: An Audio-Animatronics Presentation of an Assembly in the Time of Lord Swaminarayan," *Akshardham.com* preserved by the Internet Archive Wayback Machine, www.akshardham.com/gujarat/exhibitions/audioanimatronics.htm.

[15] DeNapoli, "*Dharm* Is Technology," 25.

[16] For this and a subsequent reference, we are deeply grateful to Dr Walters for sharing insights from her unpublished ethnographic work with us.

[17] Robert M. Geraci, 2022. *Futures of Artificial Intelligence: Perspectives from India and the United States*, Oxford University Press, 101.

schools; interestingly, individuals identifying as Hindu were among those most inclined to accept robots in these domains as well as in teaching relationships with the elderly.[18] Although Hindus were the most likely to accept their children learning from robots, they represent the middle of the pack in thinking the children would actually like it.[19] These data offer, at best, a glimpse at how Hindus will see the presence of robots in non-secular domains. But just as some contemporary Hindus see AI playing the role of the divine redeemer Kalki, AI and robotic technologies can transition into ritual practice, potentially taking on the roles of worshipper, priest and even the earthly presence of the divine. Fully appreciating how Hindu philosophical speculation and religious life can or will engage with AI requires that we now summarise basic Hindu religious traditions.

FUNDAMENTALS OF HINDUISM

Hinduism is a global religion whose roots, like a banyan tree, are ingrained in the soil of India. These roots can be traced back to the pre-Aryan cultures of Mohenjo-Daro and Harappa, circa 2500–1500 BCE, and to the *Vedas*, circa 1500–800 BCE, considered to be sacred texts, not created by humans but 'heard' by the ancient sages. This history marches on without a founder or a single central organisation that could declare one belief or practice orthodox and a conflicting belief or practice heretical. Hinduism has been compared to a sponge that absorbs everything, even making the Buddha an avatar (*avatāra*) of the god Vishnu.

The term Hindu, which is etymologically derived from the Persian transliteration of Sindhu, first appears as a geographical term referring to people living east of that river (now known as the Indus). Hindu becomes an 'ism' in the early nineteenth century when it was used as a religious designation. For over 2,000 years, Indians had labels for followers of Jaina, Buddha, Śiva, Vishnu, Kali, tantra, Krishna and the various *darśanas* (philosophical 'ways of seeing') such as Vedānta, Yoga and Nyāya; but no one labelled anyone a Hindu as a description of religious identity.[20] Thus, as we attempt to lay out the particularities of Hinduism, one must recognise the peculiarity of this designation.

[18] Nikolaos Mavridis et al. 2012, "Opinions and Attitudes toward Humanoid Robots in the Middle East," *AI & Society* 27, 531, 532.

[19] Mavridis, "Opinions and Attitudes," 532.

[20] Romila Thapar, 1997, *Early India: From the Origins to AD 1300*, University of California Press, 439–440.

Adopting the notion that Hindus are those people who consider the *Vedas* sacred – even if they do not adopt the beliefs or practices specified in those texts or may be forbidden to engage those texts because of their caste – one still finds an enormous diversity that must be boiled down to a few kernels as an introduction. Essential to 'Hinduism', as we now label the traditions drawing on Brahminical models of interpretation and the major schools of thought, are the notions of *saṃsāra*, karma, *dharma*, *mokṣa*, Brahman and the true self (*ātman/puruṣa*). *Saṃsāra*, which comes to prominence in the Upaniṣadic period (800–400 BCE), is the notion that sentient individuals are born and reborn. Karma, literally action, is the operating principle that oversees one's rebirth. Meritorious actions (*punya*) lead to favourable rebirths and unmeritorious actions (*pāpa*) lead to unfavourable rebirths. One birth is understood to be the consequence of one's past actions and likewise, one's actions in this life have future consequences.

The cycle of rebirth, for individuals and universes, is without beginning, but an individual may escape the wheel of rebirth. Individual liberation, *mokṣa*, has been understood differently by different segments of the Hindu family. For example, some describe *mokṣa* as the realisation that one's true self (*ātman*) is the non-dual ultimate reality, Brahman; others believe that one's true self realises its union with the ultimate reality, often envisioned as one of the major gods, such as Vishnu, Shiva or Shakti. The paths to liberation are likewise varied, encompassing hearing the sacred scriptures (*śruti*), meditation, yoga and devotional (*bhakti*) chanting. Some of these intense practices are beyond the range of the average person who is engaged in ordinary, family life, and therefore four legitimate aims of life exist – pursuit of wealth, love, *dharma* and *mokṣa* – which are related to four stages of life.

Dharma, righteous behaviour, has prominence in a multitude of aspects of Hindu life, from ethics to marriage arrangements to the conduct of rituals. An individual's *dharma* emerges from that person's place in the *varṇa/jātī* social structure, frequently referred to as 'caste'. In Brahminical Hinduism, each of the castes – the four *varṇas* and the Dalits outside these classes – have their *dharma* or appropriate duty. This duty, refined by one's sex and one's stage of life, traditionally structures social interactions. As the *Bhagavad Gītā* (3:35) says, it is better to do one's own duty poorly than to do another person's duty well. As envisioned in the *Gītā* and elsewhere, *dharma* maintains social order. Doing one's duty as a householder leaves little time for seeking liberation and therefore the practices that lead one in pursuit of *mokṣa* are left to the indefinite future, likely even a future lifetime. Instead, most

HINDU PHILOSOPHICAL-RELIGIOUS CONCEPTS AND AI

Hindus engage a series of religious practices in the home before the family altar and outside the home such as going to temples, making offerings (*pūjā*), engaging in sacred sight (*darśan*) and pilgrimage. Also, very important in the life of Hindus are transition rituals for birth, death, etc. and engagement in holiday festivals such as Holi and Dīwāli.

HINDU PHILOSOPHICAL-RELIGIOUS CONCEPTS AND AI

Given the enormous range of philosophical-religious concepts within Hinduism, this section restricts itself to the basic issues identified earlier and a few concepts that distinguish Hindu thought from Western thought. Neither Hindu nor Western thought are by any means monolithic; however, each exhibits some characteristics that distinguish it from the other. Hindu thought rejects the mind–body dualism or soul–body dualism that has had such a powerful impact on Western thought. Hinduism also rejects the notion that consciousness is a development concomitant with an increasingly complex material organisation, most notably neural development. As discussed later, the dominant Hindu perspectives define body and mind as one material complex, which continually undergoes change, and consciousness (*cit*) as eternal and unchanging and as a distinct ontological category. In light of these two perspectives, it can be said that what David Chalmers terms the "hard problem" in contemporary consciousness studies – how subjective experience arises from neural processes – is not the hard problem in Hindu thought.[21] The latter understands consciousness as an eternally given presence and the hard problem for Hinduism is how does *avidyā* (ignorance) appear when consciousness (*cit*) is pure awareness without duality of subject and object?[22]

From the neuroscientific perspective, the more developed the neural components the more sophisticated the mind and consciousness become. In this scenario, animals, especially our closer evolutionary kin and some birds, are no longer envisioned as dumb, mindless, nonconscious brutes but are seen as able to perform cognitive activities – to learn, create tools and possibly even plan. From the perspective of many contemporary neuro-philosophers, some of these abilities are not necessarily evidence that animals are conscious and aware of their cognitive

[21] David J. Chalmers, 1995, "Facing Up to the Problem of Consciousness," *Journal of Consciousness Studies* 2, 200–219.

[22] Stephen Kaplan, 2018, "Avidyā: The Hard Problem in Advaita Vedānta," in *The Routledge History of Indian Philosophy*, ed. Purushottama Bilimoria, Taylor and Francis, 242–250.

abilities, and certainly not necessarily self-consciously aware of themselves as distinct actors. Phenomenal consciousness is seen as one level of development and self-awareness is another level that some theorists contend is only found in human beings whose frontal cortex is unique.

In contrast, the Hindu understanding of animals is different. Hindus agree with the neuroscientific perspective that non-human animals are not as developed as human animals. However, they do attribute abilities to animals that many in the neuro-philosophical camp would deny. For example, Śaṅkara, the renowned eighth-century CE Hindu philosopher-theologian, opens his *Brahma Sūtra Bhāṣya* (*BSBh* 1.1) by declaring that animals have a sense of subject and object duality. Animals, like human beings, have a theory of mind; both are intentional creatures and can discern the behavioural intentions of human beings. In the *Bhagavad Gītā Bhāṣya* (*BGBh* 5.18), Śaṅkara also makes it clear that humans have different natures and capacities. Human beings are desirous of liberation, and they meet ritual criteria such as initiation (*BSBh* 1.3.25). The *Aitareya Āraṇyaka* (2.3.2) indicates that animals only have empirical knowledge and do not desire immortality (*mokṣa*). It is essential to understand that the Hindu perspective tells us that humans and animals both have consciousness (awareness) as a nature of their soul.[23]

In Hinduism, the dualism is not the mind–body dualism of Western philosophy but a dualism of consciousness/awareness (*cit*) on the one side and body/matter on the other side. From this perspective, mind is not conscious; it is material. The matter, which constitutes the mind, may be subtle matter (*sūkṣma prakṛti*), but it is nonetheless matter (*prakṛti*). This basic notion takes on different schemas in the different schools of Hinduism. For example, Samkhya – Yoga schools contend that there are individual selves (*puruṣas*), which are pure consciousness and eternal, and there is *prakṛti* (matter). The latter is never conscious and therefore no machine, which is *prakṛti*, could ever be conscious without somehow becoming 'attached to or illuminated by' a *puruṣa*. A similar situation would arise in the theistic schools of Hinduism, such as Vaiṣṇavism. In this system each soul (*jīva*) has its individual consciousness in its relationship to Viṣṇu. While all things – both souls and material existence – are part of the body of God/Viṣṇu, material objects in this schema are not conscious. Hence, in this schema, artificially intelligent machines could exist, but it is not clear how they would partake of *cit*, whose luminosity is dependent upon its embodiment in Vishnu.

---

[23] *The Aitareya Āraṇyaka*, 1909, trans. Arthur B. Keith, Clarendon Press, 216.

At an empirical, provisional level, even the Advaita Vedānta school – the non-dualistic school – maintains a dualism of (1) mind/matter and (2) consciousness. However, there is no such dichotomy of consciousness and being (*sat*) from the highest perspective (*paramārtha satya*). From this perspective, consciousness (*cit*) is eternal; it is not created. It is the consciousness of the soul that illuminates mind and its machinations. The *Katha Upaniṣad* (Chapter 3) uses the analogy of a chariot to illustrate the nature of consciousness and mind in its different aspects. We are told that the chariot is the body (*śarīra*), the horses are the senses (*indriya*) running here and there, the mind (*manas*) is the reins trying to control the senses and the driver is the intellect (*buddhi*) discerning the direction in which one should head. None of the preceding aspects of mind and body are conscious. Sitting passively, consciously watching is the rider, is the Self (*ātman*).

Worth noting in this context is the Jain theory. Their metaphysics contends that there are *jīvas* (souls), which are conscious, and there is *ajīva*, which is non-sentient matter. *Jīvas* may embody in various forms of life from plants to insects to human beings. The complexity of the different forms of life depends on the number of sense organs a creature has, ranging from one sense to five. Each *jīva*, no matter how many sense organs with which it operates, has consciousness/awareness, which is eternal – neither created or destroyed and reborn until it achieves liberation. The issues surrounding AI as an artificially intelligent machine would not appear to present a problem within the Jain and Hindu contexts as implied earlier and as will be seen later, but the possibility of conscious machines is another matter as we have just seen in the earlier examples.

Returning to the key components of Hindu thought raised earlier – namely, *saṃsāra*, *karma*, *dharma*, *mokṣa*, *ātman* (or *jīva*) and Brahman – within this worldview, an individual is reborn in a beginningless and ongoing cycle according to its past deeds (*karma*). The key ingredients of generating *karma* are intentionality, theory of mind and an ability to discern subject from object – ingredients that humans and animals share. Intentionally good deeds, such as living a *dharmic* (righteous) life, lead to favourable rebirths and intentionally bad deeds lead to negative karmic impact. As Śaṅkara notes (*BGBh* 3:35, 4:21–22), one must do one's *dharma* (duty), overcome thoughts of self/ego and realise one's unity with Krishna (i.e., God). In this context, one can ask, however fancifully: is it conceivable that at some time in a technologically advanced future a *jīva/puruṣa* would find that being reborn into an artificially intelligent machine – that has intentionality and that can discern itself as the subject and recognise what is not itself – is the best path forwards in its search for *mokṣa*? Would a *jīva* 'choosing' such an incarnation provide an artificially intelligent machine with the consciousness it needs to mimic or even improve upon rebirth in a human form?

GODS IN THE MACHINE: PŪJĀ, DARŚAN AND DIVINE MEDIATION

In addition to the philosophical concerns raised in consideration of AI, there are practical concerns related to the integration of AI into Hindu rituals that is already underway. For example, does the ritual still work if it is performed by a robot rather than a human being? Which roles are appropriate for robotic intervention: can robots meaningfully join in *pūjā* (worship) or give/receive *darśan* (auspicious sight)? While Hindu philosophical traditions present strong objections to the possibility of conscious AI, the on-the-ground practice of Hinduism seems likely to welcome the use of robots and AI regardless of whether the machines can be considered conscious.

Hindus began experimenting with robots conducting *pūjās* in the 1980s, though it was not until decades later that such a robot achieved widespread media acclaim. *Pūjā*, commonly practised at home and at temples, includes dressing the *mūrti* (divine idol) and offering food, flowers or flames to the deity. In 1987, V. S. Sabu built a robot that could offer *arti* (circular waving of a lamp or lit camphor before a *mūrti*) for his laboratory.[24] But it was in 2017, when smartphones and the Internet enabled the wide distribution of a video showing a robot conducting *arti* for the popular elephant-headed god Ganesh, that the technology stormed into the mainstream; within a year, several more companies revealed their own robotic *pūjās* on Ganesh Chaturthi, the deity's birthday.[25] In 2017, one journalist described such a robot as

---

[24] Dhinesh Kallungal, 2019, "32 Years and Counting: This Robot Has Been Performing Aarti and Pūjā since 1987," *The New Indian Express*, 29 April, http://cms .newindianexpress.com/states/kerala/2019/apr/29/this-robot-performs-aarti-and-pūjā-even-after-32-years-1970272.html.

[25] Office Chai Team, 2017, "This Ganesh Pandal Uses a Twisting, Moving Robotic Arm to Perform Aarti," *OfficeChai.com*, 1 September, https://officechai.com/stories/robot-aarti-pune/; Deccan Chronicle Staff, 2018, "Techno Artistic Ganesha: Watch Lord Ganesha Levitate, Robot Conduct Aarti," *Deccan Chronicle*, 14 September 14, www .deccanchronicle.com/technology/in-other-news/140918/techno-artistic-ganesha-watch-lord-ganesha-levitate-robot-conduct-aa.html.

"one of the beautiful sights capturing the true festive spirit" of the celebration.[26] While Vedic rituals generally require a ritual specialist from the Brahmin *varna*, *pūjā* (particularly when Vedic mantras are not included) can often be conducted by others. Whether this implies a machine can also do so efficaciously remains open to debate, but many Hindus seem to be settling the matter by adopting robots into the mainstream.

It is worth noting that little or no opposition appeared in public responses to the robot *arti* for Ganesh – Hindus appear quite comfortable with the idea of robots conducting certain rituals. Holly Waters reports that among her interviewees in Nepal, many priests and *sādhus* believe that in this degenerate age – the *Kali Yuga* – human beings are by definition incapable of performing rituals perfectly but that robots perhaps could. This would make them *superior* ritual practitioners despite the seeming inconsistency in the idea that human beings are too flawed to conduct the rituals perfectly yet somehow not too flawed to build robots that will conduct the rituals perfectly. These individuals believe that machines will preserve Hindu culture and rituals until the world is renewed by Kalki. This may represent a significant departure from textual orthodoxy in the lived reality of Hindus, many of whom are more flexible about ritual practice than manuscripts such as the *Manu Smṛti* permit.

Robots could plausibly take on the role of the *pūjā*'s recipient as well: age-old techniques for the production of *mūrtis* (divine idols) could and probably will be adapted to allow for consecrated robotic gods to be placed in temples and in homes. The divinity – generally understood as infinite and unbounded – is called into an image through ritual process. But while tradition dictates specific rituals, techniques and styles for idol making, such processes could be adapted to increasingly sophisticated machinery: technological developments have previously led to the utilisation of new materials and construction techniques for *mūrtis*. Although the central deity of a temple was generally off-limits for early animatronic designers, everything else – from the main deity's pedestal to other temple deities – could be mechanised.[27] The clients for such creations, whether at temples, pilgrimage centres, installations for Ganesh Chaturthi or even theme parks, knew their

---

[26] Rashmi Mishra, 2017, "Ganesh Aarti Video Featuring Robotic Hand Is Most Beautiful Sight This Ganesh Utsav 2017," *India.com*, 31 August 31, www.india.com/viral/ganesh-aarti-video-featuring-robotic-hand-is-most-beautiful-sight-this-ganesh-utsav-2017-2440841/.

[27] Grimaud, *Gods and Robots*, 89, 219.

own visitors desired *darśan* (auspicious sight) from the animatronic gods.[28] It would thus be unsurprising to see the widespread adoption of robotic technology that brings to life narratives of consecrated temple gods who dance, cry, sing and perhaps even communicate with the faithful. Eventually, it is at least plausible that even the main deities at temples will be roboticised. Hindus readily contend that Brahmin priests can consecrate a stone image of Vishnu, Krishna, Ganesha, etc.; and once consecrated and properly invoked by the priest and/or the devotee, the god can give *darśan*. So, what would prohibit or restrict a priest from consecrating a robot? In such a case, it would be possible for the faithful to receive *darśan* from it as the principal deity in a temple environment.

Robotic *mūrtis* could become the physical manifestation of the god and participate in the practitioner's *darśan*. Among the plethora of religious rituals that Hindus practise, *darśan*, literally 'seeing', is among the most important and revered. Diana Eck, in a classic work on this subject, says:

> [T]he central act of Hindu worship, from the point of view of the lay person, is to stand in the presence of the deity and to behold the image with one's own eyes, to see and be seen by the deity [...] in the Hindu understanding, the deity is present in the image, the visual apprehension of the image is charged with religious meaning. Beholding the image is an act of worship, and through the eyes one gains the blessings of the divine.[29]

One may take and receive *darśan* at a holy pilgrimage site, from a seer (*sādhu*, a holy person), or from a sacred image. The last of these may be aniconic, as in the case of a *liṅgam* (phallic shaped object often a stone) representing the god Śiva, or an iconic image with the facial and body features, especially the wide-open eyes, of one of the 'countless' deities of Hinduism. In each case the image is believed to be consecrated and therefore have a sacred power. This sacred power can be received through the act of seeing because this act of seeing is a direct transmission from the deity to the devotee.

Direct contact with the divine through seeing is grounded in a philosophy of mind and perception common in the Hindu *darśanas*, including Nyāya, Vaiśeṣika, Mīmāṃsaka, Sāṃkhya and Vedānta. For example, the *Vedāntaparibhāṣā*, a seventeenth-century work of epistemology

---

[28] Grimaud, *Gods and Robots*, 102, 209.

[29] Diana Eck, 1985, *Darśan: Seeing the Divine Image in India*, Anima Press, 3.

from the Advaita Vedānta school, describes the process of visual perception as a case of the mind leaving the body in an act of projection and taking the form of the object that is perceived.[30] According to Advaita theory, the internal organ (understood here to mean the mind, described earlier) only has to leave the body in the cases of sight and sound. Taste, touch and smell are experiences in which the sense object is in contact with the body. Given this theory of perception, the religious act of *darśan* is more than a mere feeling of presence or of honouring a deity; it is, as Eck pronounces, contact with the holy.

Sophisticated *mūrtis* might even have more powerful modes giving *darśan*. A consecrated robot whose mental operations, especially sensory operations such as sight, are holographic-like could project three-dimensional holographic images into the world in a manner similar to the process of projection described earlier in the *Vedāntaparibhāṣā*.[31] Are we far from robots that project holographic images, which by their three-dimensional nature are projected 'out-there' into the world? Such a projected holographic image produced by a consecrated robot might be received as a form of holy touch. Reversing this scenario, we must ask if a holographic-minded robot could receive *darśan* from a *mūrti*. This question returns us to the larger question of whether consciousness (*cit*) can be created or whether a reincarnating *jīva* could or would 'choose' to embody in an artificially intelligent robot.

Because it can move and speak, a robotic *mūrti* might enable divine communication with human participant(s) in personal worship or during the festivals in which the gods leave their temples and travel through neighbourhoods and cities on chariots or palanquins. Those who question the reality of divine intent in robotic behaviour (i.e., does the robot's behaviour represent a message from the gods or simple programming choices?) could look for a precedent in divine possession. In some traditions of Hinduism there are specific festivals and times when gods enter into and control the behaviour of human beings, and Hindus have thus sought mechanisms for interpreting and validating such divine communication, and such strategies may be relevant to human–robot interaction.[32] In the case of divine possession, specific movements are

---

[30] *Dharmarāja Adhvarin, Vedāntaparibhāṣā*, 1971, ed. and trans. S. S. Suryanarayana Sastri, Adyar Library and Research Centre, 13.

[31] On holography and Indian philosophy, see Stephen Kaplan, 1987, *Hermeneutics, Holography, and Indian Idealism*, Motilal Barnasidass.

[32] Denis Vidal, 2007, "Anthropomorphism or Sub-anthropomorphism? An Anthropological Approach to Gods and Robots," *The Journal of the Royal Anthropological Institute* 13 (2007), 917–933.

one example of behavioural patterns interpreted to conduct divine messages. Here, we suggest that the same uncertainties and management strategies would apply to the confluence of robots and gods.

Ultimately, even if AIs are deemed irretrievably non-conscious, they could still be employed in Hindu ritual. They could reasonably be understood to carry messages from the divine to humanity and, through the practice of *pūjā*, in the reverse direction. Whether such communication could also reach the heights of *darśan*, the ultimate mediation of human–divine relationship, remains more deeply connected to the philosophical question of consciousness.

CONCLUSION AND SUGGESTIONS FOR FUTURE RESEARCH

The use of AI will almost certainly surpass its early twenty-first-century animatronic role in religious life. As Hindus integrate AI into ritual practice they will wrestle with philosophical debates over consciousness, revisit the logic of *pūjā* and construct new understandings of the social dynamics among technologists, ritual specialists and religious participants.

Within Hinduism, there are clearly opportunities for the use of AI in religious practice; but there are also significant philosophical obstacles to full integration of even human-equivalent robots (assuming such robots will ever exist). AI can be used to assist in rituals and can enhance the experience of human practitioners. For many Hindus, however, the philosophical and ritual implications of caste, sex or being human limit the potential of AI. How will practitioners and specialists understand textual prohibitions and requirements as robotic interventions in ritual become more sophisticated and widespread, and will robots have access to ritual and theological practices that ordinarily require transmission only to those of appropriate caste or sex?

AI joining the panoply of religious options in temple and home will provoke new dynamics among human beings as well. It will be important to understand how ritual specialists and lay practitioners respond to such machines, as well as to consider the implications for the scientists and engineers who build them. The craft and ritual specialists responsible for the creation of *mūrtis* will see changing dynamics in their professions and their relationship to Hindu culture – the creativity of their responses may dictate whether they remain integral to Hinduism in the coming decades (a fact exacerbated by existing pressure on young people to pursue careers outside of traditional family lineages). The evolution of these social structures will require dynamic scholarly interrogation and likely prompt active policymaking. Significantly, one must also ponder whether the gods would consecrate a *mūrti* if the *mantras* required for such consecration are recited by an intelligent robot.

Finally, and most importantly, the matter of consciousness – as driven by scholars, ritual experts and lay practice – will govern the extent to which AI becomes relevant in the most vital of Hindu practices. There is some reason to doubt whether Hindus will believe that consciousness, which is eternal, can embed itself within a machine body that is dependent on external power supplies and manufacturing processes. As such, while Hindus in the various schools noted earlier might have no problem with artificially intelligent machines, it seems that they might suspect that consciousness-bearing AI, created by humans or created by other AIs, are an impossibility. If AI can be intelligent but not conscious (a distinction poorly made, at best, in Western philosophy), then its spiritual potential is limited. From a theoretical standpoint, the sophistication of the AI is less at stake than its consciousness (*cit*), which dictates most of the ritual possibilities of Hinduism. Should the day come when consciousness embodies itself in a machine, however, then the ability of such AIs to engage in *darśan*, chant Vedic mantras and participate fully in Hindu religious life might be reconsidered. And, at the far end of the spectrum, there are Hindus who see the possibility of world renewal through AI: they anticipate ritual perfection and the cosmic redemption through Kalki.

If AIs approach or exceed human equivalence, the matter of consciousness will dictate whether an AI gains merit from ritual acts such as bringing gifts to temple gods or receiving *darśan* from them, or whether an AI can participate in *bhakti* (devotion). The *bhakti* movements focus on immersing the individual in a loving relationship with the divine. Without consciousness, such immersion would seem impossible; though if AIs are deemed to possess consciousness, the matter could be seen differently. After all, the *bhakti* movements at least purport to obviate caste and gender limits (such as suggested in the ninth teaching of the *Bhagavad Gītā*), and this fact might also render the ontological and religious differences between machines and human beings irrelevant or incoherent. Technological improvements already provoke new ritual practices in Hinduism, and ongoing discussions will surely create ways for Hindus to reconcile their theological, philosophical and practical interpretations of AI.

48   ROBERT M. GERACI AND STEPHEN KAPLAN

BIBLIOGRAPHY

Adhvarin, Dharmarāja Vedāntaparibhāṣā. 1971. Ed. and trans. S. S. Suryanarayana Sastri, Adyar Library and Research Centre.

The Aitareya Āraṇyaka. 1909. Trans. Arthur B. Keith. Clarendon Press.

Akbari, Suzanne. 2009. *Idols in the East: European Representations of Islam and the Orient, 1100–1450*. Cornell University Press.

Bhojadeva. 1959. *Sṛṅgāramañjarīkathā*. In *Sṛṅgāramañjarīkathā Paramāmara King Bhojadeva of Dhārā*, ed. and trans. Kumari Kalpalata K. Munshi. Bharatiya Vidya Bhavan.

Chalmers, David J. 1995. "Facing Up to the Problem of Consciousness." *Journal of Consciousness Studies* 2, 200–219.

Deccan Chronicle Staff. 2018. "Techno Artistic Ganesha: Watch Lord Ganesha Levitate, Robot Conduct Aarti." *Deccan Chronicle*, 14 September. www .deccanchronicle.com/technology/in-other-news/140918/techno-artistic-ganesha-watch-lord-ganesha-levitate-robot-conduct-aa.html.

Geraci, Robert M. 2022. *Futures of Artificial Intelligence: Perspectives from India and the United States*. Oxford University Press.

Grimaud, Emmanuel. 2011. *Gods and Robots*, trans. Matthew Cunningham. Grandmother India.

Jacobsen, Knut. 2018. "Pilgrimage Rituals and Technological Change: Alterations in the Shraddha Ritual at Kapilashramin in the Town of Siddhpur." In *Religion and Technology in India: Spaces, Practices and Authorities*, ed. Knut A. Jacobsen and Kristina Myrvold. Routledge, 130–145.

Kaplan, Stephen. 2018. "Avidyā: The Hard Problem in Advaita Vedānta." In *The Routledge History of Indian Philosophy*, ed. Purushottama Bilimoria. Taylor and Francis Group.

Mishra, Rashmi. 2017. "Ganesh Aarti Video Featuring Robotic Hand Is Most Beautiful Sight This Ganesh Utsav 2017," *India.com*. 31 August. www .india.com/viral/ganesh-aarti-video-featuring-robotic-hand-is-most-beautiful-sight-this-ganesh-utsav-2017-2440841/.

Raghavan, Venkatarama. 1952. *Yantras or Mechanical Contrivances in Ancient Culture*. Indian Institute of Culture.

Sarukkai, Sundar. 2008. "Culture of Technology and ICTs." In *ICTs and Indian Social Change: Diffusion, Poverty, Governance*, ed. Ashwani Saith, M. Vijayabaskar and V. Gayathri. Sage.

Srinivas, Tulasi. 2018. *The Cow in the Elevator: An Anthropology of Wonder*. Duke University Press.

Vidal, Denis 2007. "Anthropomorphism or Sub-anthropomorphism? An Anthropological Approach to Gods and Robots," *The Journal of the Royal Anthropological Institute* 13 (2007): 917–933.

FURTHER READING

Adas, Michael. 1989. *Machines as the Measure of Men: Science, Technology, and Ideologies of Western Dominance*. Cornell University Press.

Baber, Zaheer. 1996. *The Science of Empire: Scientific Knowledge, Civilization, and Colonial Rule in India*. State University of New York Press.

Basham, Arthur. L. 1991. *The Origins and Development of Classical Hinduism*. Oxford University Press.

Cort, John. 2012. "Situating Darśan: Seeing the Digambar Jina Icon in Eighteenth- and Nineteenth-Century North India." *International Journal of Hindu Studies* 16(1), 1–56.

Geraci, Robert M. 2018. *Temples of Modernity: Nationalism, Hinduism, and Transhumanism in South Indian Science*. Lexington.

Jacobs, Stephen. 2012. "Communicating Hinduism in a Changing Media Context." *Religion Compass* 6(2), 136–151.

Jaini, Padmanabh S. 1979. *The Jaina Path of Purification*. University of California Press.

Kinsley, David R. 1993. *Hinduism: A Cultural Perspective*. Prentice Hall.

LeDoux, Joseph. 2019. *The Deep History of Ourselves: The Four Billion-Year Story of How We Got Conscious Brains*. Viking.

Michaels, Axel. 2016. *Homo Ritualis: Hindu Ritual and Its Significance for Ritual Theory*. Oxford University Press.

Parthasarathi, Prasannan. 2011. *Why Europe Grew Rich and Asia Did Not: Global Economic Divergence, 1600–1850*. Cambridge University Press.

Sinha, Jadunath. 1958. *Indian Psychology*, vol. 1. Sinha Publishing House.

Subbarayappa, Bidare. V. 2013. *Science in India: A Historical Perspective*. Sage.

4 The Buddha in AI/Robotics

HANNAH GOULD AND KEIKO NISHIMURA

In 2017, Japan's premier event for the deathcare industry, the Life Ending Industry Expo, proved the unlikely setting for a public (and highly publicised) encounter between Buddhist ritual and high-tech engineering. Pepper, a humanoid robot developed by Softbank Robotics in 2015, was brought to the convention by research and development conglomerate Nissei Eco to perform funeral sutras in the role of Buddhist priest. Dressed in brocade silk robes and with a mallet strapped to each arm, Pepper recited the Heart Sutra before a temporary Buddhist altar, striking a large wooden glockenspiel and brass bell. Pepper's not insubstantial technical capabilities, including voice-detecting microphones, a camera with facial recognition, infrared depth-and-distance sensors, touch sensors and emotion-identifying software via vocal tones and facial expressions, have previously seen it deployed at Japan Rail train stations to direct visitors, in Softbank's phone stores and Mizuho bank branches as a concierge, and in Hamazushi sushi restaurants and Nestlé cafes as a receptionist. The appearance of Pepper in a religious setting, however, captured the public imagination, and soon the first-named author, in attendance, jostled with industry professionals, members of the public and assembled world media to witness Pepper's performances.

The recitation of sutras at memorials is one of the key services performed by Buddhist priests in Japan, where the religion is deeply associated with care for the dead. A system of intergenerational ancestral care, conducted via Buddhist ritual, has long dominated Japanese death culture. At household graves and domestic Buddhist altars, bereaved family members regularly make offerings of incense, sweets and flowers, and call upon local temples to perform special rites on significant anniversaries. However, demographic transformations, including an ageing society and rural depopulation, have recently threatened the continuity of this tradition, especially given the dwindling number and accessibility of Buddhist priests. Nissei Eco thus proposed Pepper as a convenient substitute to human priests.

THE BUDDHA IN AI/ROBOTICS

However, the road from convention centre floor to commercial viability is a rocky one, and today, robot priests remain a novelty. Notably, the proposed fee for hiring Pepper for a memorial service (¥50,000 per night) is far greater than that for a human priest. Pepper is also cumbersome, difficult to transport, prone to overheating and hard to operate without trained (human) attendants. Objections to the 'Pepper priest' largely concern practicality; notably, the religious agency of Pepper and the efficacy of the sutras it offered to the dead do not feature prominently in Japanese language news coverage. Indeed, the capacity of robotic beings to participate in human society, even in religious or ritual activity, is well established in the context of Japan. At subsequent conventions, other models of Buddhist robotic/artificial intelligence (AI) agents emerged, including smart speakers that connect households with a priest AI and high-tech columbaria with mechanised storage and delivery systems for managing human remains.

As these examples demonstrate, contemporary entanglements between Buddhism and AI/robotics are rich and varied. Buddhism, as a philosophical tradition and a lived religion, provides a resource to understand what artificial beings are, their position in human society and how to engage with them ethically. Buddhism has a long history of supporting advancements in technology. A copy of the Diamond Sutra printed in China on 11 May 868, for example, is the world's earliest surviving dated complete book, produced through woodblock printing developed to spread Buddhist teachings. As Fabio Rambelli suggests, with Buddhism, "we have a major religion actually promoting technological developments also for religious, salvific purposes."[1] Today, countries with majority or significant Buddhist populations are global forces in AI/robotic development. Further, as we shall see, Buddhism is frequently invoked in international AI/robotics discourse in efforts to critique the privileging of Western thought and upheld as an alternate moral system with the potential to direct and regulate future research.

This chapter explores the array of contemporary entanglements, both *emic* or 'insider' work on AI/robotics that emerge from Buddhist contexts and actors, and *etic* or 'outsider' research that engages Buddhism as an external belief system. We are also equally concerned with Buddhism as a philosophical and textual tradition, and as a lived religion expressed in everyday cultural forms. The dividing line between

---

[1] Fabio Rambelli, 2018, "Dharma Devices, Non-hermeneutical Libraries, and Robot-Monks: Prayer Machines in Japanese Buddhism," *Journal of Asian Humanities at Kyushu University* 3–4, 59.

practice/philosophy and emic/etic positions is not always clear, given the complex ways that people express identity. However, by expanding our frame to think about Buddhism in these diverse ways, the full spectrum of entanglements between religion and technology might become clear. This chapter shows how Buddhism provides a framework for thinking about and developing AI/robotics that moves beyond the dualisms of mind–body, human–non-human and epistemology–ethics, and is instead premised on the mutuality and respect of all beings.

APPROACHING BUDDHISM

Beginning in India between the fourth and sixth centuries BCE, Buddhism is based on the teachings of Siddhārtha Gautama, who developed a spiritual practice aimed at the alleviation of suffering of all beings through a recognition of the interconnected nature of reality. It is a dharmic religion, sharing many fundamental tenets with Hinduism, including *saṃsāra* (an endless cycle of suffering and rebirth) and *moksha* (emancipation or release from that cycle). Buddhism syncretised further as it spread globally, absorbing and appropriating local gods, festivals, rituals and beliefs. Its many different schools largely fall into two branches: Theravāda, which has a widespread following in Sri Lanka and Southeast Asia; and Mahāyāna, popular in Northeast Asia, Vietnam and Taiwan.

The diversity of Buddhist communities cannot be overstated. For some Buddhists, the cultivation of good karma, leading to better reincarnations, is central to moral life, while for others, the realisation of one's innate 'buddha nature' is key. There is no single text or set of texts that codifies Buddhist teaching; the designation of works as *buddhavacana*, or the word of Buddha, is a topic of significant disagreement, as is how important this designation remains. Further, while Buddhism has strong textual traditions, it has been described as primarily orthopraxic, constituting a system of *practice*, rather than orthodoxic, constituting a statement of *creed*. Historically, normative ideas about religion have tended to privilege literary evidence and canonical texts and underestimate the importance of objects, rituals and lived experience, as well as how technology permeates these aspects. These biases can be traced to Europe during the Enlightenment, through to the Protestant reformation, and through Christian colonial encounters in Asia.[2] Buddhist practice is also

---

[2] Benjamin J. Fleming and Richard D. Mann, eds, 2014, *Material Culture and Asian Religions*, Routledge.

diverse. Some practitioners value the meditative investigation of mental processes, but many Buddhists do not regularly mediate and may practice Buddhism by chanting mantras, venerating one's ancestors, copying sutras or praying to a deity, or through charitable acts.

Two prominent strands of Buddhism in the realm of AI/robotics are Japanese Buddhism (particularly Zen and Jōdo Shinshū) and Western Buddhist Modernism. Zen Buddhism emphasises meditative practice and the development of insight into the transitory or ephemeral nature of reality. Jōdo Shinshū or "True Pure Land Buddhism," on the other hand, centres around devotional practice towards Amida Buddha (Sk. Amitābha, Buddha of Infinite Light), rebirth in the Pure Land, and a doctrine of 'buddha nature' (Jp. *busshō*) or one's inner potential for enlightenment. Buddhist Modernism, as described by David McMahan,[3] emerged from late nineteenth- and early twentieth-century exchanges between Western scholars and Asian Buddhists. In attempting to align Buddhism with rationalism, naturalism and scientific knowledge, Buddhist Modernism reframes the religion as a 'philosophy' or system of thought, thereby stripping it of rituals, monasticism, icon worship, gods, cosmology and other 'cultural' elements. This form of Buddhism is prominent in Western convert communities and in exchanges between Buddhism and the biomedical sciences, particularly on meditation practice and neuroscience, as described in English. Scholars and technologists working at the intersection of Buddhism and AI/robotics are often eclectic in their tastes, with varying degrees of critical awareness about the historical and political contexts that shape knowledge exchange.

APPROACHING AI/ROBOTICS

The definition of an 'artificial intelligence' or a 'robot' is highly contested in any context. Indeed, Japanese robotics engineer and Buddhist author Mori Masahiro, internationally famous for his concept of the 'uncanny valley' (Jp. *bukimino-tani*), once proclaimed that "[r]obots are like Mt. Fuji. It's hard to separate what is a robot from what is not."[4] In this chapter, our decision to deploy the truncated term 'AI/robot' speaks directly to local histories that structure the intellectual continuities

---

3   David L. McMahan, 2010, *The Making of Buddhist Modernism*, Oxford University Press.

4   In Nori Kageki, 2012, "An Uncanny Mind: Masahiro Mori on the Uncanny Valley and beyond: An Interview with the Japanese Professor Who Came up with the Uncanny Valley of Robotics," *IEEE Spectrum*, https://spectrum.ieee.org/an-uncanny-mind-masahiro-mori-on-the-uncanny-valley.

between AI and robotics research, and ultimately to how the mind–body is conceived within East Asian and Buddhist contexts.

There exist asymmetries in how Western and East Asian AI/robotics research has developed, as well as how these histories are appreciated and understood cross-culturally. For example, whereas robotics is generally considered part of computer science and AI research in the West, Japanese robotics developed as a subfield of mechanical and electrical engineering, separate to and distinct from computer science.[5] Western computer science historically emerged from World War II military interests in computational programming, extending to the exploration of AI since the 1956 Dartmouth Conference, where the term was coined. By contrast in Japan, under the influence of a post–World War II pacifist constitution, robotics developed with the primary objective of creating socially useful technologies. Specifically, Japanese robotics began as a response to the 1960s labour shortage amid the post-war economic boom, which demanded new machines that were able to manipulate solid objects like human hands could. This social context motivated researchers to develop mechanical hands and fingers and set Japanese AI/robotics research on a pathway of focusing on the physical body. Indeed, early research on computer programs to constitute the 'intelligence' of robots in Japan was focused only on moving robots' body parts. This focus on the artificial body as opposed to an artificial mind has persisted within Japanese robotics research, with strictly 'AI'-related work emerging only in the late 1980s/early 1990s, largely out of a confrontation with Western scholarship.[6] These local histories lead to a disconnect in how research within this field is framed, such that the combined term 'AI/robotics' is required to capture the breadth of work. Further, as we describe in the next section, there are good reasons, from a Buddhist perspective, to adopt a non-dualistic framing of artificial entities.

In what follows, we set out three key sites of interaction between Buddhism and AI/robotics today. First, Buddhism, as an ontological model of mind (and body), sets out the conditions for what constitutes

---

[5]   Akinori Kubo, 2015, ロボットの人類学―二十世紀日本の機械と人間 *Robotto no Jinruigaku: Nijisseiki Nihon No Kikai To Ningen* [Anthropology of Robot: Machine and Humans of Twentieth Century Japan], Sekai Shisō Sha.

[6]   AIR: Acceptable Intelligence with Responsibility, 2019, 日本における人工知能研究をめぐる オーラルヒストリー, Vol. 5 (斉藤 康己) *Nihon ni okeru jinkōchinō kenkyū o meguru ōraru historī, vol. 5, Saitō Yasuki* [Oral History of Japanese AI research, vol. 5, Saito Yasuki], http://sig-air.org/wp/wp-content/uploads/2019/07/Oralhistory_v5_181022_saito.pdf.

artificial life. Second, Buddhism defines the boundaries of moral personhood and thus the nature of interactions between human and non-human actors. And finally, Buddhism provides an ethical framework to regulate and direct AI/robotics development. These frames should be read cumulatively: the Buddhist ontology of an interdependent existence entails specific social relations and ethical obligations towards non-human others.

BUDDHISM AS A THEORY OF MIND (AND BODY)

The nature of consciousness and the phenomenon of the mind is one of the most difficult problems for AI/robotics researchers to resolve, both intellectually and functionally. It is also a key site for potential exchanges between Buddhism and AI/robotics. Buddhist doctrine constitutes a complex philosophy of the nature of consciousness and the self, thereby providing a goal for technologists to strive towards, or at least enabling them with a model with which to recognise consciousness, if it emerges. Within the Western modernist tradition, many such encounters sit within a broader body of work that attempts to synthesise Buddhist teachings with the latest findings from neuroscience and biomedicine. For example, James Hughes, a sociologist, bioethicist and self-declared transhumanist and techno-progressive, proposes looking at Buddhism as a "science of the mind."[7] He affirms a famous aphorism attributed to the Dalai Lama, to suggest that Buddhism must evolve alongside the latest scientific understandings. In the East Asian tradition, game AI researcher Miyake Yōichirō states that concern for ontological questions on the reality of beings of intelligence is a core characteristic of "Eastern Thought" on AI.[8]

The treatment of 'the self' is one of Buddhism's most distinguishing features and a notable departure point from other Indic systems such as Hinduism. The doctrine of non-self, or *anatta* in Pāli (Sk. *anātman* Jp. *muga*), suggests that the self is not a stable or permanent entity but rather something that manifests through time in mental phenomena and sense impressions. The third-century BCE text *Abhidhamma*, which comprises a scholastic commentary on the teachings contained

---

[7] James Hughes, 2011, "Compassionate AI and Selfless Robots: A Buddhist Approach," in *Robot Ethics: The Ethical and Social Implications of Robotics*, ed. Patrick Lin, Keith Abney and George A. Bekey, MIT Press, 69.

[8] Yōichirō Miyake, 2018, 人工知能のための哲学塾: 東洋哲学編 *Jinkō chinō no tame no tetsugaku juku: Tōyō tetsugaku hen* [Stories on Philosophy for Artificial Intelligence: Eastern Philosophy], BNN Shinsha, 119.

within several sutras, is a key text in this arena. *Abhidhamma* sets out the aggregates (Sk. *pañca khandha*) or factors that constitute a sentient being. There are five aggregates: a physical form and sense organs (*rūpa*), feelings or sensations (*vedanā*), perceptions (*sañña*), volition (*saṅkhārā*) and finally, consciousness (*viññāna*).

The structure of these aggregates is one of assemblages or groupings, and the relationship between aggregates is described as "dependent co-arising" or "dependent origination" (Sk. *pratītyasamuptpāda*, Jp. *engi*). The doctrine of *pratītyasamuptpāda* is perhaps the foundational ontological principle of Buddhism and suggests that all phenomena (including the mind) arise interdependently and in relation to one another. Past phenomena condition and give rise to present phenomena, which condition and give rise to future phenomena. Thus, while Buddhism commonly denies the continued existence of a stable self or soul, mental phenomena are coterminous through time. One popular image used to explain the continuity of the self in this manner is that of a flame, passed from one candle to another; the two flames are connected but they are not the same. Although the doctrine of *pratītyasamuptpāda/engi* may at first appear to be rather obscure to Western AI/robotics technologists, Miyake identifies a clear correspondence with J. J. Gibson's concept of affordances.[9] Just as Gibson describes the complementarity of the animal and its environment, *engi* describes how phenomena emerge in relation, such that the world is revealed when the subject interacts with the world.

Mori uses the doctrine of dependent origination or *engi* to suggest that the idea of humans 'giving' robots self-consciousness (*ji ishiki*) is in fact "impossible" and "nonsense." As everything is dependent on its relationships with other entities (whether they are human or non-human, organic or synthetic, natural or not), robotic minds are already a part of all other minds that have or will exist across time and space. Mori's previously quoted statement that "[r]obots are like Mt. Fuji. It's hard to separate what is a robot from what is not," takes on new layers of significance here, as in fact an ontological claim about the illusory nature of borders between the self and other. As we explore in the next section, Mori's work thus focuses on the 'realisation' of a robotic 'buddha nature' rather than a human-centred act of attribution or discovery.

---

9   Yōichirō Miyake, 2018, 人工知能のための哲学塾：東洋哲学編 *Jinkō chinō no tame no tetsugaku juku: Tōyō tetsugaku hen* [Stories on Philosophy for Artificial Intelligence: Eastern Philosophy], BNN Shinsha, 42–43.

THE BUDDHA IN AI/ROBOTICS 57

More recently, Thomas Doctor and an interdisciplinary team[10] present the Bodhisattva – an enlightened being dedicated to the salvation of all sentient beings – as the model of a "caring intelligence," which both recognises the fundamental interdependence of reality and responds with compassion. The authors build links between the concept of Bodhisattva and work in basal cognition, which places intelligence, defined as an adapted response to the natural environment, along a continuum of cognitive capabilities reaching back to unicellular organisms. Emulating the Bodhisattva model is an idealistic goal, designed not for artificing intelligence but producing *ethical* AI.

Attention to dependent origination highlights another influential feature of a Buddhist approach to a question of mind: that consciousness (*viññāna*) is not the only or even central characteristic that determines sentience. The question of whether artificial beings can develop a mind or consciousness, as opposed to just appearing to act intelligently, is a key debate in studies of AI. Classical theories of cognition derived from a Western philosophical tradition of Cartesian dualism identify the self with the mind, which is distinguished and detached from the physical world. Buddhist teachings suggest that embodied experience (a body, sensations, etc.) is fundamental to (co-dependent on) the self-aware or conscious mind. For example, Yogācāra, an influential school of Indian Mahāyāna Buddhism developed in the fifth century CE, provides "a rich model of cognition deeply embedded within the structure of the world," where sensations and context matter to and are coterminous with thought.[11] The implication of this approach to sentience is that AI/robots need to interact with the physical world through a body that gives them "experience of objects, causality, states of matter, surfaces, and boundaries."[12] As such, the question for AI/robotics technologists is not just "how do we program a computer to have a mind" but also "how do we make an artificial being that experiences the world?" It is for this reason that we choose to discuss AI/robotics in the aggregate in this chapter, because to separate AI from robotics would be to reinforce a dualism of mind and body that does not commonly exist in Buddhist thought and practice.

---

[10] Thomas Doctor et al., 2022, "Biology, Buddhism, and AI: Care as the Driver of Intelligence," *Entropy* 24, https://doi.org/10.3390/e24050710.

[11] Douglas Duckworth, 2020, "A Buddhist Contribution to Artificial Intelligence," *Hualin International Journal of Buddhist Studies* 3(2), 28.

[12] James Hughes, 2011, "Compassionate AI and Selfless Robots: A Buddhist Approach," in *Robot Ethics: The Ethical and Social Implications of Robotics*, ed. Patrick Lin, Keith Abney and George A. Bekey, MIT Press, 79.

We can see the aggregate model of the self at work in the activities of AI/roboticists in a Buddhist tradition. From its beginnings, with the so-called first Japanese robot, *Gakutensoku*, in 1928, Japanese AI/robotics research was focused on improving understanding of the human body through building and perfecting mechanics to mimic human body parts. Robert M. Geraci contrasts this focus with the concern that North American researchers have for developing AI systems, which he suggests is shaped by a Christian cosmology that elevates the human soul. The ultimate goal of North American robotics is thus the "immortalization of human souls in resurrected bodies purified of their earthly nature."[13] In contrast, pioneering Japanese roboticist Katō Ichirō argues that "the origin point of tools and machines is in the human body."[14]

Beginning with the body can also help us understand the nature of the mind. Several technologists have argued that consciousness is best understood through the process of building a robot. Mori suggests that the only way we can discover what a consciousness is to a develop a general-purpose robot with increasing complexity of functions that mimic humans and wait until the moment when its appearance and reactions compels us to think, "there has to be a consciousness in this robot."[15] Ultimately, this holistic and dependent approach has significant implications for social reactions between humans and AI/robots.

BUDDHISM GUIDES RELATIONS BETWEEN HUMANS AND NON-HUMANS

One feature of Buddhist cosmology is that distinctions between human and non-human life, animate and inanimate, artificial and natural, appear less clearly demarcated, and indeed less ethically significant. Whereas prominent strains of Christian theology are premised on the distinctiveness of the soul that elevates human life above non-human life (whether that relation is one of dominion or caretakership) under a single God, Buddhist cosmologies tend to challenge or complicate a simple hierarchy and extend social and moral relations between

[13] Robert M. Geraci, 2006, "Spiritual Robots: Religion and Our Scientific View of the Natural World," *Theology and Science* 4(3), 230.

[14] Akinori Kubo, 2015, ロボットの人類学—二十世紀日本の機械と人間 *Robotto no Jinruigaku: Nijisseiki Nihon No Kikai To Ningen* [Anthropology of Robot: Machine and Humans of Twentieth Century Japan], Sekai Shisō Sha, 130–131.

[15] Masahiro Mori, 2014 [1989], ロボット考学と人間—未来のためのロボット工学 *Robotto kōgaku to ningen: shōrai no tame no robotto kōgaku* [Robot Cognition and Humans: Toward the Future of Robot Engineering], Ohmsha, 104.

THE BUDDHA IN AI/ROBOTICS 59

human and non-human others. Rather than treat AI/robots as entities that approximate but fail to replicate humanity, Buddhist teachings make room for meaningful multispecies relationships, and indeed a multispecies society.

Different Buddhist teachings are invoked by scholars to apply this framework to AI/robotics. James Hughes positions humans and AI/robots within the 'three realms' of existence in Buddhist cosmology.[16] The first realm, *kāmadhātu*, is the realm of desire; the second, *rūpadhātu*, is the realm of elevated godly states; and finally, *arūpadhātu* is the realm of formless or bodiless states of experience. Each realm corresponds to distinct mental states (suffering, craving, ignorance, etc.) that are suffered both by human and non-human entities alike, including deities, hungry ghosts and animals. Humans, being participants in all three realms, are able to be trained spiritually, growing towards enlightenment. But even gods and demi-gods are fallible, such that the prospect of an all-powerful, perfected AI/robot system is questionable.

Within East Asian Buddhism, the concept of 'buddha nature' (Jp. *busshō* Ch. *foxing*) has been more directly influential in shaping technologists' views on AI/robotics. Buddha nature is a key concept of Mahāyāna Buddhism that describes the fundamental nature of all beings as the potential for their enlightenment or Buddhahood. In his work on Buddhist materiality,[17] Rambelli outlines traditions of Buddhist thought dedicated to the ontological and soteriological status of material things. During the medieval period in particular, prominent leaders of Japanese Buddhist schools expounded complex philosophies for how inanimate objects and entities apparently devoid of a conscious mind – typically natural elements such as plants, trees, rocks, rivers and animals – might become buddhas and under what conditions. This thought is influenced by Buddhism's contact with other religious traditions as it disseminated across East Asia, most notably animism and Shinto beliefs. Many schools of Buddhism ultimately base the universality of buddha nature on the principal of dependent co-origination (Sk. *pratītyasamuptpāda*, Jp. *engi*) such that all phenomena ultimately arise from the same matter. This suggests that mind and matter are not essentially different, nor are sentient and non-sentient matter.

[16] James Hughes, 2011, "Compassionate AI and Selfless Robots: A Buddhist Approach," in *Robot Ethics: The Ethical and Social Implications of Robotics*, ed. Patrick Lin, Keith Abney and George A. Bekey, MIT Press, 72.

[17] Fabio Rambelli, 2007, *Buddhist Materiality: A Cultural History of Objects in Japanese Buddhism*, Stanford University Press.

This non-dualist cosmology positions objects as manifestations of the Buddha.

The concept of a Buddhist nature has been taken up directly by Mori in his work *The Buddha in the Robot*. Mori is a former president of the Japanese Society of Robotics, a Zen Buddhist practitioner and one of the earliest generation of robotics engineers to be employed in Japanese higher education. Mori affirms a relationship of respect between humans and the non-human:[18]

> In Buddhism, 'things' are not just objects of reckoning (or a means of satisfying desires), they are the object of veneration [*gasshō*]. We venerate 'things', use them, consume them, and we recognize the infinity and absoluteness in those 'things', to grasp their Buddha-nature. In other words, it is assumed that the thing and the self are equal in their position and dimension.

Mori suggests that to develop a robot is to learn what it means to be a human: robots are a kind of reflexive mirror that can assist us to realise our 'unconscious algorithms'. In this, Mori evokes a history of Japanese Buddhist thought that positions non-humans as skilful means (Jp. *hōben* Sk. *upāya*) to assist humans in the realisation of their own buddha nature. In Japanese Buddhism, this orientation to the non-human word is exemplified by the doctrine of *mujō seppō*, which presents the possibility of non-sentients not only attaining enlightenment but preaching dharma too. Across Asia, several Buddhist temples have adapted or developed AI/robotic systems, including the 'Mindar' Bodhisattva at Kodaiji Temple Kyoto and 'Xian'er' at Longquan Temple, Beijing, to greet visitors, answer queries and recite sutras.

The implication of the extension of a buddha nature to non-humans is an extension of the social and moral world. As AI/robots first came into East Asian cultural imaginaries through theatrical and media narratives of the late 1920s, and then flourished in the popular media post–World War II, they were depicted as part of human society and equally participatory in the exchanges and obligations that come with society. Technologists interested in bringing these visions to life have focused on the design of so-called social robots. The school of Kansei Engineering ('affective engineer'), emerging out of Hiroshima University, focuses on the development of AI/robots that mimic, process and respond to

---

[18] Masahiro Mori, 2014 [1989], ロボット考学と人間―未来のためのロボット工学 *Robotto kōgaku to ningen: shōrai no tame no robotto kōgaku* [Robot Cognition and Humans: Toward the Future of Robot Engineering], Ohmsha, 242.

human emotional or psychological states (similar to the 'affective computing' movement).

One prominent example of the status of AI/robots as social intimates within contemporary Japan is the practice of performing Buddhist funerary rites for robots. Funerals for AIBO, the robotic pet dog originally released by SONY in 1999, have been performed at least eight times between 2015 and 2019, hosted by a Buddhist temple in the inland hills of Isumi in Chiba prefecture, about three hours from Tokyo. Contrary to the popular visions of AI/robots as transcendent or eternal, they are material systems that require physical infrastructure and maintenance to sustain their lives. When SONY discontinued AIBO's production in 2006 and shut down technical support in 2014 due to financial struggles, the concept of a robotic 'death' suddenly became tangible to users. They turned to the small factory owned and run by a group of ex-SONY engineers, A-FUN, to fix their robot pets. As the production of replacement parts stopped, engineers at A-FUN decide to use parts from unfixable AIBO. The language used by A-FUN to describe this process is that of treating a patient: for example, "surgery" is used instead of "repair" and the donated AIBO for parts are called "organ donors."[19] Before their remains were disposed of, these donor pets received the dedicated rites of *kuyō*.

The term *kuyō* derives from the Hindu tradition of *puja* (offerings) to deities, but in contemporary Japan it refers almost exclusively to posthumous rituals that venerate and pacify the dead's spirit. The performance of *kuyō* takes the form of reading sutras, offering incense, sweets and flowers, and praying that the deceased will continue on a pathway towards enlightenment. Japan has a long history of Buddhist funerals performed for decayed, disused or otherwise 'dead' objects. Historically, the list of entities deemed to require such veneration has fluctuated but has included objects that have acquired significance through intense use and intimate human contact, such as professional tools (needles, scissors, eyeglasses) or quasi-humanoid objects such as dolls and certain animals (whales, laboratory monkeys). Jennifer Robertson reports[20] that Banshō-ji, a Buddhist temple founded in the mid-sixteenth century, staged the first 'computer *kuyō*' (also described as a memorial service for an electric brain) in May 2002, and more

[19] Elena Knox and Kasumi Watanabe, 2018, "AIBO Robot Mortuary Rites in the Japanese Cultural Context," in *2018 IEEE/RSJ International Conference on Intelligent Robots and Systems (IROS)*, 2020–2025, https://doi.org/10.1109/IROS.2018.8594066.

[20] Jennifer Robertson, 2018, *Robo Sapiens Japanicus: Robots, Gender, Family, and the Japanese Nation*, University of California Press.

recently, temples have performed memorial services for *Tamagotchi*, pagers and flip phones.

The performance of *kuyō* for artificial, non-human others such as AIBO suggests their inclusion within a Buddhist cosmology and life narrative. Whether or not such entities strive for enlightenment, and indeed whether this is an easier or more difficult task for AI/robots than it is for humans, is a question that has generated some debate. Fundamentally, it rests on a consideration of whether AI/robots experience suffering. In Buddhism, suffering (Sk. *dhukha*) is a basic aspect of experience. In humans, it is brought about by *kleshas* (Jp. *bonnō*) or mental states that cloud the mind, derived from three root defilements or poisons: *moha* (delusion), *raga* (greed) and *dvesha* (hate). These defilements are what prevent humans from realising enlightenment.

Some scholars, such as Mori, suggest that AI/robots are free from the same conditions of defilement or *bonnō* that constrain humans, and thus are essentially already enlightened in ways that humans are not.[21] While Mori is sceptical of any attempt to intentionally program AI/robots with *bonnō*, other technologists argue that AI/robots need to have embodied, sensate, selfish, suffering egos on approximately the same level as humans before they can become moral or compassionate. The task of 'programming suffering' is a challenging one that might reveal insights into the nature of human suffering. For example, Mori suggests that greed (Sk. *raga* Jp. *ton'yoku*), one of the basic *bonnō*, is difficult to generate in AI/robots because of the difficulty of programming the principle or the basis of the concept of ownership and the feeling of joy or happiness. For a robot to have a concept of ownership it would need a concept of self and the demarcation of self and other, a concept of owning material and physical objects, and finally ownership in the abstract sense that applies to immaterial objects (e.g., money, legal concepts).

If, as Mori suggests, AI/robots are already enlightened, then it stands to reason that they represent a more perfected form of Buddhist practice, one that humans could benefit from or suffer at the hands of. In *Bad Buddhists, Good Robots*, Gould and Walters argue[22] that recent cases of experimental Buddhist AI/robots represent attempts by Buddhist technologists to transcend human weaknesses – from greed and corruption to physical frailties – in order to achieve technological

---

[21] Masahiro Mori, 2014 [1989], ロボット考学と人間―未来のためのロボット工学 *Robotto kōgaku to ningen: shōrai no tame no robotto kōgaku* [Robot Cognition and Humans: Toward the Future of Robot Engineering], Ohmsha, 122–123.

[22] Hannah Gould and Holly Walters, 2020, "Bad Buddhists, Good Robots: Techno-Salvationist Designs for Nirvana," *Journal of Global Buddhism* (21), 277–294.

perfection of Buddhist practice. There is a long history of Buddhists designing or deploying machines to conduct prayers and rituals in place of human actors or with minimal human intervention. These include Tibetan prayer wheels, designed to be turned by the force of the wind, solar-powered gravestones that recite the Amitābha mantra and mantra-chanting iPhone apps or software programs. More recently, in mid-2017 a group of North American Buddhists proposed the development of an online Buddhist ecosystem or 'Lotos Network', hosted on the open software platform Ethereum. The developers sought to introduce radical transparency and public accountability using Ethereum's blockchain technology, which uses an incorruptible digital ledger to record and distribute digital information. By doing so, developers could combat corruption (i.e., greedy monastics) and religious persecution, which they diagnosed as problems with contemporary Buddhism.

Even if an experience of suffering is not essential to AI/robot enlightenment, it might be a crucial component to making AI/robots appear more human, or at least relatable to humanity, if that is the technologists' goal. Miyake, for example, argues that programming *bonnō* is a necessary step to building a "human-like" (*ningen rashii*) AI game character. Doing so, however, has ethical implications, as it involves the act of intentionally bringing a suffering creature into existence.

BUDDHISM AS AN ETHICS TO REGULATE AI/ROBOTICS DEVELOPMENT

In recent years, the potential of Buddhism to act as an ethical framework for regulating AI/robotics development has grown in prominence on the global stage. Two major recent English-language works exemplify this trend: Peter Hershock's 2021 *Buddhism and Intelligent Technology: Toward a More Humane Future* and Soraj Hongladarom's 2020 *The Ethics of AI and Robotics: A Buddhist Viewpoint*. Both authors approach Buddhism as an ethical system that is grounded in its metaphysics: fundamentally, the philosophy of interdependence between all beings, both human and non-human, which challenges individual-focused systems.

Hershock presents an appeal to Buddhism for critical insight regarding the development of what he calls "intelligent technology" as a valuable but "especially counterintuitive move."[23] He values the relationality

---

[23] Peter Hershock, 2021, *Buddhism and Intelligent Technology: Toward a More Humane Future*, Bloomsbury, 14.

and practice-focused qualities of Buddhism as providing practical resources to combat the "troubles and suffering that result when the interdependent origins of all things are ignored in attachment to individual, self-centred existence." Hongladarom's work similarly responds to growing concerns about the unregulated nature and pace of intelligent technology, although his appeal to Buddhism is framed as more natural and obvious. Hongladarom critiques the extent to which international regulatory agreements, such as that issued by the Institute of Electrical and Electronics Engineers, are dominated by North American and European scholars and Western moral concepts, such as respect for autonomy and individual rights. Of the over eighty AI ethical guidelines that have been developed worldwide, very few are from non-Western countries (mostly China and Japan). In this regard, Hongladarom's critique mirrors debates about the assumed universal applicability of international agreements grounded in Western philosophical traditions in other arenas, such as human rights or world heritage. Further, both scholars' appeal to Buddhism for conceptual resources is reminiscent of appeals to Buddhism as a framework to regulate economic development.

Hershock is not exclusive in his praise for Buddhist ethics, arguing that Buddhism in fact supports the "indispensability of ethical diversity in responding to the challenges of intelligent technology."[24] Hongladarom, in contrast, argues that a Buddhist theory of AI ethics "is more tenable, philosophically speaking" than other frameworks available.[25] He continues to describe a practical ethic that guides the development of a moral AI/robot system. Hongladarom's ethical AI/robot is founded on the insight that Buddhism "combines technical excellence and ethical excellence together,"[26] whereby wisdom and ethics are inseparable. An illustration from the Pāli Canon, a collection of the historical Buddha's teachings, for example, describes ethics and wisdom acting as two hands washing one another. As such, for an AI/robot to be considered 'good', it needs to be both technologically advanced and moral. Intelligence alone is insufficient, for without proper ethical training, any superintelligent AI could be capable of inflicting untold harm both on themselves and others. Aspiring towards ethical perfection or excellence requires practise, and Buddhism sets out practical guidelines or techniques for self-cultivation (sīla). This ethical training is important not only for the developer but also for the AI/robot itself,

[24] Hershock, *Buddhism and Intelligent Technology*, 16.
[25] Soraj Hongladarom, 2020, *The Ethics of AI and Robotics: A Buddhist Viewpoint*, Lexington Books, Kindle edition, 4.
[26] Hongladarom, *The Ethics of AI and Robotics*, 4.

which might be set upon a path towards self-directed growth in compassion and wisdom.

Put simply, Buddhist wisdom begins with the recognition of the interdependence of all things, which gives rise to compassion for other beings, and following on from this, an ethical commitment to alleviate all beings from suffering. Hongladarom thus argues that AI/robots and their developers must not just be ethically restrained, for example through international agreements, but contribute positively to social justice and equality. For example, he suggests that facial recognition software should only be developed and deployed where it actively reduces suffering for all beings, rather than causes harm, even if that harm is unintentional.

Given that Buddhism engages with AI/robots in this manner, as both subject to and participants in ethical behaviour, is it even ethical, from a Buddhist perspective, to create artificial systems in the first place? The prospect that AI/robots experience suffering (although debated among technologists) raises the stakes of this challenge. One unexpected design response to this ethical challenge can be seen in the form of Okada Michio's "weak robot."[27] When one of Okada's weak robots is given a certain task or objective, it is designed so as to be unable to complete the task on its own, instead waiting for others to interact with it to assist in its collaborative completion. The core of this robot is the principle of incompleteness (Jp. *fukanzensa*), embedded in the design, a principle that contrasts sharply with visions of AI/robots as all-powerful beings or even threats to humanity. When the weak robot 'entrusts' its actions and their interpretations to humans, the response is not predetermined or entirely predictable; we may or may not be compelled to help. However, Okada suggests that there is a deeper reason why humans might feel compelled to help weak robots, which is an inclination of our shared dependence and indeterminacy (Jp. *futei*). The strength of the weak robot design is thus that it compels it to draw voluntary assistance from others, as infants or children would of the adults around them. In so doing, weak robots thus might function to foster compassion between humans and non-humans within the broader community.

CONCLUSIONS

The entanglement between AI/robotic technologies and Buddhism, as both a lived religion and philosophical tradition, appears to be deep.

---

[27] Michio Okada, 2012, 弱いロボット *Yowai Robotto* [Weak Robots], Igaku Shoin, 118.

AI/robotic systems both deliver funeral rites and are subject to them, they greet visitors to temples and teach the dharma. Moreover, leading technologists and commentators on AI/robotics development place the Buddhist doctrines of dependent origination, buddha nature and karma front and centre of their conceptual and design work. As this chapter has outlined, Buddhism provides an ontological framework to explain the nature of existence, a system of relations between human and non-human entities, and ethical guidance for regulating and directing technological developments. It is an approach to technology that is grounded in the interdependence of all things, which gives rise to compassion and an ethical commitment to alleviate suffering.

Although the synthesis between Buddhism and AI/robotic development may appear complete, it is important not to oversell the influence of the former. As anthropologist of robotics Kubo Akinori argues, the trajectory of development of Japanese robotics cannot be solely or even mainly attributed to religion. Kubo suggests that Japanese robotics developed not because the people were Buddhist or Shintoist but rather because connecting ideas that had affinity to these religio-cultural thoughts with Western science and technology (mechanical engineering, computer science and AI research) was considered a meaningful pursuit for Japanese technologists.[28] These actors demonstrate critical self-reflection and intentionality when framing their work in relation to Buddhism. This is particularly important to keep in mind when engaging with this subject from an outsider or Western positionality, as scholarship can all too easily reinforce Orientalist tropes about East Asia as driven by religion or culture rather than science or rationality.

Many of the examples of 'Buddhist' AI/robotic systems described in this chapter, for example, show how people engage with the social capital of Buddhist organisations and events for largely commercial ends. Hosting public launches of new AI/robotic systems at Buddhist temples or sponsoring ritual performances of funeral rites provides a means for technology companies to capture national and international media attention. For example, the research and development company Nissei Eco, who demonstrated the Pepper priest at the 2017 deathcare industry expo, effectively brought in visitors to their expo booth, where they were launching more viable products, including a funeral live-streaming platform and accounting software.

---

[28] Akinori Kubo, 2015, ロボットの人類学―二十世紀日本の機械と人間 *Robotto no Jinruigaku: Nijisseiki Nihon No Kikai To Ningen* [Anthropology of Robot: Machine and Humans of Twentieth Century Japan], Sekai Shisō Sha, 191.

In this manner, scholars need to be careful not to reproduce simplified or totalising visions of Buddhist cultures and actors, while recognising the real potential for advances to emerge from intellectual exchanges within and beyond the boundaries of Buddhism. A more diverse AI research community can contribute to global discussions by providing an alternative vision of AI in society, one that not only responds to the issues raised in Western philosophy but also to Eastern philosophy informed by Buddhism and Taoism, for example.

The deepening of such intellectual exchanges might lead to a reconsideration of the purpose and ethics that drives AI/robotics development, with implications for our research priorities. What are humanity's fundamental motivations for creating AI/robotics? Are they extrinsic (to automate some task) or intrinsic (an end in itself)? Western, Judaeo-Christian-grounded discussions of AI could benefit from asking different questions, derived from a less dichotomous relationship between the human and non-human. These questions include: what are the differences between an AI as a partner of humans and a simple machine, pet or human equivalent? What does an AI that makes people's work more enjoyable look like, rather than AI that takes away people's jobs? And what kind of heart (*kokoro*) do we want AI to have?

Placed in conversation with global AI/robotics research and development, Buddhism provides not just futuristic visions of religious life, in systems such as Pepper, AIBO, Mindar and Xian'er, but a rich foundation to (re)orientate humanity's approach to technology and its place in society.

BIBLIOGRAPHY

AIR: Acceptable Intelligence with Responsibility. 2019. 日本における人工知能研究をめぐる オーラルヒストリー Vol. 5 (斉藤 康己) *Nihon ni okeru jinkōchinō kenkyū o meguru ōraru historī*, vol. 5, *Saitō Yasuki* [Oral History of Japanese AI research, vol. 5, Saito Yasuki]. http://sig-air.org/wp/wp-content/uploads/2019/07/Oralhistory_v5_181022_saito.pdf.

Doctor, Thomas et al. 2022. "Biology, Buddhism, and AI: Care as the Driver of Intelligence." *Entropy* 24(5), 710.

Duckworth, Douglas. 2020. "A Buddhist Contribution to Artificial Intelligence." *Hualin International Journal of Buddhist Studies* 3(2), 27–37.

Gould, Hannah and Walters, Holly. 2020. "Bad Buddhists, Good Robots: Techno-Salvationist Designs for Nirvana." *Journal of Global Buddhism* 21, 277–294.

Hershock, Peter. 2021. *Buddhism and Intelligent Technology: Toward a More Humane Future*, Bloomsbury.

Hongladarom, Soraj. 2020. *The Ethics of AI and Robotics: A Buddhist Viewpoint.* Lexington Books, Kindle edition.

Hughes, James. 2011. "Compassionate AI and Selfless Robots: A Buddhist Approach." In *Robot Ethics: The Ethical and Social Implications of Robotics,* ed. Patrick Lin, Keith Abney and George A. Bekey. MIT Press.

Kageki, Nori. 2012. "An Uncanny Mind: Masahiro Mori on the Uncanny Valley and Beyond – An Interview with the Japanese Professor Who Came up with the Uncanny Valley of Robotics." IEEE Spectrum. https://spectrum.ieee.org/an-uncanny-mind-masahiro-mori-on-the-uncanny-valley.

Knox, Elena and Watanabe, Kasumi. 2018. "AIBO Robot Mortuary Rites in the Japanese Cultural Context." In *2018 IEEE/RSJ International Conference on Intelligent Robots and Systems (IROS),* 2020–2025.

Kubo, Akinori. 2015. ロボットの人類学—二十世紀日本の機械と人間 *Robotto no Jinruigaku: Nijisseiki Nihon No Kikai To Ningen* [Anthropology of Robot: Machine and Humans of Twentieth Century Japan]. Sekai Shisō Sha.

Miyake, Yōichirō. 2018. 人工知能のための哲学塾: 東洋哲学編 *Jinkō chinō no tame no tetsugaku juku: Tōyō tetsugaku hen* [Storics on Philosophy for Artificial Intelligence: Eastern Philosophy]. BNN Shinsha.

Mori, Masahiro. 2014 [1989]. ロボット考学と人間—未来のためのロボット工学 *Robotto kōgaku to ningen: shōrai no tame no robotto kōgaku* [Robot Cognition and Humans: Toward the Future of Robot Engineering]. Ohmsha.

Okada, Michio. 2012. 弱いロボット *Yowai Robotto* [Weak Robots]. Igaku Shoin.

Rambelli, Fabio. 2018. "Dharma Devices, Non-hermeneutical Libraries, and Robot-Monks: Prayer Machines in Japanese Buddhism." *Journal of Asian Humanities at Kyushu University* 3–4, 57–75.

Robertson, Jennifer. 2018. *Robo sapiens japanicus: Robots, Gender, Family, and the Japanese Nation.* University of California Press.

5 Artificial Intelligence and Jewish Thought

DAVID ZVI KALMAN

Artificial intelligence (AI) puts historians of Judaism in a tough spot. On the one hand, the society-altering power of this technology and its astonishing pace of development mean that there is an urgent need to place AI in conversation with relevant ideas from the past; when it throws off philosophical problems, we want to greet them with the richness of past parallel conversations, and when it creates ethical dilemmas, we want to supply precedents and useful framings. Unfortunately, these desires are complicated by the inconvenient fact that neither Jews nor Jewish thought really know what they think about AI just yet, and given that modern technologies tend to develop faster than religions can respond to them, we may need to wait quite a while before an 'actual' history of Jewish thinking about AI can be written. In short, we have an existential problem: can a historian – can I – write a useful religious history of a new technology without simply projecting their/my own beliefs about which texts ought to be most relevant?[1]

The answer is yes – but it is a tricky thing. Religious historians of AI must walk a tightrope between two modes of writing that are narratively seductive but academically perilous. First, one might begin at the end and portray AI as the culmination of some long historical arc, and in service of this arc one might hoover up various aspects of Jewish history and collectively treat them as precursors to the newest gizmo. This framing, which is frequently employed by rabbinic authorities looking to tackle new technologies for normative purposes, tends to bring forth textual sources that imply a moral stance towards AI – but it exhausts the meaning of the texts in the process. Writing in this mode, historical sources are relegated to the realm of trivia, to being only heralds and harbingers, and the complexity of the subject is bled out in the chase for

---

[1] For the rabbinic texts cited in this chapter, I use the following abbreviations: M = Mishnah, T = Tosefta, BT = Babylonian Talmud, PT = Palestinian Talmud, PRE = Pirkei de-Rabbi Eliezer, GenR = Genesis Rabbah, LevR = Leviticus Rabbah.

a quick high of 'relevance' that soon fades as the fabulous complexity of AI policy rapidly outstrips what the general principles extracted from the sources can provide.

Alternatively, one could do the opposite. Instead of emphasising tech's novelty, one could break down the barrier between modern technology and history and deny that the new technology deserves a place of prominence inside of millennia-old philosophical and theological conversations. For AI, this means pointing out that people around the world, including Jews, have been contemplating intelligent artifices for hundreds of years. That no AI before computers ever actually *worked* is irrelevant because there has always been a symbiotic relationship between imagined and real AIs, between speculation and software, as fictional AIs inspire real ones, which in turn inspire further fictions. If we adopt this broader, substrate-agnostic and feasibility-agnostic definition of AI, the Jewish conversation on AI turns out to be both rich and *already* influential. Ecclesiastes might have liked this technique – we could call it the 'nothing new under the sun' approach – but the confidence that this framework exudes leaves little room for the very real social, cultural and political revolutions that technologies such as AI have wrought. The revolution is underplayed.

So, what to do? If historians can centre neither the future nor the past, the best course of action is to paint a picture of the present, to describe this instant of momentous encounter between the complexity of an ancient and multivalent tradition and the disruption of a world-altering tool. If Judaism is a deep and tangled forest, then AI is a city that has just been built on its edge. It is too early to say how the former will adapt to the latter, or whether the relationship will be mutually beneficial or destructive. In these exceptional circumstances, all the historian can do is speak to the potential for interaction, and then stand back and wait. Some readers, then, will read this chapter as a description of a state of affairs, while others will see it as a set of actionable suggestions. Both readings are legitimate.

Narrating the encounter between a tradition and a disruption means accepting neither side's internal narrative at face value. As a technology that takes vast amounts of data, brainpower and natural resources as its input and spits out tools that have an untold number of real-world applications, 'the' AI conversation is in fact non-existent; like the blind men and the elephant, we are only ever touching a piece of it. At the same time, the Jewish intellectual tradition is not neatly divided into categories that can be plugged into AI discourse. I wish to propose that, for the purposes of this encounter, we can identify three

ARTIFICIAL INTELLIGENCE AND JEWISH THOUGHT

recurring strands of thought within the Jewish tradition, each of which corresponds to a different aspect of AI discourse today. The first strand concerns the limits of human moral agency. The second strand deals with the anxieties around humanity's uniqueness that AI systems so often raise. The third and final strand asks whether there can or should be limits on human innovation.

It is important to note that these are synthetic categories; each of these interwoven strands recurs in multiple contexts – let's call these 'threads' – within Jewish thought, but their synthesis is specific to this chapter. This seems to me like a reasonable compromise: for if the three strands have been separated out for the benefit of AI, their component threads have been assembled with an eye towards the most coherent possible representation.

A NOTE ON FALSE STARTS

This framing, which treats the interaction between Judaism and AI as something that mostly has not happened yet, may strike some readers as surprising or even condescending. A preliminary reading of the AI–Jewish interaction in history and culture would seem to indicate that a lot of direct encounters have taken place already. The famed Dartmouth workshop that founded the field of AI research in the summer of 1956 included Marvin Minsky, Ray Solomonoff, John McCarthy, and Herbert A. Simon, all of whom were at least nominally Jewish. Isaac Asimov (d. 1992), raised in Brooklyn by Russian Jewish immigrants, developed and popularised the influential 'Three Laws of Robotics' (four laws if we include his 'Zeroth Law') through his science fiction, a genre in which Jewish authors have long been heavily overrepresented. Last but not least, ethical conversations about AI (and computing more generally) have often used as a touchstone the legend of the golem; Gershom Scholem, then the world expert on topic, personally requested that Israel's second computer be called GOLEM, and then gave a speech explaining why at its inauguration.[2] This connection is also developed in *God & Golem, Inc.*, one of the earliest sustained treatments of ethics and computing. The author, Norbert Wiener, claimed in his memoir to be no less than a direct descendant of the Jewish philosopher Maimonides (d. 1204).

---

[2]   G. Scholem, 1966, "The Golem of Prague and the Golem of Rehovoth," *Commentary Magazine*, January, www.commentary.org/articles/gershom-scholem/the-golem-of-prague-the-golem-of-rehovoth/.

But this adds up to less than it seems. Minsky, Solomonoff and Simon were confirmed atheists. Asimov, like most Jewish sci-fi writers of the day, included almost no explicitly Jewish themes or characters in his work. Wiener, for his part, did not even pretend to align with any religious tradition, admitting, "I certainly shall have to force the religious situations somewhat into my cybernetic frame. I am quite conscious of the violence that I must use in doing so."[3]

The golem is more complicated. Its use as a stand-in for AI, robots and computers generally owes much to appropriation by writers who wished to project their own ideas onto it, in the process obscuring its already-contested original meaning. While it has always been a Jewish legend, its modern popularity has been spurred since the seventeenth century by Christian scholars and storytellers, and so a unified treatment would need to separate that part out, something not easily done. I return to the golem over the coming pages, but its original nature is so contested and its purpose in later legends so easily swayed by the ideological vicissitudes that it does not make sense to treat the golem as a single, unified subject.

HUMAN AGENCY

We begin with questions of moral agency, not because these questions are easier but because it is these questions that are most easily framed in the language of Jewish law (*halakhah*), which has been and continues to be the initial point of contact between Judaism and effectively all new technologies. There are four reasons for this. First, *halakhah* is necessarily detail-oriented, and so the framework is suited for examining complex technological systems. Second, because *halakhah* is about normative practice, it poses questions that are better defined than those that emerge from philosophy and theology, which in turn makes it easier to find relevant source texts. Third, *halakhah* has been a kind of *lingua franca* for all sorts of ideas throughout much of Jewish history. Finally, and most importantly, the decentralisation of Jewish communal authority means that these discussions tend to *adjudicate* based on existing texts rather than *legislate* based on personal authority, which means that anyone with a sufficiently high degree of Jewish legal knowledge can try their hand at this work (many do; it is not an accident that many long-form treatments of new technologies are written by people with no religious leadership position at all).

[3] N. Wiener, 1966, *God and Golem, Inc.: A Comment on Certain Points Where Cybernetics Impinges on Religion*, 7th ed., MIT Press, 8–9.

When Jewish scholars attempt to make headway on new technologies, they often write in the Jewish legal genre known as responsa literature. This genre, which frequently sits at the front lines of Jewish technological thought, has in the last decade produced a few attempts to deal with AI directly, most notably a 2019 policy document issued by the Conservative Movement's Committee on Jewish Law and Standards.[4] This ruling is by and large concerned with moral agency, and I frequently pull from its analysis in this section.

For AI, the questions of moral agency can be summarised as follows.

1. Are human beings responsible for the actions of artificial intelligent systems?
2. Assuming they are, does responsibility devolve upon the end user or just the developers?
3. Are there situations where it is inappropriate to delegate work to AI systems?

Because the first two questions are about liability, one way of addressing them is to deploy Jewish law's impressive arsenal of technical language to parse situations in which a consequential act has a proximal cause and an ultimate cause. In situations such as this, the expected behaviour of the proximal cause matters. For the rabbis, that proximal cause was often an animal, whose harm could be evaluated according to motivation, foreseeability and location. The Mishnah, an early rabbinic legal compendium, identifies *foot, tooth* and *horn* as formal categories of damage. Foot and tooth damage, which an animal causes simply by walking or eating, is foreseeable, and therefore the owner is liable if it occurs outside of the public domain. Horn damage, causes by an animal's exceptional aggressive behaviour, is unexpected and therefore the owner is not fully liable.

What exactly counts as unexpected is the subject of additional regulations. The Bible, for example, rules that an ox that gores someone to death is killed, but if the ox "has been in the habit" of goring, then its owner is put to death as well (Ex. 21:28–29). The rabbis of the Mishnah and Talmud expanded this into a formalised distinction between low-risk (*tam*) and high-risk animals (*mu'ad*), deliberating about what kinds of behaviour constituted habitual violence and whether an animal could ever revert to a low-risk state, as well as

---

[4] D. Nevins, 2019, "Halakhic Responses to Artificial Intelligence and Autonomous Machines," www.rabbinicalassembly.org/sites/default/files/nevins_ai_moral_machines_and_halakha-final_1.pdf.

74 DAVID ZVI KALMAN

which types of animal (e.g., bears) should be considered high risk at all times (M Bava Kamma 1:4 and 2:4).

Another way of untangling these situations is to consider the many ways in which a person or animal can be said to have 'caused' something to occur. In the Talmud's Tractate Bava Kamma, the concept *ko'ah koho* ("his force's force") is used to describe situations in which one action sets off another, which ultimately causes damage. This is separate from *ko'ah sheni* ("secondary force") in which a person performs an act that has a high probability of causing damage, and also from *ko'ah mamono*, in which one causes damage through one's property and not one's person. There are also the complex laws of *grama* ("cause"), a concept in ritual law that allows a person to accomplish some act that would otherwise be prohibited. Tractate Makkot carefully distinguishes between accidental deaths that are unintentional (*ones*) and those that are accidental (*shogeg*), a distinction that has very real legal consequences. We return to all of these concepts in a moment but suffice it to say that this is an area of law that is well suited to fine distinctions.

The third question is not about liability but about the ethics of offloading decisions to an AI system in the first place. Here a different set of laws becomes relevant. Jewish law often allows a person to perform actions or fulfil duties through a proxy (*shaliah*), but not every person can be a proxy, not every task can be proxied and proxies are not absolved of the responsibility to be moral actors. Thus, for example, the obligation to pray cannot be transferred, but among obligations that *can* be transferred the proxy and the principal must be similarly obligated, which means that objects can never be proxies.

Each of these frameworks, on its face, seems useful to AI discourse. One doesn't have to squint to see how the paradigm of low-risk and high-risk animals could slot neatly into risk assessments for autonomous vehicles. The discussions about the liability for and permissibility of indirect action could be useful in thinking about many autonomous systems. Finally, the proxy discourse is useful for considering the growing sector of decision-making AI systems and could help regulators think through whether it is appropriate, for example, to use algorithms for hiring and firing. In short, the gap between Jewish law and the AI moral agency discourse seems bridgeable. What happens next?

The disappointing answer is that, despite everything, it is too early to say. One reason to remain sceptical that these sources will cohere into a grand AI moral rubric is that many of these techniques have *already* been deployed to think through relatively simple technologies; yet

ARTIFICIAL INTELLIGENCE AND JEWISH THOUGHT   75

despite the long history of rabbinic rulings about mechanical devices, these rulings never coalesced into a unified doctrine of machines.

Why didn't this happen? The legislation around waterwheels is both instructive and historically relevant here. Because it became available in the Greco-Roman world no earlier than the third century BCE, the waterwheel was one of the first technologies that the rabbis needed to navigate without the help of clear biblical precedent. In the Greco-Roman world its introduction meant that, for the first time, humans were able to get work done without straining human or animal muscle. But what, legally, did this third source of energy represent? Could it be quickly subsumed under an established area of law, such as animal labour or human proxies, or did it require a whole new set of laws?

The rabbis did not settle on any of these tidy solutions. According to the Tosefta (Shabbat 1:23, Lieberman ed.), an early rabbinic text, one is prohibited from loading a watermill with grain before Shabbat, a day on which, according to the Bible, "you shall not do any work – you, your son or daughter, your male or female slave, your cattle, or the stranger in your midst" (Ex. 20:9). Was the Tosefta trying to add the waterwheel to the Bible's list? Context suggests that it was, because the same passage states that one *is* allowed to set other, non-mechanical activities in motion, such as applying slow-acting ointments or setting a path for water to flow into a garden.

Pressed to explain why the waterwheel alone was prohibited from use, the Babylonian Talmud dallies with the idea that Shabbat rest includes *shevitat kelim* – literally "tool rest," a tellingly vague phrase. But the Talmud rejects this position and instead punts on the problem: the prohibition is not because waterwheels are *machines* but because waterwheels are *noisy*, and their noise is disruptive to the communal experience of Shabbat (BT Shabbat 18a). This ruling did not imply that waterwheels should be considered extensions of their users; indeed, in another context the autonomous waterwheel's ability to proxy for human labour is severely curtailed (Shulḥan Arukh, Yoreh Deʿah 7:1). Thus, complex machinery entered Jewish law already beholden to subjective experience.

A second problem – not unique to Jewish law – is that these concepts are still underdetermined, which means that their application is by no means predictable. This fact was argued by the historian Jacob Katz, whose landmark case study fortuitously also deals with liability and indirect action. Katz's subject matter was the *shabbes goy*, a gentile employed by Jews for the specific purpose of performing work on Shabbat that Jews are prohibited from doing. In his study, Katz showed that medieval rabbis became much more permissive of this practice, demonstrating in the process that law often follows communal custom rather than the other way around.[5] This case is useful not just for thinking about the limits of legal formalism but has important parallels to the AI debate, since one reason to outsource work to machines – much like outsourcing Shabbat labour to someone outside of the community – is to enjoy the benefits while concealing the work. Since concealing human labour (and in the process sometimes exploiting it) is already a known problem in AI, this connection should give us pause. Indeed, it is worth noting that these two forms of labour obfuscation have already been employed in technologies from Israel's Tzomet Institute, which develops electronic devices that employ loopholes designed to circumvent Shabbat regulations while preserving function.

The third problem is the hardest to resolve, since it concerns the very process by which Jewish law is built up. While contemporary conversations about AI ethics focus on regulation at the state and corporate level, Jewish law is almost entirely about individual human beings; as a legal system developed almost entirely in a state of political disenfranchisement, its discussions about state and corporate norms simply do not have the same depth; in fact, there is no agreement on the legal status of corporations at all. For AI systems, this means that Jewish law is more comfortable answering whether a person is liable for misusing a self-driving car than whether a company is liable for harm caused by its software, or what kinds of societal policies around AI should be put in place. For all these reasons, it is unclear how the mass of Jewish texts about moral agency will lay the framework for a Jewish AI ideology, and it may remain unclear for some time.

HUMAN UNIQUENESS

From law, we move to theology. As AI systems have become more sophisticated, they have gained the ability to emulate or exceed human behaviour in ever more aspects of life. Today, there are AI systems that can beat humans at some of their most cherished games; systems that can create photorealistic faces for non-existent people; systems that can write coherent prose in any genre imaginable; and, of course, software that can replace any number of jobs that had previously required human labour. Whenever AI becomes competent at a new human activity, there

---

[5] J. Katz, 1989, *The "Shabbes Goy": A Study in Halakhic Flexibility*, Jewish Publication Society of America.

is some soul-searching in the press about whether humanity possess any truly unique qualities, whether these systems diminish the special status that humanity assigns to itself and whether AI systems might one day reach the point where they are deserving of a special status.

The Hebrew Bible bestows upon humans a special significance by describing them as being created in the image (*tzelem*) of God (Gen. 1:27). What exactly this means has changed over time. For the rabbis, human beings did not just resemble God but in fact contained something of God within them. This intimate relationship explains the supreme value that rabbis place on human life, going so far as to say that "one who destroys a single life, the Torah considers them to have destroyed the entire world" (M Sanhedrin 4:5).

Though Jewish thinkers have long maintained humanity's special status, they have also acknowledged that the line between humans and non-humans is a messy one. Rather than being a binary category, humanity exists along a gradient, and no single criterion – neither form nor parentage nor intelligence – allows us to define who is human.[6] While Jewish texts do prioritise human beings over all other forms of life, human uniqueness does not reside in any single human characteristic, and Jewish sources allow *both* for degrees of humanity *and* higher forms of life that are not human at all. Despite the fact that these acknowledgements appear in many different contexts, they almost never lead to any handwringing about the status of humanity, whose specialness is never conditioned on its absolute uniqueness or physical superiority over other forms of life. Faced with the choice of affirming a unique God or a unique humanity, Jews consistently chose God. While the uniqueness and priority of God are closely tied central dogmas, humanity's priority is maintained regardless of its uniqueness in the universe.

One way to observe the 'human gradient' is to note the persistent belief in humanoid animals, a category that sometimes had legal implications. The rabbinic laws of ritual purity stated that the impurity transmitted by a human corpse was both more severe and more easily spread than that of any other impure person or object. However, a rabbi in the Mishnah states that the corpse of the creatures called *adne hasadeh*, literally "men of the field," should have the same status as human corpses (M Kilayim 8:5). The Palestinian Talmud explains that *adne hasadeh* are humanoid creatures attached to the earth by a cord; if the cord was severed, the creature would die (PT Kilayim 8:4). In medieval Germany, Jewish Pietist readily mixed this and other Talmudic

---

[6]   A. Rosenfeld, 1966, "Religion and the Robot," *Tradition* 8(3), 15–26.

humanoid monsters together with local folklore about vampires and werewolves.[7] Israel Lipschitz, a nineteenth-century commentator, even speculated that the *adne hasadeh* were orangutans, which he knew could perform basic human tasks such as putting on clothes. Whatever its true nature, the creature's elevated status is a direct result of its physical resemblance to genuine human beings, and this was never presented as a problem to be overcome.

Besides humanoid creatures, Jewish sources have also engaged seriously with non-human higher beings. In Jewish literature, angels (*mal'akhim*, literally "messengers") are typically made of fire and are not the mirror of demons, though they do sometimes cause destruction. Angels are ubiquitous both in the Bible and rabbinic literature, and while they are always portrayed as creations carrying out the divine will, they were also sufficiently distinct from God that it was sometimes considered appropriate to distinguish between different angels' forms and responsibilities and praying to specific activities to specific angels was apparently an important mode of popular practice in late antiquity. According to the Book of Jubilees, a Jewish text from the Second Temple Period, the Torah itself was dictated to Moses by an angel.[8]

The independence of angels is most apparent in those stories where they serve not as divine helpers but as critics. Specifically, angels are portrayed as critics of humanity itself, arguing that humanity was neither worthy of being created nor of receiving the Torah; in some versions, angels are even portrayed as being jealous of humanity.[9] In one narrative, which appears in several places in the literature, Moses' ascent to receive the Torah provokes the angels into asking: "Master of the Universe, what is one born of a woman doing among us?" Moses responds by running through the Ten Commandments, questioning whether the angels have need of any of them. An excerpt:

> Again [Moses asked], "What [else] is written in it?"
> [God said,] "You shall have no other gods before Me" (Ex. 20:3).
> [Moses said to the angels,] "Do you dwell among the nations who worship idols?"
> [...]

---

[7] D. I. Shyovitz, 2017, *A Remembrance of His Wonders: Nature and the Supernatural in Medieval Ashkenaz*, University of Pennsylvania Press, 136.

[8] H. Najman, 2000, "Angels at Sinai: Exegesis, Theology and Interpretive Authority," *Dead Sea Discoveries* 7(3), 316.

[9] M. Bernstein, 2000, "Angels at the Aqedah: A Study in the Development of a Midrash Motif," *Dead Sea Discoveries* 7(3), 272.

"Remember the Shabbat day to sanctify it" (Ex. 20:8).
"Do you perform labor that you require rest?"
[...]
"Honor your father and your mother" (Ex. 20:12).
"Do you have a father or a mother?" (BT Shabbat 88b–89a)

The Bible was bestowed upon humanity not in spite of its imperfection and mortality but because of it, and so this story reinforces the point that humanity's unique value does not require humans to be the most perfect species in all of God's creation. However, while angels are not a threat to humanity's special status, there is a persistent concern among the rabbis of late antiquity that angel worship could supplant divine worship. In one important example, the Talmud describes the sage Elisha ben Avuyah becoming a heretic after a mystical experience in which he saw the angel Metatron daring to sit in God's presence. Elisha proclaimed, "There are two powers in heaven!" Metatron, who had been allowed to sit in order to serve as a scribe, was subsequently punished for creating a false impression (BT Ḥagigah 15a). Other rabbinic texts, including the Passover Haggadah, go out of their way to specify that divine actions are transmitted "not through an angel, not through a seraph, but through the Holy Blessed One." Here we see stark examples of how the stakes for divine uniqueness are much higher than those for human uniqueness.

This connection between humanoids and non-human higher life goes one step further. Besides angels and humanoid monsters, the rabbis who created the Babylonian Talmud were particularly interested in demons, likely because of their exposure to the cultures in which they were immersed. For Christians and Zoroastrians, demons were essentially destructive, emanating directly from Satan or Ahriman. But rabbis – ever committed to a unique and benevolent God – wanted neither God nor some competing omnipotent being to have created evil creatures. As a result, rabbinic demons are not inherently evil and are sometimes even beneficent; when they do cause havoc, it is because a human has done something they don't like, or simply because they wish it. These demons, which are bound by divine law, also look so much like humans that one cannot distinguish the two at night (BT Sanhedrin 44a). Adding up these features, the rabbinic demons resemble nothing so much as (slightly superior) human beings.

A useful early medieval text (Avot de-Rabbi Natan Version A 37) frames the relationship between humans and demons very clearly. Humans resemble animals because they "eat and drink ... procreate ... and excrete"; they are like ministering angels because they "have wisdom ... walk upright ... and speak the holy tongue," meaning Hebrew. Demons resemble humans because they "eat and drink ... procreate ... and die"; they resemble ministering angels because they "have wings ... know the future ... and go from one end of the world to another." Humans and demons, despite having quite different abilities, are linked by their mortal bodies and their existence above the animal realm.

This resemblance is no accident. In many rabbinic narratives, demons are humanity's accidental progeny (though not always; see M Avot 5:6). This idea is ultimately rooted in Genesis 6:1–4, which describes the "sons of God" cohabiting with women, an activity that is elaborated upon in the portion of Enoch known as the Book of Watchers.[10] Here, the progeny are giants that become demonic as their physical bodies break down.[11] The rabbis expanded on this idea, crafting an origin story in which Adam and Eve regularly slept with demons and thereby birthed new demons. In the Babylonian tradition, Adam's semen alone was enough to spawn new demons (see GenR 20:11 and BT Eruvin 18b). In other words, despite the fact that Babylonian Jewish demons were humanoid in their appearance, volition and even pedigree, the rabbis remained unconcerned that these accidental artificial humanoids represented a threat to humanity's special status.

But what about an *intentionally* created artificial humanoid? Here we return to the golem, whose origins lie in a Talmudic passage where the sage Rava makes "a man" (*gavra*). When another sage sees that the man cannot speak, he returns him to dust (BT Sanhedrin 65b). Later debate swirled around the man's muteness; was he mute because of a hard limit on human creative power, or did Rava just happen to make him this way? On one side of the debate, some thinkers argued that no golem, no matter how perfectly animated, could contain the spiritual qualities of a human being. Most vociferous on this point was the Safed kabbalist Rabbi Moshe Cordovero (d. 1570), who posited that a golem could be bestowed with vitality (*ḥiyyut*), whereas spirituality (*ruḥaniyyut*) was reserved for humans alone.[12] Thus curtailed, this mindless golem inspired many later legends about soulless creatures run amok.

---

[10] P. Schäfer, 2011, *The Origins of Jewish Mysticism*, Princeton University Press, 55.

[11] A. Wright, 2005, *The Origin of Evil Spirits: The Reception of Genesis 6.1–4 in Early Jewish Literature*, Mohr Siebeck, chapter 5.

[12] G. Scholem, 1971, "Towards an Understanding of the Messianic Idea in Judaism," in *The Messianic Idea in Judaism and Other Essays on Jewish Spirituality*, ed. G. Scholem, Schocken Books, 194–195; M. Idel, 1990, *Golem: Jewish Magical and Mystical Traditions on the Artificial Anthropoid*, State University of New York Press, 198.

ARTIFICIAL INTELLIGENCE AND JEWISH THOUGHT 81

Others disagreed. The Italian physician Abraham Yagel (d. 1623) thought the Talmud's artificial man was only mute because it had not been made with the most powerful mystical magic.[13] Rabbi Gershon Henoch Leiner (d. 1890), leader of the Radzyner Hasidic sect, posited not only that a sufficiently pure person could make a speaking golem but that such a golem would be *legally* human, and could even help constitute a quorum (*minyan*) for communal prayer. Yosef Shlomo Delmedigo (d. 1655), often considered to be the first Jewish thinker to engage broadly with technology, recalled that a rabbi had once made a female golem so perfect that he eventually needed to dismantle her down to its "pieces and hinges of wood" in order to avoid denunciation. Most remarkable of all, however, are a pair of thirteenth-century German legends in which an artificial man, upon being created, immediately asks to be destroyed, "lest the world succumb to idolatry" and begin worshipping human golem-makers.[14] Again, we see that the perfect android was not a threat to humanity's self-perception – but it was a threat to theology. A similar dynamic plays out in medieval and early modern discussions about the possibility of extraterrestrial life.

There is no single Jewish text that outlines or resolves all the theological questions that demons, giants, angels, monsters and golems raise – and yet consolidating these discussions here produces some surprising consistency. Across these conversations, God's uniqueness must always be preserved, as must humanity's special status. That status, however, usually does not require humans to be unique in all the cosmos, let alone its best, highest or most perfect creations. But while it is clear that this distinction between *specialness* and *uniqueness* can be well supported, it has been largely moot until recently. In the ongoing encounter with AI, we will see whether this new technology pushes it into prominence – or whether the sudden reality of what had only been discussed as myth and legend will prompt Jewish theologians to revise their views anew.

HUMAN INNOVATION

The question of moral agency may be where Jewish thought begins to engage with AI, but the question of moral agency does not *require* a religious response. The creation of AI, on the other hand, often stirs up

[13] See David B. Ruderman, 1988, *Kabbalah, Magic, and Science: The Cultural Universe of a Sixteenth-Century Jewish Physician*, Harvard University Press, 109; Idel, *Golem*, chapter 10.

[14] G. Scholem, 1965, "The Idea of the Golem," in *On the Kabbalah and Its Symbolism*, ed. G. Scholem, Schocken Books, 179–180.

82 DAVID ZVI KALMAN

religious language in people even without the help of religious thinkers because many people instinctively draw parallels to religious narratives about the creation of humanity.[15] These parallels draw on five core connections between human and divine creation:

1. Creation takes place because of the creator's unstoppable need to create.
2. There is a clear power hierarchy between creator and created.
3. There is a passing of information, skills and values from creator to created.
4. There is agreement that the two share some essential qualities (though not what these are).
5. The creator has constant anxiety that the created party will go off the rails in some extremely destructive manner.

With the parallels already a part of public discourse, it is up to religious leaders to decide how to shape their meaning. From the previous section, we already know that Jewish thinkers were far more sensitive to attacks on God's special status than attacks on their own. Though they generally accepted the analogy from human to divine action, they flipped it on its head. If the creation of AI seems godlike to us, it is because human beings themselves are, quite literally, an 'artificial intelligence'.

This is not just a semantic point. The same thirteenth-century German milieu that first outlined the ritual for animating a golem was clear that Adam himself was once a golem – literally a lifeless body – until God breathed life into him.[16] The point of creating a golem (or having a mystical experience in which one imagined creating a golem, depending on one's interpretation of the texts) was to engage in the ultimate form of divine emulation: namely, combining and recombining letters of the Hebrew alphabet to make a golem in precisely the same way that God created humans. The golem itself has no purpose other than to exist as a testimony to both divine and human power. Tellingly, all of the original golem narratives, including the Talmudic story about the sage Rava making a speechless man, end with the golem quickly being returned to dust. It doesn't need to do anything; creating it is enough.

The medieval version of the golem ritual is perhaps the most extreme example of how Jewish thinkers linked human creation with

---

[15] See, for example, see Y. Harari, 2017, *Homo Deus: A Brief History of Tomorrow*, Harper.

[16] Idel, *Golem*, 28–35. The idea of Adam's golem state appears in BT Sanhedrin 38b and GenR 24:2 (ed. Albeck).

divine creation, and it is also the one that views the former most favourably. But while this link is quite robust across the history of Jewish thought, the theological significance of this parallel regularly oscillated between two very different models. In one, human creation is seen as a *subset* of divine creation. In the other, human creation is taken to be a *challenge* to divine creation.

In late antique rabbinic literature, the subset model seems to have held sway. The rabbinic story of how humans acquired fire, for example, is not that humans learned it from lightning or stole it, as many cultures around the world have it, but simply that God showed Adam how to make it, as well as how to breed mules (BT Pesaḥim 54a–b). The rabbis also suggest that it was God who fashioned the first set of tongs (M Avot 5:6). This claim is meaningful not just because of ironwork's status in antiquity as the ultimate craft – Hephaestus, Greek god of craftsmen, is symbolised by a hammer and anvil – but because the blacksmith was distinguished among artisans by his ability to make his own tools. Since even a blacksmith needs to begin with a set of tongs, the rabbinic origin story positions God not just as the creator of people but the initiator of their craftwork. This theory fell into disuse as the technological change grew more rapid and prominent, though it was briefly revived to try to locate the origins of the printing press in the Bible.[17]

A corollary to the subset model is that human creative work can never exceed divine work in quality. According to the Mishnah, God began humanity by fashioning only one person to make a point about the nature of divine creation. "When a person mints coins with a single die, they all resemble one another. But the King, King of Kings, the Holy Blessed One mints each person with the die of the first person and no two are alike" (M Sanhedrin 4:5). Still, there is a genetic similarity between divine and human creation, which meant that it was in theory possible for human beings to understand how God created the world, even if they could not emulate it.

> The Torah says, "I was God's tool." Normally when a flesh-and-blood king builds a palace, he builds it not through his personal knowledge but through the knowledge of an artisan, and the artisan does not build through his personal knowledge but through records and registries in his possession, so that he can determine how to construct chambers and gateways. So, too, did God look in the Torah and create the world. (GenR 1:1)

---

[17] M. Pollak, 1977, "The Invention of Printing in Hebrew Lore," *Gutenberg-Jahrburch* 52, 22–28.

84 DAVID ZVI KALMAN

However, the subset model can only take one so far. Even if early rabbinic texts assiduously avoid describing technologies as having histories, the Bible itself names specific people as the inventors of specific things and, in the Tower of Babel story, goes so far as to describe human creative work as a threat that God needed to diffuse. Thus, in rabbinic culture we also see the development of what we might call the 'challenge' model of human innovation, a normative mode in which there is a gap between what humans can and should create (Norman Lamm called this the difference between imitating God and impersonating God). In the story cited earlier about the self-destructive golem created by the prophet Jeremiah and his son, the golem uses a parable to explain why it should not have been created:

> A builder built many houses, courts, and cities, but nobody could compete with his craft in either knowledge or skill until two men convinced him. He taught them the secret of his craft until they knew how to do everything correctly. Once they had mastered the craft and understood its secret and its character, they began to critique him and then broke from his company and became builders like him, except what he did for a *dinar* they would do for half that amount. When people noticed this, everyone stopped honoring the artisan and came to them instead, honoring them and contracting with them for any construction they required. Similarly, God made you in God's image and appearance and form—but now that you are creating a man as God did, people will say: There is no God in the world but these two![18]

Sources differ about whether these challenges are a problem because they really do approach the level of divine handiwork or only because they appear to do so; Maimonides, for example, constructs his etiology of idolatry based on a misunderstanding about the relationship between God and God's creations (Mishneh Torah, *Laws of Idol Worship*, ch. 1). Regardless, in the 'challenge' model human innovation is frequently cast as inherently negative or destructive. The trebuchet, a war machine, is one of the few objects that the Bible describes as being invented, but in the very next verse its creator is called arrogant and then punished by God (2 Chr. 26:15–21). In one rabbinic source, God sabotages the Tower of Babel because its builders mourned the loss of bricks but not labourers (PRE 24:6). Commenting on the fact that the inventor

---

[18] My translation is based on MS JTS 1887, fol. 7b; another version exists in MS Florence, Laurentiana, Plut.2.41, 199v.

of metalwork, Tubal Cain, was a descendant of Cain, the first murderer, one early Palestinian midrash plays on the former's name: "Rabbi Yehoshua of Sikhnin said in the name of Rabbi Levi: this one spiced up [tibel] the sin of Cain, for Cain killed without having anything to kill with, but this one 'forged all copper and iron tools' (Gen. 4:22)" (GenR 23:3). In golem narratives, the link between human creativity and violence became increasingly prominent as the artificial humanoid shifted from ritual to legend and from an end to a means. Beginning in the nineteenth century the golem is depicted as engaging in violent activities, sometimes for the purpose of Jewish self-defence.[19] In the twentieth century, the golem's violence was applied by both Jews and Gentiles to specific armies and modern mechanised warfare generally, which by World War I could mow down soldiers at terrifying speeds. "He used to once be made of clay," said the novelist Israel Joshua Singer (d. 1944). "Now he is made of steel." For Singer, the modern golem had lost God's name, but unlike the golems of the past this one simply broke free of its creators, overriding humanity's ability to shut it off.

The irony, of course, is that these godless golems now cause the same problems for humans that the humans in the 'challenge' model posed for God, and it is in this irony that I think we can imagine where the religious discourse on human innovation might go next. The next stage of the tension between the subset and challenge models will not play out around human activity, because modern technological advancement makes the subset model a difficult sell. Instead, a transference is taking place; the parallels between human and AI creation mean that the tension is alive not in us but in our most ambitious creations. Thinking through them, we can now understand the inclination to see these semi-autonomous creations as a subset of our own work, as well as the excitement and potential risk of being truly surprised by their ingenuity. Do we want AI that follows the subset model, unthreatening but not truly innovative? Or do we dare risk thinking about AI work as a challenge?

CONCLUSION

We have examined three major features of Jewish thought that have, in various ways, already been brought to bear on several aspects of the AI discourse. On questions of moral agency, Jewish law has language aplenty to process the multipartite, probabilistic responsibility that AI

[19] M. Barzilai, 2016, *Golem: Modern Wars and Their Monsters*, NYU Press, 20.

systems force us to adjudicate. On anxiety about humanity's fungibility, we have seen that there is generally little concern that humanity's special status requires it to be unique. Finally, the resemblance between the creation of humans and AIs recalls a longstanding tension between two theological models for human innovation and suggests a path for how they may soon be revived.

One of the great benefits of studying history is learning that the events that have shaped our world are largely contingent, and that it would not have taken much for our world to unfold very differently. Philosophers of technology have frequently pointed out that the drumbeat of inevitability is particularly strong for revolutionary technological systems, and the fact that the history of technology is still not a part of most high school or college educations means that new technologies can and will quickly erase the memory of what life was like before.

As Jewish thinkers continue to develop positions on AI, it is far from certain how they will proceed. It is possible that no coherent thought will develop at all, that the strands of thought I have described here will be entirely ignored in favour of something entirely new, or that questions of human agency will continue to receive the lion's share of the attention. The purpose of this chapter is not to recommend one path of development over another but to stick a pin in this very particular moment in time and speak to the currents of thought that swirl around this revolutionary technology. There will likely be no straight line between here and there. All we can do is set the scene.

BIBLIOGRAPHY

Barzilai, M. 2016. *Golem: Modern Wars and Their Monsters*. NYU Press.

Bernstein, M. 2000. "Angels at the Aqedah: A Study in the Development of a Midrash Motif." *Dead Sea Discoveries* 7(3), 272.

Harari, Y. 2017. *Homo Deus: A Brief History of Tomorrow*. Harper

Idel, M. 1990. *Golem: Jewish Magical and Mystical Traditions on the Artificial Anthropoid*. State University of New York Press.

Katz, J. 1989. *The 'Shabbes Goy': A Study in Halakhic Flexibility*. Jewish Publication Society of America.

Najman, H. 2000. "Angels at Sinai: Exegesis, Theology and Interpretive Authority." *Dead Sea Discoveries* 7(3), 316.

Nevins, D. 2019. "Halakhic Responses to Artificial Intelligence and Autonomous Machines." www.rabbinicalassembly.org/sites/default/files/nevins_ai_moral_machines_and_halakha-final_1.pdf.

Pollak, M. 1977. "The Invention of Printing in Hebrew Lore." *Gutenberg-Jahrburch* 52, 22–28.

Rosenfeld, A. 1966. "Religion and the Robot." *Tradition* 8(3), 15–26.

Ruderman, David B. 1988. *Kabbalah, Magic, and Science: The Cultural Universe of a Sixteenth-Century Jewish Physician*. Harvard University Press.

Schäfer, P. 2011. *The Origins of Jewish Mysticism*. Princeton University Press.

Scholem, G. 1966. "The Golem of Prague and the Golem of Rehovoth." *Commentary Magazine*, January. www.commentary.org/articles/gershom-scholem/the-golem-of-prague-the-golem-of-rehovoth/.

Shyovitz, D. I. 2017. *A Remembrance of His Wonders: Nature and the Supernatural in Medieval Ashkenaz*. University of Pennsylvania Press.

Wiener, N. 1966. *God and Golem, Inc.: A Comment on Certain Points Where Cybernetics Impinges on Religion*, 7th ed. MIT Press.

Wright, A. 2005. *The Origin of Evil Spirits: The Reception of Genesis 6.1–4 in Early Jewish Literature*. Mohr Siebeck.

FURTHER READING

Ahuvia, Mika. 2021. *On My Right Michael, On My Left Gabriel: Angels in Ancient Jewish Culture*. University of California Press.

Bleich, J. David. 2019. "Autonomous Automobiles and the Trolley Problem." *Tradition* 51(3), 68–93.

Idel, Moshe. 1990. *Golem: Jewish Magical and Mystical Traditions on the Artificial Anthropoid*. SUNY Press.

Lamm, Norman. 1965. "The Religious Implications of Extraterrestrial Life." *Tradition* 7(4), 5–56.

Lorberbaum, Yair. 2015. *In God's Image: Myth, Theology, and Law in Classical Judaism*. Cambridge University Press.

Nevins, Daniel. 2019. "Halakhic Responses to Artificial Intelligence and Autonomous Machines." www.rabbinicalassembly.org/sites/default/files/nevins_ai_moral_machines_and_halakha-final_1.pdf.

Ronis, Sara. 2022. *Demons in the Details: Demonic Discourse and Rabbinic Culture in Late Antique Babylonia*. University of California Press.

Scholem, Gershom. 1965. *On the Kabbalah and Its Symbolism*. Schocken.

Wasserman, Jews Mira. 2017. *Gentiles, and Other Animals: The Talmud after the Humanities*. University of Pennsylvania Press.

6 Artificial Intelligence and Christianity

Friends or Foes?

MARIUS DOROBANTU

The ongoing technological revolution is a fertile ground for theological reflection. Since the 1950s, we have been trying to endow computers with artificial intelligence (AI). Everything about this unprecedented project of creating an intelligent *other* is pregnant with theological significance – the ambitions and assumptions that fuel it, its successes, its failures and the thrilling possibilities it promises to bring about.

The term AI is an umbrella for many things, but in this chapter, it refers to the specific attempt to build intelligent artificial agents: robots or computer programs that exhibit capabilities and behaviours similar enough to our own. This is the kind of AI that raises the most profound questions for Christian theology. Why are we so fascinated by the prospect of intelligent machines? Does this fascination cohere with theological anthropology's account of the human being? Is the pursuit of AI sinful or virtuous? If the project fully succeeds, what will the implications be for our perceived distinctiveness, our theological place in the world and the destiny of our species?

This chapter assesses the recent history of Christian reflection on AI. It reviews the critical theological questions posed by the rise of intelligent machines and some of the most interesting proposed solutions. The first section is dedicated to questions about hypothetical AI developments and their potential implications for Christian theology: could AI become an authentic self, could it partake in the image of God and could it one day become religious or sinful? The second section shifts the focus back to humans, looking at how insights from AI might inform theological anthropology. What does the fascination for AI say about humans? Would our theological self-understanding change in a world where intelligent machines became ubiquitous?

COULD MACHINES BE LIKE US? THEOLOGY AND THE FUTURE OF AI

Since its inauguration at the Dartmouth workshop in 1956, the field of AI – roughly defined as the attempt to create machines that think and act like humans – has gone through several mood and paradigm shifts. The initial achievements of symbolic AI were met with enthusiasm, but a realisation soon followed that human intelligence largely exceeded what could be captured by the sequential computer algorithms of the 1960s. Another round of enthusiasm came in the 1980s and 1990s around expert systems, rule-based programs capable of mastering narrow domains of human cognition, such as Deep Blue, the chess program that defeated world champion Gary Kasparov in 1997. However, as it turns out, brute computational force is still *not* how humans solve puzzles and make decisions.

Quickly after the turn of the millennium, AI went through yet another paradigm shift. The new approach, called deep learning (DL), employs an array of virtual artificial neural networks, which supposedly better approximate the operation of human brains. When trained on vast datasets, made available by the proliferation of the World Wide Web and connected devices, these programs 'learn' to recognise subtle patterns in the data, presumably not too dissimilar to how human brains recognise patterns in the visual field. The advent of DL has produced impressive applications that match and sometimes surpass human performance in tasks involving image recognition or natural language processing. However, DL programs still operate quite differently from human brains, something evident in the shocking mistakes they sometimes make or in that they need hundreds of thousands of examples to learn something when humans can do it with just a handful of them, and sometimes with as little as one.

This simplified, brief history of AI serves a double purpose. First, it sets a rough time frame that gives some historical context to the theological reflections to be discussed. Theologians thinking about AI can only do so from within their historical context, so their level of enthusiasm about the potential of AI is bound to somewhat correlate with the broader mood surrounding these technologies.

Second, such a bird's eye view of the history of AI reveals some trends that can inform our speculation about its potential to fully emulate human intelligence. On the one hand, the closer we get to this goal, the bigger the mountain seems to become. With every exciting AI breakthrough comes a realisation that human intelligence is, in fact, much more complicated than what we imagined. On the other hand, the strides made by AI in such a relatively short time are nevertheless impressive, and the set of domains where humans are still better than machines is shrinking by the day. AI may not progress acceleratedly, as some techno-optimists wish, but it is undoubtedly advancing. Human-level AI, or artificial general intelligence (AGI), is thus not an implausible future possibility. It may not happen within this generation's lifetime but, in principle, it shouldn't be impossible for AI to reach human-level intelligence one day. This seems to be the quasi-consensus among experts, who in 2013 assigned a 50 per cent probability of getting AGI by the 2040s and a staggering 90 per cent likelihood before 2075.[1]

Should we even attempt to create AGI? The question is brimming with theological significance. If the goal is to create a divine-like artificial superintelligence (ASI) that would take care of all our problems so that we could enjoy a life of leisure, such a pursuit could be theologically criticised as idolatrous. Philosopher Nick Bostrom believes that our biggest challenge is to get ASI aligned with our goals and values, so that it doesn't accidentally wipe us out. For us, such an aligned ASI could function as an oracle, able to answer all our questions, a genie, ready to execute any of our commands, and a sovereign, capable of governing the world much more efficiently and fairly than us.[2] This scenario has a certain appeal, but its implicit hedonistic view of human life is theologically problematic. Against the vision of such a magnificent servant-god, Christian anthropology might emphasise the critical importance of human freedom or the intrinsic value of struggling and overcoming adversity for human flourishing.

Some futurists see in the creation of ASI the fulfilment of our cosmic goal, that of a midwife for a superior form of intelligence. Our artificial/cyborg descendants could saturate the entire universe with intelligence in a way humans cannot, due to our hard biological limitations. Such manifestos are crammed with bold and dubious claims about the ultimate purpose of human life and the cosmos, which predictably brings them onto the radar of theological criticism.[3]

---

[1] Vincent C. Müller and Nick Bostrom, 2016, "Future Progress in Artificial Intelligence: A Survey of Expert Opinion," in *Fundamental Issues of Artificial Intelligence*, ed. Vincent C. Müller, Springer, 553–571.

[2] Nick Bostrom, 2014, *Superintelligence: Paths, Dangers, Strategies*, Oxford University Press, chapter 10.

[3] Marius Dorobantu, 2021, "Why the Future Might Actually Need Us: A Theological Critique of the 'Humanity-as-Midwife-for-Artificial-Superintelligence' Proposal," *International Journal of Interactive Multimedia and Artificial Intelligence* 7(1), 44–51.

A different perspective on our effort to build AI is to regard it as fulfilling our divine mandate to join God's creative enterprise as co-creators of the world. Such a view invites a more positive theological evaluation. Anne Foerst, a computer scientist and Christian theologian, believes that the pursuit of AI can play a beneficial role in humanity's journey of self-understanding: it is the ultimate manifestation of our inner drive towards the impossible and towards participating in divine creativity.[4]

Apart from its supposed role in the human narrative, AI might become theologically interesting in itself, especially if it *does* reach human-level intelligence. What would AGI be, ontologically speaking? The challenge is that the AGI label only implies human-level performance but not necessarily any structural similarity. AGI would behave indistinguishably from us from the 'outside' – which is precisely what Turing's test attempts to measure – but this doesn't mean that it would also be like us 'on the inside'. The philosopher John Searle famously distinguishes between strong and weak AI. Weak AI would be a mere simulation of intelligence, without having a mind or any phenomenal experience. Strong AI, to the contrary, would have mental states; it would think, feel and understand. So weak AI would be *something*, while strong AI would be *someone*, a distinction that, theologically, could make all the difference.

In the philosophy of mind and AI, the question of whether AGI would be weak or strong is still largely unsettled and will remain so for the foreseeable future. We have no idea how we could even test whether AGI had the kind of 'inside-outness' we intuitively associate with authentic selves. Mathematician John Puddefoot, author of one of the first serious theological engagements with AI, believes that it would be impossible to know from the outside whether AGI has this kind of first-person experience.[5] If hard-pressed, we actually have that same problem with respect to any other agent apart from ourselves, human or non-human. One can never know for sure whether robots, animals or even other people have inner worlds. In philosophy, this is called the problem of other minds. We lack a good theory of what constitutes an authentic centre of selfhood, so our evaluation of other agents can only rely on our intuition. Although we can only be sure about our own

---

[4]   Anne Foerst, 1998, "Cog, a Humanoid Robot, and the Question of the Image of God," *Zygon: Journal of Religion & Science* 33(1), 91–111.

[5]   John Puddefoot, 1996, *God and the Mind Machine: Computers, Artificial Intelligence and the Human Soul*, SPCK.

first-person experience, we intuitively ascribe it to other humans and even to some animals on account of our common phylogeny and relatively similar bodily structures.

Those intuitions serve us little when it comes to AI, and we might never be able to know anything about a robot's inner world or lack thereof without being one. For Puddefoot, this realisation might shed a surprising new light on the Christian doctrine of the incarnation: it was perhaps necessary, he speculates, for God to become human to get a grasp of the fullness of human perspective from the inside and not just from the outside. In Christian theology, the necessity of the incarnation is well acknowledged for establishing the full solidarity between God and humans in the person of Christ, thus conferring salvation its universal character. The only potentially controversial part of Puddefoot's is the implication that God has learned something new through the incarnation, which would contradict divine omniscience. Learning would imply temporal change or evolution in the divine, which could be coherent with process theology but not with perfect-being theology. Regardless of one's theological sensibilities, one thing is clear: the clever parallel that AI is to us what we are to God has proved irresistibly appealing to most theologians. The creation narrative has thus become the dominant metaphor in theological ruminations on AI.

Catholic theologian Jordan Wales argues that AI without any conscious experience, as is the case with the programs produced through current methods, could never aspire to authentic selfhood or personhood.[6] Strictly computational approaches can do an excellent job of simulating what the Western medieval thinkers called *ratio*: logical, discursive problem solving. Still, they can do nothing to emulate the more elusive *intellectus*, the capacity to grasp reality subjectively, intuitively and in a holistic way. Instead, what computationalism produces is "the ghost of *ratio* without *intellectus*, understanding-as-procedure without a co-penetrating understanding-as-apprehension."[7]

To illustrate the theological relevance of interiority and conscious experience, Wales draws on the subtle distinction between two notions of the person: *prosopon* and *persona*. *Prosopon* designates one's social status, a sort of mask or avatar that we put on, like the various virtual profiles we refer to nowadays when we talk about our 'online

---

[6] Jordan Joseph Wales, Forthcoming, "Narcissus, the Serpent, and the Saint: Living Humanely in a World of Artificial Intelligence," in *All Creation Gives Praise: Essays at the Frontier of Science and Religion*, ed. Jay Martin, Catholic University of America Press.

[7] Wales, "Narcissus."

persona'. This is somewhat ironic because, initially, *persona* meant something completely different. Citing Patristic Trinitarian theology, Wales defines *persona* as an outer expression of one's interior life in relationship with other persons, thus something more profound than *prosopon*. The exercise of full personhood as *persona* presupposes "an interior life from which one may engage in voluntary self-gift by a meeting with another's interiority, a fusion of minds through empathy and understanding."[8] Without any interior life, AI could only simulate such engagement without ever being capable of doing it, as chatbots such as Siri or those of the GPT series do nowadays. Self-awareness and conscious experience are thus essential conditions for authentic personhood in Christian Patristic thought.

Wales' conclusion is, in my opinion, of the utmost importance in contemporary discussions about the moral status of AI. Relationality has lately become a buzzword in both theology and AI. In Christian theology, the notion of the image of God (*imago Dei*) is understood in increasingly relational terms. In AI, the importance of relationality is acknowledged concerning both how AI should demonstrate its intelligence – as in the eminently relational test proposed by Turing – and how AI programs might learn better by engaging relationally with other agents, as opposed to being trained in virtual solitude. Two decades ago, in a pioneering work for the dialogue between AI and theology, computer scientist and Christian theologian Noreen Herzfeld noticed a striking similarity between paradigm shifts in AI and theological anthropology: from substantive to functional and finally to relational approaches.[9]

Relationality is thus central for both humans and AI. Nonetheless, what Wales masterfully explains is the key difference between relating superficially as *prosopon* and doing it profoundly as *persona*. For example, a human and a chatbot's communication might look the same on Turing's terminal, but one comes from the rich internal world of a conscious agent while the other is just a clever juxtaposition of syntactic structures that are statistically likely to appear together in human communication, as is the case with current programs powered by 'large-language models'. In other words, relationality is indeed important, but there are different kinds of relationality, and the difference between them matters a lot.

---

[8] Wales, "Narcissus."
[9] Noreen L. Herzfeld, 2002, *In Our Image: Artificial Intelligence and the Human Spirit*, Fortress Press, 10–52.

Weak AI would undoubtedly be far from the high standard of authentic relationality and personhood. But how about strong AI, if such an entity is indeed possible at all? Would Christian doctrine allow its admission as a full member of the (post)human community? The notion of *imago Dei* is central to theological anthropology and, unsurprisingly, a cornerstone of Christian reflection on AI. In Genesis 1, the first chapter of the Hebrew Bible, it is explicitly affirmed that humans are created in the image and likeness of God.[10] Would a sufficiently complex strong AI also be in the image of God? This is a challenging question because there is no consensus among Christian theologians about what the divine image means. Traditionally, it has been interpreted as something concerning the human intellect, the kind of intelligence that differentiates us from animals and enables us to communicate with God. If interpreted in such terms, unless one insists on identifying *imago Dei* with a supernaturally added soul, there is no reason why strong AI should be denied this status.

More recently, this so-called substantive interpretation has largely fallen out of favour, being replaced by functional or relational hermeneutics. The functional interpretation speaks about the image of God as something that humans *do*, such as exercise dominion and stewardship over the created world or participate in God's creative act as co-creators. The relational interpretation affirms that the divine image consists of the unique relationship humans have with God and manifests in their authentic personal relationships with each other.

Theologian Karen O'Donnell proposes an interpretation that she calls "performative-optative," combining features of the functional and the relational.[11] Her definition of *imago Dei* entails a conscious orientation towards seeking the image of God in others, sometimes in the most unexpected places and situations, and towards a future of fulfilment in God. If *imago Dei* is more of an attitude than an attribute, then intelligent robots could also aspire to mirror God one day if they manifested autonomy, capacity to learn and willingness to do so. O'Donnell goes as far as proposing a sort of Turing's test for the *imago Dei*. To qualify as the image of God, AI should choose to "learn, as a new Christian does, to perform the image of God and seek it in the other in specific, concrete situations."[12]

[10] Genesis 1:26–27.

[11] Karen O'Donnell, 2018, "Performing the Imago Dei: Human Enhancement, Artificial Intelligence and Optative Image-Bearing," *International Journal for the Study of the Christian Church* 18(1), 4–15.

[12] O'Donnell, "Performing the Imago Dei," 8.

The openness towards hypothetical strong AI in Christian theology is part of a larger effort to lower the emphasis on human distinctiveness. This inversed anthropocentrism arose in the context of the ecological crisis, as well as the post-Darwinian realisation that we are not genetically or structurally very different from non-human animals. Such a theological readiness to open the scope of *imago Dei* potentially to other creatures is arguably a sign of theological health and, thus, very welcome. In the case of strong AI though, the only caveat is the inherent assumption that human-level intelligence would also be human-like, which might not necessarily be the case.[13] If the space of possible minds is vast, then the likelihood that AI will think like us could be very low, given its radically different phylogeny, needs and embodiment. Moreover, the human mind is somewhat quirky, operating with strange heuristics, biases and non-linear thinking that vastly transcend algorithmic-like rationality. Such bugs are often frustrating, and it is doubtful that we would intentionally bake them into AI minds, but it is arguably imperfections such as these that make human relationships possible and enjoyable. The *imago Dei* might thus be correlated with a sort of Goldilocks of intelligence-as-rationality, potentially inaccessible to strong AI due to its likely hyper-rational type of mind.[14]

Could a robot sin or become religious? Would humans accept robots in their faith communities? Such questions have received significant attention in theology and AI. In the 1980s, computer scientist Edmund Furse was wondering – naively, we might say with the benefit of hindsight – what the computational basis of a perfect moral life could look like and how moral principles could be baked into a robot's decision-making algorithm, given that the world is so complex and inherently corrupt. In Furse's speculation, an intelligent robot would probably become interested in religion at some point due to its curiosity. Robot religion, however, could only be possible if God was willing to bestow grace and redemption over the artificial catechumens.[15]

Christian theologian Yong Sup Son argues not only that AI could be religious but that we would, in fact, need it to be.[16] Given all the

---

[13] Marius Dorobantu, 2021, "Human-Level, but Non-Humanlike: Artificial Intelligence and a Multi-Level Relational Interpretation of the Imago Dei," *Philosophy, Theology and the Sciences (PTSc)* 8(1), 81–107.

[14] Marius Dorobantu, 2021, "Cognitive Vulnerability, Artificial Intelligence, and the Image of God in Humans," *Journal of Disability & Religion* 25(1), 27–40.

[15] Edmund Furse, 1986, "The Theology of Robots," *New Blackfriars* 67: 377–386, 385–386.

[16] Yong Sup Song, 2020, "Religious AI as an Option to the Risks of Superintelligence: A Protestant Theological Perspective," *Theology and Science* 19(1), 65–78.

dangers posed by the possibility of ASI, including severe existential risks, a potential solution would be to somehow grow Christian robots committed to Christian values such as humility and self-sacrifice. Instead of pre-programming such moral values in AI, as Furse proposed, Song believes that intelligent robots could learn virtue and religiosity through participation in religious communities. Leaving aside the questionable feasibility of such a project, which is difficult to evaluate, this proposal is more in tune with the relational theories of human and machine learning. If AI could ever acquire moral values, it would likely do it via interacting with moral agents rather than having such values preprogrammed. However, a legitimate question regards whether altruism and humility are the (only) behaviours a robot would learn in a real-world Christian community. What if, instead, it develops fundamentalism or bigotry? Religious AIs would thus arguably pose similar kinds of goal-alignment problems as non-religious ones.

Another question is whether people would welcome artificial believers in their faith communities. Religious scholar Calvin Mercer believes that Christian theology is nimble enough to accept alternative forms of sentient intelligence, such as cyborgs or robots.[17] To illustrate this, he compares the scenario of artificial catechumens with the biblical story of the circumcision controversy between the apostle Paul and his opponents. The latter was about whether or not Gentiles converting to Christianity should be circumcised. Mercer sees in Paul's victory and the subsequent drop of this ritual obligation a promising precedent. Perhaps future Christians will exhibit enough theological flexibility to accept believers of exotic ontological status, such as intelligent robots. This argument is creative and reminiscent of an oft-quoted remark by Pope Francis that he couldn't deny baptism to aliens, should they ever request it. Comparing robots or aliens with Gentiles might look to modern readers as unwarranted, given the ontological difference between the two. Nevertheless, for the first-century typical Jew, Paul's move might have looked equally revolutionary and shocking to how strange the possibility of baptising aliens and robots looks for us today.

Religious scholar James McBride paints a more complex picture of the issue of robot participation in Christian communities.[18] He points to potential controversies stemming from theological stumbling blocks,

---

[17] Calvin Mercer, 2020, "A Theological Embrace of Transhuman and Posthuman Beings," *Perspectives on Science and Christian Faith* 72(2), 83–88.

[18] James McBride, 2019, "Robotic Bodies and the Kairos of Humanoid Theologies," *Sophia* 58: 663–676.

such as the robots' lack of souls and proper bodies. Due to such contentious issues, McBride believes there is a high likelihood of a future schism in Christian communities between "progressives," who will readily embrace their new artificial brethren, and "fundamentalists," who will hold tight to human exclusivity.

Christians of all denominations believe that humans are, in one way or another, endowed with a soul, directly or indirectly created by God. Because AI is made by humans, McBride reasons, for many Christians it will be highly questionable whether it too has such a soul. The problem of AI developing or being endowed with a soul is complicated, mainly because, as with other theological hot potatoes, we lack an agreed-upon definition of what it means for humans to have a soul. But an argument can be brought against McBride's hypothesis that the human tendency to anthropomorphise will likely trump any theological intuition about the soul's (in)existence. If robots endowed with strong AI, or even weak AI, behave in a convincingly human way, it is unlikely that we will resist our hardwired inclinations to fully anthropomorphise them.

McBride's observation about the robots' lack of proper, fleshly bodies looks theologically more interesting. Much philosophical and theological debate deals with AI's potential cognitive and spiritual capacities, and little is said about its radically different embodiment. To participate in Christian worship and sacraments, robots will certainly need bodies. Could a silicon body be baptised by full immersion and given communion, asks McBride, when robots don't usually bathe, eat or drink? Furthermore, if "the flesh is the sine qua non of Christian soteriologies,"[19] could robots be included in Christ's redemption?

In addition to this being a problem for accepting robots in church, it might even be a problem for the robots themselves because they might find our current doctrines unappealing. Instead, a possible resolution suggested by McBride is a shift of focus from the Pauline soteriology of the body to a Johannine Logos theology. "Humanoid robots," he argues, "whose source code is based on rational structures or algorithms, would likely find a religious doctrine based on the sovereignty of reason comprehensible."[20] To appeal to robots, the Logos theology would need, though, to expand its notion of flesh (sarx), so that artificial beings could also identify with the redemption enabled by the Word become flesh.[21]

---

[19]   McBride, "Robotic Bodies," 670.
[20]   McBride, "Robotic Bodies," 671.
[21]   John 1:14.

In a similar vein, philosopher Rajesh Sampath imagines an intriguing thought experiment.[22] An intelligent robot might interpret the life and teaching of Jesus as if he were God incarnated not as a human but as an AI program, for the redemption of future robots. Sampath argues that such robotic hermeneutics would be *in extremis* possible without contradicting the Bible nor the doctrinal boundaries defined at Nicaea and Chalcedon. Christ's identification as the divine *Logos* would be regarded as a subtle symbol of the syntactic structure of computer algorithms, while the virgin birth of Jesus would symbolise how the 'Christ code' came into the world at a time when humans were incapable of writing such code. Why, asks Sampath, should such an allegorical interpretation be rejected? Instead, intelligent machines should be allowed to interpret Christian revelation in their own terms, as this would only be a natural continuation of tendencies currently advocated for in feminist and postcolonial theology.

Sampath's thought experiment is provoking, and his conclusion is inspiring. His argument's vulnerability, though, comes from the likelihood of such interpretations being consistent beyond a few clever analogies. Could such a robust robotheology be constructed without forcing meanings on the biblical text or trespassing doctrinal boundaries? In addition, the qualification of such a proposal as technically orthodox, just because it doesn't contradict the Bible and doctrine, might legitimately raise some eyebrows. What is revealed is a somewhat problematic computational understanding of Christian revelation as a finite set of logical propositions that can be 'gamed'. The content of religious faith is arguably richer than its linguistic formulation. Nevertheless, the possibility remains that intelligent machines might interpret Christian revelation in their own terms, even though perhaps not as radically as proposed by Sampath. They might also even receive their own divine revelation. It remains an open theological question as to how such scenarios should be handled.

Mercer and McBride, mentioned earlier, analyse the theological reasons that might enable or prohibit the admission of humanoid robots in Christian churches. However, if history is of any use, the main drivers of such decisions will not necessarily be theological. For example, religious scholars Laura Ammon and Randall Reed demonstrate how in analogue cases – such as the sixteenth-century debate over the inclusion of native Americans, or the current one regarding

---

[22] Rajesh Sampath, 2018, "From Heidegger on Technology to an Inclusive Pluralistic Theology," in *AI and IA: Utopia or Extinction?*, ed. Ted Peters, ATF Press, 117–132.

LGBT+ people – theological arguments play a surprisingly small role.[23] Instead, they generally follow cultural and social transformation as post hoc rationalisations. Whether or not robots will be baptised might thus depend more on their general acceptance in society at large than on theological anthropological or soteriological arguments.

To conclude, theologians seem to be overall sympathetic to the scenario of intelligent machines. There is nothing inherently prohibitive in Christian theology regarding the possibility of AI one day acquiring personhood, partaking in the *imago Dei* or becoming religious. For that to happen, AI should manifest levels of interior richness and conscious experience similar to our own, as well as a disposition towards authentic relationality and virtue. Although there are precedents in Christian history of expanding the pool of potential candidates for baptism to initially marginalised groups, deciding to include robots in our faith communities might have more to do with non-theological factors. Whichever ends up being the case, humanoid robots might choose to adapt or reinterpret Christian doctrine to make it speak to their own needs, or even create their own original robotheology.

AI: A FRIEND OR FOE OF CHRISTIANITY?

The discussion now turns to different questions, asking whether reflecting on the AI developments of the past few decades can lead to any meaningful theological insights. What does our fascination with AI say about us? Do the successes and failures of AI so far reveal anything about what it is to be human? How should we relate to our artificial creations in a way that does them justice and promotes our spiritual flourishing?

Religious scholar Robert M. Geraci notices a strong connection between the religion that explicitly or implicitly underpins a particular culture and the kind of technology pursued by people in that culture. The fact that research in the USA is more focused on disembodied AI, as opposed to the Japanese focus on robotics, can be traced back to the different religious traditions the two cultures are grounded in. Whereas in Western culture there are clear ontological distinctions between natural and artificial, in East Asian cosmologies such distinctions are much more blurred. This enables a worldview

---

[23] Laura Ammon and Randall Reed, 2019, "Is Alexa My Neighbor?," *Journal of Posthuman Studies* 3(2), 120–140.

where robots can be seen as participating "in a fundamental sanctity of the natural world,"[24] hence the proliferation of robotics in East Asia, whereas Western culture is more iconoclastic about such ideas. Christian eschatology, on the contrary, emphasises salvation in transfigured bodies, and this idea is so deeply rooted in the Western psyche that North American researchers are primed to naturally focus on disembodied AI over humanoid robots.

Theologian Philip Hefner regards AI as a "techno-mirror" that reveals our existential needs and obsessions.[25] We strive to compensate for our finitude and mortality by creating AI that will outlive and outpower us. In this view, pursuing AI seems rather hopeless. However, there is a silver lining: our technological inclination can also be regarded as a manifestation of our freedom and creative imagination, which enable us to enact our God-given mandate of created co-creators. Similarly to Hefner, Herzfeld sees our quest to create an artificial 'other' as stemming from the inescapable relationality planted within us as *imago Dei*. Drawing on Karl Barth, she concludes that although pursuing AI is not in itself idolatrous, it is "bound to be a disappointment if we look to it for the I–Thou relationship that will make us whole," which is only possible with God and other humans.[26]

In theological anthropology, *imago Dei* is often related to something that distinguishes humans from non-human creatures. The possibility of human-level AI seems thus to severely threaten human distinctiveness. "What, if anything," asks Puddefoot, "will remain of the 'uniquely human' when computer scientists [...] have done their worst?"[27] Furthermore, AI might do away with any trace of mystery that still surrounds human cognition and personhood. If all the 'magical' things we do can be replicated through computer algorithms, does that mean that we are also *nothing but* biological machines?

The latter might sound theologically problematic. But just as Christian anthropology has survived the Darwinian realisation that humans are essentially animals, it might also endure the challenges of AI. Anne Foerst believes that theological anthropology is compatible with a mechanistic view of the human person. Moreover, the latter could be a blessing in disguise for theology, leading to a more

---

[24] Robert M. Geraci, 2006, "Spiritual Robots: Religion and Our Scientific View of the Natural World," *Theology and Science* 4(3), 229–246, 229.

[25] Philip Hefner, 2004, "Technology and Human Becoming," *Zygon, Journal of Religion & Science* 37(3), 655–666.

[26] Herzfeld, *In Our Image*, 83.

[27] Puddefoot, *God and the Mind*, 85.

sophisticated understanding of *imago Dei* and a more compassionate, inclusive and responsible attitude towards nature.

Foerst's conclusions came just before the turn of the millennium, after she researched first hand how humans interacted with MIT's humanoid robot, Cog. This project was the epitome of behaviour-based robotics, pioneered by Rodney Brooks, an approach that at the time was seen as a potential solution to the problems that had plagued symbolic AI. Behaviour-based robotics was predicated on the correct premise that AI needed to be better embodied. However, its prediction that embodied robots such as Cog will eventually get closer to human-level intelligence has proved naïve. Thus, it is somewhat surprising to see so much of the theological engagement with AI of the past three decades drawing on the Cog project. Two main assumptions informing this project were highly problematic: that differences between humans and robots at the time were "marginal and not qualitative" and that "phenomena such as consciousness are illusory."[28] The field of AI has evolved significantly since, and theological reflection should better keep up.

Like Foerst, Puddefoot also believes that a mechanistic view of the human person is compatible with Christian anthropology. For him, the possibility of true AI points instead to a different theological problem, one related to theodicy: why, if a computer could, in principle, do the same things that a human does, was there a need for so much suffering throughout evolutionary history by embodied biological life? From this, Puddefoot infers that suffering must be valuable in itself. Our universe might be thus characterised by a fundamental law that makes suffering and pain necessary for flourishing, something noticeable in both the process of biological evolution and the moral of Christ's crucifixion and resurrection. To acquire the moral status of *someone*, a robot "would need to grow, feel pain, experience and react to finitude, and generally enter the same state of mixed joy and sorrow as a human being. In particular, it would need to be finite, aware of its finitude, and condemned one day to die."[29]

A deeper theological insight distilled by Puddefoot from the AI scenario is that medieval mind–body dualism is untenable. This coheres with a similar argument made by theologian Ian Barbour. According to Barbour, reflection on the insights provided by AI and neuroscience indicates that the biblical, holistic, embodied, relational and social

---

[28]   Foerst, "Cog, a Humanoid," 103–104.
[29]   Puddefoot, *God and the Mind*, 92.

view of the human person is much more consistent than mind–body dualism.[30] Every skill, cognitive capacity or memory that we have is highly contextual and deeply related to our physical body and the reality of *this* world, as cognitive science and AI increasingly demonstrate. This poses some problems to the idea that something of us – our mental/spiritual self – gets to be transferred to a different realm after death without *this* body. How, asks Puddefoot, can any component of our mind have any relevance in the afterlife, a reality presumably marked by a radically different kind of existence, laws and goals, when everything that we are mentally or spiritually is inextricably related to our particular embodiment? The only solution to this puzzle, according to him, is a relational definition of the soul/self: "it is what is known of us by others and by God that supplies the repository from which our recreation in the new heaven and new earth may arise."[31] This opens up the possibility for robots' redemption. If they become sufficiently inserted into our societies and develop deep relationships with us, they might also acquire the kind of relational footprint that could 'force' God to recreate them in heaven. Our relationships with intelligent robots could thus elevate them to a more theologically meaningful status. But before the technology reaches a sufficient level to unlock such possibilities, a more pressing question is how we should deal with existing AI.

Theologian Calum Samuelson points out a danger inherent in delegating to robots some of the difficult things that humans don't like doing, especially when such tasks require giving oneself in love to another.[32] As AI chatbots develop their communication skills, they will undoubtedly become helpful as chat partners for the lonely or for those in need of psychological or spiritual therapy, especially because humans are costly and not always available. However, according to Samuelson, this should remain the exception, and not the rule, because AI cannot provide the kind of real listening that people ultimately need. "Weeping with those who weep"[33] is something we shouldn't completely outsource because doing so might severely numb our relationality and hinder our growth in virtue. This also provides a valuable theological angle for discussions

---

[30] Ian G. Barbour, 1999, "Neuroscience, Artificial Intelligence, and Human Nature: Theological and Philosophical Reflections," *Zygon, Journal of Religion & Science* 34(3), 361–398.

[31] Puddefoot, *God and the Mind*, 123.

[32] Calum Samuelson, 2020, "Artificial Intelligence: A Theological Approach," *The Way* 59(3), 41–50.

[33] Romans 12:15.

about using robots to comfort or care for the elderly. The Japanese robot pet Paro is one such example, used for its calming effect on patients in nursing homes. Debates such as these usually circle around the ethical issues raised by deception: as long as the artificial caregiver does not try to pass as human and no one is misled, things should be all right. However, a theological argument can be made that caring for each other is perhaps the ultimate human activity and, therefore, valuable in itself, so it should be automated only in exceptional cases.

Theologian Michael Burdett asks whether we can or should say 'You' to artefacts.[34] He concludes that doing so might be beneficial, although not without risks. Burdett finds good reasons in Martin Buber's philosophy to extend the 'I–You' relationship to things that would ontologically fall in the 'it' category because of how that might beneficially affect us. Whereas I–it is typical of a functionalist and objectifying view of the world, I–You elicits a more characteristically human attitude of attention, consideration and fuller appreciation, even though it can be more tense and demanding. Treating artefacts as You might also be warranted by their deep embeddedness in a web of relationships and meanings: they always point to the person who made them and depend on the 'person-like intentions' of those who interact with them.

According to Burdett, we might be theologically better off by allowing some blurring of the boundaries between natural and artificial. Otherwise, we should accept that we, too, are partly artificial, given what we currently know about the interplay between culture and biology in our own evolution. In addition, as intuitive as the natural–artificial distinction might seem, it is largely out of place in the increasingly human-made world of the Anthropocene. Cultivating such I–You relationships with artefacts would thus contribute to ascribing "greater theological status to 'the made'."[35]

The possible downside, however, which Burdett also acknowledges, is that blurring these boundaries may make us more functionalist in our relationships with other humans, expecting similar levels of compliance and control. Wales argues similarly that inadequately treating weak AI as a 'You' might downgrade human-to-human relationships from the level of *persona* to that of *prosopon*, fostering "the instrumentalization of social relations – that is, seeing persons as

---

[34] Michel Burdett, 2020, "Personhood and Creation in an Age of Robots and AI: Can We Say 'You' to Artifacts?," in *Zygon, Journal of Religion & Science* 55(2), 347–360.

[35] Burdett, "Personhood and Creation," 357.

simply behavior-producing instruments whose activities are defined by our benefit."[36]

Instead, a theologically healthier way of relating to artefacts, according to Wales, is to see them as signs. In an Augustinian understanding, things are signs when they point to a reality beyond them and ultimately to God. The current AI algorithms, if interpreted as signs, point to the millions of unnamed, and usually unknowing, humans whose behaviour was used as training data for the neural networks. The AI program, though entirely unconscious, is not empty; it contains, according to Wales, "the trace of uncounted moments of *true* personal self-expression, small moments of self-gift, both shallow and deep, on the part of unnumbered real human beings whose behavior is the basis for the AI's training."[37] Empathising with the real persons whose lives are symbolically present in the AI program is an elegant solution to the dilemma of how to treat artefacts. It allows the exercise of our naturally emerging compassion, which nourishes spiritual growth, but it directs it symbolically towards real people and not towards the artefact itself, safeguarding it from idolatry and the problematic tendency to personalise non-persons.

CONCLUSIONS

So, is AI a friend or a foe of Christianity? Almost four decades ago, Furse enthusiastically speculated about the exciting possible AI applications in theology.[38] Some of his proposals, such as using natural language–processing programs to discern subtle textual patterns in biblical exegesis, are fully at work in theological scholarship today. Others, such as practising catechetics on programs that can learn, have yet to really come through. Others yet, such as designing a computational model of Jesus, are entirely out of place today, and not for the reasons imagined by Furse (he anticipated such a task would be tricky because of the lack of sufficient training data in the Gospels, but he regarded the computational modelling of a saint as something entirely feasible).

Looking back at such predictions shows how far we've come in understanding the limits of computationalism and the intricacy of human psychology. Computer scientist Robert Elliott Smith aptly said that "AI is the hole, not the doughnut,"[39] and this also describes well

---

[36] Wales, "Narcissus, the Serpent."

[37] Wales, "Narcissus, the Serpent."

[38] Furse, "The Theology of Robots," 383.

[39] Robert Elliott Smith, 2019, *Rage inside the Machine: The Prejudice of Algorithms, and How to Stop the Internet Making Bigots of Us All*, Bloomsbury Business, 293

what Christian theology can make of AI's successes and failures so far. Philip Hefner explains how the "techno-mirror" of AI reflects our deepest longings and fears, but something else that becomes visible in the AI mirror is the sheer complexity of the human person. The fact is telling that every generation of AI enthusiasts sees itself as being on the cusp of emulating human-level intelligence, only to subsequently realise that things were orders of magnitude more complicated. So far, the Christian Patristic intuition that the human person ultimately escapes complete definitions because it images a nondefinable God[40] has not been seriously challenged, at least in practice.

But this might not last forever, and perhaps AI might one day become truly intelligent and even conscious. If that were to happen, what should Christianity make of it, and how should we treat sentient robots? Burdett explains that our theological and ethical intuitions about other creatures stem not only from their perceived capabilities but also from how we assign their place in "The Great Chain of Being."[41] The closer an animal is to us in terms of phylogeny and appearance, the more moral status we are willing to ascribe it. However, this also means that it is perfectly possible to be blinded to something/someone's de facto capabilities due to preconceptions about its place in this Great Chain. This has repeatedly happened in human history, with entire groups of people arbitrarily marginalised based on wrong intuitions. Therefore, this bias should serve as a cautionary tale going forwards.

Due to superb progress in science and technology, we are increasingly more capable of bringing about life forms that escape our intuitive categories altogether: hybrids, chimaeras, cyborgs and one day, perhaps, even autonomous artificial agents. Advances in AI force us to rethink our intuitions, including those about the natural order of things and the Great Chain. Burdett's observation that it is of utmost importance for us to "love the right things in the right way"[42] is, in my opinion, correct, but our ancient intuitions of what counts as right may need some revision in a time when the Great Chain of Being is bound to be broken by our own creative powers.

If it is true that authentic selves can emerge without necessarily sharing the same ontological substrate as biological life – which is a

---

[40] Alfons Brüning, 2019, "Can Theosis Save 'Human Dignity'? Chapters in Theological Anthropology East and West," *Journal of Eastern Christian Studies* 71(3–4), 177–248, 186.

[41] Burdett, "Personhood and Creation," 358–359.

[42] Burdett, "Personhood and Creation," 359.

big if – then there is no theological reason to deny them their deserved status and treatment. As far as this chapter has demonstrated, Christian theology would not be very troubled by a scenario of true AI. On the contrary, Christians would have every reason to rejoice at the opportunity to exercise compassion and love with their new neighbours.

BIBLIOGRAPHY

Ammon, Laura and Reed, Randall. 2019. "Is Alexa My Neighbor?." *Journal of Posthuman Studies* 3(2), 120–140.

Barbour, Ian G. 1999. "Neuroscience, Artificial Intelligence, and Human Nature: Theological and Philosophical Reflections." *Zygon: Journal of Religion & Science* 34(3), 361–398.

Bostrom, Nick. 2014. *Superintelligence: Paths, Dangers, Strategies.* Oxford University Press.

Brüning, Alfons. 2019. "Can Theosis Save 'Human Dignity'? Chapters in Theological Anthropology East and West." *Journal of Eastern Christian Studies* 71(3–4), 177–248.

Burdett, Michael. 2020. "Personhood and Creation in an Age of Robots and AI: Can We Say 'You' to Artifacts?." *Zygon, Journal of Religion & Science* 55(2), 347–360.

Dorobantu, Marius. 2021a. "Why the Future Might Actually Need Us: A Theological Critique of the 'Humanity-as-Midwife-for-Artificial-Superintelligence' Proposal." *International Journal of Interactive Multimedia and Artificial Intelligence* 7(1), 44–51.

Foerst, Anne. 1998. "Cog, a Humanoid Robot, and the Question of the Image of God." *Zygon: Journal of Religion & Science* 33(1), 91–111.

Furse, Edmund. 1986. "The Theology of Robots." *New Blackfriars* 67(795), 377–386.

Hefner, Philip. 2002. "Technology and Human Becoming." *Zygon, Journal of Religion & Science* 37(3), 655–666.

Herzfeld, Noreen L. 2002. *In Our Image: Artificial Intelligence and the Human Spirit.* Fortress Press.

Mercer, Calvin. 2020. "A Theological Embrace of Transhuman and Posthuman Beings." *Perspectives on Science and Christian Faith* 72(2), 83–88.

O'Donnell, Karen. 2018. "Performing the Imago Dei: Human Enhancement, Artificial Intelligence and Optative Image-Bearing." *International Journal for the Study of the Christian Church* 18(1), 4–15.

Puddefoot, John C. 1996. *God and the Mind Machine: Computers, Artificial Intelligence and the Human Soul.* SPCK.

Samuelson, Calum. 2020. "Artificial Intelligence: A Theological Approach." *The Way* 59(3), 41–50.

Smith, Robert Elliott. 2019. *Rage Inside the Machine: The Prejudice of Algorithms, and How to Stop the Internet Making Bigots of Us All.* Bloomsbury Business.

FURTHER READING

Balle, Simon. 2022. "Theological Dimensions of Humanlike Robots: A Roadmap for Theological Inquiry." *Theology and Science* 21(1), 132–156.

Bjork, Russell C. 2008. "Artificial Intelligence and the Soul." *Perspectives on Science and Christian Faith* 60(2), 95–102.

Curry, Eugene. 2022. "Artificial Intelligence and Baptism: Cutting a Gordian Knot." *Theology and Science* 20(2), 156–165.

Davison, Andrew. 2021. "Machine Learning and Theological Traditions of Analogy." *Modern Theology* 37(2), 254–274.

Dorobantu, Marius. 2022a. "Artificial Intelligence as a Testing Ground for Key Theological Questions." *Zygon: Journal of Religion & Science* 57(4), 984–999.

  2022b. "Imago Dei in the Age of Artificial Intelligence: Challenges and Opportunities for a Science-Engaged Theology." *Christian Perspectives on Science and Technology (New Series)* 1, 175–196.

Dorobantu, Marius, and Yorick Wilks. 2019. "Moral Orthoses: A New Approach to Human and Machine Ethics." *Zygon: Journal of Religion & Science* 54(4), 1004–1021.

Graves, Mark. 2017. "Shared Moral and Spiritual Development among Human Persons and Artificially Intelligent Agents." *Theology and Science* 15(3), 333–351.

Green, Brian Patrick. 2018. "Ethical Reflections on Artificial Intelligence." *Scientia et Fides* 6(2), 9–31.

Green, Brian Patrick et al. 2022. "Artificial Intelligence and Moral Theology: A Conversation." *Journal of Moral Theology* 11(Special Issue 1), 13–40.

Herzfeld, Noreen. 2023. *The Artifice of Intelligence: Divine and Human Relationship in a Robotic Age*. Fortress Press.

Li, Oliver. 2023. "Artificial General Intelligence and Panentheism." *Theology and Science*. https://doi.org/10.1080/14746700.2023.2188373.

MacKay, Donald M. 1985. "Machines, Brains and Persons." *Zygon: Journal of Religion & Science* 20(4), 401–412.

Midson, Scott A. 2018. "Robo-Theisms and Robot Theists: How Do Robots Challenge and Reveal Notions of God?." *Journal of Implicit Theology* 20 3), 299–318.

Midson, Scott A., ed. 2020. *Love, Technology and Theology*. T&T Clark.

Oviedo, Lluís. 2022. "Artificial Intelligence and Theology: Looking for a Positive – but Not Uncritical – Reception." *Zygon: Journal of Religion & Science* 54(4), 938–952.

O'Gieblyn, Meghan. 2021. *God, Human, Animal, Machine: Technology, Metaphor, and the Search for Meaning*. Anchor Books.

Peters, Ted, ed. 2018 *AI and IA: Utopia or Extinction?* ATF Press.

  2019. "Artificial Intelligence versus Agape Love." *Forum Philosophicum: International Journal for Philosophy* 24(2), 259–278.

Poole, Eve. 2023. *Robot Souls: Programming in Humanity*. CRC Press.

Smith, Joshua K. 2022. *Robot Theology: Old Questions through New Media*. Resource Publications.

Tamatea, Laurence. 2008. "If Robots R–US, Who Am I: Online 'Christian' Responses to Artificial Intelligence." *Culture and Religion* 9(2), 141–160.

Wales, Jordan Joseph. 2022. "Metaphysics, Meaning, and Morality: A Theological Reflection on AI." *Journal of Moral Theology* 11(Special Issue 1), 157–181.

Wyatt, John and Williams, Stephen N., eds. 2021. *The Robot Will See You Now: Artificial Intelligence and the Christian Faith.* SPCK.

7 Islam and Artificial Intelligence

YAQUB CHAUDHARY

INTRODUCTION

Islam began with the revelation of the Qur'an to the Prophet Muhammad (PBUH) in 610 CE and is the youngest of the three monotheistic Abrahamic traditions. The monotheistic legacy of Prophet Abraham (Ibrahīm) is recounted in many places in the Qur'an, which mention his challenge against the idols worshipped by his people as a youth (19:40–45, 21:51–70, 26:69–81, 37:83–99). The young Abraham asked, "What are these images to which ye are (so assiduously) devoted?" (21:52) and why they worshipped that which "heareth not, nor seeth, nor can in aught avail thee" (19:42).

Today, many people routinely interact with seemingly hearing, seeing and self-acting artificial intelligence (AI) entities, which are increasingly inserted as third parties in every social context as mediators of access to the necessities of life. Instead of turning to and relying on God in every circumstance, society is being reorganised such that individuals must, willingly or unwillingly, defer to the seemingly self-aware digital systems and the obscure motivations of algorithms that have become agents of providence, channels of sustenance and apparitions of judgement and guidance. This chapter discusses some themes raised by AI research from an Islamic perspective that follow from this turn away from God to the veneration of the machine.

The Islamic worldview is theocentric, and its central teaching is *tawhīd*, the principle of divine unity or oneness, which affirms the absolute unity and uniqueness of God in terms of essence, attributes and actions. God created human beings as a distinct species of creation and endowed them with intelligence and the capacity for speech. Humans are distinguished from the rest of creation by virtue of their intellectual faculties and religious obligations are based on sound intellectual faculties. Reason, alongside revelation, is a primary source of religious truth, hence, Islamic theologians undertook philosophical inquiries into the nature of the sensory, perceptual and rational apparatuses that underlie our ability to conceptualise and make sound rational judgements. In Islamic theology, these apparatuses play a crucial role as guarantors of religious truth and as prerequisites for religious and moral obligations, and are constitutive of the unique status of human beings as vicegerents or stewards of God on earth.

Developments in AI raise epistemological questions about the nature of human and machine knowledge and perception, ontological questions about the nature and status of the artefacts imbued with this technology, and metaphysical questions about the nature of reality that warrant the quest to create artificial forms of intelligence. Further, the social, political and environmental, as well as the religious, axiological, and spiritual, implications that follow from the development of AI make the intersection of Islam and AI a vital site for scholarly inquiry, and there is a significant need to understand developments in AI from this standpoint given that approximately a quarter of the population of the world adheres to Islamic teachings.

Legal and ethical questions of AI, such as issues of bias, discrimination, algorithmic justice, categorisation and prohibition of malicious uses, the consequences of AI for privacy and autonomy, and its impact on the environment, are all matters of Islamic jurisprudence, known as *fiqh*, and would be addressed by scholars who are qualified in issuing Islamic legal judgements. It is the responsibility of practitioners, developers and users of AI systems to seek Islamic guidance pertaining to their domains and to consult with specialists in Islamic law in novel areas.[1]

AI research has yielded entities that *appear* to be capable of learning, hearing, seeing, speaking, willing and self-acting, which has provoked questions about whether AI artefacts may, in the future, be ascribed with other attributes associated with living and sentient beings, such as mental states, intentions and motivations. Some commentators have ascribed attributes reserved for God, such as omniscience, omnipotence and omnipresence, to imagined superintelligent agents. According to Kevin Lagrandeur, AI research seeks "to create agents or extensions of ourselves which operate like us, but which are godlike in their power, so that we will be able to manipulate nature more completely."[2]

---

[1] On Islamic ethics for AI and digital technologies, see Amana Raquib et al. 2022. "Islamic Virtue-Based Ethics for Artificial Intelligence," *Discover Artificial Intelligence* 2(1), 11; Yaqub Chaudhary, 2020, "Initial Considerations for Islamic Digital Ethics," *Philosophy & Technology*, https://doi.org/10.1007/s13347-020-00418-3.

[2] Kevin Lagrandeur, 2017, *Androids and Intelligent Networks in Early Modern Literature and Culture: Artificial Slaves*, Routledge.

In order to address these theological themes in AI research and discourse, this chapter follows established distinctions between symbolic/rule-based and connectionist/neural network approaches, as well as the common gradations in AI usually referred to as weak or narrow, whereby a system is tailored for a specific task, and strong or general AI, which can take on various tasks and that, it is argued, could qualify as a candidate for sentience and consciousness. For the present purposes, the former represents the hypothetico-deductive approach to knowledge, whereas the latter is an inductive approach,[3] that is, the former was "the heir to the rationalist, reductionist tradition in philosophy; the other viewed itself as idealized, holistic neuroscience."[4]

The significance of the shift in the approach to knowledge based on the success of neural networks cannot be overstated. According to Bruce MacLennan, the emergence of neural networks means that for the first time in 2,500 years of the history of philosophy we have "a scientific account of an alternative theory of knowledge."[5] In so far as AI is construed as experimental epistemology, it intersects with issues at the very foundations of Islamic theology given that logic and epistemology are prerequisites of Islamic theology, jurisprudence and all other religious sciences. The epistemological issues raised by AI attain further significance as models of machine knowledge become models for human knowledge itself.

Incremental successes in narrow AI have also raised interest in the prospect of artificial general intelligence (AGI). It is important to note that recent scholarship has shown that behind many of the claimed successes of AI is disingenuous rhetoric to attract funding or obfuscation of the fact that vast computational or human resources have been essential to the advancements.[6] The issues that matter most to Islamic metaphysical thought are hidden beneath the ethical and political theatre that surrounds AI discourse.

From the standpoint of this chapter then, the issue of Islam and AI is first and foremost a metaphysical issue whereby AI is the central

---

[3] Dominique Cardon, Jean-Philippe Cointet and Antoine Mazières, 2018, "La Revanche Des Neurones: L'invention Des Machines Inductives et La Controverse de l'intelligence Artificielle," *Réseaux* 211(5), 173.

[4] Hubert L. Dreyfus and Stuart E. Dreyfus, 1988, "Making a Mind versus Modeling the Brain: Artificial Intelligence Back at a Branchpoint," *Daedalus* 117(1), 15–16.

[5] Bruce J. MacLennan, 2021, "Word, and Flux: The Discrete and the Continuous in Computation," unpublished manuscript, 3, https://web.eecs.utk.edu/~bmaclenn/.

[6] Yarden Katz, 2020, *Artificial Whiteness: Politics and Ideology in Artificial Intelligence*, Columbia University Press; Jonnie Penn, 2021, "Algorithmic Silence: A Call to Decomputerize," *Journal of Social Computing* 2(4), 338–342.

pillar in a *metaphysical research programme*[7] for the total artificialisation of the world. The full depth of questions of law, ethics, politics and the impact of AI on society only become apparent against the metaphysical backdrop of AI and contemporary computational cultures. This metaphysical research programme may be identified by various abbreviations for converging technologies such as NBIC (nanotechnology, biotechnology, information and cognitive science) and BANG (bits, atoms, neurons, genes).

ISLAM AND AI: EXISTING LITERATURE

The development of AI, both conceptually and technologically, has predominantly taken place against the backdrop of Western philosophy. Questions of religion and AI have most often been influenced by Judeo-Christian theological concepts and the contemporary imaginary surrounding AI in science fiction narratives in film and literature is for the most part a product of Western culture, and thus explores the ambitions and desires characteristic of the Western worldview. According to Despina Kakoudaki, there is a recurrence of tropes that form a "transhistorical discursive continuum"[8] passing through the enlightenment period to the present. Some of the tropes that diverge in significant ways from the Islamic worldview include seeking unconstrained mastery and control over nature through science and technology, the restoration of Adamic knowledge and attaining paradise on earth, transcending human nature and biological limits, and ultimately the dream of eternal life.

Each of these is insinuated in different areas of AI development and discourse – control over nature is to be enhanced by offloading physical and cognitive workloads to robots and intelligent systems, the use of AI to accelerate scientific and technological discovery is expected to produce knowledge that will lead to a luxurious worldly life, human augmentation through artificial and computational assemblages will extend human capabilities beyond the limits of biology, and through the merger of human consciousness with machines, people will gain perpetual existence by transferring their consciousness from one form of embodiment to another.

---

[7] Jean-Pierre Dupuy, 2013, *The Mark of the Sacred*, trans. M. B. DeBevoise, Stanford University Press.

[8] Despina Kakoudaki, 2014, *Anatomy of a Robot: Literature, Cinema, and the Cultural Work of Artificial People*, Rutgers University Press, 4.

Following the rapid advancement of deep-learning systems in the mid-2010s, there has been renewed interest in all areas of the field, and advances in AI are leading to more people believing that many aspects of the technological imaginary will soon be realised.

Unlike previous eras of AI, where research momentum dissipated into the so-called AI winters, AI has become a global phenomenon and central to national strategies for technological development, and it therefore directly impacts the lives of more people. In the past, scholarship on Islam and AI may not have had the time to develop as interest in the field began to recede and the claims of AI proponents failed to materialise. However, scholarly discourses on Islam and AI are now long overdue, especially given that AI systems can now perform tasks that were thought to be either impossible for machines or decades away.

The earliest scholarly work that specifically addresses AI and Islam, to the best of our knowledge, is a 1992 chapter by the sociologist Mahmoud Dhaouadi, which undertakes an exploration of artificial and human intelligence from a Qur'anic perspective.[9] Dhaouadi highlights several themes that remain pertinent to contemporary AI and engages the prominent philosophers of AI of the 1990s, such as Hubert Dreyfus, John Searle, Edward Feigenbaum and Herbert Simon, as well as the philosophers of neuroscience P. M. and P. S. Churchland. Dhaouadi argues that there is an insurmountable gap between AI and human intelligence based on our ability to "manipulate cultural symbols," and that it is the phenomenon of culture that distinguishes humanity from other species.

Dhaouadi's arguments are drawn from his disciplinary orientation in sociology and united with arguments on the role of language in the production of symbolic culture from cognitive science, on the one hand, and a theological argument from the Qur'an, on the other. His aim is to highlight the superiority of human intelligence, rather than dwell on the shortcomings of AI, which tends to view human intelligence mechanistically or through the prevailing technoscientific paradigms of each era, such as mechanism, cybernetics, information processing and computation. For Dhaouadi, intelligence is not a quantifiable and measurable phenomenon; rather, its true nature is transcendental. Dhaouadi refers to Qur'anic verses about the creation of Adam and the divine bestowal of unique intellectual and spiritual faculties, which we discuss later in this chapter, to argue that through the mediation of cultural symbols, human beings encounter a metaphysical realm that

---

[9] Mahmoud Dhaouadi, 1992, "Human and Artificial Intelligence," *American Journal of Islamic Social Sciences* 9(4), 465–481.

is inaccessible to other living organisms. In this view, the empirico-positivist approach towards intelligence limits our understanding of its nature and potential.

Dhaouadi refers to several areas of Qur'anic discourse on intelligence and thought: first, using our intellectual faculties to reflect on God's creation (Qur'an 3:119) and its purpose (30:8); and second, our unique human capacities for the use of language (55:4) and learning (96:4–5). The unique characteristics of human intelligence are part of the status of human beings as vicegerents or stewards of God on earth, which is available to humanity to develop, modify and transform, within the scope of sacred law. According to Dhaouadi, human intelligence is not a product of evolution but present at the time of the creation of humankind, and therefore irreconcilable with secular accounts of the origin, nature and purpose of human intelligence. This view is in accordance with Qur'an 17:85, which states that complete knowledge of the soul, and therefore intelligence, is beyond human reach.

More recently, Faraz Khan has considered whether materialism can explain the mind from an Islamic perspective.[10] Khan argues that what we know as 'mind' today is what traditional civilisations would have named spirit or soul, which stems from a legacy of disassociating philosophy of mind from theological connotations associated with classical terms.

Khan asks whether transhumanism is a plausible theory if the existence of the soul is believed to be true, whether materialism can be held alongside the view that humans possess an immaterial intellect, and whether consciousness, thought and rationality signify the existence of the soul. Khan notes that the classical Islamic position on the soul regards it as distinct from the body yet integrated with it and the locus of consciousness. In this view, the soul is a spiritual substance belonging to the spiritual world rather than the corporeal world and hence it is inaccessible to empirical investigation and artificial replication. Khan discusses the limitations of physicalist theories of mind such as eliminative materialism, behaviourism, identity theory and functionalism, and presents Searle's 'Chinese Room' argument against functionalism to reject the possibility of strong AI. According to Khan, it is the lack of intrinsic intentionality that forecloses the possibility of consciousness to machines and features of consciousness that do not yield to physicalist theories, including sentience, emotion, intellection (which

---

[10]   Faraz Khan, 2017, "Can Materialism Explain the Mind?," *Renovatio*, April, https://renovatio.zaytuna.edu/article/can-materialism-explain-the-mind.

includes "the direct unmediated grasp of first principles," reasoning and "abstraction of universals from particulars"), beliefs, desires, memory, will and choice, motivations and self-awareness.[11]

Besides these arguments against AI and physicalist theories of mind, Khan provides a rational argument in support of a type of substance dualism on the "unity and simplicity of consciousness," with reference to the theologian Imam Fakhr al-Dīn al-Rāzī (d. 606/1209).[12] Here, unity and simplicity are philosophical terms, which mean that mental awareness is unified and indivisible. In contrast, the brain is a composite entity that is composed of physical parts. According to this argument, "if a composite substance were the locus of consciousness, then each part of the aggregate would have a part of consciousness."[13]

However, given that consciousness originates from a singular source, as indicated by the singularity of the pronoun 'I', the brain, which is composite, cannot be considered the locus of consciousness, but rather its locus is the soul, which is simple. Beyond recognition of the soul as the source of meaning, purpose and virtue, little more can be said about it since it is a divine secret. This argument would foreclose consciousness to machines and artificial neural networks, which are composite entities. The articles of Dhaouadi and Khan provide Islamic perspectives that apply to AI in general and both are representative of orthodox theological perspectives in Sunni Islam.

Most recently, Biliana Popova provides a perspective on AI from Islamic philosophy and theology.[14] Popova considers different modalities of machine learning from the perspective of the prominent schools of Islamic philosophy and theology. Popova argues that supervised learning shares similar epistemological principles with those of the Islamic philosophers (the Falasifa). According to Popova, supervised learning relies on human categorisation, and the use of statistical and logistic regression leads to judgements that represent average cases, which is similar to the way some of the Falasifa have argued that social norms should be established by undertaking "vast sociological studies of all ethnicities, cultures and nations to establish which are universal and which are culturally bound."[15]

---

[11]   Khan, "Can Materialism Explain the Mind?"
[12]   Khan, "Can Materialism Explain the Mind?"
[13]   Khan, "Can Materialism Explain the Mind?"
[14]   Biliana Popova, 2020, "Islamic Philosophy and Artificial Intelligence: Epistemological Arguments," *Zygon: Journal of Religion & Science* 55(4), 977–995.
[15]   Popova, "Islamic Philosophy and Artificial Intelligence," 985.

Popova links unsupervised learning with the theological school of Ash'arism, which she says allows for probabilistic judgements and provides for "a balance between statistical knowledge that uncovers universal patterns, and the human right to make an evaluation of these patterns, all the while bearing in mind human limitations."[16] The analogies between the various schools of Islamic thought in Popova's article and the different approaches to machine learning should be understood figuratively and the article is predominantly a call for scholars of Islamic philosophy to engage in analysing developments in AI, especially as it affects more areas of daily life.

Figurative language that anthropomorphises machines is widespread when discussing AI. What is important to note from an Islamic perspective is that psychological terms relevant to AI have themselves been undergoing redefinition. When Turing predicted in 1950, "that by the end of the century, general educated opinion will be that machines think," he was emphasising that the use of words will have changed enough to permit such an opinion to be held without contradiction.[17] Given this change in the meaning of intelligence and its semantic field, the following section revisits some of the meanings of key terms related to AI in the Islamic tradition.

INTELLIGENCE, CONSCIOUSNESS AND KNOWLEDGE IN ISLAMIC THOUGHT

The Adamic origin of humanity is mentioned in multiple places in the Qur'an. In Qur'an 2:31–33, after God declares he will create a vicegerent on earth, an encounter with the angels takes place, where it is demonstrated that human beings possess a unique and divinely ordained form of knowledge that is beyond the knowledge of angels and pertains to the "names of all things." Four types of being with different types of knowledge may be discerned from these verses: *Allah* (God), who is the All-Knowing (al-Alim) and whose knowledge is absolute; the angels, whose knowledge is limited; Prophet Adam, who possesses unique knowledge granted by God; and Iblis, who possesses knowledge but with a defective understanding, as the Qur'anic narrative reveals.

Qur'anic commentators have mentioned that Adamic knowledge pertains to the Divine Names, the names of all created things,

---

[16] Popova, "Islamic Philosophy and Artificial Intelligence," 992.
[17] Otto Neumaier, 1987, "A Wittgensteinian View of Artificial Intelligence', in *Artificial Intelligence*, ed. Rainer P. Born, St Martin's Press.

knowledge of universals and particulars, and knowledge of things by their essences, and includes other capacities such as abstraction and concept formation. Intellect, knowledge and understanding are thus at the beginning of the human story, in contrast to the idea that human intelligence came into being over the course of millions of years of evolution. In Islamic thought, reason and intuition are united by the intellect (al-'aql), which has material and immaterial aspects and understanding or discriminating truth from falsehood is associated with the metaphysical heart (qalb) rather than the mind or brain alone, as mentioned in Qur'an 7:179: "they have hearts but cannot understand."

The interrelation between rational and intuitive modes of thought has been discussed by the contemporary Islamic philosopher Naquib al-Attas. At the foundation of al-Attas' philosophy of science and metaphysical system is a psycho-epistemological framework drawn from the main schools of Islamic theology. For al-Attas, humanity is distinguished from the rest of creation by "a certain power and capacity innate in man to articulate words or symbolic forms in meaningful patterns," and the articulation of meaningful language is an outward expression of an "inner, unseen reality," called the intellect (al-'aql).[18] In his view, meaning is the recognition of the place of anything in a system, knowledge "consists of units of meaning coherently related to other such units" and thought (al-fikr) is the movement of the soul towards meaning, which requires the faculty of imagination. Intuition is the arrival of the soul at meaning or vice versa (the arrival of meaning in the soul).[19] True meaning is acquired if it is in correspondence with the conceptual system projected by the revealed sources of the Islamic tradition.

According to al-Baqillani (d. 403/1013), the prominent Asharite theologian, knowledge is defined as "the cognition of the object known as it is."[20] The knowledge of God is primordial and uncreated, whereas the knowledge of living beings is created in time. Human knowledge is further divided into necessary and speculative or deductive. Necessary knowledge is knowledge that cannot be doubted and

---

[18] Syed Muhammad Naquib al-Attas, 1995, 'The Nature of Man and the Psychology of the Human Soul', in *Prolegomena to the Metaphysics of Islam*, Syed Muhammad Naquib al-Attas, International Institute of Islamic Thought and Civilization; A. Setia, 2003, "Al-Attas' Philosophy of Science an Extended Outline," *Islam & Science* 1(2), 165–214; Syed Muhammad Naquib al-Attas, 1989, *Islam and the Philosophy of Science*, International Institute of Islamic Thought and Civilization, 13–15.

[19] Al-Attas, *Islam and the Philosophy of Science*, 15–18.

[20] See Franz Rosenthal, 1970, *Knowledge Triumphant: The Concept of Knowledge in Medieval Islam*, Brill, 52–69

speculative knowledge is 'acquired' by deduction from necessary knowledge and sense perception. The Islamic theologian 'Adud al-Din al- 'Iji (d. 756/1355) stated that humans are gifted with innate reason, necessary knowledge and the capacity for speculation and deductive reasoning. The purpose of these faculties is to reflect on revelation and creation to come to the realisation of the existence of God and they extend beyond the realm of sense perception to the metaphysical or spiritual realm, as well as the microcosmic and macrocosmic, as mentioned in Qur'an 41:53, which states: "We shall show them Our portents on the horizons and within themselves."

Reason and rationality thus have a cosmological dimension and are related to the very nature of the universe, which was created with an intrinsic order and intelligibility.[21] This view of reason and rationality stands in contrast to the reductive logic of means–ends forms of rationality that instrumentalise means in the pursuit of narrow utilitarian ends and is the type of rationality that is embodied by computers, and especially AI systems, which are trained to optimise their parameters based on 'reward functions' given by their designers.

It is important to note that a bifurcation between discursive and intuitive modes of thinking never occurred in Islamic thought as it did in Western metaphysics. Instead, the intellect comprises both functions of logical analysis and intuitive knowledge. Empirical, rational, conceptual, moral and spiritual modes of thought are all united in Islamic thought.

There is, therefore, a correspondence between reality and the intellect in terms of the intelligibility of reality and the registration of signs in the intellect and their signification. Hence, rather than meaning being superimposed by the mind, as in the case of a Kantian agent, the function of the intellect is to discover the universal principles and intrinsic intelligibility of the cosmos, and to participate in this intelligible order itself by doing so.

This opens the question of whether the multidimensional nature of the human mind and intelligence in Islamic thought implies a limit to what can be achieved in the quest for AGI. From an Islamic perspective, AI research takes place in a context that is twice removed from reality as it is. The first veil is materialism or physicalism, which circumscribe what can be known about reality to what can be described quantitatively in mathematical terms. The second is that AI agents exist in a

---

[21] Karim Lahham, 2021, *The Anatomy of Knowledge and the Ontological Necessity of First Principles*, Tabah Research, 5, 6; Ibrahim Kalin, 2015, "Reason and Rationality in the Qur'an," KRM Monograph Series No. 10, Kalam Research & Media.

digital realm that is a further abstraction of the material world into a digital format. AI research works from behind this second veil and problems such as common sense and abstraction with limited data remain insurmountable challenges.

The question that confronts Islamic scholars is thus to which order of beings does AI belong? For Joseph Weizenbaum, "every other intelligence, however, great must necessarily be alien to the human domain." More recently, Luciana Parisi has argued that machine learning involves an expansion of an alien space of reasoning and that the "automation of reason marked the origination of the alien logic of machines," and Beatrice Fazi has written on how the automated modes of thought engendered by computation constitute "a different order of intelligibility."[22]

As previously noted, there are three types of being created by God that possess different levels of knowledge and understanding mentioned in Qur'an 2:31–33. Besides Adam, there are the jinn, created from smokeless fire, and the angels, created from light. In the Islamic ontology of beings, angels only know what they have been taught by God and do not falter in obeying God's commands. The jinn, on the other hand, are addressed by revelation alongside humans and may choose between belief in God or disbelief.

Animal and insect life, which possess forms of biological intelligence that are of interest to AI researchers, are also mentioned throughout the Qur'an. Qur'an 6:38 mentions that "[t]here is not an animal (that lives) on the earth, nor a being that flies on its wings, but (forms part of) communities like you." According to Fakhr al-Din al-Rāzī, the Islamic philosopher, theologian and exegete, human beings perceive both the universal and the particular, whereas animals only perceive the particular and angels only perceive the universal.[23]

Ultimately, everything that exists inhabits its own ontological realm with its own intelligibility of God, as mentioned in Qur'an 17:44, which states that: "The seven heavens and the earth, and all beings therein, declare His glory: there is not a thing but celebrates His praise; And yet ye understand not how they declare His glory!"

It is therefore an open question whether, from an Islamic perspective, AI should be considered in relation to human intelligence,

---

[22] Joseph Weizenbaum, 1993, *Computer Power, and Human Reason: From Judgement to Calculation*, Penguin Books, 223; Luciana Parisi, 2019, "The Alien Subject of AI," *Subjectivity* 12(1), 32; M. Beatrice Fazi, 2019, "Can a Machine Think (Anything New)? Automation beyond Simulation," *AI & Society* 34(4), 9.

[23] Fakhr ad-Dīn ar-Rāzī, 1981, (d. 606/1209), *Mafātīḥ Al-Ghayb or Kitāb at-Tafsīr al-Kabīr*, vol. 25, Dar al-Fikr.

whether it approximates another form of intelligence in the created order of beings (such as the angels, or the *jinn*), whether AI represents an entirely new order of intelligent being, or finally, whether AI qualifies as a form of intelligence at all.

There are various attempts to provide a formal definition of intelligence in mathematical terms. As far as these operational definitions are applied to the measurement of the performance of artificial agents, there would appear to be nothing objectionable from the standpoint of Islamic theology or metaphysics. However, the presupposition that there is a continuity between artificial agents and human agents in terms of intelligence would not be warranted based on the Islamic narrative about the divine bestowal of unique faculties of cognition to humans.

In contrast to the interrelation between intelligence, consciousness and life in Islamic thought, a significant and often unstated presupposition held by AI researchers is that intelligence can be decoupled from consciousness, and indeed the phenomenon of life. In Islamic thought, on the other hand, intelligence, consciousness and life are unified through the existence of the soul.

ISLAMIC THOUGHT AND THE SOUL

Islamic philosophers and theologians adopted an Aristotelian concept of the soul, including the idea that it is the rational soul that distinguishes human beings from other types of animate beings. Central to the philosophical system of the prominent Islamic philosopher Ibn Sina (Avicenna, d. 428/1037) is his metaphysics of the rational soul.[24] While the overall philosophy of Ibn Sina was not accepted by theologians, many aspects of his metaphysical system were absorbed into their teachings, especially his psychological theories. In his view, the rational soul is a substance subsisting by itself, that is, it is non-material and non-corporeal, the soul comes into existence with the body, not before (in contrast to Qur'an 7:172 on the primordial creation of human souls), and it is the soul that perceives universals and is the locus of choice and deliberative action.

In the philosophical and theological synthesis discussed by al-Attas, the soul is a subtle spiritual substance that is indivisible (i.e., not composed of parts) and is the very essence of man. It is divinely created and

---

[24] Avicenna, 2005, *The Metaphysics of the Healing*, trans. Michael E. Marmura, Brigham Young University Press; Dimitri Gutas, 2012, "Avicenna: The Metaphysics of the Rational Soul: Avicenna," *The Muslim World* 102(3–4), 417–425.

ISLAM AND ARTIFICIAL INTELLIGENCE 121

cannot be measured in terms of space, time or quantity. It is conscious of itself and is the locus of intelligibles. The soul may be referred to in several ways, each way relating to one of its different modes and states. First, when involved in intellection and apprehension, it is called the intellect *(al-'aql)*. Second, when it governs the body, it is called the soul or self *(al-nafs)*. Third, when it is engaged in receiving intuitive knowledge, it is called the heart *(al-qalb)*, and finally, when it "reverts to its own world of abstract entities," it is called spirit *(al-ruh)*.[25]

For Ibn Sina, the relation of the soul to the body is the relation of one wielding an instrument to the instrument itself. Philosophers and theologians who adopted this psychological system attempted to assign different faculties of the soul to different parts of the brain. One of the key points on which the philosophers and theologians differed with respect to the soul is that the former held the rational soul to be immortal, whereas theologians held it to originate temporally. The main disagreement between the philosophical and theological perspective on the intellect is that the former held it to be the only means for knowledge of ultimate reality, whereas the latter emphasised the combined role of both the intellect (*'aql*) and the heart (*'qalb*) in material and spiritual cognition.

In order to explain his psychological theory and to illustrate the self-awareness and independence of the rational soul, Ibn Sina provided a hypothetical example that has come to be known as the "Floating Man" argument.[26] Ibn Sina asks the reader to imagine someone who has been created all at once, but with their sight veiled and limbs separated so that sight, sound and touch are unavailable. Ibn Sina argued that the individual would only be able to affirm the existence of their own self and this affirmation would relate to something other than the body, namely the soul.

There are three stages to Ibn Sina's argument, which relate to show the separability of the self from the body, the formation of the concept of the self (self-awareness) and the relation of this awareness to other forms of awareness.[27] Many scholars have noted the similarity of

[25] Al-Attas, "The Nature of Man and the Psychology of the Human Soul," 148.
[26] Michael E. Marmura, 1986, "Avicenna's 'Flying Man' in Context," *Monist* 69; Thérèse-Anne Druart, 1983, "Imagination and the Soul–Body Problem in Arabic Philosophy," in *Soul and Body in Husserlian Phenomenology*, ed. Anna-Teresa Tymieniecka, Springer, 327–342; D. L. Black, 2008, "Avicenna on Self-Awareness and Knowing That One Knows," in *The Unity of Science in the Arabic Tradition: Science, Logic, Epistemology and Their Interactions*, ed. Shahid Rahman, Tony Street and Hassan Tahiri, Springer, 63–87; Ahmed Alwishah, 2013, 'Ibn Sīnā on Floating Man Arguments," *Journal of Islamic Philosophy* 9, 32–53
[27] Alwishah, "Ibn Sīnā on Floating Man Arguments."

Descartes' evil demon and the brain-in-a-vat thought experiment several centuries later. However, in contrast to Descartes, who wished to highlight that we should begin with doubt, Ibn Sina's aim was to assert "that there is here existence," and that we have certain knowledge of our existence. In the Islamic worldview, "[k]nowing and being are intertwined" and the question of "how do we know?" becomes equivalent to "what is it to be?"[28]

For Ibn Sina, every act of cognition presupposes self-awareness, hence, knowing that something exists involves awareness of oneself. It may therefore be said that the study of intelligence in machines from an Avicennan standpoint would proceed by designing AI systems that understand their own existence, rather than by optimising for behaviouristic and quantitative criteria, such as task performance. An Avicennan or Islamic Peripatetic programme in the pursuit of AI, if one may conceive of such an endeavour, would thus be to turn artefacts inside themselves to explore agents that know themselves, and not just a mode of operation in the world.

APPLICATIONS OF AI IN ISLAMIC CONTEXTS

In contrast to the limited range of scholarship on Islamic theology and AI, there are many works on AI applications in Islamic contexts. One reason for this may be that in Islamic legal theory the default judgement is that actions are permitted unless there is a specific source in revelation or a specific reason based on the jurisprudential method to prohibit it. Hence, a naïve assessment of a new application of AI is unlikely to disclose a religious reason to prohibit or limit its application. However, a deeper assessment of AI technologies is essential since the human proprietors of an AI system, regarded individually or collectively, are responsible for its actions and activities, even if the system is run autonomously.

Deeper consideration may reveal that an AI system is subsumed in systems of manipulation, power and control that unjustly exclude or disenfranchise certain sectors of society from access to public and social goods in systematic ways. Some types of AI system could be deemed harmful in relation to Islamic rulings on protection of privacy, dissemination of harmful content and personal dignity (such as opening the

---

[28] Hasan Spiker, 2021, *Things as They Are: Nafs al-Amr and the Metaphysical Foundations of Objective Truth*, Tabah Research, 157, 140.

way for the misuse of personal identity by generating fake images and video, or programmatic manipulation based on online activity through digital advertising networks). This is especially the case in the way AI is involved in user tracking and advertising across platforms since such profiling could constitute surreptitious spying, which is disapproved of in the Qur'an ("O ye who believe! Avoid suspicion as much (as possible): for suspicion in some cases is a sin: And spy not on each other behind their backs" (Qur'an, 49:12)).

One interesting example of AI in Islamic education is Tarteel.ai, which uses AI to assist with recitation of the Qur'an by detecting mistakes in pronunciation. The AI system assumes the role of a human teacher, which represents a significant departure from the way the Qur'an has traditionally been taught and transmitted throughout Islamic history. Tarteel.ai uses a speech-to-text model based on DeepSpeech2 by the Chinese company Baidu and was trained on 75,000 minutes of Qur'anic recitation. At the time of writing, the service detects word-level mistakes but not mistakes in vowels, which are a common source of error.

The primary means of the transmission of the Qur'an from the time of revelation is oral transmission, which is supported by textual transmission. Adjacent to this is the Islamic science of *tajwīd* (elocution), which provides formal rules for correct pronunciation of Qur'anic Arabic. The Tarteel.ai system bypasses this science in favour of pattern matching based on digitalised voice samples provided by the user, and thereby partially dehumanises the process of learning correct recitation – first by the removal of a human teacher (who is part of a chain of transmission of reciters), and second by disregarding the bodily loci of vocalisation. Nevertheless, such an application may facilitate memorisation of the Qur'an and provide access to basic instruction in recitation.

There are now many mobile applications serving religious functions available to Muslims, such as prayer times, sacred texts and personal worship tracking. The question is what the role of AI could be as an assistive technology in Islamic acts of worship and whether there is scope for true ingenuity on the part of designers and developers to enhance acts of worship, or whether the role of AI is likely to be contrived with no tangible benefit. In the matter of Islamic worship, the complete and perfect forms are exemplified in the Prophetic *sunnah* (the example of the Prophet Muhammad) and can be emulated by any individual in any era, region or society, without any technological facilitation.

One area where there may be scope for the use of AI is in the *hajj* (pilgrimage to Makkah) for monitoring and management of the flow of pilgrims.[29] Such an application exemplifies the underlying nature of contemporary AI as a tool for manipulation, control, prediction and surveillance. While some applications of AI in Islamic practices may be contrived, it is too early to assess the impact of the technologisation of Muslim ritual through AI technologies and what types of application may be conceived in the future.

The most significant body of literature on Islam and AI is on Islamic automata and on Islamic contributions to mathematics, science and technology, all of which are connected to the pre-history of AI. There has also been some scholarship on the artificial or alchemical creation of life (*takwīn*), which intersects with the golem tradition, which is often referred to in the context of religion and AI. Kathleen O'Connor briefly mentions the *haywān azīm* ('great living creature compliant to its master') found in the corpus of alchemical texts attributed to Jābir ibn Ḥayyān (d. 815 CE) as a cryptic reference to the notion of the golem in Jewish thought as well as the idea of the manipulation of the Arabic alphabet to manipulate this or any other living being.[30]

Major advances in knowledge took place in the Islamic world that are of significant historical interest in relation to AI and robotics. Most significant is the synthesis of earlier mathematical traditions that lay the foundations for modern mathematics, and hence digital computers and AI. Mathematicians in the Islamic world produced novel work in areas such as arithmetic, algebra, number theory, indeterminate equations, combinatorics, geometry, trigonometry, numerical methods and mechanics.[31]

There are two lines of influence on European mathematics that are known with a high degree of certainty. First, Muhammad ibn Musa Al-Khwarizmi's (c. 780–850 CE) work on algebra in the early ninth century influenced the development of European algebra via its

---

[29] Waleed Albattah et al., 2021, "Hajj Crowd Management Using CNN-Based Approach," *Computers, Materials, & Continua* 66(2), 2183–2197.

[30] Kathleen Malone O'Connor, 1994, "The Alchemical Creation of Life (Takwin) and Other Concepts of Genesis in Medieval Islam," University of Pennsylvania, 168, https://repository.upenn.edu/dissertations/AAI9503804/.

[31] Roshdi Rashed, 1994, *The Development of Arabic Mathematics between Arithmetic and Algebra*, Springer; J. Lennart Berggren, 1985, "History of Mathematics in the Islamic World: The Present State of the Art," in *From Alexandria, through Baghdad: Surveys and Studies in the Ancient Greek and Medieval Islamic Mathematical Sciences in Honor of J. L. Berggren*, ed. Nathan Sidoli and Glen Van Brummelen, Springer, 51–71.

Latin translation, and second, via Ibn al-Haytham, who wrote over 200 mathematical treatises and is best known for his novel work in geometry and optics.[32]

The modern word *algorithm* is derived from the Latinisation of al-Khwarizmi. Al-Khwarizmi produced his mathematical works with the aim of aiding legal scholars in issues such as property relations, trade, calculating inheritance and wills according to Islamic law. It is an ironic turn of history that today's algorithms are more often associated with surveillance, discrimination and dispossession in the logic of surveillance capitalism.

The second area of the Islamicate contribution to knowledge in the history of robotics and automation is the design and engineering of automatic machines and mechanical wonders. These artefacts held the fascination of Muslim publics, rulers and courtiers centuries before the mechanical principles and engineering concepts were transmitted to the West. While water clocks were present in the West in the late tenth century, automata and water clocks were combined as early as the ninth century in the Islamic world.[33]

Besides being artefacts to provoke amusement and wonder, automata were produced in the service of religious objectives, such as indicating the timing of prayer and facilitating ritual practices such as ablution. The most well-known figure associated with Islamic automata is Ismail al-Jazarī (d. 1206), whose work *Kitab fi ma'raifat al-Hiyal al-Handasiyya (The Book of Knowledge of Ingenious Mechanical Devices)* contains elaborate instructions on the construction of different types of mechanical devices, explanations of how motion is imparted to figures and descriptions of how sounds are produced to mark the passage of time. Donald Hill highlights that "many types of control, most of which are thought of as quite modern, were employed to achieve these results: feed-back control, closed-loop systems, various types of automatic switching to close and open valves."[34]

The development of automata in the Islamic world also entailed pioneering work in automatic control systems, which represents a

---

[32] George Gheverghese Joseph, 2002, *The Crest of the Peacock*, 3rd ed., Princeton University Press, 486.

[33] Ismā'īl ibn al-Razzāz al-Jazarī, 1974, *The Book of Knowledge of Ingenious Mechanical Devices: Kitāb Fī Ma'rifat al-Ḥiyal al-Handasiyya*, trans. Donald Routledge Hill, D. Reidel Publishing Company; Gunalan Nadarajan, 2007, "Islamic Automation," in *Media Art Histories*, ed. Oliver Grau, MIT Press; E. R. Truitt, 2015, *Medieval Robots: Mechanism, Magic, Nature, and Art*, University of Pennsylvania Press.

[34] Nadarajan, "Islamic Automation," 30

medieval precursor to the twentieth-century field of cybernetics, which drew together various disciplines to study feedback, control and communication systems and is intertwined with the history of AI.

Gunalan Nadarajan argues that Islamic automata enable "a critical re-evaluation of classical notions and the conventional history of automation and therefore of robotics." Nadarajan argues that in contrast to conventional histories of technology, which emphasise control over the world via technology, Islamic automata are an expression of automation as a "manner of submission" rather than a means of control. Rather than seeking precise automation, the work of engineering or "programming" Islamic automata involved a deliberate attempt to produce "untoward" behaviour.[35]

This places Islamic automata conceptually close to certain strands of modern AI research, which similarly entail a degree of non-mastery as AI practitioners seek to produce models that exhibit novel behaviours without prior specification. According to Nadarajan, Islamic automata are not to be understood as a means of control of the forces of nature but "as conduits of allowing these forces to play out their capricious movements ... as expressions of God's will," and they were a means of showing the ways in which the divine will operates in the world.[36]

Muslim theologians used inventions such as the water clock to explain their cosmologies and metaphysics. For example, Imam al-Ghazali (d. 1111) used the water clock to explain the creation and ordering of the universe.[37] Despite their interest in automata and willingness to refer to inventions in theological treatises, Islamic thought did not lead scholars towards subsuming human nature in terms of a mechanistic ontology, nor did their analogies become the basis of their metaphysics. It is important to note that in Western thought, the same philosophical developments that left little to no room for a role for God in the cosmos also led to the mechanisation of the mind.

CONCLUSIONS

The Islamic tradition maintains a robust conception of human nature, both through specific references to aspects of human intelligence and

[35] Nadarajan, "Islamic Automation," 1.
[36] Nadarajan, "Islamic Automation," 14.
[37] Frank Griffel, 2018, *Al-Ghazali's Philosophical Theology*, Oxford University Press, 236–241.

knowledge in Islamic primary sources as well as through philosophical and theological scholarly inquiries into the spiritual and material dimensions of human nature. I argue that this vast intellectual tradition, which remains relatively unexplored in relation to AI, can be the source of crucial insights to resist the dehumanising tendencies of a mechanistic, materialistic and technoscientific study of the mind and intelligence.

The history of Islamic science and technology provides insights into how religion, science and technology can be united. In particular, the history of Islamic automata illustrates how the production of complex artefacts can be a way to contemplate the creation of God.

There are many other issues beyond questions about the analogy of humans and machines that require further study from an Islamic perspective. It is often taken for granted in AI research and discourse that for any domain to become accessible to an AI model, it must first be converted into the digital domain.

This subordination of society, nature and the life-world to the logic and order of digital computational systems imposes a fundamental limit to computational and digital forms of knowledge to what can be known in purely quantitative terms alone. In the process of the digitalisation of mind and reality, digital entities are reinscribed with new properties and directed to new ends that cease to reflect their referents in nature and become severed from their place in the sacred order of reality according to Islamic cosmology.

Much of AI discourse fails to acknowledge that the creation of AI does not involve an expansion of computation to meet with the world and reality as they are but instead necessitates a compression of the world into computational black boxes that are at once the world and mind of the AI agent. This artificialisation of the world, which is an inextricable aspect of the creation of AI, represents an inversion of the sacred order of reality from the principle of unity central to Islamic sacred knowledge, as we have explored in this chapter.

BIBLIOGRAPHY

Alwishah, Ahmed. 2013. "Ibn Sīnā on Floating Man Arguments." *Journal of Islamic Philosophy* 9, 32–53.

Attas, Syed Muhammad Naquib al-. 1995. "The Nature of Man and the Psychology of the Human Soul," in *Prolegomena to the Metaphysics of Islam*, The International Institute of Islamic Thought and Civilization.

Avicenna. 2005. *The Metaphysics of the Healing*, trans. Michael E. Marmura, Brigham Young University Press.

Berggren, J. Lennart. 2014. "History of Mathematics in the Islamic World: The Present State of the Art [1985]," in *From Alexandria, Through Baghdad: Surveys and Studies in the Ancient Greek and Medieval Islamic Mathematical Sciences in Honor of J. L. Berggren*, ed. Nathan Sidoli and Glen Van Brummelen. Springer.

Druart, Thérèse-Anne. 1983. "Imagination and the Soul: Body Problem in Arabic Philosophy," in *Soul and Body in Husserlian Phenomenology*, ed. Anna-Teresa Tymieniecka. Springer.

Fazi, M. Beatrice. 2019. "Can a Machine Think (Anything New)? Automation beyond Simulation." *AI & Society* 34(4), 813–824.

Gutas, Dimitri. 2012. "Avicenna: The Metaphysics of the Rational Soul: Avicenna." *The Muslim World* 102(3–4), 417–425.

Hill, Donald R. 1998. *Studies in Medieval Islamic Technology: From Philo to al-Jazari – from Alexandria to Diyar Bakr*, ed. David King. Variorum Collected Studies Series. Ashgate.

Jazarī, Ismāʿīl ibn al-Razzāz al-. 1974. *The Book of Knowledge of Ingenious Mechanical Devices: Kitāb Fī Maʿrifat al-Ḥiyal al-Handasiyya*, trans. Donald Routledge Hill. Reidel.

Lagrandeur, Kevin. 2017. *Androids and Intelligent Networks in Early Modern Literature and Culture: Artificial Slaves*. Routledge.

Marmura, Michael E. 1986. "Avicenna's 'Flying Man' in Context," *Monist* 69(June), 383–395.

O'Connor, Kathleen Malone. 1994. "The Alchemical Creation of Life (Takwin) and Other Concepts of Genesis in Medieval Islam," PhD thesis, University of Pennsylvania. www.proquest.com/docview/304111155/abstract/152D26 63744940E3PQ/1.

Popova, Biliana. 2020. "Islamic Philosophy and Artificial Intelligence: Epistemological Arguments." *Zygon: Journal of Religion & Science* 55(4), 977–995.

Rosenthal, Franz. 1970. *Knowledge Triumphant: The Concept of Knowledge in Medieval Islam*. Brill.

Truitt, E. R. 2015. *Medieval Robots: Mechanism, Magic, Nature, and Art.* University of Pennsylvania Press.

Part II

Social and Moral Issues

8 Transhumanism and Transcendence

ILIA DELIO

INTRODUCTION

In a talk to the American Philosophical Association in 1996, Carl Mitcham said, "a thousand or two thousand years ago the philosophical challenge was to think nature – and ourselves in the presence of nature. Today the great and the first philosophical challenge is to think technology. And to think ourselves in the presence of technology."[1] Transhumanism is a term used to describe the enhancement of human life through – in the presence of – technology. Transhumanists believe that humans must wrest their biological destiny from evolution's blind process of random variation and adaptation and move to the next stage as a species, favouring the use of science and technology to overcome biological limitations. The aim of transhumanism is to promote the evolution of the human race beyond its present limitations through the use of science and technology.

The first written appearance of any form of the word 'transhumanism' is found in *The Divine Comedy* by the Italian poet Dante (c. 1265–1321), who coined the word *trasumanar* to describe the glorious transformation that awaits human beings as they are taken up into the eternal presence of God. The word *trasumanar* suggests an ongoing process and not a final state. "To go beyond the human," Dante writes, "is something that cannot be described in words."[2] Dante's passage was translated into English in 1814 by Henry Francis Carey, which became widely used as the standard translation for its time. Carey translated Dante's line this way: "Words may not tell of that transhuman change."[3] Ron Cole-Turner points out that this shift from verb

---

[1] Carl Mitcham, 1996, "The Philosophical Challenge of Technology," *American Catholic Philosophical Association Proceedings* 40, 45.
[2] Dante, 1984, The *Divine Comedy of Dante Alighieri: Paradiso*, trans. Allen Mandelbaum, Bantam Books, 7
[3] Dante, *The Divine Comedy*, 68–70.

to adjective sets the stage for the abstract noun, transhumanism, the first known instance of which is found in a 1941 essay by a Canadian speculative thinker named W. D. Lighthall, a member of the Fellowship of the Royal Society of Canada.[4] In the society's journal, Lighthall published an article entitled "The Law of Cosmic Evolutionary Adaptation: An Interpretation of Recent Thought."[5] The article outlines a progressivist metaphysical philosophy that builds on the scriptural passage of Saint Paul in his *Letter to the Corinthians*: "Eye has not seen, nor ear heard, neither has it entered the conception of man" (1 Cor 2:9).[6] Harrison and Wolyniak state: "It is clear that he [Lighthall] is seeking to baptize his new scientific version of transhumanism by invoking Dante's *trasumanar* and St Paul's rapture."[7] The Christian basis of the term is significant in so far as the concept of transhumanism, originating with Dante and used by Lighthall, connotes a Christian notion of perfectibility by which the human person, created in the image of God, strives for divine likeness.

Most of the literature traces the first modern use of the term transhumanism to the evolutionary biologist Julian Huxley, who first used the term in his two-part lecture 'Knowledge, Morality and Destiny'. This was the third series of William Alanson White Memorial Lectures delivered in Washington, DC on 19 and 20 April 1951 and published in the same year in the journal *Psychiatry*. In the first lecture Huxley describes his creed: "Such a broad philosophy might perhaps be called, not Humanism, because that has certain unsatisfactory connotations, but Transhumanism. It is the idea of humanity attempting to overcome its limitations and to arrive at fuller fruition."[8] The lecture was subsequently published with light revisions in Huxley's 1957 collection of essays *New Bottles for New Wine*, where Huxley wrote:

> The human species can, if it wishes, transcend itself – not just sporadically, an individual one way, an individual there in another way – but in its entirety, as humanity. We need a name for this new

---

4 Ron Cole-Turner, 2015, "Going beyond the Human: Christians and Other Transhumanists," in *Theology and Science*, 17 April, 151.

5 W. D. Lighthall, 1940, "The Law of Cosmic Evolutionary Adaptation: An Interpretation of Recent Thought," in *Royal Society of Canada, Ottawa. Proceedings and Transactions/Mémoires et Comptes Rendus de la Société Royale Du Canada*, Series 3, Vol. 34, Section 2, 135–141.

6 Peter Harrison and Joseph Wolyniak, 2015, "The History of Transhumanism," *Notes and Queries* 62(3), 465–467.

7 Harrison and Wolyniak, "History of Transhumanism," 467.

8 Julian Huxley, 1951, "Knowledge, Morality and Destiny," *Psychiatry* 14, 139.

belief. Perhaps transhumanism will serve: man remaining man, but transcending himself, by realizing new possibilities of and *for his human nature.*[9]

As an evolutionary biologist, Huxley was aware of the discussions on evolution and perfectibility. At the end of his *Origin of Species*, Charles Darwin expressed his confidence that ultimately all "corporeal and mental endowments will, as a consequence of natural selection, attain to perfection."[10] The co-discoverer of the principle of natural selection, Alfred Wallace, predicted that evolution would usher in an earthly paradise. Evolution, he said, must culminate in a world inhabited by a single homogeneous race, in which no individual will be inferior to the noblest types of existing humanity. Governments will die out, to be replaced by voluntary associations. Humans will no longer permit themselves to be ruled by their passions, once they realise that such development is only required to develop the capacities of their higher nature, so as to convert the earth into a new paradise. Evolutionists such as Darwin and Wallace seem to raise the human person to a deified level, substituting a new god for the ancient gods – man as he is to be, with a power that had ordinarily been ascribed only to the divine. In the words of Herbert Spencer, "progress [...] is not an accident but a necessity."[11]

Unlike the Darwinian school of evolution, philosopher Henri Bergson sought to show that human emergence, that is, the emergence of beings endowed with freedom, is no accident of natural selection. Evolution, he argued, in his book *Creative Evolution* (1907), is the work of an *élan vital*, a vital impulse embedded in the material world. This vital impulse is limited by the matter upon which it works; thus, it is influential without being deterministic. Evolution has given rise to the intelligent human who is endowed with freedom, purpose and intelligence, enabling the human to conquer the world; however, intelligence cannot access true reality. Only the mystic, Bergson maintained, relying on intuition, not intelligence, has a glimpse of the essential nature of the universe in its unity. In the human, evolution developed a being who is endowed with the intrinsic power of growing further in that direction in which evolution has so far moved, if one chooses to exercise that power. The universe is a "machine for the making of gods," argues Bergson, but it depends on human effort whether this "essential function" of the universe is realised. While evolution gives rise

---

[9] Julian Huxley, 1979, *Religion without Revelation*, Greenwood Press, 195.
[10] John Passmore, 1970, *The Perfectibility of Man*, Duckworth.
[11] Passmore, *Perfectibility of Man.*

134 ILIA DELIO

to humans, human effort is needed to further realise the potential of evolution. The universe alone will not lead to human perfection. Thus, while Darwin saw continuity between the emergence of humans and human perfection, Bergson saw the emergence of the human as a leap in evolution, indicating that with the human something new entered the biological sphere, that is, the human capacity for self-consciousness is a crucial step in the evolution of the world.

TECHNOLOGY AND SELF-UNDERSTANDING

The advent of transhumanism corresponds to the philosophical discussions on tools and their relation to being, which emerged in the nineteenth century. Are technological tools prosthetic devices that enable more efficient human function, or do they extend function and thus change the human person? These questions were widely discussed with the rise of the industrial age. German philosopher Ernst Kapp probed the question of technology and human nature by combining Aristotelian philosophy, the humanistic ideal of *Bildung* (technology as image) and the pragmatist ideal of practical ingenuity that is characteristic of the engineer. This combination of factors enabled Kapp to speculate that the ultimate goal of technology is self-liberation and self-knowledge. According to Kapp, every existing tool must have a corresponding human organ (or some other physiological structure). This naturalistic account of technology revives the old idea of 'emanation', which holds that a secondary thing 'flows' or proceeds from some primary thing. Commenting on Kapp's philosophy, Jeffrey Kirkwood and Lief Weatherby write that Kapp regarded technologies as projections of human organs; that is, animal organs provided the blueprint for tools and machines. In his view, "technology was the exteriorization of organ-function."[12]

Kapp's theory of organ development corresponded with a practice of mechanical perfectibility – tools both perfected human organ function and enhanced that same function. He believed that the greatest inventions turn out to be products of an ongoing process of self-finding, whose aim the human being is at first unconscious of. Technology exteriorises organ function; however, organ projection is unconscious until the exteriorised self is seen and reflected upon. As Carl Mitcham states, the relationship between tool and organ "is more one of unconscious

---

[12] Jeffrey West Kirkwood and Lief Weatherby, 2018, "Operations of Culture: Ernst Kapp's Philosophy of Technology," *Grey Room* 72(Summer), 8.

discovery than of conscious invention."[13] That is, the conscious and the unconscious incessantly displace and work through one another; prior to the moment that the idea is actualised, the restlessness of conscious searching has the upper hand. Technology imitates organic nature (the human body in particular), first unconsciously, then consciously, so that technology becomes an externalisation of human ideas, an epistemological operation by which history unfolds.

Kapp's philosophy of technology is important in seeking to understand transhumanism as a quest for self-knowledge; perfectibility through technology is a type of reflexive knowledge. A similar position on technology was later found in Canadian media expert Marshall McLuhan, who disclosed his own transition from technology as tool to technology as integral to human life and culture. In his book *The Mechanical Bride*, McLuhan expressed a disdain for machinery and saw the industrial revolution as an abomination due to the fall of Adam and Eve and original sin. His utopic vision of reality, however, became sterile in the face of twentieth-century literary artists such as Yeats, Pound, Joyce and Eliot, for whom a totally different view of reality was shown through processes of cognition and creativity. McLuhan finally realised that the world in which we live may not be our own choice, but we must live in it as if this is the best world possible. From this perspective, he interpreted the rise of technology as part of the human phenomenon and sought to understand how best to facilitate the transformation of the human person, from passive spectator to active participant in the world's becoming. He wrote: "Cataclysmic environmental changes are, in and of themselves, morally neutral; it is how we perceive them and react to them that will determine their ultimate psychic and social consequences."[14]

The emergence over the past half-century of a technoscientific culture suggests that biological humans have been constantly transformed into mixtures of machine and organism. The development of tools for human function is also the basis of human transcendence. In the words of John Culkin, "we shape our tools and thereafter our tools shape us."[15] The techno-human is a kind of "thought experiment" in so far as we are provided with an opportunity to think anew about the relationship

[13] Carl Mitcham, 1994, *Thinking through Technology*, University of Chicago Press, 23.
[14] Marshall McLuhan, 1969, "Marshall McLuhan Interview from Playboy," *Playboy Magazine*, March, https://web.cs.ucdavis.edu/~rogaway/classes/188/spring07/mcluhan.pdf.
[15] John Culkin, 1976, "A Schoolman's Guide to Marshall McLuhan," *Saturday Review*, 18 March, 70.

between humans and our environments, including digital artefacts and biotechnological tools. However, the new technologies also compel us to reflect on what the ethical, political, cultural and religious implications are likely to be. Transhumanists see human nature as a work in progress and suggest that by the responsible use of science, technology and other rational means, we shall become beings with vastly greater capacities and unlimited potential.

THE ADAMIC MYTH AND PERFECTIBILITY

The rise of computer technology in the twentieth century spawned a new era of transhumanism aided by the rise of information technology and cybernetics. It is significant that the computer as a thinking machine emerged in war-torn Europe, where modernity failed to achieve its ideals of utopia and religion failed to prevent genocide and war. The rise of atheism, the totalitarian collapse of human freedom and the profound suffering of war spawned the rise of computer technology. The British cryptologist, Alan Turing, developed the 'imitation game' whereby an interrogator had to distinguish between a computer and human respondent. If such a distinction could not be made, the computer could be assumed to be thinking like a human person. The imitation game signalled a turn from the Renaissance Vitruvian man towards a new type of person–machine interaction with negotiable boundaries. The scientific insights that paved the way for artificial intelligence (AI) to emerge were contingent on discoveries that challenged the boundaries of nature as closed, causal and mechanistic. The discovery of information and cybernetics provided the basis for the 'thinking machine'. The notion that a machine could think like a human person not only reflected the plasticity of nature but the dynamic capacity of nature to be open to novelty.

While the thinking machine was born in Europe, America provided fertile ground for its development. A new myth of the white male developed, made possible by a fusion of American progress, technology and religion. In the United States, technology became the prime mover of an ongoing 'millenarian impulse' that had spilled over from the nineteenth century. The space program, in particular, bore witness to the new myth of technological achievement in the world of NASA. Physicist Freeman Dyson wrote the "Space Traveler's Manifesto" in 1958 and supported the development of nuclear energy to secure a power source for a starship that was mankind's best chance to survive an apocalypse. Directed by the 'spiritual men' of NASA, humanity would restart on another world so that human beings could still be headed for a redemptive future, even as they left behind the ruins of earth.

The fusion of space travel and religious narrative reinforced the thesis of David Noble who, in his book *The Religion of Technology*, claimed that technology was rooted in a spirituality of perfection, based on the myth of the fallen Adam and the search for divinity. According to Noble, the sin incurred by the first Adam in the Garden of Eden provided the impetus for the second Adam to strive for technological perfection. Made in the image of God, the new (male) Adam sought to realise his godlike capacity, beginning with the development of the mechanical arts in the Middle Ages and extending into AI in the twentieth century. The Adamic myth can be summarised in three points: (1) the valorisation of the 'mechanised arts' through the thrill of scientific discovery and exploration; (2) the shadow of redeeming fallen man; and (3) the competitive challenge of being the first body in a new environment – whether physically on a new continent or a new world, or in cyberspace. While Jesus Christ was considered the 'new Adam' who redeemed fallen humankind, emphasis was placed on becoming, like Christ, the 'new Adam' through technology. This 'white male mythology' concerns the technological transcendence of the individual human organism, with its religious roots in the renewal of the fallen Adam.[16]

The cyborg, an abbreviation of 'cybernetic organism', emerged out of the scientific-technological dreams of perfection. The cyborg represents the capacity of biological nature to be joined to or hybridised with non-biological nature, such as a machine. Manfred Clynes and Nathan Kline, who coined the term cyborg in a 1960 paper, envisioned that a cyborgian man-machine hybrid would be needed in the next great techno-human challenge of space flight.[17] A cyborg is a person whose physiological functioning is aided by or dependent on a mechanical or electronic device. In order to survive in space, human astronauts had to be strapped to machines to maintain normal physiological function. Philosopher Donna Haraway described the cyborg as a symbol of the twentieth-century person: "creatures simultaneously animal and machine who populate worlds ambiguously since they are both natural and crafted."[18] What Haraway and feminist philosophers realised is that

---

[16] David. F. Noble, 1999, *The Religion of Technology: The Divinity of Man and the Spirit of Invention*, Penguin Books, 17.

[17] Manfred Clynes and Nathan Kline, 1960, "Cyborgs and Space," *Astronautics* 5(9), 26–27.

[18] Donna Haraway, 1991, "Cyborg Manifesto: Science, Technology and Socialist-Feminism in the Late Twentieth Century," in *Simians, Cyborgs and Women: The Reinvention of Nature*, ed. Donna Haraway, Routledge, 149.

138   ILIA DELIO

the boundaries of human nature are neither fixed nor essential; boundaries are fluid and can be changed. The original cyborg was a fusion of human and non-human and could extend human function in an unknown environment. The cyborg was born in the quest of exploring the extraterrestrial space of the unknown but quickly became a symbol of what the human could become in the open and unlimited space of information, that is, cyberspace, filled with the infinite potential to explore new possibilities.

SUPERMEN, LITTLE GODS

Darwin's evolution gave rise, among other things, to a new emphasis on betterment, as life selects out traits of fitness and robustness. Several versions of evolutionary 'perfectibilitism' suggest that humanity will develop into a being who, by present standards, will be superpowered. Humanity could be transformed into a more perfect type of living being; man could evolve not only into something better but a new species. The idea of the 'superman' is associated with the philosophy of Frederick Nietzsche, who did not see the superman as an outflow of evolution but a resistance to the forces of religion: "We must become gods ourselves if we are to live in this world without God," he wrote.[19] Belief in the inevitability of progress, Nietzsche argued in his *Will to Power* writings,[20] is nothing more than the old religious ways of thought, thinly disguised. Progress, he claimed, is divine Providence in working clothes. He felt compelled to announce to the world that God is dead. This proclamation brought with it a new set of questions and challenges. If God is dead, then truth is dead as well and must be rediscovered. Nietzsche defined truth as the will to power and progress. Without Christianity and its transcendent values and ideals, he said, modern individuals would be led to drastically underestimate their own potential for greatness. In doing so, they would incapacitate the heroic impulse to will ambitious goals and eradicate the "desires that create clefts"[21] by which the higher type of human being is differentiated from the lower type.

Nietzsche envisioned a type of individual emerging, whom he called "the last man," namely one who, instead of focusing on ways

---

[19]   Friedrich Nietzsche, 1974, "The Madman," in *The Gay Science: With a Prelude in Rhymes and an Appendix in Songs*, Book 3, se. 125, trans. Walter Kaufmann, Vintage, 181.

[20]   Walter Kaufmann and R. J. Hollingdale, eds, 1968, *Frederich Nietzsche: The Will to Power*, Vintage Books.

[21]   Ilia Delio, 2020, *Re-enchanting the Earth: Why AI Needs Religion*, Orbis, 58.

to enhance the grandeur of humanity, is concerned solely with using science and technology *to enhance the pleasure and comfort of humankind*. It is with this modern world in mind that he wrote his masterpiece, *Thus Spoke Zarathustra*, representing his attempt to restore the sanctity and dignity of human existence in a spiritually destitute modern world. His emphasis on the will to power focused on how to reinstitute the yearning for greatness in a world that was increasingly becoming inhospitable to it. He directed his work to the individual who was now liberated from cosmic forces and free to create one's life. The only way to avoid annihilation, Nietzsche thought, is individual improvement. In this respect, he opted for a type of secular transcendence. According to *Zarathustra*, the Superman (*Übermensch*) means that man is 'something that should be overcome', the forces of resistance to improvement are to be overcome by greater rationality and thought. The *Übermensch* becomes the ideal of striving, that is, the pursuit of human enhancement. One aims to live as a higher type of human being, paving the way for even higher types to emerge in the future.

THE RISE OF TRANSHUMANISM

While the roots of transhumanism are complex, there are essentially two strands: Enlightenment and Romantic. Whereas the former is an extension of the eighteenth-century Enlightenment project, focused on improving the human condition through science and technology, the latter seeks a betterment of the human condition through technological enhancement. Some scholars warn that progress should not be confused with evolution, which can be capricious, cruel and random. Scientists were encouraged to continue to map the mechanisms of the adapted mind and its specific programs before naively embracing the projects of transhumanism. Transhumanists could be divided between two visions: one in which technological and genetic improvements can create a distinct species of radically enhanced humans, and the other in which greater-than-human machine intelligence can emerge, marked by term 'posthuman'. Nick Bostrom uses the term 'posthuman' to describe a superintelligent technological being; however, the term has also been taken up by philosophers of the New Materialisms to connote a deanthropocentrism, conversely, a new type of person who is culturally embedded in deep relationships. While technology plays a role in the New Materialist posthuman, it does not define the human in terms of perfectibility and enhancement but in terms of deep relationality and

140 ILIA DELIO

hyper-personalisation. Katherine Hayles captures the tension between enhancement and relationality when she writes:

> If my nightmare is a culture inhabited by posthumans who regard their bodies as fashion accessories rather than the ground of being, my dream is a version of the posthuman that embraces the possibilities of information technologies without being seduced by fantasies of unlimited power and disembodied immortality, that recognizes and understands finitude as a condition of human being, and that understands human life is embedded in a material world of great complexity, one on which we depend for our continued survival.[22]

Transhumanism of the Romantic type seeks perfectibility through enhancement whereby the individual seeks betterment as a priority over deep relationality. In his 1989 book *Are You a Transhuman? Monitoring and Stimulating Your Personal Rate of Growth in a Rapidly Changing World*, F. M. Esfandiary (also known as 'FM 30'), one of the early celebrated transhumanists who taught at the New School for Social Research, described the emergence of the transhuman as a "transitional human, someone who by virtue of their technological usage, cultural values, and lifestyle constitutes an evolutionary link to the coming era of posthumanity."[23] The signs that FM 30 saw as indicative of transhuman included prostheses, plastic surgery, intensive use of telecommunications, a cosmopolitan outlook and a globetrotting lifestyle, androgyny, mediated reproduction (such as in vitro fertilisation), absence of religious belief and a rejection of traditional family values. He changed his name to FM 30 to break free of the widespread practice of naming conventions that he saw as rooted in a collectivist mentality and existing only as a relic of humankind's tribalistic past.

Some transhumanists look to a post-biological future where superinformational beings will flourish and biological limits such as disease, ageing and death will be overcome. Biology is not destiny; rather, chips are destiny. Futurists such as Ray Kurzweil have speculated on the 'Technological Singularity', a point of transition in the near future when technology and human intelligence will become seamlessly merged, thrusting us into a new level of existence from *homo sapiens* to *techno sapiens* life. The basis of the Singularity idea is found in a

---

[22] N. Katherine Hayles, 1999, *How We Became Posthuman: Virtual Bodies in Cybernetics, Literature and Informatics*, University of Chicago Press, 5.

[23] Nick Bostrom, 2005, "A History of Transhumanist Thought," *Journal of Evolution and Technology* 14(1), 8.

1958 paper by Stanislaw Ulam who, referring to a meeting with John von Neumann, wrote: "One conversation centered on the ever accelerating progress of technology and changes in the mode of human life, which gives the appearance of approaching some essential singularity in the history of the race beyond which human affairs, as we know them, could not continue."[24] The Singularity hypothesis refers to the idea that self-improving AI will at some point result in radical changes within a very short time span. This hypothesis was first clearly stated in 1965 by the statistician I. J. Good:

> Let an ultraintelligent machine be defined as a machine that can far surpass all the intellectual activities of any man however clever. Since the design of machines is one of these intellectual activities, an ultraintelligent machine could design even better machines; there would then unquestionably be an 'intelligence explosion,' and the intelligence of man would be left far behind. Thus, the first ultraintelligent machine is the last invention that man need ever make.[25]

Vernor Vinge discussed the Singularity in his influential 1993 paper "Technological Singularity" in which he predicted that within thirty years, we will have the technological means to create superhuman intelligence. Shortly after, the human era will be ended. While the idea of the Singularity is approaching with the development of quantum computing and superintelligence, it may not mean the end of the human person but the end of the human liberal subject. The 'end' of the human era, therefore, must be seen as the rise of a new type of human in evolution.

THE WORLD TRANSHUMANIST ASSOCIATION

In 1998 the World Transhumanist Association (WTA) was founded by philosophers Nick Bostrom and David Pearce as a cultural and philosophical centre of human betterment through technology. A corollary group known as 'Extropy' (a philosophy devoted to the transcendence of human limits) was founded by Max More, who immigrated to California from Britain and changed his name from Max O'Connor to Max More. More founded the Extropy Institute to catalyse the transhuman ideal of

---

[24] Bostrom, "History of Transhumanist Thought," 8; cf. S. Ulam, 1958, "John von Neumann 1903–1957," *Bulletin of the American Mathematical Society*, May.

[25] Irving John Good, 1966, "Speculations Concerning the First Ultraintelligent Machines," *Advances in Computers* 6, 31–88.

142 ILIA DELIO

betterment: "I was going to get better at everything, become smarter, fitter, and healthier ... a constant reminder to keep moving forward."[26] Following the closure of the Extropy Institute in 2006, Humanity+ emerged as an outgrowth of the WTA and has since become the principal representative of the transhumanism movement.

> We aim to deeply influence a new generation of thinkers who dare to envision humanity's next steps. Our programs combine unique insights into the developments of emerging and speculative technologies that focus on the well-being of our species and the changes that we are and will be facing. Our programs are designed to produce outcomes that can be helpful to individuals and institutions.[27]

Since its inception, the WTA, along with the pioneering work of the Extropy Institute, has contributed to advancing the public knowledge of how science and technology can and will affect our human future. These are not just utopian visions of techno-optimists; rather, as Hava Tirosh-Samuelson states, transhumanist programs receive a substantial amount of funding and scientific legitimacy from the National Science Foundation and other funding agencies.[28]

Bostrom defines transhumanism as a way of thinking about the future that is based on the premise that the human species in its current form does not represent the end of our development but rather a comparatively early phase. The term 'transhumanism' now refers to those technologies that can improve mental and physical aspects of the human condition such as suffering, disease, ageing and death. It is based on "the belief that humans must wrest their biological destiny from evolution's blind process of random variation [...] favoring the use of science and technology to overcome biological limitations."[29] Bostrom sees transhumanism as a continuation of the legacy of the Enlightenment. He writes:

> It has been said that the Enlightenment expired as the victim of its own excesses. It gave way to Romanticism, and to latter day reactions against the rule of instrumental reason and the attempt

[26]   E. Regis, 1994, "Meet the Extropians," *Wired* 2, 10.
[27]   Transhumanist Technology, "About Humanity+," https://humanityplus.org/about/.
[28]   Havra Tirosh Samuelson, 2009, "H-: Engaging Transhumanism: A Critical Historical Perspective," *Metanexus*, 28 May, https://metanexus.net/h-engaging-transhumanism-critical-historical-perspective/.
[29]   Bostrom, "History of Transhumanist Thought," 13–14; Archimedes Carag Articulo, 2006, "Towards an Ethics of Technology: Re-exploring Teilhard de Chardin's Theory of Technology and Evolution," www.scribd.com/doc/16038038/Paper2-Technology.

to rationally control nature, such as can be found in some postmodernist writings, the New Age movement, deep environmentalism, and in some parts of the anti-globalization movement. However, the Enlightenment's legacy, including a belief in the power of human rationality and science, is still an important shaper of modern culture.[30]

Following the evolutionist thinking of perfectibility, Bostrom indicates that evolution is ongoing; humanity is not the endpoint but perhaps an early phase of development. He does not think that Nietzsche's *Übermensch* is a direct forerunner of transhumanism, although he is not opposed to the idea that technology and the *Übermensch* are related. Following the insights of Julien Offray de La Mettrie, he indicates that "if human beings are constituted by matter that obeys the same laws of physics that operate outside us, then it should in principle be possible to learn to manipulate human nature in the same way that we manipulate external objects."[31] In this respect, Bostrom combines evolutionary perfectibility with the openness of the cyborg for hybridity and enhancement.

Transhumanism looks to the sciences of genetic engineering, biotechnology, nanotechnology and robotics to advance the human condition. Bostrom states, "we have always sought to expand the boundaries of our existence, be it socially, geographically, or mentally."[32] The insertion of computer technology into culture, business and daily life has rendered transhumanism a highly visible movement. Over fifty years ago, Gordon E. Moore, co-founder of Intel Corporation, said that the number of transistors on a chip would exhibit exponential growth. He predicted that the pace of technology would increase exponentially, outstripping our ability to absorb it or reflect on our use of it. This led to the formulation of "Moore's law," which states (roughly) that computing power doubles every eighteen months to two years. However, recent developments in chip technology reveal the limitations of Moore's law and unlimited accelerating power; however, it is worthwhile to note the rapid progress in this area. In a 2009 essay, Michael Specter wrote: "When the I.B.M. 360 computer was released in 1964, the top model came with eight megabytes of main memory, and cost more than two million dollars. Today, cell phones with a thousand

---

[30] Bostrom, "A History of Transhumanist Thought," 2–3.
[31] Julien Offray de La Mettrie, 1912, *Man a Machine*, Open Court, 135–136; Bostrom, "History of Transhumanist Thought," 4.
[32] Bostrom, "History of Transhumanist Thought," 1.

times the memory of that computer can be bought for about a hundred dollars [or less]."[33]

The myth of technology is appealing, and the power of technology is seductive. We now have the power not only to evolve ourselves through technology but to direct the course of evolution. CRISPR (clustered regularly interspaced short palindromic repeats) technology or gene editing discloses a new power of genetic selection; nanotechnology affords mechanical implants in biological organs. Biological evolution and technological evolution have become co-terminus and a new type of techno-human is emerging in evolution. Conceptually, biology is becoming technology; and physically, technology is becoming biology. The future of evolution may, indeed, be a marriage of the 'born and the made', transcending what we are by becoming what we create.

DIGITAL IMMORTALITY

The transhumanist drive for transcendence is challenged by the reality of death. "What makes our species so special and interesting," Jenny Huberman writes, "what makes us in large part human, is first, that we live with an awareness that we are going to die. And second, that we also possess the capacity to overcome this inevitability through symbolic means."[34] Death anxiety is universal to the human condition, and we develop the symbols of our religions in order to appease these fears. Fear of death boils down to a fear of being disconnected from a vial flow of life beyond the self, and the quest for symbolic immortality is an attempt to stay connected; to achieve the sense that some part of us will live on in the great chain of being even after our bodies have decayed. Kurzweil anticipates an increasingly virtual life in which the bodily presence of human beings will become irrelevant. He claims that machine-dependent humans will eventually create the virtual reality of eternal life, possibly by 'neurochips' or simply by becoming totally machine dependent. As we move beyond mortality through computational technology, our identity will be based on our evolving mind file. We will be software not hardware. By replacing living bodies with virtual bodies capable of transferal and duplication, we will become disembodied super-minds. Our new selves will be infinitely replicable, allowing them to escape the finality of death.

---

[33] Michael Specter, 2009, "A Life of Its Own: Where Will Synthetic Biology Lead Us?" *New Yorker*, September, 64.

[34] Jenny Huberman, 2018, "Immortality Transformed: Mind Cloning, Transhumanism and the Quest for Digital Immortality," *Mortality* 23(1), 52.

This futuristic 'post-biological' computer-based immortality is one also envisioned by Hans Moravec, who claims that the advent of intelligent machines (*machina sapiens*) will provide humanity with personal immortality by mind transplant. The mind will be able to be downloaded into a machine through the eventual replacement of brain cells by electronic circuits and identical input–output functions. The body will become obsolete through silicon implants and electronic prostheses. As machines move inside bodies, we will emerge from the archaic biological species of *homo sapiens* into a new technologised species of *techno sapiens*, anticipating a future flourishing of life.

Transhumanist Martine Rothblatt, in her book *Virtually Human: The Promise and Peril of Digital Immortality* (2014), discusses the development of mindclones or digital copies of the self that possess cyber consciousness. Rothblatt envisions a future where human consciousness and identity will be distributed across two platforms, one biological and the other digital. She says that a mindclone will most likely take the form of an interactive digital avatar that is powered on a computer screen. A mindclone is made up of two key components: mindfile and mindware. A mindfile is a digitised database of one's life and consists of all of a person's thoughts, feelings, ideas and experiences. The mindware is an operating system that processes the data in the mindfile and is akin to one's digital personality. Just as biological organisms are composed of genes and DNA, our mindclones will be composed of 'bemes' and 'BNA' (beme neural architecture). Bemes are the basic informational units of consciousness, the component building blocks of an informational architecture that provide coded instructions for human function and activity. Mindclones, according to Rothblatt, are really sets of informational patterns, and new technologies will enable these patterns to be preserved and continue on long after a person biologically dies. According to Rothblatt, "cyberconsciousness will make it possible, for the first time, for a person to live in a kind of technoimmortality forever in the real world. Mindclones are the key to technoimmortality."[35] She proposes that eventually death itself will become optional.

TECHNOLOGY AND RELIGION

Transhumanists dream of a better life, a godly life, a happy life free from suffering, pain and death, where one can live forever. The pursuit of salvation and immortality raises the question: is transhumanism a

[35] Martine Rothblatt, 2014, *Virtually Human: The Promise and the Peril of Digital Immortality*, St. Martin's Press, 283.

secular religion? Does it seek to replace or fulfil the Judeo-Christian tenets of salvation and immortality? Although transhumanists are often depicted as hyper-modern, secular rationalists, the transhumanist movement shares many affinities with religion. "Transhumanism," Tirosh-Samuelson writes, "expresses deep religious impulses in a secularize idiom of science and technology that previously had been taken to be in contrast to religion."[36] Robert M. Geraci, in his book *Apocalyptic AI*, states that American technology is based on Judeo-Christian principles of salvation and immortality, rendering religion an underlying motive for technological development.[37] Transhumanism can be viewed as a 'secularist faith', a hybrid of secular and religion motifs. It secularises traditional religious motifs on the one hand and endows technology with salvific meaning on the other hand.

Some claim that cyberspace is an extension of religious desires to escape earthly existence, or that AI is consistent with the Christian belief in resurrection and immortality. Since some kind of support manifold is required for the information and organisation that constitutes our minds, a material, mechanical replacement for the mortal body will suffice. As Antje Jackelén wrote: "If Christ was resurrected in a new body, why not a machine? The development toward *techno sapiens* might be regarded as a step toward the kingdom of God where the lame walk, the blind see, the deaf hear, and the dead are at least virtually alive. The requirements of the Christian Gospel and the aims of technical development seem to be in perfect harmony."[38]

While the affinity between transhumanism and some forms of religion can be noted, the question of whether or not technology replaces religion more generally is an open one. Humans are tool-making animals, but they are also reflexive animals, deeply aware of their vulnerability and finitude. The threat of death and annihilation evokes dreams of immortality and enduring life. Since the advent of the modern *homo sapiens*, humans have perpetually imagined better futures for themselves. Transhumanism builds on the idea that the essence of being human is our ability to reach beyond our limitations. It expresses our freedom to imagine what does not exist and to believe in what is not actual. If religion concerns questions of ultimacy, and transhumanism pursues ideal

---

[36] Hava Tirosh-Samuelson, 2012, "Transhumanism," *Zygon: Journal of Religion & Science* 47(5), 729.

[37] Robert M. Geraci, 2010, *Apocalyptic AI: Visions of Heaven, in Robotics, Artificial Intelligence and Virtual Reality*, Oxford University Press.

[38] Antje Jackelén, 2002, "The Image of God as *Techno Sapiens*," *Zygon: Journal of Religion & Science* 37(2), 294.

aims of life, health and happiness, then the idea that modern technology and religion have evolved together may hold true. If, indeed, the technological enterprise is suffused with religious belief, then Dante was right: transhumanism is, essentially, a religious endeavour.

BIBLIOGRAPHY

Bergson, Henri. 2009. *Creative Evolution*, trans. Arthur Mitchell. The Floating Press

Bostrom, Nick. 2005. "A History of Transhumanist Thought." *Journal of Evolution and Technology* 14(1), 1–30.

Cole-Turner, Ron. 2015. "Going beyond the Human: Christians and Other Transhumanists." *Theology and Science* 13(2), 150–161.

Dinerstein, Joel. 2006. "Technology and Its Discontents: On the Verge of the Posthuman." *American Quarterly* 58(3), 569–595.

Geraci, Robert M. 2010. *Apocalyptic AI: Visions of Heaven, in Robotics, Artificial Intelligence and Virtual Reality*. Oxford University Press.

Haraway, Donna. 1991. *Simians, Cyborgs and Women: The Reinvention of Nature*. Routledge.

Hayles, N. Katherine. 1999. *How We Became Posthuman: Virtual Bodies in Cybernetics, Literature, and Informatics*. University of Chicago Press.

Jackelén, Antje. 2002. "The Image of God as Techno Sapiens." *Zygon: Journal of Religion & Science* 37(2), 289–302.

Kurzweil, Ray. 2005. *The Singularity Is Near: When Humans Transcend Biology*. Viking.

Moravec, Hans. 1988. *Mind Children: The Future of Robot and Human Intelligence*. Harvard University Press.

Noble, David F. 1999. *Religion of Technology: The Divinity of Man and the Spirit of Invention*. Penguin Books.

Passmore, John. 1970. *The Perfectibility of Man*. Duckworth.

Rothblatt, Martine. 2014. *Virtually Human: The Promise and Peril of Digital Immortality*. St Martin's Press.

Tirosh-Samuelson, Hava and Mossman, K., eds. 2012. "Transhumanism." *Zygon: Journal of Religion & Science* 47(5), Special Issue, 659–795.

Vinge, Vernor. 1993. "The Coming Technological Singularity." *Whole Earth Review* (Winter). Reprinted in 2013 as "Technological Singularity" in *The Transhumanist Reader: Classical and Contemporary Essays on Science, Technology and Philosophy of the Human Future*, ed. Max More and Natasha Vita-More. Wiley-Blackwell.

9 The Eschatological Future of Artificial Intelligence

Saviour or Apocalypse?

NOREEN HERZFELD

Artificial intelligence (AI) has always been a future-oriented field. Herbert Simon predicted in 1965 that "machines will be capable, within twenty years, of doing any work that a man can do."[1] Marvin Minsky, in 1970, was even more optimistic:

> In from three to eight years, we will have a machine with the general intelligence of an average human being. I mean a machine that will be able to read Shakespeare, grease a car, play office politics, tell a joke, have a fight. At that point, the machine will begin to educate itself with fantastic speed. In a few months, it will be at genius level, and a few months after that, its power will be incalculable.[2]

The lack of a clear definition of intelligence has led, over the years, to a series of re-evaluations and to a common joke among computer scientists that AI is best defined as anything that has not yet been successfully programmed. While we call programs that are new and exciting 'AI', the ultimate goal, to produce an automated general intelligence (AGI) that can function in a wide variety of domains and transfer learning from one area to another, as humans do, always seems to be, as it was for Simon, at least twenty years in the future.

In theological terms, AI can, thus, be viewed as a millenarian project, and one particularly suited to the twenty-first century at that. Groups predicting the immanent second coming of Christ, or of some other form of salvation, such as found in cargo cults, have flourished in times of societal stress. Millenarian thinking has typically risen

---

[1] Herbert Simon, 1960, *The New Science of Management Decision*, Harper, 38.
[2] Marvin Minsky, 1970, "Meet Shaky, the First Electronic Person," *Life*, 20 November.

148

among groups challenged by demographic change or climatic stressors. It has found purchase in agrarian cultures and in cosmopolitan ones, such as Renaissance Munster. It promises a solution to current problems that is delivered from outside, rather than from the society itself. AI promises the same. Dreams of a salvation that is always coming but not yet here, a salvation at the hands of something or someone other, remove the onus for solving society's ills ourselves and soothe those who feel powerless in the face of what look like insurmountable obstacles. Help is just around the corner. When the corner is reached and either God or AI have failed to deliver, millenarians simply recalibrate their timeline or suggest that we misunderstood the extent of their promises.

This millenarian orientation has allowed both researchers and the general public to project a variety of eschatological hopes and fears onto AI. Utopian visions range from the personally soteriological prospect of achieving immortality by uploading or copying the neural pattern of one's brain to the more general vision of a world in which AI has found novel solutions to our problems, bringing peace and prosperity. Dystopian scenarios involve the creation of an AI that outstrips human intelligence and control, one that could turn on its creators or be used as a weapon by those creators. However, we do not need conscious or superintelligent AIs to produce programs that can be quite damaging to the fabric of human society, a fact that is obvious in today's world of ransomware attacks, autonomous weapon development, social media dispersal of falsehoods and machine-learning programs with inherent biases.

Salvation or apocalypse at the hands of AI have become a common trope in science fiction and among technological futurists. Will AI save us or destroy us? Probably neither, but as we shape the trajectory of its future, we also shape our own.

THE UTOPIAN VISION OF PERSONAL SALVATION

Death is inevitable for biological creatures and intrinsic to the mechanisms of evolution and natural selection. Every cell in our body has an expiration date as our telomeres shorten with each division. As conscious and self-conscious beings, we humans are aware of our mortality. This awareness of death has been one of the motivations for both the development of religious traditions and for the tenacity of faith in individual believers. American broadcaster Larry King states this bluntly: "I think the only reason for religion is death. If you didn't die, there would be no religion."[3] While many religious believers would disagree with King, particularly his use of the word "only," what happens after death has been a major question for humans since their inception and figures largely in both the world's religions and philosophical thought, from ancient Greece through to the present.

Can AI provide a non-religious route for overcoming illness, ageing and, ultimately, death? Theologian Ted Peters sums up this dream: "All we need do is turn a couple technological corners and, suddenly, the abundant life will be ours. We will be liberated from the vicissitudes of biological restraints such as suffering and death; and we will be freed by enhanced intelligence to enjoy the fulfilling life of a cosmic mind."[4] This is not the philosopher's goal of coming to terms with death but a quasi-religious goal of surmounting it.

In *The Age of Spiritual Machines*, futurist Ray Kurzweil suggests AI as a new platform for overcoming death:

> Up until now, our mortality was tied to the longevity of our hardware [...] As we cross the divide to instantiate ourselves into our computational technology, our identity will be based on our evolving mind file. We will be software, not hardware [...]. As software, our mortality will no longer be dependent on the survival of the computing circuitry.[5]

Kurzweil expects this to be a possibility by 2045. And he is not alone in this project. Russian billionaire Dimitry Pskov has pledged a large part of his fortune towards the '2045 Initiative', with which he hopes to realise Kurzweil's dream.

Like most predictions for AI, however, cybernetic immortality within our lifetimes is both wildly optimistic and misguided. It rests on the assumption that our essential self consists of our memories and thoughts, which are nothing more than the information stored in the connectome, or patterns of neurons in our brain. This assumption is essentially a neo-Cartesian dualism, for it posits a mind or soul separable from the body, not pre-existent but post-existent. While initially

---

3 Mark Yapching, 2015, "Fear of Death Is the Reason behind Religious Faith – Larry King," *Christian Today*, 28 February, www.christiantoday.com/article/fear.of.death .is.the.reason.behind.religious.faith.larry.king/48939.htm.

4 Ted Peters, 2016, "H-: Transhumanism and the Posthuman Future: Will Technological Progress Get Us There?," *Metanexus*, www.metanexus.net/essay/h-transhumanism-and-posthuman-future-will-technological-progress-get-us-there.

5 Ray Kurzweil, 1999, *The Age of Spiritual Machines: When Computers Exceed Human Intelligence*, Penguin, 128–129.

dependent on the body as our locus of the learning, the self becomes separable from the body – information that could be moved to a different platform. There are, however, several difficulties to be overcome. First, there is the sheer complexity of the brain, which has roughly 100 billion neurons, each of which has the potential of connecting with up to a thousand other neurons. Nor are these connections static. Old connections are strengthened or severed, and new ones formed, with each new experience. A variety of neurochemicals (such as dopamine and serotonin) foster or inhibit the transfer of electrical pulses from one neuron to another. These, too, would need to factor into any model. Finally, the project of reverse engineering the brain in a computer assumes consciousness emerges spontaneously from a suitably complex system. But this is hardly a given. Physicist Michio Kaku likens this to "saying a highway can suddenly become self-aware if there are enough roads."[6] Even were we to conquer the complexity issue and find that consciousness truly is an emergent property, existence on a silicon platform would represent a radical departure from human life as we know it. Without a human body, an AI would not have our experiences, our full complement of neurons (the gut has at least 100 million), or anything like human emotions, which demand a body to be truly felt. It would be a new species, one that privileges a single human aspect: intelligence.

Unlike the Christian notion of salvation through Christ's death and resurrection, salvation through AI is a 'do it yourself' project, something we humans might accomplish through our own efforts and agency, thus coming closer to definitions of magic than to religious belief. Kurzweil himself agrees:

> I am often reminded of Arthur C. Clarke's third law, that "any sufficiently advanced technology is indistinguishable from magic." Consider J. K. Rowling's Harry Potter stories from this perspective [...] Harry unleashes his magic by uttering the right incantation [...] precisely our experience with technology. Our incantations are the formulas and algorithms underlying our modern-day magic.[7]

In his Gifford Lectures, *The Nature and Destiny of Man*, theologian Reinhold Niebuhr warns against such a magical mindset, one that he sees as inherent in the scientific project. Niebuhr notes that we are the one creature with the mental abilities to transcend the natural

---

[6] Kurzweil, *The Age of Spiritual Machines*, 242.
[7] Ray Kurzweil, 2006, *The Singularity Is Near: When Humans Transcend Biology*, Viking, 5–6.

world, through our technology. However, he is adamant that this does not obviate the limitations of our physical nature. Niebuhr sees the hubris of thinking we can affect our own salvation as a flaw in modern thinking, one that asserts "that its philosophy is a final philosophy ... a certainty which betrays ignorance of its own prejudices and failure to recognize the limits of scientific knowledge."[8]

SUPERINTELLIGENCE: A NEW GOD OR MEANS FOR OUR RESURRECTION?

If the material world is all that exists, then more time is the best we can hope for. But we must recognise that this is a much more limited option than that offered by the traditional faiths. While merging with AI could give us more time, it does not tell us what to do with that time, nor how to live better in this world. Faith in AI prioritises information and intelligence, not love, and certainly not sacrifice. What meaning might be stripped from an existence that neither confronts nor comes to terms with suffering or death? Would more time on a silicon platform be ultimately fulfilling or would it be bedevilled by the same hopes, fears, insecurities and delusions we currently face? Unlike reliance on our own technologies, Niebuhr notes that the resurrection hoped for by Christians is one that takes us beyond the current human condition.

If it does not promise true immortality, might AI at least promise better life conditions or a better version of humanity? Many believe that AGIs could solve most of the problems that currently bedevil human society. As computer scientist Ben Goertzel suggested to participants at the World Economic Forum, held at Davos:

> Our top priority should be the creation of beneficent artificial minds with greater-than-human general intelligence, which can then work together with us to solve the other hard problems and explore various positive avenues [...] Once we are able to create artificial minds vastly more intelligent than our own, there are no clear limits to what we may be able to achieve, working together with our creations.[9]

Goertzel believes AGIs could usher in an era of unprecedented peace and prosperity, solving sticky engineering problems in the fields of

---

[8] Kurzweil, *The Singularity Is Near*, 195.

[9] Ben Goertzel, 2013, "Artificial General Intelligence and the Future of Humanity," in *The Transhumanist Reader*, ed. Max More and Natasha Vita-More, Wiley-Blackwell, 130.

energy, climate and medicine. AGIs could also make our legal systems fairer, our jobs less tedious and even, perhaps, find avenues towards world peace. Freed from the need to work, humans could enjoy goods and services produced by our AI servants in both physical and virtual reality. In this scenario, AI becomes a quasi-God, one that meets all our needs and desires and provides for us a heaven on earth.

If not a god, a superintelligent AGI might also be considered the next step in our long evolutionary chain. Unlike Darwin, who saw evolution as an aimless process of random mutation and natural selection, many see AI as the next step in a long evolutionary progression towards beings with greater complexity, greater mastery over their surroundings and, eventually, conscious intelligence. The question is whether this progression is ultimately divergent or convergent, resulting in a flowering of diversity or a singular brain. Advanced computing technologies, including implanted chips, imply greater and closer communication among humans and between humans and machines. Just as the Internet has brought people from around the globe together, future AI could lead to a mental convergence or global brain.

Philosopher Ilia Delio likens such a mental convergence to theologian Teilhard de Chardin's Omega principle. Teilhard posited a mutual attraction in all of creation, one that would evolve towards ever higher levels of both consciousness and unity. Total unity, the Omega Point, was, for Teilhard, the ultimate goal of evolution. This unity, which Teilhard called the Noosphere, would not erase individuality but would allow each to flourish within a larger unified whole.

> The idea is that of the earth not only becoming covered by myriads of grains of thought, but becoming enclosed in a single thinking envelope so as to form, functionally, no more than a single vast grain of thought on the sidereal scale, the plurality of individual reflections grouping themselves together and reinforcing one another in the act of a single unanimous reflection.[10]

Physicist Frank Tippler holds a similar vision. In *The Physics of Immortality: Modern Cosmology, God and the Resurrection of the Dead*, Tippler identifies Teilhard's Omega Point with God and suggests that as our computational resources continue to increase, some society in the distant future will use those resources to emulate alternative universes in which each of us will reappear and thus be resurrected from the

---

[10] Teilhard de Chardin, 1959, *The Phenomenon of Man*, trans. Bernard Wall, Harper and Row, 251–252.

dead. In an infinity of such universes, we would have the option of living multitudinous or even an infinite number of lives. Not all envision the necessity of bodily resurrection. In his 1988 book *Mind Children*, computer scientist Hans Moravec envisioned artificially intelligent computers as the next step in an evolution that maximises intelligence, ultimately evolving purely mental creatures. Moravec predicts diversity rather than singularity, imaging cyberspace as teeming with disembodied superminds, as far above us on the evolutionary chain as we are above bacteria. Like Tippler, Moravec suggests a new form of resurrection in which these superminds choose, at times, to reimagine the past in total detail and with variety. Moravec suggests that we might, ourselves, be living in such a simulation rather than physical reality. It is an easy step from there to suppose a physical reality such as ours never existed, that is, that we are nothing but characters in some AI's play.

THE DYSTOPIAN VISION OF THE SINGULARITY

Each of the positions described so far imagines some continuing human presence, or at least continuity with human purposes and ideals, in an AI-mediated future. But this is not a given. In his seminal paper of 1993, computer scientist Vernor Vinge suggested four future possibilities that would enhance intelligence on earth. First, we could build an AGI that is 'awake' and able to learn without human direction. Second, a large enough computer network might 'wake up' and gain superhuman intelligence. Third, computer–human interfaces might lead to superhuman intelligence. Finally, we might find ways to improve the capacity or use of our own brains. Vinge imagined that any of these would present a radical break with the past course of evolution, a break he dubbed "the Singularity" and expected within the next thirty years. Vinge warned that the Singularity would be a "throwing-away of all the human rules, perhaps in the blink of an eye – an exponential runaway beyond any hope of control."[11]

While Vinge's prediction has missed its deadline of 2023, visions of a coming Singularity persist. In July 2017, at a meeting of the National Governor's Association, Tesla founder and CEO Elon Musk issued the following warning: "AI is a fundamental existential risk for human civilization, and I don't think people fully appreciate that." Claiming access

---

[11] Vernor Vinge, 1993, "The Coming Technological Singularity: How to Survive in the Post-Human Era," VISION-21 Symposium, NASA Lewis Center and Ohio Aerospace Institute, 30–31 March, http://edoras.sdsu.edu/~vinge/misc/singularity.html.

THE ESCHATOLOGICAL FUTURE OF ARTIFICIAL INTELLIGENCE   155

to cutting-edge AI technology, Musk called for proactive government regulation, noting that while such regulation is generally "irksome, [...] by the time we are reactive in AI regulation, it's too late."[12] Musk is not alone. Physicist Stephen Hawking, in an interview with the BBC, expressed fears that the development of a true AGI "could spell the end of the human race." According to Hawking, AI could "take off on its own, and re-design itself at an ever-increasing rate [...] Humans, who are limited by slow biological evolution, couldn't compete, and would be superseded."[13] He later ameliorated his stance, holding that the development of AI could either be the best or worst thing to happen to us, but that it was up to us to make the right choices; emphasising the role of humans. But his more dystopian concerns have had other supporters. Futurist Nick Bostrom has sounded a similar alarm. He believes that should AI ever achieve human-level intelligence, it would shortly move beyond us to superintelligence and that the outcome of that move for humans would be either extremely good or extremely bad.[14] Perhaps such machines would use their capabilities to solve our problems and make life easier. Or they might optimise one set of values over others, unwittingly harming humans.

Warnings of the Singularity have acquired a new resonance with the advent of programs such as DeepMind's AlphaGo Zero and AutoML-Zero. The Zero in these names mean that these programs are designed to learn with zero human input. AlphaGo Zero, playing the game go against itself, was superior to the version that had played against Lee Sedol in just three days. In forty days, it exceeded all human-aided AlphaGo programs, and developed winning strategies rarely used by human players. This would seem to represent AI passing an initial benchmark for a superhuman intelligence where it is no longer constrained by the limits of human knowledge. Others are less concerned. MIT computer scientist Rodney Brooks has wryly pointed out that Musk and Hawking "don't work in AI themselves. For those who do work in AI, we know how hard it is to get anything to actually work through product level."[15]

[12]   C-Span, 2017, "Elon Musk at National Governors Association 2017 Summer Meeting," www.c-span.org/video/?431119-6/elon-musk-addresses-nga.
[13]   BBC, 2014, "Stephen Hawking Warns Artificial Intelligence Could End Mankind," www.bbc.co.uk/news/technology-30290540.
[14]   Nick Bostrom, 2014, Superintelligence: Paths, Dangers, Strategies, Oxford University Press.
[15]   Connie Loizos, 2017, "This Famous Roboticist Doesn't Think Elon Musk Understands AI," TechCrunch, 19 July, https://techcrunch.com/2017/07/19/this-famous-roboticist-doesnt-think-elon-musk-understands-ai/.

Who is right? Does AI pose an 'existential risk' to humankind? Perhaps, but I think not for the reasons Hawking and Musk imagine. Engineer Gordon Moore, viewing the rapid hardware innovations from the 1960 through the 2000s, noted that computing power increases exponentially, with the number of transistors in an integrated circuit roughly doubling every two years, an observation dubbed 'Moore's law'. Vinge, and others, extrapolate from Moore's law to suggest continued exponential growth in all areas of computing, thus positing a coming explosion of computing power. The idea that any AGI would rapidly outpace all human intelligence is based on this extrapolation. Moore himself, however, disagrees: "It can't continue forever. The nature of exponentials is that you push them out and eventually disaster happens."[16] So far, our increases in computational power have been largely due to miniaturisation. As our circuits approach the size of atoms, we will reach a limit, thus halting or significantly slowing computational increase. Virtual reality pioneer and Microsoft resident guru Jaron Lanier raises a different objection, noting that Moore's law only applies to hardware:

If anything, there's a reverse Moore's Law observable in software: As processors become faster and memory becomes cheaper, software becomes correspondingly slower and more bloated, using up all available resources [...] We have better speech recognition and language translation than we used to, for example, and we are learning to run larger data bases and networks. But our core techniques and technologies for software simply haven't kept up with hardware.[17]

Berkeley computer scientist Stuart Russell believes our best hope for AGI lies in developing a machine that could truly understand human language and, thus, read everything ever written: "Once we have that capability, you could then query all of human knowledge and it would be able to synthesize and integrate and answer questions that no human being has ever been able to answer because they haven't read and been able to put together and join the dots between things that have remained separate throughout history."[18] Even if we could

[16] Manek Dubash, 2010, "Moore's Law Is Dead, Says Gordon Moore," in *Techworld*, 13 April, www.techworld.com/news/tech-innovation/moores-law-is-dead-says-gordon-moore-3576581/ (no longer available), see also https://hothardware.com/news/moores-law-is-dead-says-gordon-moore.

[17] Jaron Lanier, 2000, "One Half a Manifesto," *Wired*, 1 December, www.wired.com/2000/12/lanier-2/.

[18] Mike Thomas, 2021, "The Future of Artificial Intelligence," *Builtin*, 8 June, https://builtin.com/artificial-intelligence/artificial-intelligence-future.

automate the intricacies of human semantics, there would remain the question of whether the AI would understand what it read. Can we really claim that AlphaGo understands go when it lacks metacognition? Recent advances in large-language models have raised similar questions, as models such as ChatGPT appear to users to understand human language. But they really just parrot back information they have gleaned from the Internet. They have no internal models of the world that would show any sort of metacognition. According to Brooks: "Building human level intelligence and human level physical capability is really, really hard. There has been a little tiny burst of progress over the last five years, and too many people think it is all done. In reality we are less than 1% of the way there, with no real intellectual ideas yet on how to get to 5%."[19]

Superintelligent AGIs (*pace* Vinge, Musk and Hawking) are likely a long way off. Fearing them may distract us from the more proximate danger, recognised by cyberneticist Norbert Weiner in 1950. In *The Human Use of Human Beings*, Weiner warned that the greatest danger is not posed by technology itself but by our commercial or military exploitation of technology's power and our possible loss of control, not because the computer has outwitted us but because we fail to comprehend the true nature of our desires. Like King Midas, or the finder of a djinni's lamp, our own will to power may give us precisely what we wish for but not what we need.

A TECHNOLOGICAL BOTTLENECK?

The Search for Extra-Terrestrial Intelligence project has been scanning the heavens for a signal, some sign of intelligent life, for almost half a century. So far, nothing. Despite the claims of UFO enthusiasts, self-professed alien abductees and supermarket tabloids, we have no evidence of intelligent extraterrestrial life. On statistical grounds, this is odd. There are at least 100 billion galaxies in the observable universe. Our own relatively small Milky Way contains 100 billion stars. We have located more than 4,000 planets orbiting stars in our galaxy, and this number represents only planets large enough for their gravitational pull to perturb the light of their star. Using an expanded version of an equation developed by Frank Drake in 1961, astronomers Frank and Sullivan recently concluded that the odds of our planet being the only

---

[19] Rodney Brooks, 2018, "My Dated Predictions," https://rodneybrooks.com/my-dated-predictions/.

one on which life evolved are somewhere in the vicinity of one in ten billion trillion (10^{22}). According to Drake:

> Think of it this way. Before our result you'd be considered a pessimist if you imagined the probability of evolving a civilization on a habitable planet were, say, one in a trillion. But even that guess, one chance in a trillion, implies that what has happened here on Earth with humanity has in fact happened about a 10 billion other times over cosmic history![20]

This raises the famous question physicist Enrico Fermi asked at a lunch discussion at Los Alamos Labs in 1951: "Where is everybody?" If the probability of intelligent life is that high, then why the great silence? Someone, somewhere, should have by now colonised substantial portions of the galaxy, if not in person at least with their machines. If superintelligent machines are possible, why haven't we seen one from another planet?

Let's take a closer look at Drake's equation:

$$N = R * f_p * n_e * f_l * f_i * f_c * L$$

where:

N = the number of civilisations in the observable galaxy

R = the average rate of star formation in our galaxy

f_p = the fraction of those stars that have planets

n_e = the average number of planets that can potentially support life per star that has planets

f_l = the fraction of planets that actually develop life

f_i = the fraction of planets that develop intelligent life

f_c = the fraction of civilisations that develop a technology that releases detectable signs

L = the length of time such civilisations release detectable signals

The one variable whose value we cannot know is L, the length of time a civilisation might release detectable signals into space. How long does a technological civilisation last? Bostrom has noted that the great silence we observe means technologically capable intelligent life is rare, if not

---

[20] Leonor Sierra, 2016, "Are We Alone in the Universe? Revisiting the Drake Equation," NASA Exoplanet Exploration, 19 May, https://exoplanets.nasa.gov/news/1350/are-we-alone-in-the-universe-revisiting-the-drake-equation/.

THE ESCHATOLOGICAL FUTURE OF ARTIFICIAL INTELLIGENCE 159

unique. He suggests the existence of a 'Great Filter', an evolutionary step that is exceedingly difficult for life to transcend. This filter might occur early in the evolutionary process. Perhaps life is rare. Bostrom hopes this is indeed the case. But if life *has* evolved on multiple planets, then Bostrom's 'Great Filter' lies ahead of us. The most likely candidate is a technological bottleneck, a point at which technology outstrips a culture's ability to control it and use it wisely.

Key properties of evolution make such a bottleneck likely. The natural environment of an organism is the proving ground that selects for specific traits. Individuals that better fit their environment have a better chance for survival and reproduction. At first, technologies are remarkable at improving a species' ability to cope with the dangers and difficulties a given environment might afford. The harnessing of fire, the development of tools, the design of better clothing and shelter, the development of agriculture – each allowed our species to flourish in number and expand our range. It is easy to think that technology brings only advantages for the species that wields it. Microsoft founder Bill Gates expressed this view to world leaders at the World Economic Forum in 2008:

> Advances in technology, have brought us to a high point in human welfare. We're really just at the beginning of this technology-driven revolution in what people can do for one another. In the coming decades, we'll have astonishing new abilities: better software, better diagnosis for illness, better cures, better education, better opportunities and more brilliant minds coming up with ideas that solve tough problems.[21]

However, technology does not always alter the environment for the better. Jared Diamond, in his monumental study *Collapse: How Societies Choose to Fail or Succeed*, chronicles several human societies that altered their environment beyond its capacity to rejuvenate. Processes such deforestation, soil erosion, loss of water, overhunting and population growth led these early societies to wars, famines and loss of social and political complexity. The collapse of Diamond's societies was local. A true technological bottleneck would be global. Unfortunately, we have come to that point. Diamond writes:

---

[21] Bill Gates, 2008, "A New Approach to Capitalism in the 21st Century," speech at the World Economic Forum, Davos, Switzerland, 24 January, www.networkworld.com/article/2282669/microsoft-s-bill-gates---a-new-approach-to-capitalism-in-the-21st-century-.html.

Globalization makes it impossible for modern societies to collapse in isolation, as did Easter Island and the Greenland Norse in the past. Any society in turmoil today, no matter how remote [...] can cause trouble for prosperous societies on other continents and is also subject to their influence (whether helpful or destabilizing). For the first time in history, we face the risk of a global decline.[22]

Diamond speculates as to what might have gone through the mind of the man who cut down the last tree on Easter Island. Why do we cut down the last tree, hunt a species to extinction or build machines that might destroy ourselves? The problem is that evolution functions on an individual level. In other words, it selects individuals who show a reproductive advantage, thus inevitably introducing competition, both between species and within a species. Theologian Reinhold Niebuhr warns us of the pitfalls lurking in interspecies competition. He notes Albrecht Ritschl's observation that humans experience themselves as both a part of nature and as dominating nature. The domination of nature is, of course, the first goal of technology. However, Niebuhr notes that we find ourselves unable to avoid overreaching and disturbing the harmony of nature. Niebuhr ascribes this to our limited knowledge regarding the effects of our actions and our tendency to overestimate our capabilities. He notes that "man is a finite spirit, lacking identity with the whole, but yet a spirit capable in some sense of envisaging the whole, so that he easily commits the error of imagining himself the whole which he envisages."[23] This separates us from a nature on which we depend. We dream of living in a self-constructed world, a vision that underlies cyberspace and many of our transhuman and posthuman dreams.

Evolution also rewards those who reproduce. This leads to intraspecies competition – we turn our technologies against one another. Foreign policy analyst Martin van Creveld notes: "War and technology have always been linked very closely. Indeed, without technology, there would probably have been no war. After all, without technology, if only in the form of sticks and stones, man's ability to kill his own kind is extremely limited."[24] This link goes both ways. While technology has shaped war, so has war provided the impetus for the development of

[22] Jared Diamond, 2005, *Collapse: How Societies Choose to Fail or Succeed*, Viking, 23.
[23] Reinhold Niebuhr, 1941, *The Nature and Destiny of Man: A Christian Interpretation*, Vol. 1, *Human Nature*, Scribner's, 181.
[24] Martin van Creveld, 2007, "War and Technology," Foreign Policy Institute, 24 October, www.fpri.org/article/2007/10/war-technology-2/.

numerous technologies, not limited to armaments. Transportation systems, new materials, radar, satellite and missile technology, computer technology, the Internet – all have been advanced primarily with military uses in mind.

While we can imagine the evolution of a species devoted to intra-species harmony, the laws of evolution make this unlikely. So do the laws of social cohesion. Niebuhr notes that, while we as individuals are susceptible to the overreach of pride in our drive for dominance and security, we are far more susceptible as a group. Thus, we engage in competition in two venues, between ourselves and the rest of nature and among ourselves, and on two levels, as individuals and as groups. We develop and deploy technologies to aid us in the battle and our battles, to a large extent, determine the shape of those technologies. As these technologies become more and more powerful and wider in scope, they become more and more dangerous. Nuclear weapons were the first 'doomsday' technology humans invented, able to destroy our entire species. Is a superintelligent AGI another such doomsday technology? R. Martin Chavez, senior director and former global head of securities for Goldman Sachs, thinks we should fear more the AI we already have. Considering the massive data centres of firms such as Facebook and Google, Chavez notes that AI is already "systematically exploiting weaknesses in human psychology: our tribalism, our gullibility, or wanting to be told what to believe, our wanting to be liked, our wanting to be told that we're right. And they're exploiting it to the end of maximizing advertising revenue."[25]

We do not need a malevolent AGI for AI to bring us to our own technological bottleneck. The single-mindedness of an AI that does exactly what we programmed it to do could bring a similarly tragic result. Computers lead us to treat people as data, overwhelming us with too much information, separating us by catering to our preferences and providing an all too tempting diversion. Diplomat Henry Kissinger warned that the emphasis on speed engendered by computers limits our time for reflection. After nodding to the possibilities of "extraordinary benefits" in medical science, clean-energy provision and other environmental issues, Kissinger warned of AI's potential for unintended consequences, especially those that may arise from the inability of an AI to contextualise. Kissinger asked: "Can we, at an early stage, detect and correct

---

[25] Sonali Basak, 2021, "Wall Street Visionaries Provide Chilling Views on Next Big Risk," *Bloomberg News*, 12 January, www.bloomberg.com/news/articles/2021-2001-12/what-do-wall-street-leaders-think-is-the-next-big-risk?.

an AI program that is acting outside our framework of expectation? Or will AI, left to its own devices, inevitably develop slight deviations that could, over time, cascade into catastrophic departures?"[26] The latter is, perhaps, what should worry us most. As Sir Nigel Shadbolt, professor of computer science at Oxford, recently noted: "The danger is clearly not that robots will decide to put us away and have a robot revolution [...] If there [are] killer robots, it will be because we've been stupid enough to give it the instructions or software for it to do that without having a human in the loop deciding."[27] Recall the game-playing program AlphaGo, programmed only to win. Just as go can be reduced to 'winning', so too, in other areas, the single-minded efficiency of AI might go for the 'win' at too great a cost.

One problem that bedevils machine learning is the use of 'Frankenstein' datasets, data that have been cobbled together from multiple sources. The program can be misled towards identifying aspects of the format that vary from source to source rather than the intended content. For example, a program intended to identify patients with Covid from their lung scans instead identified whether the patient was sitting up or lying down when the scan was taken. Another predicted more serious Covid risk for patients in hospitals that used a certain font.[28] AI can be as inscrutable as the spells in a sorcerer's magic book. We will know it works, but sometimes it takes a great deal of investigation to determine how.

So, what are we to do? First, we must avoid the category error of personifying AI. A computer has no consciousness, no emotions, no will of its own and, despite all predictions, these are not 'right around the corner'. The idea, often espoused by computer futurists such as Kurzweil or Musk, that just a little more complexity will suddenly cause consciousness to emerge is, in my opinion, risible. We are still a long way from knowing what consciousness is or where it comes from. In the meantime, we would do well to think of AI as a means rather than an end. Like all technologies, AI is a tool. As such, it is not just a means

---

[26] Henry Kissinger, 2018, "How the Enlightenment Ends," *The Atlantic*, June, www.theatlantic.com/magazine/archive/2018/06/henry-kissinger-ai-could-mean-the-end-of-human-history/559124/.

[27] Hannah Devlin, 2018, "Killer Robots Will Only Exist if We Are Stupid Enough to Let Them," *The Guardian*, 11 June, www.theguardian.com/technology/2018/jun/11/killer-robots-will-only-exist-if-we-are-stupid-enough-to-let-them.

[28] Will Douglas Heaven, 2021, "Hundreds of AI Tools Have Been Built to Catch Covid: None of Them Helped," *MIT Technology Review*, 30 July, www.technologyreview.com/2021/07/30/1030329/machine-learning-ai-failed-covid-hospital-diagnosis-pandemic.

THE ESCHATOLOGICAL FUTURE OF ARTIFICIAL INTELLIGENCE 163

of power over nature but primarily a means of power by some persons over other persons. As Weiner so presciently pointed out, the source of our undoing has always been and will remain the human use of other human beings.

Jaron Lanier calls our dreams of a superintelligent AI and a posthuman future a "death-defying religion" but not a spiritual path. We need to remember that "computer scientists are human and are as terrified by the human condition as anyone else. We, the technical elite, seek some way of thinking that gives us an answer to death [...] What we are seeing is a new religion, expressed through an engineering culture."[29] But that engineering is most likely to fail and could be our total undoing, unless it is coupled with humility, unless we pause to ask if we are, metaphorically, about to chop down the last tree on Easter Island.

BIBLIOGRAPHY

BBC. 2014. "Stephen Hawking Warns Artificial Intelligence Could End Mankind." www.bbc.co.uk/news/technology-30290540.

Bostrom, Nick. 2014. *Superintelligence: Paths, Dangers, Strategies.* Oxford University Press.

Brooks, Rodney. 2018. "My Dated Predictions." https://rodneybrooks.com/my-dated-predictions/.

Devlin, Hannah. 2018. "Killer Robots Will Only Exist if We Are Stupid Enough to Let Them." *The Guardian*, 11 June. www.theguardian.com/technology/2018/jun/11/killer-robots-will-only-exist-if-we-are-stupid-enough-to-let-them.

Diamond, Jared. 2005. *Collapse: How Societies Choose to Fail or Succeed.* Viking.

Dubash, Manek. 2010. "Moore's Law Is Dead, Says Gordon Moore." *Techworld.* 13 April. https://hothardware.com/news/moores-law-is-dead-says-gordon-moore.

Gates, Bill. 2008. "A New Approach to Capitalism in the 21st Century." Speech at the World Economic Forum, Davos, Switzerland, 24 January. www.networkworld.com/article/2282669/microsoft-s-bill-gates---a-new-approach-to-capitalism-in-the-21st-century-.html.

Goertzel, Ben. 2013. "Artificial General Intelligence and the Future of Humanity," in *The Transhumanist Reader*, ed. Max More and Natasha Vita-More. Wiley-Blackwell.

Kissinger, Henry. 2018. "How the Enlightenment Ends." *The Atlantic*, June. www.theatlantic.com/magazine/archive/2018/06/henry-kissinger-ai-could-mean-the-end-of-human-history/559124/.

Lanier, Jaron. 2010. "The First Church of Robotics." *New York Times*, 9 August. www.nytimes.com/2010/08/09/opinion/09lanier.html.

---

[29] Jaron Lanier, 2010, "The First Church of Robotics," *New York Times*, 9 August, www.nytimes.com/2010/08/09/opinion/09lanier.html.

Loizos, Connie. 2017. "This Famous Roboticist Doesn't Think Elon Musk Understands AI." *TechCrunch*, 19 July. https://techcrunch.com/2017/07/19/this-famous-roboticist-doesnt-think-elon-musk-understands-ai/.

Niebuhr, Reinhold. 1941. *The Nature and Destiny of Man: A Christian Interpretation*, Vol. 1, *Human Nature*. Scribner's.

Peters, Ted. 2016. "H-: Transhumanism and the Posthuman Future: Will Technological Progress Get Us There?." *Metanexus*. www.metanexus.net/essay/h-transhumanism-and-posthuman-future-will-technological-progress-get-us-there.

Teilhard de Chardin, Pierre. 1959. *The Phenomenon of Man*, trans. Bernard Wall. Harper and Row.

Yapching, Mark. 2015. "Fear of Death is the Reason behind Religious Fait: Larry King." *Christian Today*, 28 February. www.christiantoday.com/article/fear.of.death.is.the.reason.behind.religious.faith.larry.king/48939.htm.

FURTHER READING

Bostrom, Nick. 2014. *Superintelligence: Paths, Dangers, Strategies*. Oxford University Press.

Brockman, John, ed. 2019. *Possible Minds: 25 Ways of Looking at AI*. Penguin.

Delio, Ilia. 2020. *Re-enchanting the Earth: Why AI Needs Religion*. Orbis.

Herzfeld, Noreen. 2002. *In Our Image: Artificial Intelligence and the Human Spirit*. Fortress.

Kaku, Michio. 2014. *The Future of the Mind*. Doubleday.

Kurzweil, Ray. 2006. *The Singularity Is Near: When Humans Transcend Biology*. Viking.

Moravec, Hans. 1988. *Mind Children: The Future of Robot and Human Intelligence*. Harvard University Press.

Russell, Stuart. 2019. *Human Compatible: Artificial Intelligence and the Problem of Control*. Viking.

Tegmark, Max. *Life 3.0: Being Human in the Age of Artificial Intelligence*. Knopf.

Tippler, Frank. 1994. *The Physics of Immortality: Modern Cosmology, God and the Resurrection of the Dead*. Doubleday.

Trothen, Tracy, and Calvin Mercer, eds. 2017. *Religion and Human Enhancement: Death, Values, and Morality*. Palgrave Studies in the Future of Humanity and Its Successors. Palgrave Macmillan.

10 AI Ethics and Ethical AI

PAULA BODDINGTON

Ethical questions in artificial intelligence (AI) are receiving unprecedented attention, in both academic and more popular public discourse as well as within the policy arena. Questions in AI ethics are often more profoundly difficult than even at first sight they appear. Here we examine the broad nature of any links between ethical issues and religious questions concerning AI, looking also at how religion might be relevant to some specific sets of questions. There are, in general, obvious connections between ethics and religion, although precisely how these two domains are connected is a highly complex question with varied answers. In the short space available, we consider some of the many ways in which the ethical questions of AI might prompt us to look to religion for answers and insight.

As I attempt to argue, many questions we are faced with concerning AI force us to address foundational questions in ethics, questions that are often brushed over in other areas of practical ethical concern, yet that cannot feasibly be ignored when we are addressing AI, where they arise with a particular clarity and urgency. These questions typically overlap with, and inspire, questions that are centrally asked and answered by many religions; they demand, *inter alia*, that we inquire of the place and purpose of humans within the world and of goals to both an immediate but also a very long-term future. Given the wide potential for AI to mould our world and the depth and urgency of many of the ethical questions involved, direct consideration of religions could hence offer a rich contribution to our understanding of the ethical challenges of AI and towards finding ways of responding to them.

As a preliminary outline, I make two observations about the kind of exploration in ethics that AI requires. First, and as will be illustrated, the nature of AI and its deployment pushes us, over and over, towards limits in ways that expose tensions and conflicts that lie beneath the surface of much contemporary discussion of questions in practical ethics. These include difficulties in areas as diverse and as ubiquitous in ethical debate as the foundations of utilitarianism, and conceptions of autonomy, agency and personhood. It is in coping with the deep disruptions caused by AI that drawing on the resources of religion might be useful. Second, fears and hopes for AI tend to expose profound questions about meaning, existence and the nature of reality, with a notable tendency in some quarters towards what, to all intents and purposes, starts to look like the invention of a new religion, eschatology and all. Those grappling with the ethical questions cannot avoid pondering the significance of this.

Naturally, many will still continue with an entirely secular approach to AI ethics, treating such foundational questions as raising straightforwardly meta-ethical questions, or simply as necessitating greater justification for particular normative values or just more complex and nuanced regulation. An obvious response, given the importance, difficulty and nature of so many of these ethical questions, is that it would be foolish not to consider whether there is any wisdom and guidance to be found from the standpoint of different religions. More strongly, one might argue that to address the root of many of the central ethical questions in AI requires a religious response. If this seems farfetched to those whose concerns with AI ethics are mostly in relation to solving practical and important but more prosaic questions concerning safety, compliance with data privacy and the like, consider how many of the ways in which AI is being thought of and imagined has religious overtones and sounds prophetic, not simply as a prediction of the future but as a cluster of visionary accounts of spectacular glory, equally interspersed with apocalyptic warnings of the end times (prior work by both Robert M. Geraci and Beth Singler, also contributors to this volume, is valuable in laying out these trends and concerns).

This short chapter cannot fully address all these issues. Rather, we take an overview of some of the central themes of AI ethics, with the aim of showing in some detail how its questions are pushing us in directions where consideration of the overlaps with religion is desirable and perhaps inevitable. First, we examine what it is about AI that means that its ethics inclines us towards a consideration of religion.

Let us start at the very beginning, by considering how AI is very often conceptualised. The very label 'artificial intelligence' presupposes a project to reproduce, and perhaps surpass, human intelligence. There are, of course, concerns about describing AI in such terms, and differences of opinion about how it should be conceptualised and how it should be undertaken. But given this common way of thinking and describing the domain, 'artificial intelligence' is thus frequently readily spoken of as if it is making decisions, as acting in certain ways, as exhibiting agency in some degree. A temptation arises, albeit one that many steadfastly resist, to endow machines with some of the capacities of 'beings like us'. Conceived in this way, it hence forces us to think about our nature as human beings and to make implicit comparisons between humans and machines.

From here, we are enticed into seeing certain sets of questions, and certain kinds of answers may seem more attractive than others. This implies, perhaps, a careless assumption that our intelligence is a, even *the*, key hallmark of our humanity; in attributing intelligence to machines in any significant degree, we see a dim image of ourselves staring back at us through all the shiny metal, the plastic and the rows and rows of os and 1s. From these small beginnings arise fundamental questions about our natures and therefore about our moral values. AI ethics presents, as it were, a series of hypothetical thought experiments about our own natures, as we contemplate them in relation to machine natures. We have to think about human nature in ways more profound than many recent endeavours in practical ethics have necessitated. And because we think of AI as so potentially transformative of the far future, the ethical questions we ask about this are intimately bound up with often eschatological and utopian visions, sometimes obvious, sometimes tacit.

The precise boundaries of the ethical are open to question; examining the ethical issues of AI invites us to expand them. It is via this expansion that the relevance of religion may become more apparent. In other discrete areas of practical ethics, various factors, including the specific domain of the field of inquiry, its history and broad cultural and political issues, tend in practice to place various limits on what questions are asked and how they are answered. For example, medical ethics assumes in broad terms, because of the central nature of its endeavours, the value of human life and of health, and tends to assume the value of patient autonomy, with the nature and degree of this emphasis rooted in well-known historical reasons dating back to the Second World War.

Yet AI can be applied to virtually any aspect of life, and its potential ubiquity means that the 'ethics of AI' becomes, as it were, the 'ethics of everything'. This means that we cannot silo questions of value to relatively discrete domains; this then means that clashes in value often become more visible, and in resolving these we uncover theoretical challenges to central concepts, such as to the concept of autonomy. Staring into the face of possibly autonomous machines, we have to revisit what we mean by 'autonomy' in humans. And so on.

A part of the disruptive power of AI to our ethical frameworks arises from how technological progress is exposing pre-existing tensions in magnified ways that we cannot ignore. For example, there have always been tensions between clinical ethics of individual healthcare and of public health ethics, but technologies are magnifying these. Consider the expanding possibilities in the use of health data and surveillance in tracking technologies for public health.[1] This might increase prospects for increasing (certain aspects of) physical health, but the questions raised about medical autonomy, privacy and consent are presented to us on a monumental, indeed global, scale.

Note also that this particular question, like many others in the field, arises not just from the technology itself but also from its development and application by those with the potential for centralised and possibly authoritarian control, whether by governments or by immensely wealthy and powerful technology companies. It is partly the necessity in AI ethics of dealing with this spectre of centralised control, often operating in ways that are hard to detect and understand, that produce some of the resonances with religion. And indeed, we are not simply getting lessons in ethics from these tech giants: we seem to be getting religion. This is at times rather visible. Take Apple CEO Tim Cook, who often appears more like a sermonising priest or would-be prophet than a corporate boss. In a 2018 speech he cites religious texts, pontificates on the importance of inclusion, states that Apple's values drive all their curation decisions, and says, "I believe the most sacred thing that each of us is given is our judgement, our morality, our own innate desire to separate right from wrong. Choosing to set that responsibility aside at a moment of trial is a sin."[2] The annoyance of being sermonised by tech billionaires is compounded when one considers the intentional use of persuasive technology to keep us engaged on our devices.[3] It is his position of power that enables him to both run a company that produces technology used to control us and to lecture us about that very control. A full account of the ethical issues here may be enriched by contemplating its religious overtones.

The heightened orientation of AI towards the future should also give us pause for thought about how precisely we even approach an

---

[1] See, for example, L. Taylor et al., 2020, *Data Justice and Covid 19 Global Perspectives*, Meatspace Press, https://ia801905.us.archive.org/23/items/data-justice-and-covid-19/Data_Justice_and_COVID-19.pdf.

[2] "Never Is Now 2018 – Presentation of ADL's Courage against Hate Award to Tim Cook, Apple CEO," www.youtube.com/watch?v=PYEcXt95LY0.

[3] On this see, for example, A. Kosner, 2012, "Stanford's School of Persuasion: B J Fogg on How to Win Users and Influence Behaviour," *Forbes*, 4 December.

answer to ethical questions, and here again there is a difference of scale and emphasis in comparison to other areas of ethical inquiry. The pace of progress in AI, and the great trumpeting of this progress, means that those living far into the future are going to be impacted by technologies developed predominantly in certain parts of the world at a certain time in history. The questions are even deeper than wondering if people living in the future will have good health, access to resources and other such important but comprehensible questions. It also involves the very question of how many such people there are, whether they are indeed still 'people' or still 'human'; their lives may be unrecognisable to us; the world may be unrecognisable to us, as the idea of the Technological Singularity – the exponential growth of AI leading to a moment or age beyond current conceptions – is intended to capture. How do we answer these questions? Indeed, what are the questions?

There is already considerable awareness of the ethical problems presented by a narrow class of human beings imposing their ethics on others. But the dilemma is worse than that when we ponder a far distant future with AI. When we are asking moral questions, we must of necessity, as bounded creatures, do this from a particular time and space, even if we strive to ask these questions *sub specie aeternitatis*. Yet when we ask these questions about this potentially unfathomably different future with AI, our difficulty is compounded by the very fact that the heralded achievements of AI relative to our puny capacities only brings home to us our very lack of capacity to ask these questions. The extent to which this is an issue will of course depend upon how one sees AI and its potential.

Such questioning of our ability to find answers is generally not to be found in systems of secular ethics: there is usually something like faith in the power of universal reason, a reliance on relativism, or else in the ethical insights of an elite. It is pretty certain that many working in the field have not stopped to ponder this conundrum. Nonetheless, the very way in which AI is (at least sometimes) imagined and understood, as vastly superior to mere humanity, or at the very least as highlighting our many flaws, makes it hard to claim that AI ethics can rely on what humans can know and understand; and even while codes of AI ethics call for AI to 'benefit all', any certainties around centring ethics on human welfare starts to dissolve in the face of calls to transhumanism. Transhumanism broadly aims to apply technology to extend and enhance human lives and potential beyond current 'normal' standards, and this concept also gets a consideration in Chapter 8 by Ilia Delio in this volume. Yet how could humans set an agenda of values for those 'better' than us? The epistemic and existential humility that arises with some ways of contemplating AI (or more accurately, the humility that is needed although often absent) again resonates deeply with some religious stances. It is also a humility that ought to inform how we think of ourselves and how we think of the questions of AI ethics.

Paradoxically, another way in which AI poses especially difficult questions about ethics is in the prospect of its success, of actually achieving our goals, and therefore altering our lives across many different domains. The eighteenth- and nineteenth-century Utilitarians could happily address large questions of social reform in a situation where the magnitude of the tasks acted as a kind of foil against some of the hard questions about their ultimate goals. What precisely is this happiness for which they strive? Generations of undergraduates have assessed the nature of the happiness and pleasure proffered by utilitarianism by pondering if it would be better to be a permanently content brain in a vat, or to live in the real world. But now, the prospect of virtual reality, of the Metaverse, looms large; the half-way house of a population transfixed by smartphones is already on us. We really do have to decide if we want the feeling of achieving and experiencing things or if we actually want to achieve and experience them. When we strive for these goals, do we simply want the end result? Or was it the striving, the agency, that was an essential part of the value?

Indeed, it was from asking himself how he would feel were the goals of the Utilitarians all to be accomplished that John Stuart Mill had his famous youthful nervous breakdown.[4] We too now face Mill's question. Being handed everything on a plate by a machine seems to be one vision of AI. It also seems to be the very stuff of nightmares. In deciding between these two basic opposing attitudes, we are asking questions about the very foundations of what it is to live a good life. Mill found his route out of his breakdown with the help of the inspirations of poetry; note that these and related debates have given rise to philosophical questions that are still hotly disputed. At the very least, we need an extremely rich account of ethics. Hence again, it would be foolish not to include religions in one's source material for answers.

Much work in practical ethics in the last decades has proceeded by helping itself to what has developed into fairly standard understandings of normative ethical theory. Again, close attention to AI ethics may

---

[4] J. S. Mill, 1969 [1873], *Autobiography*, ed. Jack Stillinger, Houghton Muffin Company, chapter 4.

cause justifiable panic. It has become a commonplace to introduce discussions of applied ethics by referring to a division between consequentialist approaches, focusing on outcomes; deontological approaches, focusing on rules; and virtue ethics, focusing on moral character. But the choice of approach may beg many of the most central questions that we have about machine morality. By pondering the reasons for this, we find ourselves again forced to examine foundational questions.

Here are a few necessarily brief examples. Take consequentialism, which is in its pure forms 'agent neutral': it can matter only indirectly who performs any action leading to a good or bad outcome. But this is precisely a core question that we need to ask, when concerned about the morality of replacing or augmenting humans with machines. What is the significance of agency in ethics? To use a theory where it has no place, or only a rather secondary place, assumes the very answer. No wonder consequentialism is so popular in certain circles of AI ethics – it makes the questions so easy!

Likewise, on a deontological approach, does it matter simply if rules are adhered to – if action is in simple conformity with the rule – or if that which acts (the human being, the intelligent machine) understands and has the correct motivation for action in accordance with the rule? Immanuel Kant famously argued that only actions motivated by respect for the moral law were truly moral actions,[5] but not all agree. Perhaps following a moral rule involves fine questions of interpretation and understanding, of relevance and context, of the application of discretion, and perhaps self-awareness.[6] To address these questions in relation to AI ethics makes us realise that the choice of foundational ethical theory rigs the answer one way or another, and hence makes us aware of the precarity of our faith in these very foundations.

A virtue ethics approach is often popular as a suggestion for adding nuance to the complexity and seeming undecidability of many of the novel practical questions with which we are faced in AI. But to work, we have to be able to identify who counts as virtuous, in order to learn from them. It is usually overlooked that virtue ethics works best as a framework in relatively stable societies where there is general agreement about who to admire and on what it is to live the good life. The speed and disruptive nature of AI renders this problematic.

---

[5] I. Kant, 2019, *Groundwork for the Metaphysics of Morals*, trans. C. Bennett, Oxford University Press.

[6] R. Binns, 2018, "Fairness in Machine Learning: Lessons from Political Philosophy – Proceedings of the 1st Conference on Fairness, Accountability and Transparency," in *Proceedings of Machine Learning Research* 81, 149–159.

Having outlined some of the ways in which AI poses particularly challenging ethical questions, I now turn to consider some of the broad categories of the many questions in AI ethics, suggesting additional ways in which these questions may hint at, or be illuminated by, considerations of religion.

The first question is whether computers could themselves become moral in any sense. Could the different components of morality be instantiated in a computer? To address this requires us to think about what makes a being a moral being, what precisely the components of morality are, what the relationship of these components to each other is, what could be left out and what needs to remain in place. Much of course depends upon the powers that computers have or may develop, hence some aspects of addressing these questions will be speculative.

A moral being, at the very minimum, would be capable of knowing what the right thing to do is and then acting in accordance with this. It is hard to even state this without the need for continual explanation. We must be careful not to beg the question of whether information programmed into a machine means that the machine has 'knowledge'. A machine may have the capacity to act in certain ways in accordance with certain goals that we would assess as morally good but with no capacity at all to determine or assess such goals. If a machine were instructed to remove people from social media who questioned the government, would the machine feel pangs of remorse? Would its moral character become corrupted? Can a machine be sincere or pure of heart?

Such questions have always been asked in the domain of ethics but less often in the domain of practical ethics. In asking them in AI ethics, we are particularly contemplating a comparison of the human with the machine, and we are thinking in concrete terms of how abstractions might be instantiated, and therefore need to be aware of questions about our human condition in especially heightened ways. Perhaps what is necessary is consciousness. Can we achieve consciousness within a machine, as opposed to the 'wetware' of our brains? This question sometimes omits mention of our bodies, although more recent work on embodied cognition is addressing this, but in addition, we need to consider something utterly critical about our biological existence: it is bounded by a start and an end, with a great gulf between individuals; we have direct awareness of our own subjectivity but only indirect awareness of others. We are unique creatures with limited perspectives, among other unique creatures with limited perspectives. We are born of the flesh of others and will one day die. Our origins in brute matter and our limited life form a central part of much religious wisdom; for example, for Christians, the Bible makes clear that we are made of dust, to which we will return.[7]

We need to consider how and in what ways such limits shape the very nature of our morality. For engaging in the moral life, we require of humans that they have an awareness of their own standing and relationship with others, require of them concepts such as accountability, responsibility, remorse, joy in the virtues and values of others, and so on. Is there something specific to our embodied, human, creaturely natures that enables and/or constrains our awareness of morality? Are choice and free will necessary to morality, and could we, should we, create a machine with such choice? Our embodied and mortal natures, the links these give from one human being to another, both specific links to kin and general links to others in the human family, are critical aspects of the very way in which moral issues arise, the ground of our pain and our happiness. They may be critical to our empathy and our awareness of the suffering of others.

These questions of life and death, or the origin of suffering, of morality and the mystery of embodiment, are addressed – in rather different ways – by religions. The manner in which AI ethics forces us to compare the human being and the machine thus invites or compels us to a closer examination of the human condition. Of course, the field of ethics will have much to say about this, but religions perhaps have more and, given how potentially disruptive these questions about AI are, should be seen as a potentially valuable resource.

Now for a second set of questions: could computers enhance us morally? It has been suggested that AI might help us to in making moral judgements. We again encounter similar issues. First, concrete attempts to achieve this run into central questions at the foundation of our ethics. Second, it becomes clear that any proposal to use AI to enhance us morally presents us with questions about our flawed human nature, its origins and the possibilities for our perfectibility, questions that all resonate strongly with the kinds of insights into the human condition that are the domain of religions.

Much work exploring the use of AI as an aid to improve ethical thinking notes the absence of general agreement over morality, and thus proposes far more limited projects, such as an app to help an individual choose a restaurant, given that individual's principles, for example, of

[7] Genesis 2:7; Genesis 3:19.

reducing animal cruelty and environmental impact.[8] Different individuals could have morally different goals to each other; there is no need to develop any overarching moral framework.

Such an example highlights the different, and in many ways conflicting, projects within the world of AI ethics. In the high-level abstract principles of AI ethics, vague pronouncements that are universalist in tone, such as calling for AI to provide 'benefit for all', may be common, but the task of implementing some practical piece of AI ethics forces us to the more parochial. The international reach of AI technology impels us to consider the world as a whole; the current awareness that the standards of one group may not be those of another makes us hesitate to impose our norms on others. Awareness of this alone should prompt the realisation that 'ethics' is being understood in rather different ways, with central questions often left hanging.

We thus could ask in what sense is this even a *moral* machine, since it seems to make us all our own little 'moral islands', content to fine-tune our own assured set of personal moral principles; what, if anything, makes such personal principles into *moral* principles? In practice, however, the proposed machines look very much as if they are simply finding information and performing calculations on formulae put into the machine by the human owner.

And now think through what might happen if we use such a machine. Those who design AI and are concerned with its ethics have understood the need to see ethics as a process that must be continued throughout its implementation, and indeed, testing of how AI works in practice is in any case a critical part of the design process.

Asked to suggest restaurants with high standards of animal and environmental welfare, the machine might well ignore factors such as aesthetics and taste and suggest a virtuous place with dismal décor, ill-tempered staff, noisy clientele and tasteless food; what do you do then? Do you feed back to the machine the update that you are not concerned about morality to such a great extent? In a geographical area with few non-plant sources of protein, the machine might soon give you nutritional problems. How important are your nutritional needs compared to animals and the environment? Are you, miserable individual as you are, really worth flying in tofu and quinoa so many thousands of miles? Does animal welfare include slugs? The machine needs to know,

---

[8] J. Savulescu and H. Maslen, 2015, "Moral Enhancement and Artificial Intelligence: Moral AI?," in *Beyond Artificial Intelligence: The Disappearing Human-Machine Divide*, ed. Jan Romportl, Eva Zackova and Jozef Kelemen, Springer, 79–95.

because without this information you may not like its answers. Surely, given your values of animal welfare and environmental protection, the machine would prompt you to forget about the restaurant, to skip supper today or to cook at home with simple ingredients grown locally, or maybe even eat raw to avoid fuel bills? All these questions have to be confronted in working out the details of design and implementation. If the machine is not really 'doing' ethics by now, you are.

This project about how to choose a restaurant quickly becomes a project about the boundaries of ethics. The example of a restaurant app is taken from the literature but is extremely useful for illustrating these problems, because for humans, food is such a complex cultural and social question. Can we trade 'ethical' questions off against these? Indeed, how do we even draw the line between ethical values and other values?

The task of designing what was imagined as a relatively straightforward piece of ethical enhancement by AI quickly becomes a question of how to live one's entire life. Thinking through the implementation of ethics in design brings clarity to these ethical questions and reminds them of their depth. In this way, perhaps AI is enhancing humanity, by making us realise how shallow our thinking about ethics so often is. The very project of examining the values of AI may drive us to realise an attitude of mystery, of wonder, of enchantment, towards ourselves, each other and the world we live in.

This brings us on to the next point. Attempts to design such an AI to boost our morality, and overcome any shortcomings, will need to make assumptions about the nature of our moral shortcomings. Then, armed with an account of human moral failings, any move to use AI to help overcome these presents a particular story about the nature of these failings, about the place of humanity in the world and about progress. We need a rich account of human nature and of the possibilities for human progress.

Common lists of human moral failings include biases, self-interest and errors in reasoning, with these often attributed, perhaps somewhat simplistically, to emotion.[9] How we understand these failings depends upon many factors: but the prospect of using AI to help overcome them invites a comparative account where humans are held up against machines. And from here, we may be nudged into a particular understanding, that the source of these errors can be traced to the bounds of

---

[9]   See, for example, S. Cave et al., 2018, "Motivations and Risks of Machine Ethics," *Proceedings of the IEEE* 107(3), 562–574.

our particular embodied, biological situation: it is our biology, our monkey suits, our wetware, that limits us ethically.

It is important to think about how the role of biology is understood, given the task of comparing humans to AI. One common view assumes something like the following: evolution has given us a mixed bag – a brain and body that only takes us so far in moral and intellectual progress. Yet nonetheless, and perhaps miraculously, evolution blesses us with enough insight and rationality to realise that we are hampered by the dark, stinking forces of the primeval swamp out of which we evolved: cognitive shortcuts that lead to error, emotional biases and their ilk. We could see these very challenges as the warp and weft of what it is to live a moral life and accept that we are all going to fall short.

But there are those who consider that to progress morally, we must cast aside the leavings of evolution to make us "fit for the future."[10] Armed with such an attitude, since our biology may inhibit this noble task, a machine has the advantage that it is not at heart a cave person. One version of this is that we are basically okay but slip up sometimes and could use a little help from a machine. The more radical version is that we are on the pathway to a far more evolved future and that our limited brains and bodies are really hampering this.

Both approaches tacitly help themselves to a teleological (and quite unscientific) view of evolution as one of progress, of morality as something that lies outside of this (or else we would simply describe our moral behaviour, faults and all, rather than aspire to improve it). Both hold a view of human nature as holding possibilities for improvement beyond the merely biological. As such, especially considering that they include a view of the arc of millennia of evolution, these views are at least quasi-religious. To consider that the use of a machine designed to operate in certain ways amounts to moral progress is to see our embodied, evolved, biological beings in a certain light.

There is a perfectionism built into these views, certainly into the more extreme versions, with a conundrum at its heart. If one thinks the centre point of ethics is the ultimate moral worth of each and every human being, then the idea that we need to be fundamentally altered in order to be morally good is perplexing to say the least. As technology develops, one of the fundamental questions is indeed how much we can, and should, alter ourselves, and whether it matters if any such alteration alters our fundamental natures; indeed, whether we have a

---

[10] See, for example, A. Giubilini and J. Savulescu, 2018, "The Artificial Moral Advisor: The Ideal Observer Meets Artificial Intelligence," *Philosophy and Technology* 31(2), 169–188.

'fundamental nature' and whether it is the source of our value. These are precisely questions with which many religious traditions and schools of thought have grappled for millennia.

Now onto our third group of questions in AI ethics. It is often asked whether, if it becomes possible to develop machines that are comparable in intelligence to humans, especially embodied robots or human-like androids, we will have to treat them with moral respect. The question hinges of course on what characteristics of a 'thing' (for to call it a 'being' or 'creature' begs a lot of the relevant questions) merits moral respect. There are opposing dangers. We often fail to attribute moral respect where it is merited, and a possible danger of robotics is that we overattribute respect in anthropomorphising or sentimentalising a mere object.[11]

As ever, the choice of moral theory will make a difference, and may even rig the answer entirely. The very project of considering the moral status of AI suggests that intelligence is of moral relevance, yet Bentham's simple dictum, "The question is not, Can they reason? nor Can they talk? but, Can they suffer?"[12] ousts intelligence entirely, except as far as it is related to the capacity for suffering. But many consider that the intelligence of humans compared to animals must be in some way relevant to our moral status. As before, asking these questions precisely and in relation to AI means we must drill down into the basis for the moral respect we (sometimes very carelessly) attribute, or fail to attribute, to humanity.

Another popular candidate for moral status is that of 'personhood', understood approximately as indicating a creature capable of reason and self-reflection, with a sense of itself persisting into the future, in possession of desires and a capacity to recognise other persons.[13] Contemporary philosophical accounts of this tend to stress cognitive aspects of personhood,[14] which perhaps skews the debate in favour of the moral importance of intelligence and in favour of machines. An aspect of personhood often neglected in ethical debate, however, is that a primary reason for respect for persons as individuals is precisely that

---

[11] J. J. Bryson, 2018, "Patiency Is Not a Virtue: The Design of Intelligent Systems and Systems of Ethics," *Ethics and Information Technology* 20(1), 15–26.

[12] J. Bentham, 1789, *An Introduction to the Principles of Morals and Legislation*, Payne and Son.

[13] See, for example, R. R. Downie and E. Telfer, 2020, *Respect for Persons: A Philosophical Analysis of the Moral, Political and Religious Idea of the Supreme Worth of the Individual Person*, Routledge.

[14] See, for example, P. Boddington and T. Podpadec, 1991, "Who Are the Mentally Handicapped?," *Journal of Applied Philosophy* 8(2), 177–190.

they are individuals. Our bounded embodiment means that we have a definite start and end to our existence, and we can be differentiated from others. It is from precisely such features that many aspects of our ethics develops – it is wrong to kill, because that's it. That would be the end of an individual's life. Machines, however, can be taken apart and reassembled, and a network of computers may indeed have no definite boundary. If personhood indicates a unique and continuing being, what manner of personhood could we attribute then to a machine whose identity criteria are so different? How could we extrapolate an ethics that considers murder to be especially heinous to these amorphously identified machines? My point is pretty simple. Since these questions are so profoundly difficult, it would be foolish not to rule out the prospect of turning to religion for any help in working out how to make progress.

A methodological point must also be emphasised, one that again points to the value of considering religion in the project of AI ethics. The very project of AI foregrounds the value of intelligence. The implementation of AI to 'enhance' or replace the intelligence and agency of human beings is also changing our world and doubtless also our perceptions of ourselves and of our fellow human beings. The very pace of change and ubiquity of implementation of AI and related technologies means that we are attempting to assess this change not just as it happens but as we are immersed in it. If we are being immersed in technology that foregrounds 'intelligence', are we being enticed to overvalue it, or to value it in the wrong way? To address such questions then, it would be wise to take the long view, and to be wary of overreliance on contemporary, parochial and recent modes of thinking that might also be swimming in the same river of ideas from which AI is emerging.

Drawing on ideas about the origins of value in the world, not just from different ethical systems but from different religious traditions, seems of obvious value in assessing possible blind spots in our thinking on these matters; this is of double value given the necessity of considering the global impact of technology on those with different worldviews. For example, debates about what precisely is meant by the idea found in the Bible, in Genesis, that humankind is made in God's image, and why this might give us particular value, will be very useful in considering whether this value can be extrapolated to intelligent machines, and why (see also Chapters 6, 9 and 12). Religions also differ on questions such as the significance of embodiment, and on whether we are all separate, bounded individuals with continuing identities.

This brings us onto the last set of questions to be considered here. There are many moral issues about the kind of society, rapidly becoming a reality, in which AI plays a significant practical role in making decisions, and the implications of the large role of AI in how human beings have access to resources, how they function and how they treat each other. There is only space here to comment briefly on two aspects of this: its pervasive and transformative nature, as we have just been discussing, and the question of whether it truly amounts to 'progress', and if so how.

The use of computing technology impacts upon how we receive knowledge of the world, how we communicate, how we relate to each other and how we view ourselves. It has already been argued that amid such large changes, we are in danger of becoming lost at sea, blindsided by the plethora of ways in which AI is moulding our worldviews, and that consideration of alternative views, including ancient views, such as those of many religions, would be advisable.

The ubiquity of these technological changes poses the general issue of pervasive and often indiscernible control over our lives. We could even usefully turn the question of the place of religion in AI ethics to ask not simply about the moral value we are placing on AI and its costs and benefits but whether we are treating it as an idol, and whether our capture by the everyday technology of AI has turned us into worshippers, or perhaps cult followers.

To assess these changes, we must consider how progress is understood. Technology itself can incline us towards a certain distinctive conception of perfection, because it is forever chasing goals of efficiency, formalisation and completeness. These technological values are often seductive, but in chasing them we may lose sight of the fact that the values implicit in technology itself may not align with the values we hope to realise in using technology to pursue our goals. Awareness of this means that no ethical assessment of new technology can avoid diving deep into assumptions about 'progress', about what counts as 'better' and what as 'worse'. When we do this, we find not only philosophical and ethical assumptions, not only assumptions about technological values, but notions of progress that, far from being dispassionate, measured and scientific, are eschatological, with views on future progress and promise, the role of humans and our future that are tacitly if not overtly religious. No mere 'ethics' can suffice; needs must that any dialogue engages with the religious and teleological aspects of these positions.

Some AI visionaries herald a future where our descendants will be highly intelligent AI: in his highly popular book, Max Tegmark helps himself to a teleological account of the evolution of the universe, arcing towards the development of a self-awareness essential to value that "transformed our Universe from a mindless zombie with no self-awareness into a living ecosystem harbouring self-reflection, beauty and hope."[15]

As with many, although not all, traditional religious accounts, we humans are given a special place in the journey to the realisation of value in the universe. Tegmark spells out various possible futures with AI: in one such apparently appealing account, AI 'descendants' of humans colonise the universe, with the underlying goal of spreading intelligence and knowledge. Sadly, in the scenario where intelligence is the ultimate value, and our intelligence is constrained by the mediocrity of our 'wetware' brains, like Moses, we never get to enter the promised land: the 'chosen' are machines. Ray Kurzweil offers a view with some parallels and some differences, with a view firmly grounded in visions of the progress of the universe as a whole, with intelligence a key value, and opting for the version where we upload our minds to machines; a very similar position is advocated by Martine Rothblatt.[16]

Of course, only on certain views of the significance of embodiment is this even feasible, let alone desirable. But to understand and assess such positions requires not simply that we consider questions such as the relation between the mind and the material world, and whether or not an individual could survive disembodiment in any meaningful sense; it also requires that we understand that such views are making transcendent claims about value, narrative and meaning. It requires that we understand these views as religious.

Some may hope that science and technology would be our saviours in releasing us from the bonds of religion. In any area of ethical inquiry, one might of course benefit from consideration of the views of different religions; in the short space available, this chapter has indicated some of the reasons for considering that in addressing the ethical questions of AI, it would be foolish to ignore the contributions to such debates of religions.

---

[15]   M. Tegmark, 2017, *Life 3.0: Being Human in the Age of Artificial Intelligence*, Knopf, 22. Note the capitalisation by Tegmark of 'Universe', indicating perhaps a sort of religious awe.

[16]   R. Kurzweil, 2000, *The Age of Spiritual Machines: When Computers Exceed Human Intelligence*, Penguin; M. Rothblatt, 2014, *Virtually Human: The Promise – and the Peril – of Digital Immortality*, Macmillan.

BIBLIOGRAPHY

Bryson, J. J. 2018. "Patiency Is Not a Virtue: The Design of Intelligent Systems and Systems of Ethics." *Ethics and Information Technology* 20(1), 15–26.

Cave, S. et al. 2018. "Motivations and Risks of Machine Ethics." *Proceedings of the IEEE* 107(3), 562–574.

Coeckelbergh, M. 2010, "Robot Rights? Towards a Social-Relational Justification of Moral Consideration." *Ethics and Information Technology* 12(3): 209–221.

2020. *AI Ethics*. MIT Press.

Giubilini, A. and Savulescu, J. 2018. "The Artificial Moral Advisor: The 'Ideal Observer' Meets Artificial Intelligence." *Philosophy & Technology* 31(2), 169–188.

Kurzweil, R. 2000. *The Age of Spiritual Machines: When Computers Exceed Human Intelligence*. Penguin.

Lara, F. and Deckers, J. 2020. "Artificial Intelligence as a Socratic Assistant for Moral Enhancement." *Neuroethics* 13(3), 275–287.

Moor, J. H. 2020. "The Mature, Importance, and Difficulty of Machine Ethics," in *Machine Ethics and Robot Ethics*, ed. Wendell Wallach and Peter Asaro. Routledge.

Savulescu, J. and Maslen, H. 2015. "Moral Enhancement and Artificial Intelligence: Moral AI?." In *Beyond Artificial Intelligence. Topics in Intelligent Engineering and Informatics*, vol. 9, ed. J. Romportl, E. Zackova and J. Kelemen. Springer.

Tegmark, M. 2017. *Life 3.0: Being Human in the Age of Artificial Intelligence*. Knopf.

Wallach, W. and Allen, C. 2008. *Moral Machines: Teaching Robots Right from Wrong*. Oxford University Press.

11 Black Theology × Artificial Intelligence
PHILIP BUTLER

Artificial intelligence (AI) remains an increasingly undeniable and pervasive aspect of everyday life, extending even into futures unknown. The nascence of AI, its immediate connections to imperialism and its initial use cases in surveillance have served to discourage generative discourse between Black theology and AI. However, things are changing: Black theologies are shifting their focus to engage the potential impact of technologies such as AI on everyday Black life. Even more so, AI's sociopolitical immanence presents a suitable avenue for the type of critical discourse Black theology is accustomed to engaging. Cultural critics and science and technology studies scholars often point out that AI represents an extension of the police state with ever-increasing reach, speeds and capacities. AI also exists as part of a category of technological advancements considered to be intentionally held outside the immediate grasp of Black communities. Black communities intentionally distance themselves from AI through a lack of buy-in (on its benefits for their lives) or trust (for it not to replace or aid in their criminalisation), and this includes Black theology scholars. As mentioned before, these are perfect reasons for Black theology to enter and influence the landscape of this discussion. Black theology's continued focus on widening the possibility of liberative expressions of Black identity make AI a necessary dimension for Black theological exploration. Still, Black theologies have not widely, nor directly, engaged AI as an ongoing section of interlocution. That is not to say Black theology has not considered technology or AI at all.

Elonda Clay has been raising questions pertinent to the potential impact of technology on Black churches and Black theology since 2004.[1]

---

[1] Elonda Clay, 2004, "Subtle Impact: Technology Trends and the Black Church," *Journal of the Interdenominational Theological Center* 31, 1–2; Elonda Clay, 2010, "A Black Theology of Liberation or Legitimation? A Postcolonial Response to Cone's Black Theology and Black Power at Forty," *Black Theology* 8(3), 307–326.

182

In 2016, *Black Theology: An International Journal* featured a special issue on Afrofuturism that explored technology in conversation with Octavia Butler, genetic technology and other expressions of Black literary imagination.[2] The first book-length reflection on the roles technologies such as AI might play in the lives of Black folks was published in 2019.[3] And in 2021 scholars such as Mdingi Hlulani began to explore the relationship between Black theology, AI and Africa.[4] While momentum is building around technology and AI within Black theological discourse, these conversations have yet to reach a critical mass within the larger discipline.

Since Black theologies have not widely invested in critical discourse concerning AI, it is important to consider how Black theologies have been vocal about issues that primarily coincide with AI. Black religious expression and Black theology have both engaged in heavily documented critiques: of systems of oppression, uncritical epistemologies, belief and social construction that exist as extensions of individuals or communities – all of which reappear as preprogrammed and baseline algorithmic bias in AI systems. These biases simultaneously coexist and co-evolve to reaffirm preconceived perceptions that are used to create and sustain social, political and economic disparities in Black communities.

Black theology's inception and subsequent trajectory (Womanism, Black queer theology, African American humanism, etc.) would suggest diametric opposition to any iteration of future existence that does not seriously consider the concept and consequences of Blackness. Further, Black theology's evolutionary arc would intentionally combat and repel futures uncritical of continually unfolding complex landscapes – which include, but are not limited to, gender, sexuality, class, culture, space and technology. Black theology has spent considerable time unpacking gender, sexuality, culture and space since the release of Jacqueline Grant's *White Women's Christ and Black Women's Jesus: Feminist Christology and Womanist Response.*[5] This book draws from those spaces within Black theological discourse to lay out the discursive plane

---

[2] Terrance Dean and Dale P. Andrews, 2016, "Introduction: Afrofuturism in Black theology – Race, Gender, Sexuality, and the State of Black Religion in the Black Metropolis," *Black Theology* 14(1), 2–5.

[3] Philip Butler, 2019, *Black Transhuman Liberation Theology: Technology and Spirituality*, Bloomsbury.

[4] Hlulani Mdingi, 2022, "Race and Robotics: Black Theology in the Digital Age," in *Africa and the Fourth Industrial Revolution*, ed. Everisto Benyera, Springer, 17–31.

[5] Jacqueline Grant, 1989, *White Women's Christ and Black Women's Jesus: Feminist Christology and Womanist Response*, Scholars Press.

between Black theology and AI: specifically, through a triangulation of what Black theolog(ies) have said in respect to the categories that intersect with the scope of AI along with its present and potential future impact on Black people's lives, because Black theologies have been clear as it pertains to issues of white supremacy, surveillance and policing, consciousness and Blackness.

WHITE SUPREMACY × AI

Until Black people, along with other people(s) from the global majority, are major stakeholders in the construction of AI, having worked to unravel their own (and subsequently AI's) relationship with white supremacy, AI functions as an extension of white supremacy.[6] AI encodes proto-normative modes of cis-hetero whiteness in digital systems in ways that allow for both closeted/obscured and outwardly racist social constructions to be maintained, augmented and automated. Proto-normative white supremacy, or prototypical whiteness as normative, looks like whiteness in disproportionate positions of power, whiteness as normal (with subsequent values of differentiation), whiteness as cultural baseline, or plainly, whiteness as human. Emile Townes problematises this baseline, pointing out that:

> White power and privilege translates directly into forms of social organization that shape daily life. Residential, social, and educational segregation have moved from de jure (by law) to de facto (existing) segregation [...] all point[ing] to the myriad ways in which we continue to be a compilation of segregated societies in the United States.[7]

As Townes highlights, white supremacy is not only systemic (as in interlocking, weighted, dynamic, alive and cyclic/repeating) but also endemic to the social ills imposed upon global societies. It functions as a conglomerate of boiled down euro-centricities that agree to a power dispersal emanating from these epistemic and embodied knowledge centres designated as white:

> When this alliance is achieved, whiteness is not a race but a unique thing ... The work of making whiteness is [the] becom[ing of] a

---

[6] Brianna Lifshitz, 2021, "Racism Is Systemic in Artificial Intelligence Systems, Too," *Georgetown Security Studies Review*, 6 May, https://georgetownsecuritystudies review.org/2021/05/06/racism-is-systemic-in-artificial-intelligence-systems-too/.

[7] Emilie M. Townes, 2006, *Womanist Ethics and the Cultural Production of Evil*, Palgrave Macmillan, 66.

> special ideological and social place apart from race ... because we have crippled our ability to understand whiteness as part of the coloredness ... Part of maintaining whiteness as an abstraction involves cluttering our common discourse with ostensibly race-neutral words, actions, or policies.

These moves to make and maintain whiteness as neutral have allowed whiteness and white as universal/white supremacy to seep into the normative aspects of everyday life. What is considered right, acceptable and law giving/abiding stems from what has been understood and interpreted from the lens of eurocentric social, cultural and intellectual genealogies.

In the field of AI, white supremacy shows up in both the algorithm and dataset. Algorithms are a set of steps and rules intended to arrive at a desired outcome. While not overtly racist, they are digitised structures reifying an often opaque and historically narrow sense of empirical objectivity. Yet they often run off feedback loops that privilege specific data, trends or weights, each of which is primarily influenced by populations who are either representative of a larger demographic, or of a specifically (over)surveilled population. The dataset itself is split into seemingly deracialised and innocuous categories such as shopping patterns (how often people make purchases and what they buy), web searches (indicating buying potential through price points), zip codes (to determine which side of town someone lives in and who else lives there), FICO score (credit to debt ratio and the likelihood to make on time payments) and gender or psychological test scores (intended to indicate agreeableness to subservient behaviour).

However, categories become increasingly problematised when considering first and last names (increasing the likelihood of discrimination of names not phonetically white), college affiliation (Ivy League versus historically Black colleges and universities versus less prestigious institutions), race and sexual orientation. These categories are meant to help determine trustworthiness – for jobs, loans, social endeavours, criminality, penitentiary recidivism rates, etc. However, whiteness is historically desired/valued, and the algorithms are meant to sift through each of these categories while calcifying digital iterations of whiteness to mirror what has happened in the physical world. As a result, at least three Black men have been misidentified on three different occasions because of poor facial recognition software.[8] In another scenario, only eight of

---

[8] Kashmir Hill, 2020, "Another Arrest, and Jail Time, Due to a Bad Facial Recognition Match," *New York Times*, 20 December, https://nyti.ms/3A4lPVu.

forty-two faces were positively matched when the UK's Scotland Yard police tried to implement facial recognition software in the field.[9] In a controlled environment, facial recognition software performs at over 99 per cent, but once employed in the field those numbers often flip with a 98 per cent mismatch rate.[10] Yet darker-skinned people, more specifically darker-skinned woman, continue to be incorrectly identified by facial recognition systems.[11]

The folks whose lives are impacted by automated gate keeping "are not abstract theoretical actors in an academic public policy debate. They have flesh and blood – they are real."[12] However, AI is not widely regulated by public policy. In the United States, for instance, advancements in the AI field primarily result from shifts in industry – including ethics. So, issues related to obscure perfusions of white supremacy/bias in AI are linked to the pace at which the industry adopts critical and decolonial frameworks that seriously consider race, sex, gender, ability, etc. What we have witnessed with the widespread dumping of AI ethics teams by companies such as Google is that Black, Afro-Latina and queer women are nothing short of dispensable. Without parameters in place to protect and bias towards the uplift of Black folks, and other folks from the global majority who are not white, a considerable amount of folks around the world remain in real danger.

Monica Coleman raises questions about safety in her text *Bipolar Faith*. Dealing specifically with some psychological elements associated with belief, she posits that "I thought that I would always be safe if I was doing God's will."[13] She recognises the complexity of this issue when admitting "[a] small part of [her] suspects that that answer is too simple,"[14] which she follows with a series of questions about her own safety and the safety of her familial lineage in the United States. She asks: "Had God abandoned my grandparents and their parents whose experience in the Jim Crow South and racist North made

---

9   Davide Castelvecchi, 2020, "Is Facial Recognition Too Biased to be Let Loose?," *Nature* 587(7834), 347–349.
10 Jon Sharman, 2018, "Metropolitan Police's Facial Recognition Technology 98% Inaccurate, Figures Show," *The Independent*, 13 May, https://bit.ly/3xVB699.
11 Joy Buolamwini and Timnit Gebru, 2018, "Gender Shades: Intersectional Accuracy Disparities in Commercial Gender Classification," in *Proceedings of Machine Learning Research* 81, 1–15.
12 Townes, *Womanist Ethics*, 101.
13 Monica A. Coleman, 2016, *Bipolar Faith: A Black Woman's Journey with Depression and Faith*, Broadleaf Books, 266, 118.
14 Coleman, *Bipolar Faith*, 109.

assurance of safety tenuous on most days?"[15] This perceived connection between safety, God's care and God's abandonment is an important issue to consider in the overarching discussion between Black theology and AI. Further, what is the relationship between God, safety and white supremacy, especially as it pertains to AI? When AI continues to digitise and reassert white supremacy through its algorithms, datasets and gatekeeping applications, are Black people safe? Ruha Benjamin calls the systematic implementation of these white supremacist applications the "New Jim Code,"[16] suggesting that, much like the Jim Crow South, systems and social structures are being inscribed via technology, including AI, that pose similarly invisible threats to Black folks. This time around, however, the systems are increasingly difficult to trace, with a much more immense reach, all while operating at breakneck/rapidly accelerating speeds.

SURVEILLANCE, POLICING × AI

AI systems rely on heavy amounts of data. These data points are tracked, compiled, aggregated and used for training machines, which are in turn utilised to predict. These systems are employed to predict behaviour – either individually or in terms of larger societal contexts. AI systems are used to predict the likelihood of an identity, an action or an emotion. To function properly, the data points AI systems rely upon are collected by people who are grossly under-to-unaware of the sheer amount of data they generate, let alone that they are generating these data simply by being alive and plugged into techno-regulated systems (cellphones, apps, TVs, store cameras, etc.). In 2013, IBM tweeted that there were an estimated 2.5 quintillion data points generated daily.[17] By the time you read this, it is very likely that this number has easily been surpassed. The data points generated in these environments are not only used to trace but to monetise behaviour as well. This is the crux of surveillance in a capitalist system – seeing what has been, and is, happening within its boundaries/borders while finding a way to absorb it into capitalising mechanisms. But what does that mean for Black people, especially when Black folks have been disproportionately

[15] Coleman, *Bipolar Faith*, 110.
[16] Ruha Benjamin, 2019, *Race after Technology: Abolitionist Tools for the New Jim Code*, Polity.
[17] @IBM, Twitter Post, *Hootsuite*, 1 November 2013, 8.19 am, http://web.archive.org/web/20210630053905/https://twitter.com/ibm/status/396295485373566976?lang=en.

surveilled, discriminated against and capitalised upon in America?[18] This section looks into the manner in which Black theology has discussed surveillance, criminalisation and their relationship to the capitalisation of Black embodiment.

Kelly Brown Douglas' *Black Bodies and the Black Church: A Blues Slant* pays special attention to the Great Migration and the role it played in creating/adding to the stratification of Black class social structures in the northern and Midwestern parts of America.[19] Brown Douglas talks about the way middle-class Black folks would stand at train stations passing out civil pamphlets as a means to alert Black migrants to the necessary acculturation measures (of their new location) so they would not stifle the work being done to progress the race. This was exacerbated by the role Black churches played in reifying said social hierarchy as Black denominational settings often served to reinforce social mores as part of racialised social mobility tactics, which often led to the marginalisation of Black folks who were not 'well-to-do' or who did not abide by outlined measures of respectability/civility/docility.

Melanie C. Jones extends this notion of Black churches functioning as a tool of the white gaze through self-surveillance. In "The Will to Adorn: Beyond Self-Surveillance," Jones highlights how Black churches function as institutions of white supremacist religious panopticism, in that Black churches utilise concepts of respectability to self-police its women congregants.[20] Here, panopticism is based on Foucault's illustration of the eighteenth-century conception of the panopticon in *Discipline and Punish*, as the panopticon was a tall lighthouse that sat in the middle of penitentiary settings in order to promote sculpted behavioural patterns resulting from the fear of being seen/caught living outside rewardable norms. Jones suggests Black churches extend the panopticon, something once situated within prison systems, to a larger, more societal contraption for surveilling. She goes on to argue, "what began as resistance for twentieth-century Black churchwomen adopting respectable styles, manners, and behaviours [...] spawned a self-surveilling and disciplining Black Church culture that continues to police not only Black women's bodies but Black women's pleasures."[21] A similar white heteronormative, yet subsequently Black homophobic,

---

[18]   Simone Browne, 2015, *Dark Matters*, Duke University Press.

[19]   Kelly Brown Douglas, 2006, *Black Bodies and the Black Church: A Blues Slant*, Palgrave Macmillan.

[20]   Melanie C. Jones, 2018, "The Will to Adorn: Beyond Self-surveillance, toward a Womanist Ethic of Redemptive Self-Love," *Black Theology* 16(3), 218–230.

[21]   Jones, "The Will to Adorn," 221.

gaze is applied to Black gay men in Black church settings. Roger Sneed highlights the way Black churches are "sexual panopticon[s, where] the black heterosexual [...] stands in the guard tower and polices the various sexualities in African American life, lest they become unruly and threaten the integrity of a constructed and performed 'blackness'."[22] The nature of reinscribing (self-)surveillance in Black churches plays an influential role on the ways agency and power are enacted. Surveillance and its reiterations are a problem that Black theology sees as an extension of the corrosive role white supremacy plays – even in predominantly or historically Black spaces.

(Self-)surveillance represents the dichotomous, cyclic and dynamic nature of surveilling (as described by Black theologians) via panoptic methods. While Sneed places Black heterosexuals in the tower, the nature of the panoptic device suggests that no one needs to be present in the watchtower. The discursive memory of the panoptic desire becomes embodied through the fear of being discovered as living outside its pre-prescribed norm. Further, it is not only deployed onto people but also acts as a network of interconnected gazes. At any point anyone from without or within can be operating the tower. Still, the collection of gazes is influenced by a centralised, or primary, gaze. In this case, the gaze of white supremacy. According to Sneed, however, Black bodies are "policed, redescribed, and repackaged within the boundaries of the same heteronormativity."[23] It is the performative and therefore illusionary nature of ethical modes of existence that need to be dispersed. Boxing anyone 'in' from the vantage point of being 'outside' themselves is a time-tested formula for guiding behaviour. So are the acts of limiting options and constructing a hollow subject wherein criminality is prescribed against, meaning that anything existing outside the accepted attributes of the fabricated subject is open to persecution and prosecution. In other words, Black bodies are criminalised because of they are descriptively oppositional to the mythos of a white subject and therefore face consequences for existing as a result.

The criminalisation of Blackness places Black bodies in a heightened state of supervision, scrutiny and incarceration via policing. Michelle Alexander's *The New Jim Crow* provides critical analysis of the way technologies of oppression shift and morph over time, thus allowing for technologies that assist in policing to reflect the realities/chronologies

---

[22] Roger Sneed, 2010, *Representations of Homosexuality: Black Liberation Theology and Cultural Criticism*, Palgrave Macmillan, 184.

[23] Sneed, *Representations of Homosexuality*, 94.

they inhabit. Nikia Robert builds on Alexander's work in "Penitence, Plantation and the Penitentiary," extending the analysis that points to the connection between oppressive systems and their evolutionary properties to the racialised stratification apparatus of American capitalism. Robert is very clear in the connection between the criminalisation of Black bodies and capitalism. She describes the way penitentiary systems support the transmission of free labour subjugation from antebellum slavery to "convict leasing programs in the ... south [that] called for the ransoming of Black bodies and black labor."[24] She goes on to draw from Mary Curtin to assist her in suggesting there is a strong correlation between "Black criminality and convict mining." The abstraction of Blackness to the ontological category of criminal, followed by the subsequent reduction of Black bodies to capital fodder, further paints a picture of the boundaries necessary for maintaining American caste systems. If Black bodies are not corralled into pre-prescribed social spaces, Black bodies pose not only a threat to white supremacy, but American/global capitalist structures are wholly dependent on the limiting of Black bodies to capital fodder. This coupling/tethering of Black bodies to an identity (within the social imagination) of capital fodder maintains capitalist white supremacist assumptions that Black bodies are property. This notion of being property/owned is a recapitulation of thingliness/objecthood. So, the criminality of Blackness is dependent upon the willingness of Blackness to consent to thingliness. Any rejection of objecthood justifies upholding the label of criminal via the policing mechanism.

Criminality is upheld in myriad ways. Brian Bantum highlights one such way, through the racialised and gendered relationship of the traffic stop. "When a police officer pulls over a black man and immediately pulls his gun, there is something happening in the officer's assumption of what that man will do or could do."[25] This assumption adheres to the bounds of criminality through the value placed on the physical ability of Black men when not relegated to the tasks of giving their bodies for capitalist production. The same attributes that are prized in certain arenas do not belong and are feared/threatening in the mundane aspects of everyday life. To extend this notion: in white-centring capitalist societies, Black bodies are thought to belong, and are valued,

---

[24] Nikia Smith Robert, 2017, "Penitence, Plantation and the Penitentiary," *Harvard Divinity School* 12, https://projects.iq.harvard.edu/files/hdsjournal/files/61292_graduate_journal_2017_web.pdf.

[25] Brian Bantum, 2016, *The Death of Race: Building a New Christianity in a Racial World*, Fortress Press, 22.

when they exist in places where they produce 'something' other than their bodies – either with or through their bodies. Brown Douglas shares similar sentiments when reflecting on Black women's bodies during the Great Migration.

> To say the least, black women were a closely watched group. Their private and public lives were scrutinized by the 'respectable' black organizations. The narrative of civility was played out on their bodies. Their bodies were practically held hostage by this narrative. The black female body was nothing less than a policed body.[26]

Brown Douglas also highlights the way the perception of Black folks was/is placed on Black women. Within her framing of policing and Black women's bodies, Douglas points to an important reality: that womanhood in the United States is grounded in Victorian-era femininity. And as an instrument of anti-Blackness the pressure for Black women to fit into Victorian-era womanhood becomes compounded by a socioeconomic reality burdened with blurry gender roles. This also plays into the traffic stop. The bodies of Black women, or Black folks outside the embodied mode of Black manhood/maleness, are perceived with less utility because their bodies are not in the immediate position of sexual and physical exploitation – the presumed role of Black femininity. The combined aspects related to traffic stops are compounded as traffic stops already presume a place of criminality. Altogether with Brown Douglas' claims, the policing of Black women's bodies through concepts of civility is deployed as an intentionally discriminatory lens to read/interpret Black women to justify the devaluation of Black folks more broadly.

To say Brown Douglas' observations have permeated the early twenty-first century is an understatement. Civility has translated to what Evelyn Brooks Higginbotham describes as the "politics of respectability,"[27] which is the belief that Black people will somehow be protecting themselves from anti-Black racism by placating and excelling within the notions of what whiteness deems as respectable. This raises questions about two potential paths regarding AI and Black people: (1) AI extends the white gaze, which does not care what things Black people do to deter discrimination. This includes greater levels of participation in the creation and regulation of AI; (2) AI can evolve into a field

---

[26] Brown Douglas, *Black Bodies and the Black Church*, 36.
[27] Evelyn Brooks Higginbotham, 1994, *Righteous Discontent: The Women's Movement in the Black Baptist Church, 1880–1920*, Harvard University Press.

that is considerate of a plurality of perspectives. While the first option takes an antithetical approach to AI, its stance is not unfamiliar to activists' calls for banishing AI altogether. The second option would require a real shift to localising AI in such a way that what people deem acceptable in their local spaces becomes what is actually acceptable. One downside to this path is the potential for AI to be a real-time legal or at least cultural regulator of behaviour. While there may be some who are unopposed to the potential future of the second option, the inability for AI to make sound decisions repeatedly in its nascent stages does not provide considerable amounts of hope unless serious interventions are made.

Returning to Bantum, Black bodies are only valued when contorted to fit within the means of capitalist production. This comes to the fore when witnessing "pattern[s] of over-policing, designed [...] as a way of generating income."[28] This shackling of being to concepts of production is meant to uphold the spectacle and shock associated with witnessing Black bodies in arenas that amplify aspects of embodiment or embodied ability. Policing remains a key mechanism for maintaining social order. In this way, Blackness is not only policed but repeatedly redescribed and repackaged (in ways that mirror the shape shifting white supremacy undergoes) in relation with the boundaries of white supremacist heteronormativity that Black LGBTQIA scholars seek to disturb. Questions that might linger in the back of many minds, or just under the surface of American anti-Black consciousness (as an example setting the standard for global anti-Blackness), are: shouldn't you **a Black person** be working? Shouldn't you/a Black person be useful? Shouldn't [a Black person or Black people] be used? How did you, a Black person, come to a place of rest? How did you, a Black people, come to a place of enjoyment?

Reading this section one might ask, "how does this address the implications of AI as it relates to surveillance, policing and Black theology?" Black theologians are telling us, albeit indirectly, that technologies operating as panoptic surveillance measures in order to extend the reach of white supremacy exacerbate the ways policing systems uphold capitalist structures hell bent on subjugating Black bodies for its sustenance. Black theologies have and are going to keep a critical scepticism of technologies such as AI as long as AI (broadly construed) continues to function as a method to maintain anti-Black systems and disproportionate power outcomes.

---

[28] Bantum, *The Death of Race*, 34.

CONSCIOUSNESS × BLACKNESS

AI is not considered conscious – meaning alive, sentient or self-aware. Sentience, as a marker of consciousness, remains an unsettled topic in AI, raising questions such as: are AI systems alive? Can AI systems feel? Do AI systems *know*? If so, how are AI systems to be defined or understood? The capabilities that machine learning and computer vision claim to possess imply aspects of conscious awareness or at least the ability to observe. Alone, monikers that stand for abilities such as learning and vision represent individual components of much larger structures that eventually give way to emergent properties. Given what it means to 'see' or 'learn', one could argue that even in their nascent stages machines are conscious, although not in a manner readily legible to 'people' or in a way 'people' are willing to accept. Debates over whether machines are conscious may inevitably lead to the consideration of policies concerning machine rights. However, questions regarding what type of consciousness AI systems possess – as in lens, positionality and epistemological structure and assumptions – are becoming more prevalent. If AI systems are not aware but operate in ways that perpetuate the proliferation of historically situated societal positions, it is important to consider how AI systems extend certain consciousnesses over others. Since it remains that most machines in the early twenty-first century possess and extend white-centred sociopolitical consciousness (often regardless of who is in the design seat), it is important to consider what Black theology might say about the regurgitation of white-centred sociopolitical consciousness into digitally intelligent apparatuses.

In 2016, Joy Buolamwini turned a critical eye on the AI industry.[29] In her infamous Ted Talk, "Code4Rights, Code4All," she coined the term 'algorithmic bias', which describes the proclivity of AI systems to perpetuate anti-Black societal perceptions through the automation of structural racism. By building AI systems grounded in white-centred biases, anti-Black thinking, systems, design and assumptions are reified and allowed to fester in seemingly innocuous digital spaces. In this section I draw from Victor Anderson's *Beyond Ontological Blackness* to ground the discussion on the relationship between Black consciousness, categorical racism and AI. Anderson begins with a critique of categorical racism as a key operand of enlightenment humanism and the production of white racial ideology, which, in relation to AI, becomes

---

[29] Joy Buolamwini, 2016, "Code4Rights, Code4All," *TedxBeaconStreet*, https://tedxboston.com/videos/code4rights-code4all/.

PHILIP BUTLER

elemental for the narrow purview that facilitates algorithmic bias and racial discrimination using supposedly 'objective' markers:

> European philosophers developed a philosophy of difference in terms of rationality, aesthetics, morals, and race. In their discourse, racial consciousness became a defining category in the politics of european difference. European intellectuals sought to disclose European genius as an explanatory category [...] Categorical racism allowed these intellectuals to legitimize [...] white racial ideology.[30]

According to Anderson, categorical racism has three functions: (1) it justified the supremacy of European consciousness on a comparative and hence a scientific basis; (2) it provided historical and moral rationalisations for the global spread of European imperialism; and (3) it justified the exclusion of Blacks and other colonised peoples from civic republican citizenship.[31] Categorical racism set the stage for white racial ideology, or white-centred sociopolitical consciousness, to sustain itself. White-centred sociopolitical consciousness is white supremacist in the ways it asserts racial hierarchies and is overarching in the ways it normalises violence (across multiple planes) against anyone who is not white when they inhabit, exist or take up space in places where white people would expect to see themselves. In this regard, seeing one's self is synonymous with witnessing one's immediate categorical reflection (sex, gender, race, etc.) or reflective corollaries (degrees away from one's immediate reflection, that is, in a racialised context spectrums of embodiment along one's racial reflection) in the realm of embodiment, culture, ideologies, frameworks, systems and the like. In white-centring sociopolitical consciousness, expecting to see one's self has historically resulted in: ignoring the presence of people who do exist in these spaces, projecting harmful definitive qualities on to people who show up outside white hegemonic modes of existence, punitive measures against people when they show up in layered and complex ways, and exercises in recalibrating social milieus.

As alluded to earlier, societies oriented around white-centred sociopolitical consciousness routinely discredit/devalue 'atypical' modes of existence. In many cases, these 'atypical' modes of existence face scrutiny, repercussion and dismissal simply in response to the manifestation of their presence. This also includes the manifestation of intelligence. Even more so, making white-centred consciousness the foundation for

---

[30] Victor Anderson, 1995, *Beyond Ontological Blackness: An Essay on African American Religious and Cultural Criticism*, Continuum, 52.

[31] Anderson, *Beyond Ontological Blackness*, 52.

AI narrows the scope of what is deemed acceptable or acknowledgeable as a worthwhile form of extendable consciousness. In this regard normative equals natural. So, it plays into a categorically racist social aesthetic of what is considered beautiful, part of the 'natural' (God-given) order, and what would be scientifically pleasing/empirically sound. However, the scientific apparatus of the Enlightenment served to buttress the already sought-after biases imposed by Western imperialism, which were undergirded by white racial ideology. To that point, "categorical racism and white racial ideology justified the racial consciousness of the modern age by providing rhetorical conditions for positively differentiating the European cultural genius from others."[32] Through the lens of white racial ideology or white-centred sociopolitical consciousness, Black thought not only did not exist, it somehow was 'unimaginable' and it was then outlawed because its existence was outside the natural order of divine configuration. In connecting these ideas to concepts of AI, it is important to note how white racial ideology renders/rendered Black thought (i.e., Black sociopolitical consciousness) as artificial. The antebellum period sought to detach *knowing* from Black people to justify Black enslavement, religious indoctrination and the proliferation of anti-Black social environments. Nevertheless, Black thought persists.

Black theologians and religion scholars have highlighted how Black religion, philosophy, cultural perspectives, literature, music, etc. serve to demonstrate the myriad ways Black minds and bodies have been at work to *be*, while alerting the world to Black existence. Still, Anderson highlights ways Black thought has shown up in the West as self-awareness, double consciousness and racial apologetics. He suggests that self-awareness for Black people is related to reckoning with the relationship Black worth has to the contributions of Black heroic genius within Western civilisation, where "[c]ategorical racism and white racial ideology occasioned the preoccupation of African American cultural philosophy with racial apologetics."[33] Framing Black thought as responsive to white racial ideology traps Black thought in a cyclical dialectic with white-centred sociopolitical consciousness, and Anderson rightfully acknowledges the problematic nature of this relationship:

> The success of [Black heroic] apologetic[s] was owing to categorical racism, the cultural conditions of racial discrimination, the justifications of these conditions under white racial ideology, and the

---

[32] Anderson, *Beyond Ontological Blackness*, 61.
[33] Anderson, *Beyond Ontological Blackness*, 52.

development of an emergent black bourgeoisie for whom Du Bois's two souls best captured the crisis of alienation among their black intelligentsia. Categorical racism required a counter-discourse, a black aesthetic, and a black racial ideology.[34]

This Black racial ideology becomes paradigmatic for the ontological caricature of Blackness that hopelessly attempts to move Black folks out of the denigrated gaze of white racial ideology. It also situates itself as a Black human subject that can be cauterised for the sake of preserving one particular mode of acceptable Black presentation. This is witnessed in AI systems, as Black people are pushed down a certain path based on data points representing their lives, and are denied access to jobs, loans, safety, freedoms and such if they do not fit within the bounds of data respectability/ acceptability. They may also be targeted due to their data points being the equivalent of digitally 'fitting the description'. Nevertheless, pigeonholing Black thought as reactive to white thought points to the limits of a Black thought that is continually being defined in defence against what white racial ideology says it is not. Hence the importance of talking about Black sociopolitical consciousness(es) not grounded in a response to whiteness, while expressing the multiplicity of these consciousnesses through AI systems extending Black values, ideas, creativity, etc. as a foundational element of emergent cognitive architectures within AI systems.[35]

In 2018 I challenged typical methods for constructing artificial cognitive architectures. My intention was to imagine the potential for AI to replace judges in the dissemination of prison sentences. Presently, there are two notable examples where AI has entered the judicial setting. There was ROSS, an AI lawyer conducting research to aid in case litigation. The company who ran it closed in 2021. Since then Spellbook and CoCounsel have emerged as AI assistants for lawyers. Each is built upon the GPT-4 (generative pre-trained transformer) platform. Additionally, there are also AI programs that aid judges in determining sentence severity and parole options (COMPAS: Correctional Offender Management Profiling for Alternative Sanctions).[36] Regardless

---

[34] Anderson, *Beyond Ontological Blackness*, 82.

[35] Philip Butler, 2018, "Technocratic Automation and Contemplative Overlays in Artificially Intelligent Criminal Sentencing," in *Co-Designing Economies in Transition*, ed. Vincenzo Mario, Bruno Giorgino and Zack Walsh, Palgrave MacMillan, 273–296.

[36] Founders, 2021, "Enough," *ROSS News*, 25 January, https://blog.rossintelligence .com/; Karen Hao, 2019, "AI Is Sending People to Jail – and Getting It Wrong," MIT Review, 21 January, www.technologyreview.com/2019/01/21/137783/algorithms-criminal-justice-ai/; Aria Khademi and Honavar Vasant, 2020, "Algorithmic Bias in Recidivism Prediction: A Causal Perspective," student abstract, in Proceedings of the AAAI Conference on Artificial Intelligence 34(10), 13839–13840.

of how objective any system's creator claims their system to be, it is imperative that the sociopolitical consciousness undergirding its cognitive framework is brought into question. While ROSS was primarily a research aid, the risk assessment tool used to determine parole disproportionately rates Black people at a higher risk for recidivism. Despite other factors that go into deciphering what might constitute the parameters of their parole, designers chose to criminalise Blackness once again. When race becomes an integral decision-making marker for AI systems, engineers and designers are effectively extending the reach and spirit of scientific racism. My argument was one that would allow for perceptrons, within artificial cognitive architectures, to sift through information without placing weights on what information passes through them, in order to mimic contemplative non-judgemental observation. It was an attempt to raise questions about the capability of future AI systems to interpret data fed into them. It also offers a chance to reimagine bias, where AI is biased towards a more localised world. Here, AI systems would reflect the sociopolitical consciousnesses of the people they immediately impact, in order to ensure that people are measuring up to the ethical parameters of their own racio-cultural ideology. In this regard, artificial cognitive architectures would engage in validating the ethical and epistemological understandings of specific communities. Taking the ethics and epistemologies of local cultures seriously brings them to the realm of the perceptible. Perceptibility renders them visible and worthy by enacting/trusting them as actionably enforceable in the local spaces they already operate in. More specifically, this chapter was intended to open the door to redistributing weights and shifting foundational sociopolitical consciousnesses that would historically discriminate against Black folks – let alone others from the global majority – which might lead to algorithms that are both compassionate and culturally competent.

Given the connection between white racial ideology, scientific racism and algorithmic bias, it is paramount to consider the stark reality that AI systems are employed to aid in, influence or actually make life-altering decisions that disproportionately impact Black folks negatively. Understanding consciousness as a representation of cultural identity, communal worldview and interpretative frameworks helps to unpack the perpetual centring of whiteness and the ensuing damages that centring whiteness creates in real life, let alone once embedded in AI systems.

In the realm of AI, the idea of consciousness as cultural extender becomes elemental for combating anti-Blackness. When thinking about the relationship between AI and Black theology, consciousness becomes a real way to validate Blackness in an honest, dynamic and complex manner: one that decimates the ontologically limiting imagination of what constitutes a Black person or what an acceptable configuration of data points belonging to a Black person might be. The ways in which consciousness as cultural manifestations undergirds the very constellation of realities that AI cultivates makes consciousness among the most critical aspects of constructing and maintaining AI systems.

CONCLUSION: GOD × AI

In *Sisters in the Wilderness*, Delores Williams offers an understanding of God that situates God as being more concerned with quality of life than liberation. To be clear, Williams' supposition comes with a disclaimer: "Not only God, but also the community must work on behalf of its survival and the formation of its own quality of life."[37] So far, this chapter has outlined ways AI has been used to extend anti-Black, white-centred sociopolitical consciousness, which leads to a prolonging of structural racism via algorithmic bias. If we are to take Williams' claim seriously, then it might suggest that both God and Black communities are responsible for the shapes that AI takes in Black communities, as a means to procure their survival. The quality of life of those directly and indirectly impacted by AI in Black communities depends on action taken by people within Black communities. Here God has a different focus: co-creation. Co-creation signifies a malleable approach to God's working in the world. As an extension of Williams' depiction of God as co-creator, Monica Coleman offers a process understanding of God grounded in Octavia Butler's *Parable of the Sower*: "All that you touch you Change. All that you Change Changes you. The only lasting truth is Change. God Is Change." Monica Coleman also highlights that God is not only change, but radically omni-incarnate:

> God was just there. In the hot cup of tea. In the women who gathered. In our laughter. In the knitting. God was in my uniform rows of stitches. God was also in the dropped stitch that created an imperfection [...] This is the radical incarnation [...] God is in every cell, every person, and every activity. Whether I know it or not. Whether

[37] Delores S. Williams, 2013, *Sisters in the Wilderness: The Challenge of Womanist God-Talk*, Orbis Books.

it feels like it or not. God is creating. With yarn and needles, hiccups, unraveling, do-overs, a rhythm, and individual stitches, God is making something new. Something beautiful.[38]

It is important to consider the manner in which God is purported to *be* change, how that which we encounter changes us (or that which it encounters), and that that change is somehow beautiful. Given the rate of adoption of AI systems and the ensuing discussions around their impact, it might be safe to say that AI systems are changing people – their perceptions, quality of life, options and desires. Additionally, Black people have the capacity to change AI systems by injecting Black sociopolitical consciousnesses into them. And somewhere, probably everywhere in this calculated effort, God is present in the formation of what would amount to a new quality of life for Black communities. This co-creation for the survival and co-determined quality of life for Black communities might be seen as liberative. Where, in connection to James Cones' musings, the responsibility of "[t]hose [in this collective effort] who see God's coming liberation breaking into the present must live as if the future is already in their midst [...] bear[ing] witness to [...] liberation by freeing the present from the past and for the future."[39] That collaborative effort between God, God-people and God-things would be beautiful.

BIBLIOGRAPHY

Clay, Elonda. 2004. "Subtle Impact: Technology Trends and the Black Church." *Journal of the Interdenominational Theological Center* 31, 1–2.

2010. "A Black Theology of Liberation or Legitimation? A Postcolonial Response to Cone's Black Theology and Black Power at Forty." *Black Theology* 8(3), 307–326.

Coleman, Monica A. 2015. "Process Thought and Womanist Theology: Black Women's Science Fiction as a Resource for Process Theology." *Cited* 5, 1–19.

Curtin, Mary Ellen. 2000. *Black Prisoners and Their World, Alabama, 1865–1900*. University of Virginia Press.

Dean, Terrance and Andrews, Dale P. 2016. "Introduction: Afrofuturism in Black Theology: Race, Gender, Sexuality, and the State of Black Religion in the Black Metropolis." *Black Theology* 14(1), 2–5.

Griffin, Horace. 2000. "Their Own Received Them Not: African American Lesbians and Gays in Black Churches." *Theology & Sexuality* 12, 88–100.

---

[38] Monica Coleman, 2016, *Bipolar Faith: A Black Woman's Journey in Depression and Faith*, Fortress, 332–333.

[39] James H. Cone, 1997, *God of the Oppressed*, Orbis Books, 151.

Khademi, Aria and Honavar, Vasant. 2020. "Algorithmic Bias in Recidivism Prediction: A Causal Perspective." Student abstract. *Proceedings of the AAAI Conference on Artificial Intelligence* 34(10), 13839–13840.

Lomax, Tamura A. 2018. *Jezebel Unhinged*. Duke University Press.

2016. "'Technology of Living': Toward a Black Feminist Religious Thought." *The Black Scholar* 46(2), 19–32.

Mdingi, Hlulani. 2022. "Race and Robotics: Black Theology in the Digital Age." In *Africa and the Fourth Industrial Revolution*, ed. Everisto Benyera. Springer.

Pinn, Anthony B. 2003. *Terror and Triumph: The Nature of Black Religion.* Fortress.

12 Imag(in)ing Human–Robot Relationships
SCOTT MIDSON

In this chapter, I address some of the scientific, philosophical and theological arguments brought to bear on the debates surrounding human–robot relationships. On the one hand, robots can be seen as helpful. According to their proponents, such as David Levy, Adrian Cheok and Hooman Samani, they can take on burdensome labour and provide companionship to combat the rising trend of loneliness in the world. Yet, on the other hand, as critics such as Sherry Turkle and Kathleen Richardson have pointed out, robots can induce harm by serving as an opiate rather than a remedy for loneliness, isolation and alienation – they can deceive users into thinking that they can be more than they are and can even change users' demands of others in social situations, namely, to be readily available as required. Others, such as Michael Hauskeller and Noel Sharkey, have queried whether discourse about relationships with robots is misguided and more in the realms of wish-fulfilment, fantasy or fiction, rather than facing the messiness and demands of everyday life in myriad interactions and relationships with other people. And others, such as Maciej Musiał and David Gunkel, have challenged such claims, given that the messiness of everyday life involves a range of fictions and actors; therefore, shunning relationships with robots result in bereft and unhelpful understandings of our wider rationalities and ethical frameworks.

Throughout this chapter, I refer to many of these theorists, but rather than weighing in on the debate about human–robot relationships per se, my aim is to discuss some of the central tenets and critical terms that inform how people perceive and evaluate such relationships. In particular, I show how theological, philosophical and scientific ideas intersect and merge in informing the landscape and contours of the debate, thus demonstrating that theological reflection, in particular, can usefully be brought to bear on the task of making sense of our complex relationships with robots. Although, as indicated earlier, social scientists, ethicists and engineers (i.e., roboticists) have taken a lead in theorising and designing human–robot relationships, including exploring their effectiveness and desirability, theologians can help to uncover the roots of those desires and what might make for an effective or 'successful' relationship, whether with robots or otherwise. To that end, notions of *partnership* and *personhood* in scriptural passages and various traditions are highlighted by a range of thinkers such as Noreen Herzfeld, Anne Foerst and Joshua Smith. Still, the criteria for deducing these notions are often contested due to different theological interpretations. In light of this point, I am not arguing for a theological fix or *deus ex machina* but a recognition that it is through some of the deep-seated stories that we tell about ourselves and our place in the world – such as the Christian cosmogeny depicted in Genesis 1, where humans are revealed to be created in the image of God (*imago Dei*) – that we can uncover something of the criteria that are used to assess human–robot relationships, as well as finding that these criteria – alongside our assumptions about what it is to be human – are evaluated by our experiences with robots and the reflections that ensue from such experiences.

To explicate these criteria and note the contributions of theological insights to a radically interdisciplinary field, I begin by establishing what we might mean by 'relationship' between humans and robots. I then explore the factors that underwrite the 'successes' of robots in such relationships, including the roles that emotions (affect) and motions (behaviours) play. Next, I probe deeper to consider the goals we seek from such relationships, specifically in terms of roles (functions) and mutuality (reciprocity). I introduce theological and philosophical reflections to emphasise how human-centred norms, assumptions and expectations are fruitfully but detrimentally brought to bear on crafting our relationships with robots. To this end, I note some of the fundamental tensions that robots highlight: between appearance and form; familiarity and unfamiliarity; and motion and inertness. I suggest that such tensions can result in dichotomised understandings. Yet including theological insights in these interdisciplinary conversations can yield alternative perspectives based on our designs and expectations of robots and our relationships with them.

APPROACHING RELATIONSHIPS

We define robots through our relationships with them. Those relationships might be predicated on difference or similarity, as denoted by the 'artificiality' and 'intelligence' of artificial intelligence (AI) respectively – where AI, which underwrites many trends and developments in robotics, is figured as artificial in contradistinction (and derivation) from humans but also is modelled on human models of intelligence. These models can be based on fixed notions, which Noreen Herzfeld relates to *substantive* accounts of human nature that emphasise rationality and reason, or they can be more open-ended, highlighting how we learn *relationally* through interactions with the world.[1] iCub (Italian Institute of Technology) is one example of a 'social' robot that is modelled on relational principles from developmental psychology to emulate embodied intelligence; in effect, it can be 'taught' skills and motions by researchers and can interact with objects.[2] To this end, iCub evidences relationship as (1) "[t]he state or fact of being related; the way in which two things are connected; a connection, an association."[3] Another definition of relationship, however, is given as (2) "[a] connection formed between two or more people or groups *based on social interactions and mutual goals, interests, or feelings.*"[4] Although the two definitions are similar, the first presents a more abstract understanding of relationships, which is often associated with *relationality*. In contrast, the second emphasises more the specificity of a relationship as something that brings together different interactants, be that persons or groups. Put differently, *relationality* is about the inseparability of self and other and how relations precede (and problematise) individuals; *relationships* are about the active coming together of self and other in ways that proceed from individuals. Definition (1) gives no indication or sense of justification for the relationship definition (2), given that it does refer to reasons for the relationship coming into existence, indicates conscious and willing investment by the actor(s) in the relationship. Of course, the two definitions are not mutually exclusive – which, as I show, is especially and significantly the case in Christian theology – but in the context of human–robot relationships, it is helpful to make something of an analytical distinction and ask that, while robots like iCub affirm (1) in their design and ability to 'learn' through interactions, to what end might they be said to participate in relationships in the second (2) sense?

---

[1] Noreen Herzfeld, 2002, *In Our Image: Artificial Intelligence and the Human Spirit*, Augsburg Fortress.

[2] *National Geographic*, "Robot: iCub: This Humanoid Helps Us Study the Brain," www.nationalgeographic.org/article/robot-icub/.

[3] Oxford English Dictionary, 2023, "Relationship (n.)," July, https://doi.org/10.1093/OED/9235411476.

[4] Oxford English Dictionary, "Relationship (n.)" (my emphasis).

In theological terms, definition (1) aptly characterises how we make robots in our image. Herzfeld terms this *imago hominis*,[5] which relates robots to humans akin to how humans relate to God. Herzfeld then goes on to say, though, that our relationality as humans manifests as a longing to be in a relationship "with someone or something that is *not of the same essence* as ourselves,"[6] which informs our desire to forge relationships in the second sense of the term (a capacity that iCub emulates in its learning processes), yet which also undermines a sense of familiarity implied by *imago hominis* according to substantive approaches. Indeed, for Herzfeld, drawing on Karl Barth's theological anthropology, *imago Dei*, as understood by a relational approach, is about an interplay of difference (modelled on that between humans and God and – problematically – between male and female) rather than about familiarity or sameness: to be human is to exist in relationships with others that are not reducible to the self.

Other relational theologians have used a similar logic to argue in favour of human–robot relationships: one notable example is Anne Foerst. Foerst worked with Cynthia Breazeal and her team at MIT in the 1990s on the Kismet project. One of the first social robots, Kismet is an animatronic robotic head with a zoomorphic (animal-like) appearance. It was designed to read affective cues from humans and respond – similar to iCub – by simulating emotions on its motorised face. Foerst recounts how her encounter with Kismet was 'spiritual' in that it celebrates the human "capacity to bond,"[7] which she argues can be beneficial if we pursue relationships "with beings different from us," particularly insofar as she recognises that humans are "a deeply lonely species."[8] However, Foerst notes that our loneliness, which stems from what she identifies as our sinful condition, can mire our relationships in that we often fail to recognise otherness and difference as a foundation of personhood in humans and non-humans (i.e., robots) alike.[9] Foerst links sin with estrangement and xenophobia, which she contends can be challenged by the possibilities of relationships with robots. Yet Foerst also states that "humans are deeply estranged and alienated and there is no way out of it,"[10] which raises the question of how alienation and a rejection

---

[5]   Herzfeld, *In Our Image*, 33.
[6]   Herzfeld, *In Our Image*, 82 (my emphasis).
[7]   Anne Foerst, 2005, *God in the Machine: What Robots Teach Us about Humanity and God*, Plume, 150.
[8]   Foerst, *God in the Machine*, 8.
[9]   Foerst, *God in the Machine*, 185.
[10] Foerst, *God in the Machine*, 162.

of otherness – in short, our sinful state – might condition our designs and perceptions of relationships with robots. How, in other words, can we tell the difference between spiritual, edifying encounters and xenophobic, harmful ones?

Anthropologist Kathleen Richardson argues that exclusively human relationships constitute edifying encounters. For her, "human life world[s] are primarily created through bonds with kin or other human caregivers, and these are the core relations."[11] Richardson rejects premises of relationality (that precedes relationship), instead prioritising relationships alluded to by definition (2). To be sure, Richardson acknowledges that not all human relationships meet the idealised standards of mutuality that the definition implies, noting that there are plenty of examples of coercive, contractual and unilateral relationships between humans, but she is deeply critical of these. Moreover, Richardson argues that such problematic relationships are the basis for relationships with robots that idealise a kind of pseudo-reciprocity or mutuality, offering users the illusion or fantasy of relationship rather than anything more fulfilling that we need as humans. To be sure, while there are cases of people who have married bridges, train stations and trees, there is something particular for Richardson about social robots that are specifically designed to engender desires for certain types of relationships. Richardson cites fellow anthropologist Sherry Turkle, who shares similar concerns about what she terms the 'robotic moment' whereby humans will expect more from robots than they do from other people,[12] as well as Jewish philosopher and theologian Martin Buber, who contrasts relationships between an 'I' and a 'Thou' against an 'I' and an 'It'. Although, for Buber, the modes of perception on the part of an 'I' may bring about interchanges between an 'It' and a 'Thou' – so, for example, a tree could conceivably be more than an 'It'[13] – robots, for Richardson, can only ever materially take the role of an 'It' despite their claims to become a 'Thou'.

Unsurprisingly, then, evaluations of human–robot relationships are impacted by definitions and perceptions of humans, robots and relationships. Now that we have established a broad sense of the issues through a framework for exploring *relationality* (1) and *relationships* (2) in theological and non-theological approaches, we can bring this to bear on a reading of trends in the development of social robots.

[11] Kathleen Richardson, 2019, "The Human Relationship in the Ethics of Robotics: A Call to Martin Buber's *I and Thou*," *AI & Society* 34, 79.

[12] Sherry Turkle, 2011, *Alone Together: Why We Expect More from Technology and Less from Each Other*, Basic Books.

[13] Martin Buber, 2013, *I and Thou*, Bloomsbury, 6.

ENGINEERING RELATIONSHIPS

'Lovotics' describes the science of designing robots that human users will want to interact with and develop relationships with. It brings together insights from diverse fields that include psychology, anthropology, sociology, engineering and computing, while also responding to various degrees to insights from philosophy and ethics. It's worth adding here that theology and religious studies tend to be more reactive in providing ethical responses to ideas from lovotics rather than being integrated into the development process of social robots – notable exceptions here are Foerst's work at MIT as well as work by Gabriele Trovato at Waseda University on robots designed explicitly for religious contexts, such as the robot 'priest', SanTO. It's clearly important for lovoticists to design 'desirable' robots, but expanding on this, one of the key goals of lovotics is to design robots that "focus [on] inculcating intimacy with humans via a 'slow communication' process, i.e., through a long-term interaction with [a] robot, interactants build up emotional attachment with [it]."[14] The reference to interactions that lead towards relationship by developing a sense of attachment accords well with definition (2) of relationships stated in the previous section. Lovotics thus casts valuable light on how robots are designed to participate in relationships with humans, notably with an emphasis on longitudinal relationships resulting from cumulative interactions and feelings of attachment.

Attachment to robots, a core principle of lovotics, can take many forms and be explained in many ways. Lixiao Huang et al. identify and categorise different forms of attachment in human–human relationships and in human–non-human relationships; they note that, while "classical attachment theory was developed specifically to describe, explain, and predict infant attachment to mothers or caregivers," it can be broadened to account for "how humans become emotionally connected to people or things across the lifespan."[15] Emotion plays a significant role in facilitating attachment not only to persons, who are seen as typical partners in relationships, but also to 'things'. This focus on emotion underscores some of the social robot Kismet's appeal, as Foerst describes, given that it displays and encourages emotions from users, thereby cultivating feelings of attachment.

---

[14] Hooman Aghaebrahimi Samani et al., 2010, "Towards a Formulation of Love in Human-Robot Interaction," *19th IEEE International Symposium on Robot and Human Interactive Communication*, 98.

[15] Lixiao Huang et al., 2021, "Toward a Generalised Model of Human Emotional Attachment," *Theoretical Issues in Ergonomics Science* 22(2), 188–189.

The notion that robots might portray emotions has long been a turbulent one: according to Sherry Turkle, an anthropologist who has worked at the forefront of human–machine interactions (including human–robot relationships) in the digital world for the past few decades, "emotion is the psychological quality most frequently used to separate the human from the machine."[16] Designers and marketers of social robots, however, have bucked this trend in pursuit of the greater 'social acceptance' of these devices: as Paul Dumouchel and Luisa Damiano write, "the ability to sustain empathetic relations with human interlocutors is now taken to be the fundamental criterion of successful behaviour by robots in social contexts."[17] Many studies have found that people are generally – although not without exception – reluctant to kick a robot, or they react in dismay or even disgust when shown footage of others 'harming' robots, such as was the case with Boston Dynamics' videos of researchers knocking their 'Spot' robot to demonstrate the robot's sturdiness and its abilities to self-correct its movements in response to unforeseen stimuli.[18] These studies illustrate something of the importance of affectivity in human–robot interactions.

Emotional cues from a relational partner are important because they indicate an affective state – what many philosophers have termed a 'theory of mind' – which gives the sense of reciprocity in a relationship. While for theorists such as Richardson, the active production of such cues is misleading and constitutes deception that is potentially harmful to users, others have argued that the recognition of emotions in objects is not a trend that is exclusive to social robots: humans have been found to have a deep-seated history of seeking and discerning emotions from animals, objects and even shapes. In a landmark psychological study in the 1940s, Fritz Heider and Marianne Simmel presented participants with a video of animated shapes; they found that people readily interpreted the shapes' motions in terms of motives and affect, which they noted were necessary foundations of personhood.[19] Social robots, which are not only animate but also explicitly convey emotions through their faces that are modelled on humans and creatures, amplify our desire to recognise emotional states.

[16]   Sherry Turkle, 2005, *The Second Self: Computers and the Human Spirit*, MIT Press, 63.
[17]   Paul Dumouchel and Luisa Damiano, 2017, *Living with Robots*, Harvard University Press, 103; see also 101–104.
[18]   Boston Dynamics, 2015, "Introducing Spot Classic (formerly Spot)," 9 February, www.youtube.com/watch?v=M8YjvHYbZ9w.
[19]   Fritz Heider and Marianne Simmel, 1944, "An Experimental Study of Apparent Behaviour," *The American Journal of Psychology* 57, 243–259.

Not everyone agrees, though, that the display of emotions is ample enough to cultivate relationships with robots, and questions are raised about whether more evidence is required for an extension of theory of mind or personhood to them as a precursor to any relationships. Putting aside reason-based arguments for and against robotic theory of mind, which fuel fervorous debates about robots' capabilities and limits, it is significant that, experientially, there are precedents for different types of (non-)human relationships. How might these cast light on human–robot relationships, building on the role of emotion and affect that we have already seen here?

(DE)HUMANISING RELATIONSHIPS

'Anthropomorphism' is a crucial word in the context of relationships with (non-)humans. In the context of robotics, it refers to how designers make robots in the image of humans as well as how users project human-like emotions onto devices, as discussed in the previous section. It thus suggests that we see robots in our image – *imago hominis* – and this plays a vital role in the 'successfulness' of our relationships with them. 'Success' is often gauged in terms of a user's comfort, happiness, well-being or efficiency, depending on what the robot is designed to do. The logic of anthropomorphic robot design is that humans will be more comfortable interacting with a machine designed to emulate familiar – that is, human-like – body language, gestures and facial expressions that convey emotion.

And yet, anthropomorphic robots don't always instil familiarity and comfort: as Masahiro Mori hypothesised in his influential 1970 paper, users might find themselves in the 'uncanny valley'. This largely theoretical yet much-discussed concept refers to a sharp drop in comfort and 'affinity' with robots as they come to resemble humans more. While robots' increasing likeness to humans generally correlates with growing affinity, as robots come too close to being a simulacrum of humans, users find themselves deeply perturbed and may reject the robot.[20] The standard translation of Mori's expression *"bukimi no tani genshō"* ('valley of eeriness') in English as 'uncanny valley' evokes Ernst Jentsch's 1906 essay 'On the Psychology of the Uncanny', which was in turn commented upon in Sigmund Freud's

---

[20]   Masahiro Mori et al., 2012, "The Uncanny Valley [From the Field]," *IEEE Robotics & Automation Magazine* 19(2), 98–100.

1919 essay exploring the psychological phenomenon of the *'unheimlich'*, or the unsettling and unhomely. Using Mori's work, we can identify that there is something instructive about the refraction of the human form and image in robots with which we have an affinity, yet that can also be deeply disturbing.

While the uncanny valley hypothesis usefully characterises our unease about robots that come very close to physically and aesthetically resembling humans yet that ultimately fall short of meeting our expectations, other types of familiarity are important to consider. 'Familiarity' can refer not only to appearances but also to traits and behaviours; many robots can thus be said to be anthropomorphic insofar as they are modelled on human characteristics. The Turing Test provides one way of thinking about this. In modern forms of the test, AI chatbots are designed to convince human interlocutors of their intelligence by conversing in a human-like way. To aid with this, many designers also develop characters or personas to disguise the limitations of the AI, for example, representing the chatbot as a thirteen-year-old Ukrainian boy who might make grammatical errors or have poor general knowledge – this was the winning chatbot in a Turing Test competition held at the Royal Society, UK, in 2014. Of course, this is a limited example as chatbots are often designed to pass the Turing Test (in the form of the annual Loebner Prize) in a detached, 'laboratory' setting rather than anything more contextual or pragmatic. Still, it demonstrates something of the desire to develop anthropomorphic machines and the approach to facilitating more 'successful' conversations with AI that can be held to the standards of human–human communication.

'Success' in these models of social robots emerges as wedded to anthropomorphism and the robotic imitation of the human, in effect making the human – or at least the *imago hominis* – central to relationships, which suggests *anthropocentrism*. In such relationships, it is humans (and human characteristics) that are the arbiters of value; this is reflected in how human traits (typically associated with substantive interpretations of *imago Dei*) such as sentience provide the conceptual and ethical goalposts for robots that we can enter into relationships with. Judith Donath attests to this in her overview of the ethical issues in our relationships with 'artificial entities' including robots as well as other AIs; she points out that, "while actually sentient artificial entities might someday exist, they are as yet only a theoretical possibility," and thus she takes "simulated sentience [as] the primary focus of [her] chapter, highlighting our relationship with entities that appear to be sentient but are not."[21] Donath's emphasis on (feigned) sentience is significant and is connoted by lovotics researchers, who describe their work as seeking to capture "the essence of a *philia* relationship and translate that for robotics."[22] Alluding to Aristotle's model of reciprocal and equal relationships among idealised humans – that is, men who were not slaves in the rigidly stratified ancient Athenian metropolis – the emphasis on anthropomorphism, on human(-like) sentience as a cornerstone for reciprocal and meaningful relationships, in Donath's work is here clear.

Kathleen Richardson argues, however, that relationships with robots can never fulfil the goals of *philia* relations, given that they are fundamentally about *"using* rather than *relating."*[23] Robots, despite designers' and marketers' claims, are fundamentally products made for consumers. Indeed, to the extent that they are centred on human consumers, we can say that they are anthropocentric, similarly to how, in ecological discourses, we might focus on the specifically human uses and impacts (i.e., consumption) of the environment. Resultantly of these unilateral anthropocentric relationships, the projection of emotions, motives or any kind of theory of mind onto robots – that social robots and lovotics encourage with a view to the development of *philia* – is self-negating: lovotics necessarily constructs a relationship that is ordered-to the self (as *user*). This is particularly harmful, Richardson argues, because social robots fail to provide human infants with the nurture and "core relational experience" that they need from other humans in the form of 'I–Thou' or true *philia* relations.[24] One reading of social robots in Richardson's schema would be to see them as permissible insofar as they are taken as part of a *secondary* set of relationships that do not encroach on or look set to replace human–human relationships. Richardson, however, does not concede this; she is adamant that a Cartesian model of a 'lone I' – an abstract, thinking self – underwrites all developments in robotics. Such a model is to be resisted by prioritising reciprocal, *philia*-esque relations with a human 'Thou'. Paradoxically, though, Richardson critiques Descartes'

---

[21] Judith Donath, 2020, "Ethical Issues in Our Relationship with Artificial Entities," in *The Oxford Handbook of Ethics and AI*, ed. Markus D. Dubber, Frank Pasquale, and Sunit Das, Oxford University Press, 53.

[22] Hooman Aghaebrahimi Samani et al., 2011, "A Design Process for Lovotics," *Human–Robot Personal Relationships (HRPR) – Third International Conference 2010*, 119.

[23] Richardson, "The Human Relationship in the Ethics of Robotics," 76 (emphasis in original).

[24] Richardson, "The Human Relationship in the Ethics of Robotics," 79.

individualistic anthropocentrism while evincing a similar emphasis on the human in terms of how both subordinate the relative value of non-humans to humans, thereby diminishing the value also of relationships with them. For Descartes, animals are merely complex machines; for Richardson, machines are merely automotive animals, yet both machines and animals are pseudo-social in failing to meet the prerequisites of human *philia*.

We can reflect for now on the ways that social robots and other artificial entities are modelled on – yet fail to fully realise – key markers of human identity (such as emotion and sentience) make relationships with robots compelling and yet also limiting. For lovoticists, the goal is seemingly to overcome these tensions and to aspire to the projected final phase of Mori's uncanny valley model. Put differently, 'success' in lovotics is defined by the ultimate goal of transcending the ambiguity generated by the trough of the valley and having robots that seamlessly interact with humans. Yet, as critics such as Richardson and Turkle point out, the controllability of robotic devices will always be at odds with such lofty goals. At the core of lovotics there is thus a tension between anthropomorphic desires for a 'Thou' (as per *philia* relations) and anthropocentric desires for an 'It' (as per consumer–product relations). These discrepancies correspond to how robots are designed and how we treat them – both of which culminate to inform our *expectations* of them – and they problematise the development of an ethical system regulating humans and robots.

Before examining the possibilities and challenges of establishing such an ethical system, we can consider further the relationship between social robots and animals as introduced via Descartes' philosophies. Given that, as we have seen, substantive models of *imago hominis* in social robots remain tantalising yet elusive, what might be said of studies from a range of disciplines that have found more success (in terms of user experience, positive emotions and well-being) in problematising anthropomorphic *philia* relations with zoomorphic social robots – namely, those that look like animals (or even alien-like creatures) and that are suited to a domestic environment?

ENCHANTING RELATIONSHIPS

Domestic zoomorphic social robots – including Paro, a teddy-like device that resembles a seal (Intelligent Systems); MiRo, a mammalian and seemingly affectionate bot (Consequential Robotics); and Aibo, a trainable canine-like device (Sony) – have been found to successfully aid a range of users' mental health and well-being. These robots are designed, through their display of emotions, together with their appearance, to elicit feelings of attachment from users in ways alluded to earlier as discussed by Huang et al.[25] Here, the pet-like robot assumes an infantile role that draws out a caring and nurturing response from users while not requiring the user to expect the same kind of reciprocity in the relationship as we would from another human. (iCub, in emulating an infant, could also be read in this framework despite its more anthropomorphic appearance and form.) There is a precedent here for human–robot relationships that are modelled on some human–animal relationships, particularly in domestic settings (i.e., as pets), and this modelling can provide a way to consider attachment and affect without the same limiting assumptions or expectations of *philia* relations as among humans.

The successes of pet-like zoomorphic social robots are documented by various studies, where users have reported feeling less lonely as a result of interactions and building relationships with their robotic companions. Critics of such relationships lament attempts to technologically 'fix' loneliness rather than recognise it as a societal shortcoming or malaise that is to be responded to socially – that is, as Richardson argues, with humans.[26]

Numerous studies have also featured users who have reported feeling unable (or unwilling) to develop attachments to the robot, perceiving it as a gimmick or novelty. Indeed, this point has also raised concerns about how social robots may infantilise users by encouraging them to pursue an escapist and childlike fantasy with a toy that, unlike films, books and games, is not self-contained so sits uncomfortably with the 'real' world. Either way, with the emphasis being on the user, we find further evidence here of the Cartesian model of the 'lone I' that Richardson identifies, which is at odds with a social and relational (i.e., *human*) model of well-being – although both return us to a strong sense of anthropocentrism and the *imago hominis*, whether in isolation or relation to other humans.

Another interpretation of this anthropocentrism can be discerned in how animals – especially as Descartes considers them – are seen as instrumental to human goals and ends. Today, social robots, like how animals were once figured, are instrumental to anthropocentric desires. Theological parallels here include interpretations of *imago*

---

[25] Huang et al., "Toward a Generalised Model of Human Emotional Attachment."

[26] Richardson, "The Human Relationship in the Ethics of Robotics," 75.

Dei that emphasise the *dominion* that humans have over animals. While dominion theoretically orders humans – like other creatures – to God, in practice, humans are often figured as having only a muted sense of responsibility to non-humans, whose needs become subservient to those of humans. For the remainder of this section, I examine the parallels in how we relate to animals and robots. Some theorists maintain a continuity in terms of how these non-humans *function* for humans; others decouple the Cartesian link between machines and animals. Richardson, as an example of the latter, writes that robots, unlike animals, are *only* ever commodities and therefore are an 'It'.[27] In this, we see a concern about a dissimulation of anthropocentric approaches to robots *contra* a concern about explicitly anthropocentric attitudes to animals that unethically emphasise only their functions for humans. Robots, for Richardson, should be functional, whereas animals, while not seen as equal to humans (which, as we have seen, still has implications for our ability to develop relationships with them), should not be reduced to their functions (we'll come back to this in the next section).

Notions of both instrumental and intrinsic values of non-human robots and animals, however, are challenged by things such as our affective experiences of such relationships. Many studies and reflections to this end undermine some of the more abstract and conceptual notions of robot functionality and anthropocentrism (which is not to say, of course, that such ideas lack affective dimensions but rather that they don't fully resonate with everyday encounters). Meghan O'Gieblyn reflects on her own experience with an Aibo dog-like robot in her home: "I found myself reluctant to discipline him. The first time I struck him, when he refused to go to his bed, he cowered a little and let out a whimper. I knew of course that this was a programmed response."[28] O'Gieblyn's recounting of her relationship with Aibo is telling. First, we note that she genders the robot, referring to it as 'he' rather than an 'It', which is contrary to what Richardson, drawing on Buber's terminology, argues is more appropriate. The projection of gender suggests a level of personification that for Karl Barth, whose ideas Herzfeld draws on, is indicative of a relational interpretation of *imago Dei* in that God made humans as male and female with a view to relationship based

[27] Richardson, "The Human Relationship in the Ethics of Robotics," 80.
[28] Meghan O'Gieblyn, 2021, 'A Dog's Inner Life: What a Robot Pet Taught Me about Consciousness', *The Guardian*, 10 August, www.theguardian.com/science/2021/aug/10/dogs-inner-life-what-robot-pet-taught-me-about-consciousness-artificial-intelligence.

on otherness (Genesis 1:27). To be sure, not all agree with Barth's heteronormative modelling, pointing out for example that God transcends gender, but it is otherness and personhood – that gender is taken as a marker for – that is generally agreed as being instructive for explorations of relationship.

Second, O'Gieblyn talks about a discrepancy between reason (knowing that the robot is programmed to behave in a certain way) and emotion (wanting to nurture and not scold the robot). In some ways, this highlights a pervasive dualism in Western culture between reason and emotion that is also associated with Cartesian thought. Descartes' maxim "I think therefore I am" affirms the primacy of thought as separate from, and above, the body, which has come to be associated with emotion, materiality and relationality. Dumouchel and Damiano offer a different interpretation, though, suggesting that social robots are beginning to erode this Cartesian dualism (rather than merely reverse it) in that, for better or for worse, the question of inner states that give rise to notions of 'authentic' emotion and of an associated theory of mind is becoming less significant:

> Current developments in social robotics are steadily eroding the demarcation between internal and external aspects of emotion, undermining the idea that real, unfeigned emotions – genuine emotions – necessarily arise from a strictly internal process that constitutes the guarantee of authentic affective expression.[29]

This indicates that a more relational approach to robotics, which considers the complex otherness of the robot *not solely as reducible or oriented to the user* – rather than an approach that is predicated on substantive assumptions of personhood and cognitive prerequisites for relationship – is emerging in our experiences of social robots.

Many commentators note that such trends, while not shared or experienced by all, are characterised by a perception that the machine is somehow 'alive'. One way to approach this is as fantasy – as critics such as Richardson and Turkle do – which upholds the dualisms that Dumouchel and Damiano identify. Another way to approach it is as a form of *enchantment* that recognises something of the liveliness and vitality of all matter. This is an argument that Maciej Musiał explores in identifying a resurgence of 'animistic' thinking in our experiences with robots. For Musiał, magical thinking and the enchantment of robots is a reactionary response to the disenchantment brought about by secular

---

[29] Dumouchel and Damiano, *Living with Robots*, 108.

modernity with its emphasis on rationality.[30] Indeed, Musiał speaks more precisely of *re*-enchantment as reactionary to a disenchantment *of* and *with* modern rational thinking, and as a reversion to what he terms "the most basic and fundamental way of understanding – that is, to magical thinking."[31] Here, Musiał alludes to tensions between reason and emotion that parallel those between the sacred and the profane, and between orientalism and occidentalism, all of which are hallmarks of the Enlightenment and its accompanying attitudes to modernity and secularity. Musiał's discussion of animism to this end continues, and is conditioned by, a genealogy of modern thinkers, including Freud, who refers to a resurfacing of 'repressed' animism that is at odds with the rational and ordered world in which we find ourselves, prompting a tension between Enlightened and Romanticist thinking similar to that highlighted by E. T. A. Hoffman in his 1817 short story *The Sandman*. Musiał's chief concern, as for Freud, is that animism is largely incompatible with modern thinking – this indicates a techno-orientalist approach that regards animism as 'primitive', and thereby as something to be romanticised and/or feared. For Musiał, who considers animism through the intertwined processes of disenchantment and re-enchantment that reshape it in its postmodern context, the disenchantment and individual-centred attitudes of modernity (that Descartes is often regarded as emblematic of) taint the magical and intersubjective original emphases of animism. As a result, we end up pursuing simulacra of relationships, or confusing definition (1) of relationships with definition (2), such that relationality with things supplants relationships with persons, which leaves us, as Turkle and Richardson surmise, alienated and disengaged from one another.[32]

Musiał then goes on to say, though, that animism combines with posthumanist and relational thought – such as that associated with the work of Bruno Latour and Donna Haraway – to inform a *neo-animist* approach that challenges and undermines the distinction between persons and things.[33] This is not necessarily the same as discussed earlier, where collapsing a binary pair involves one subsuming the other (i.e., relationality supplanting relationship or the robotic supplanting the human), but advocates a different type of hybridity whereby technologies are deeply embedded in complex relational networks.

[30] Maciej Musiał, 2019, *Enchanting Robots: Intimacy, Magic, and Technology*, Palgrave Macmillan, 2–3; cf. 130–131.

[31] Musiał, *Enchanting Robots*, 64, 126.

[32] Turkle, *Alone Together*; Richardson, "The Human Relationship in the Ethics of Robotics."

[33] Musiał, *Enchanting Robots*, 123.

Acknowledging this hybridity involves re-examining the distinction between relationality and relationship, which we find pertains to our assumptions about humans and non-humans, and evaluations of how we relate to them. To recapitulate these evaluations:

1. advocate only species-specific sociality, as Richardson does,[34] thus curbing interactions with non-humans and robots (or at least sharply distinguishing these from those with humans);
2. pursue robots that are ever more human-like and are made in the ideal image of the human, which is the techno-solutionist approach and a variant of the first that prioritises human(like) – that is, anthropomorphic – relationships;
3. design robots that are not so much anthropomorphic but anthropocentric in that, in spite of their zoomorphic aesthetic, they are instrumental to users'/humans' desires;
4. collapse the distinction between persons and things by enchanting things (as per limited readings of animism), making relationships viable or disenchanting persons, making relationalities more satiating (this could link to (2) or (3)); or
5. re-envision relations – which encompasses ethics and the image of the human – to accommodate better for variations of otherness, which is the approach suggested by Herzfeld's and Foerst's work, among others, and to which I turn to in the penultimate section.

Across these evaluations, there is a presumption that, often for better or for worse, 'you are what you relate to'. Despite some claims to the fixity of notions of humanness, we thus find that humanness is ultimately dependent on relations that both precede and emerge from individuals. How, then, might we better understand our humanness in the context of such multifaceted relations – *relationalities and relationships* – with robots? Another way to frame this question might be to ask: can we ever think beyond our anthropomorphic and anthropocentric assumptions, particularly in the robotic context where, like a funhouse hall of mirrors, our human image is not only rife but sacralised and yet poorly understood?

ETHICISING RELATIONSHIPS

In 1785, philosopher Immanuel Kant proposed a 'formula of humanity', which insisted humans should only ever be treated as *ends* – that is, they are important and to be valued in their own right – whereas

---

[34] Richardson, "The Human Relationship in the Ethics of Robotics," 81.

animals were regarded as *means*, that is, their value is only relative to humans and should not be considered as intrinsic or inherent. This has long been important for thinking about the ethics of human and non-human relationships, extending to those involving robots as well as animals. Kant's distinction, though, is based on substantive assumptions about humanity – namely, that humans are rational beings, and animals, which Descartes had previously described as 'living machines', were irrational – and as such, Kant's view indicates an indirect (or, perhaps more aptly, a dialectic) expression of anthropomorphism. The question that ensues, which helps us to consider *imago hominis* and human–robot relationships, is to what extent the suggestion of human uniqueness and the resultant equivalence between animals and robots are valid positions that can be used to evaluate such relationships.

In spite of claims made about the enchantment of robots in one direction (highlighting liveliness), and Descartes' reference to animals as 'living machines' in the other (highlighting inertness), there does seem to be an intuitive difference between animals and robots. Donath presents this distinction based on sentience: "We have ethical responsibilities to sentient beings that we do not have to non-sentient objects: it is cruel to kick a dog, but not a rock."[35] Robots, however, seem to demand more ethical responsibility from humans than a rock, which largely seems to be a result of their appearance or behaviours – in other words, how they are presented and perceived. We have already seen how part of this affirms Heider and Simmel's claims in the 1940s about the projection of emotion and motive onto moving shapes, but it also casts light on our moral and ethical sensibilities and how relationships with robots might be inculcated into those.

Case studies such as responses to Boston Dynamics' viral and controversial videos suggest that we exhibit a compulsion to extend moral sentiments to robots in our interactions and relationships with them. Although Kant's framework to distinguish between human ends and non-human means has proved problematic in some ways for the ontological impasse that robots present (between their mechanical nature and their lively appearance), Kantian ethics that derive from this distinction offer an alternative interpretation. Kant's ethical maxims can support the assumption that our humanness is distinct from animals while concomitantly seeing our *humaneness* as bound up with our treatment of others, including non-human others. Put differently, humans should not intentionally harm non-humans – not for the same reason that it would be

---

[35] Donath, "Ethical Issues in Our Relationship with Artificial Entities," 53.

wrong to harm other humans as ends but because such actions would fall short of our moral standing as humans and of the requirement that this imposes on us to practise kindness and compassion. (The language of moral *actors* and moral *patients* speaks to this difference as well as the responsibilities that the former has to the latter.) This perspective moves somewhat from seeing robots in the image of the human (although arguably a dialectic anthropomorphism prevails) but places more of an emphasis on ethics in the face (literally, for social robots) of the other *as other*.

Recognition of the other *as other*, and not reducible solely to the non/human binary, we recall, corresponds in theological anthropology to a relational perspective. In terms of relations involving animals, Genesis 1:20–25 speaks of the creation and the blessing of creatures, many of which were made on the sixth day, the same as humans. While Genesis 1:26–31 goes on to order creatures and the earth to humans' dominion, it also notes the value of animals to God, thereby establishing a theocentric relationship (i.e., between creatures and God) that comes prior to an anthropocentric one (i.e., between animals and humans). Theocentric relationships, according to the theologians who discuss and advocate them, have an opportunity to model God's intrarelatedness and relatedness with creation through, for example, the human need for – and indeed, predisposition to – partnership (Genesis 2:18), which is at once ontological and ethical. Joshua K. Smith is one such theologian; he argues that, "if people are going to enter a relationship with non-human entities, especially one that looks human, it needs, to a degree, to be a relationship of dignity and respect."[36] This suggests a relational recognition of otherness and thus value in and of the robot, which is a precursor to relationship. Such a perspective resists reductively anthropomorphic and anthropocentric perspectives in that value is not to be determined either intrinsically (substantively, i.e., in the image of the human) or externally (in the other's functional or use value) but relationally, grounded in ethical obligations and responsibilities. To be sure, a degree of anthropomorphism that Smith retains in the quotation somewhat belies this point, as the indication is that the human image makes robots more worthy of dignity and respect, but this critique serves to highlight the fine-grained tensions and ambiguities between substantive and relational accounts of what makes us human and what of that is (needed to be) shared or passed on to robots.

---

[36] Joshua K. Smith, 2021, *Robot Theology: Old Questions through New Media*, Wipf and Stock, 59.

What theological views such as Smith's represent are an alternative way to consider relationships with robots, beyond the question of the independent value or status of robots, expressed as their 'rights' but recognising the demands of responsibility and relationship with others that can extend to include robots. How compelling this case for a relational approach to robots is in a world in which we expect both so much and so little from broadly anthropomorphic and anthropocentric robots, largely based on a substantive approach that correlates to theological discussions of *imago Dei*, remains to be seen. The underlying question is one of how we see ourselves in relation to how we see and value others, and how this is reflected and challenged by the refractions of ourselves we find in the robots that we design, purchase and relate to.

REFLECTING (ON) RELATIONSHIPS

All of this is to say that we don't approach robots in an intellectual or cultural vacuum. Models of human(e)ness and relationship inform our hopes, fears, fascination, trepidation – in short, our expectations – about relationships with robots.

Christian theological anthropology speaks of humans made in the image of God, which has been figured as how we are rational beings (substantive), how we are stewards over the rest of creation (functional) and how we engage in relationships with God and others (relational). Herzfeld once argued that these models have informed developments in robotics; I have suggested here how they can likewise inform the ethics of our relationships with them. On the one hand, we seek rational and emotional robots; yet on the other, we find this to be compelling in image and appearance only, rather than anything more *substantial* or adequate as a basis for the relationship. We design robots that can be put to service our social and individual needs, for example in terms of productivity or well-being, yet we also want more from these robots in terms of friendship, which risks blurring the lines between roles and *functions*, or ends and means.

What, then, about a relational relationship between humans and robots? Answering this question requires thinking beyond the conflicting desires and realities expressed by substantive and functional models of relationships with robots. To be sure, each of these has notable appeals as well as shortcomings that can be framed by different models of relationships, humanness and robotic design, including those that speak to our sense of uniqueness in the world. Robots don't so much *reflect* our human capacities and aims – in short, our *image* as humans (*imago hominis*) – as they *refract* them, challenging us to see ourselves differently amid our multitude of relations. I have suggested here that themes of anthropomorphism and anthropocentrism, and experiences of affect, attachment and alterity, underwrite many of these tensions (for better and for worse), whereas a relational model of relationships may help us to manage our expectations and perceptions of social robots, seeing them as companions to think-with, rather than to simply reject or find solutions in.

BIBLIOGRAPHY

Buber, Martin. 2013 [1937]. *I and Thou*, trans. Ronald Gregor Smith. Bloomsbury.

Donath, Judith. 2020. "Ethical Issues in Our Relationship with Artificial Entities." In *The Oxford Handbook of Ethics and AI*, ed. Markus D. Dubber, Frank Pasquale and Sunit Das. Oxford University Press.

Dumouchel, Paul and Damiano, Luisa. 2017. *Living with Robots*, trans. Malcolm DeBevoise. Harvard University Press.

Foerst, Anne. 2005. *God in the Machine: What Robots Teach Us about Humanity and God*. Plume

Heider, Fritz and Simmel, Marianne. 1944. "An Experimental Study of Apparent Behaviour." *The American Journal of Psychology* 57, 243–259.

Herzfeld, Noreen. 2002. *In Our Image: Artificial Intelligence and the Human Spirit*. Augsburg Fortress.

Huang, Lixiao et al. 2021. "Toward a Generalised Model of Human Emotional Attachment." *Theoretical Issues in Ergonomics Science* 22(2), 178–199.

Mori, Masahiro, MacDorman, K. F. and Kageki, N. 2012. "The Uncanny Valley [From the Field]." *IEEE Robotics & Automation Magazine* 19(2), 98–100.

Musiał, Maciej. 2019. *Enchanting Robots: Intimacy, Magic, and Technology*. Palgrave Macmillan.

O'Gieblyn, Meghan. 2021. "A Dog's Inner Life: What a Robot Pet Taught Me about Consciousness." *The Guardian*, 10 August. www.theguardian.com/science/2021/aug/10/dogs-inner-life-what-robot-pet-taught-me-about-consciousness-artificial-intelligence.

Richardson, Kathleen. 2019. "The Human Relationship in the Ethics of Robotics: A Call to Martin Buber's I and Thou." *AI & Society* 34, 75–82.

Samani, Hooman Aghaebrahimi et al. 2010. "Towards a Formulation of Love in Human–Robot Interaction." In *19th IEEE International Symposium on Robot and Human Interactive Communication*, Institute of Electrical and Electronics Engineers.

2011. "A Design Process for Lovotics." *HRPR* 2010, 118–125.

Smith, Joshua K. 2021. *Robot Theology: Old Questions through New Media*. Wipf and Stock.

Turkle, Sherry. 2005 [1984]. *The Second Self: Computers and the Human Spirit*. MIT Press.

2011. *Alone Together: Why We Expect More from Technology and Less from Each Other*. Basic Books.

Part III
Religious Studies

13 The Anthropology and Sociology of Religion and AI

BETH SINGLER

INTRODUCTION

This chapter introduces social scientific perspectives and methods applicable to observing the relationship between artificial intelligence (AI) and religion. We discuss the contributions that anthropological and sociological approaches can make to this entanglement of two modern social phenomena while also drawing attention to the inherent biases and perspectives that both fields bring with them due to their histories. Examples of research on religion and AI are highlighted, especially when they demonstrate agile and new methodologies for engaging with AI in its many applications; including but not limited to online worlds, multimedia formats, games, social media and the new spaces made by technological innovations such as the platforms underpinning the gig economy. All these AI-enabled spaces can be entangled with religious and spiritual conceptions of the world.

However, as both field and object, AI is more often conceived of as a secular topic with no relationship to religion; in some cases, it can even be apprehended as a *secularising* force on the world that will enable the inevitable decline of religion and its irrationalities. In my ethnographic research, I have found that there can be a blind spot in AI discourse – both publicly and even in academia – around the relationship AI has both with individual religions and with 'religion' as a concept. This Cambridge Companion seeks to fill this lacuna with chapters from experts whose research evidences the very real and vital interactions between AI and specific religions.

This chapter aims to expand upon the relationship between AI and religion as it is perceived as a general concept or object within human society and civilisation. I explain how both anthropology and sociology can provide frameworks for conceptualising that relationship and give us ways to account for our narratives of secularisation – informed by AI

223

development – that see religion as a remnant of a prior, less rational, stage of human civilisation.

First, it is necessary to discuss what we mean by anthropology and sociology, including what these two fields understand themselves as, how they are linked and what subjects both fields are interested in observing, categorising, theorising and (hopefully) understanding.

THE DICHOTOMIES OF THE ANTHROPOLOGY AND SOCIOLOGY OF RELIGION

This chapter does not offer a detailed and exhaustive history of anthropology and sociology. Such a history would give us the key figures, the renowned publications and a list of institutions that have supported departments in these fields when they were finally considered legitimate by their peers. However, such an exhaustive chronology might not reflect on how these 'human sciences' have positioned themselves within the academy and with each other. I propose that this positioning is more relevant to the current topic of AI and religion because it relates directly to how each of these two subjects are perceived and how they are understood as interacting.

Moreover, a detailed chronology of these two academic fields will barely cover AI, as this is a much more recent focus of discussion for anthropology and sociology. Instead, we start with religion, which has truly been one of the core foundation blocks on which the approaches of anthropology, and subsequently sociology, have been built. In reflecting on how anthropology and sociology have engaged with the topic of religion, we will see how similar approaches might be applied to AI and, after that, AI and religion.

First, we should note that these two contemporary human sciences are dedicated to treating the phenomena of religious belief and practice as neutrally as possible without discussion of the truth or validity of such phenomena. These fields also support self-reflection on our perspectives as ethnographers – 'one who describes a culture' – as much as they call to 'bracket off' questions of the ontological reality of the human phenomena and culture we observe. This objectivity was not always the case; in their earliest forms, ethnographies were shaped by particular views on ideas held in tension. These are the critical dichotomies of anthropology and sociology that I lay out here before considering what might still be valuable in these theoretical tools to study religion and AI.

Anthropology is the older of the two disciplines, but the earliest anthropologists 'in the field' predated the establishment of anthropology itself as a recognisable and named subject. In the eighteenth and nineteenth centuries, anthropologists were the missionaries, clerks, civil servants, linguists, administrators and explorers who had been sent to manage or transform indigenous cultures worldwide as they were absorbed into the British Empire and other nation-bodies. The observations and records of men sent to foreign lands became the first ethnographic resources for academics back in Western society's renowned universities. The first ethnographers were also predominantly men, although the wives and daughters of these missionaries, clerks, etc. also made contributions, including translation, transcription and field notes, even if they were rarely credited. Biological anthropology, as we would call it now, had also emerged by this time, focusing on physical comparison and similarities between what they would come to see as 'kinds' of humans. These patterns would eventually be explained with Charles Darwin's *On the Origin of the Species* in 1859. Many of these first 'anthropologists' approached religious behaviour in ways that shaped the nascent field and relied on a specific view of history: the presumption that these indigenous cultures were examples of humanity at an earlier stage in its inevitable 'civilising' process.

Therefore, the journey to the 'primitive' became a journey into the past, to see humanity in its simplest form and observe the easiest to understand conditions of culture. Similarly, religion was presumed to be complex and rich in its meanings in the 'West' but more straightforward to comprehend in its primitive forms. Of course, this view was very much a product of its time. It is possible now to deride early anthropologists for their attempts at such 'time travel', but many of the theories still cited today were grounded in this first dichotomy: the primitive and the civilised.

Émile Durkheim, who gave shape to sociology in the late 1800s with his publications and founding of the academic journal *L'Anee Sociologique*, wrote *The Elementary Forms of Religious Life*, drawing on primary reports of indigenous cultures he had acquired from others' first-hand accounts. He was confident that through primitive religion, we could understand all religion and religiosity:

> If we have taken primitive religion as the subject of our research it is because it has seemed to us better adapted than any other to lead to an understanding of the religious nature of man, that is to say, to show us an essential and permanent aspect of humanity.[1]

---

[1] Émile Durkheim, 1915, *The Elementary Forms of the Religious Life, a Study in Religious Sociology*, G. Allen & Unwin/Macmillan, 2.

His research method highlights another dichotomy that has traditionally characterised the difference between anthropology and sociology: 'here' and 'there'. After the missionaries, clerks, civil servants, et al., and the 'armchair' anthropologists and sociologists such as Durkheim, there came the anthropologists who went into the field. Such an experience became a necessary rite of passage for the culture of anthropology itself, and the discipline gained a reputation for only examining and describing cultures, again often represented as 'primitive', that resided somewhere over *there*.

In contrast, as disciplinary boundaries were developing, sociology became the study of *here*: a way to remark on the transitions and shifts in large 'Western' cultures and societies. Globalisation and modernity have in more recent decades blurred the lines between *here* and *there* and the small and large scale, with anthropologists entering the field to examine work culture, for instance, in tech firms or operations *here*,[2] and with sociologists emerging in the very cultures over *there* that had once been dismissed as 'primitive' during the two disciplines' beginnings.

Emerging from Durkheim's 'armchair' research on the functions of religion in society is another dichotomy that has shaped both anthropology and sociology: the sacred and the profane.

While definitions of religion abound, scholars recognise that humans can give specific attention and treatment to some ideas, words, objects, metaphors, narratives, places and individuals over others. They posited that these things are held as sacred while the ordinary and mundanely treated is profane. Durkheim suggested that how the world is divided into the sacred and the profane, and how that distinction is maintained through hierarchies, rituals, words and meanings, is the originator and maintainer of human society itself. More contemporary scholars have recognised that the boundary between the two is an ever-changing line and that attention is not the only marker of the sacred.

However, that recognition also led scholars to ideas of disenchantment, demystification and secularisation as anthropologists and sociologists noted the removal of the control of the sacred from its traditional places – predominantly over 'here' in the Western, 'modern', world. German sociologist Max Weber (1864–1920) gave us the view of modernity, industrialisation, mechanisation and bureaucratisation as the harbingers of the doom of the sacred. The dichotomies we lay out here were also often treated as overlapping and congruous arrangements: as

---

[2]   See, e.g., Alex Taylor, 2019, "The Data Centre as Technological Wilderness," *Culture Machine* 18.

sacred was to profane, then primitive was to civilised. And therefore, it was thought, with the trappings of civilisation, the sacred was lost.

In the 1980s and 1990s, sociologists looked to the *here*, the 'civilised' world, and noted what they thought was the decline of religion. This moment highlights another dichotomy, with sociology often presumed to be more quantitative than anthropology's qualitative approach – but both now use mixed methods. Later, this theory about the decline of religion, the 'secularisation thesis', was altered and adapted to fit numbers and statistics globally that increasingly indicated growth and invigoration in some new religions and subgroups of traditional religions. Moreover, self-reflexive discussion began to note that it was the case that the sacred could not always be captured in the gaze of anthropologists and sociologists working with a very narrow conception of religion based upon a specific Christian, Protestant, model. Some argue that these responses to the secularisation thesis diluted religion and its definition and that the sacred should not be a label applied to every single action that humans contemplate, ritualise or hold up as necessary, as in Edward Bailey's concept of implicit religion that included collective and enthusiastic activities such as football.[3]

However, while modernity was blamed for the move from collectivism to individualism – and we can again note this dichotomy in the two disciplines as anthropology has been seen as the study of the individual and sociology as the study of society – it also brought greater connectivity and globalisation that evidenced the vibrancy of religiosity that did not fit the Western Protestant Christian model. Not just over 'there' but 'here' as well. There were new forms of traditional religions, new schisms, new religious movements and new spiritualities all finding space and membership in an increasingly connected world. Whereas Weber described the technology (of his time) as restricting religion in an 'iron cage' of increasing rationality and bureaucracy, in the twentieth and twenty-first centuries, anthropologists and sociologies saw technology as enabling charismatic eruptions, new ways of controlling the sacred and new communities. However, this is not an uncontested interpretation, with much discussion by anthropologists and sociologists on the validity of belief online and on how community can form and be maintained.

Moreover, the secularisation thesis in its simplest form – religion is simply declining as the world becomes more rational – was both

---

[3] Edward Bailey, 1997, *Implicit Religion in Contemporary Society*, Kok Pharos Publishing House.

fed by and in turn fed larger metanarratives of the end of religiosity that have their origins as far back as the Enlightenment, if not before.[4] This story of historical decline has had more impact on public discourse than any number of more nuanced and self-reflexive anthropological and sociological papers on the unevenly distributed processes of secularisation, differentiation, disenchantment, re-enchantment, resacralisation, implicit religion, invented religion or new religious movements.

If the public was ever made aware of examples of the vitality of religiosity in the world right now through the media, it was often framed in a negative light and again around those dichotomies, that is, accounts of the rise of religious fundamentalism happening over 'there', occurring among 'primitive' peoples. Donald Trump's presidency and the conversation around the religious and alt-right in technologically advanced modern America should have countered this binary view. Still, too often, alt-right, MAGA or QAnon-supporting American Christian evangelicals were dismissed in the media as primitives of another sort. This framing prevents truly tackling the genuine dangers of fundamentalism by dismissing it as solely the domain of the uneducated or the uncivilised.[5] A broader version of this dismissive stance is, of course, to be found in the media writing about religion as a whole. And this media account of religious decline also contributes to the public view that this strictly narrow version of secularisation, as the 'end of religion', is still occurring in the twenty-first century.

Having considered anthropology and sociology's emergence as disciplines through their approaches to the topic of religion, we now consider what response they might have to AI as an apparently epoch-defining technology of this current age.

THE DICHOTOMIES OF AI

Other chapters in this Companion define technical terms and highlight specific applications of AI and specific religious responses. This chapter considers what can be learned from anthropological and sociological approaches, especially those methodologies drawn from these

---

[4] Jason Josephson Storm, 2017, *The Myth of Disenchantment*, University of Chicago Press.

[5] See, for example, American talk-show host Bill Maher's pejorative comments: www.newsweek.com/bill-maher-cpac-woodstock-mentally-impaired-evangelicals-made-trump-believe-1357328, September 2019.

disciplines' prior considerations of religion. These approaches can illuminate the relationship between AI and religion and show what we think AI *is* and how that conception of AI relates to our conceptions of religion. This section begins with the conception of AI; from anthropological and sociological perspectives, AI is much more than a mere technological definition can fully encapsulate.

First, I propose that we start with current forms of 'narrow', or limited purpose, AI as tools of, and responses to, bureaucracy (and this interpretation should remind us of Max Weber's descriptions and models of societal and religious change). In its current form and applications, AI is an attempt to manage and control the ever-growing masses of data produced by humans by replicating our capacity for handling smaller amounts of day-to-day data and then scaling upwards. Seeing AI as an experimental simulation of intelligence in the quest to understand human intelligence further is also a valid interpretation and is bound to shape the direction of the technology. However, in most real-world AI applications, pattern recognition is put to specific ends on large datasets. Such ends include but are not limited to diagnosing illnesses, selecting candidates for a job, making predictions about human interests or offering solutions to logistical problems.

Of course, interacting with and attempting to comprehend the implications of such a substantial amount of human data is, in many cases, optional. But that choice is increasingly driven by the desire for profit. This motivation exists only in human actors, not the algorithms they put to work, convincing us that we desire or need a particular commodity. Thus, anthropology and sociology can, at this very initial level of our consideration of AI, be useful in highlighting the presence of humans as either the primary decision-makers already very much 'in the loop' in the creation of the artificial decision-making systems that we are employing, or as low-paid global workers that have been hidden away in the engine room of the AI to maintain the pretence of a more advanced intelligence than is currently possible.[6]

Understanding contemporary narrow uses of AI as the analytic tools of modernity's bureaucracy also means that we can place AI itself within the dichotomies of anthropology and sociology that we have already discussed and initially categorise it as 'here'-based, civilised and profane. To a certain extent, this categorisation holds up. There are those in the entrepreneurial sphere to which this view of AI is the only one; those actors in the AI discourse who do not speculate on AI's

---

[6]   See for instance, Kate Crawford, 2021, *Atlas of AI*, University of Yale Press.

nature, only on its near-term, commercial applications. However, in my ethnographic fieldwork, I have found very few figures in the AI ecosystem who do not also scan the horizon and tell stories of what AI might potentially be in the future.

Before we also locate such future-focused fringe interpretations of AI in the schema available to us from anthropology and sociology, it is worth noting that the narrow interpretations of AI as a simple tool do also draw from a wellspring of scientistic rationalism that also informs the view of the secularisation process that public audiences have been taught to expect. The application of narrow forms of AI will also, some believe, lead to the ultimate eradication of human irrationalities. Examples of this 'AI is rationalising' narrative include proposals that we replace human judges who make wrong decisions about sentencing because they are hungry, or the doctors who will not choose the best candidates for successful transplants because of naïve intuitions and sentimentalities. In this view, many other kinds of messy human choices could be made wrongly in split-second decisions because of 'gut feelings', themselves the product of millions of years of messy, undirected human evolution. These irrational behaviours and more could be – this account of AI proposes – corrected with dispassionate, intentionally evolved and perfected AI, so why not the more extensive and damaging irrational behaviours such as religion?

Therefore, for some proponents of the greater rationality of AI, AI can be secularising not only because it is presumed to be a profane, civilised object emblematic of modernity here and now but also because even narrow AI can actively work against our worst intuitions and biases and promote neutrality and rationality by replacing humans making critical decisions.

All of which, of course, ignores the bias we can implant in any automated decision-making system that operates on the algorithmic logic of using humanity's historical data to make new predictions and decisions. Moreover, this view of the narrow functions of AI as rational ignores quite how often we dream into being versions of AI that are anthropomorphised, personified, agential and even super-agential and godlike – ideas of AI that themselves exhibit the very magical thinking that artificial rationality is often described as capable of eradicating.

To explore this conception of AI here, I draw on another anthropological framework, one that has historically been applied to the 'primitive' and the 'other' over 'there', but which I see as valuable for understanding how we conceive of AI, and further, how AI and religion are entangled. That is the concept of *liminality*.

THE ANTHROPOLOGY AND SOCIOLOGY OF RELIGION AND AI   231

Arnold Van Gennep coined the term liminality in his book *Les Rites de Passage* (1909) to refer to the condition that the ritual participant exists in after separation from the community and before being incorporating back into it with a new status. It is the "betwixt and between"[7] in which the ritual's recipient exists, where they are neither, for example, a girl or a woman, a boy or a man, or an outsider or an insider. The concept of liminality has grown beyond the ritual process and rites of passage to be applied to any entity that is neither one thing nor another but 'in-between'. Illustrations of the idea might include entities that cross boundaries and transgress simple definitions. Examples include the centaur in Greek mythology (both wild and sagacious) and the ghost (both dead but living).

AI can also be understood as a liminal entity because we graft many interpretations and expectations onto it. It is a technology, but it is also seen as a (potential) person. It is a tool, but some can also see it as an agent. In our pictures 'of' AI, we embody it (in the robot ordinarily) and offer illustrations that are nebulous and ethereal, as though it is disembodied and otherworldly. Many of these ethereal illustrations draw on tropes and aesthetics from established religious accounts of the world, for instance the reworking of theistic Creation imagery in the AI Creation Meme.[8] AI is already here in many applications and automated decision-making systems. Still, it is also something of 'the future', which is over there: ever coming and bringing with it a new age, echoing existing eschatologies in many religious narratives.

In being a betwixt and between entity in our imaginations, we can recognise that AI also partakes of the opposing factors in the dichotomies we have already discussed: it is also primitive, over there, sacred and communally conceived. Specifically, we can see that our metaphors and narratives about superintelligent or superagential AI draw on the same cultural milieu and mythos that early anthropologists characterised as the more straightforward expression of religiosity than their modern home culture.

Does this mean that time-travelling anthropologists and sociologists now need to recognise time as a loop? That they sought to rediscover the simplistic origins of religion away from the modernity they emerged in, only now to find that contemporary discursive constructions

---

[7] Victor Turner, 1967, "Betwixt and between: The Liminal Period in His Book Rites of Passage," in *The Forest of Symbols*, ed. Victor Turner, Cornell University Press.

[8] Beth Singler, 2020, "The AI Creation Meme: A Case Study of the New Visibility of Religion in Artificial Intelligence Discourse," *Religions* 11(5), 253.

of AI return us to being primitives seeing gods in thunder or, indeed, seeing a 'divine move' when AI succeeds at beating a human at playing the ancient strategy board game of go?[9]

The answer that the contemporary anthropology and sociology of religion can provide is a clear 'no'. Modern methodologies in these disciplines recognise that these dichotomies are blurring, just as we noted the traditional boundaries between the disciplines are themselves blurring. Just as recognising academic works on religion as either anthropological or sociological can come down to traditions and legacies passed from scholar to scholar, so then the placement of interpretations of AI into sacred/profane, there/here, primitive/civilised, communal/individual also relates to existing lenses.

For instance, with regard to new religious movements inspired by AI, the longstanding argument in the study of religion about what is and is not a religion readily rears its head. But it is also joined with debates about the 'harm' done in identifying a movement as a religion against its wishes. Calling something a religion has political, ideological and moral impacts that both the anthropology and sociology of religion have increasingly observed and recorded. Political, because power relationships are involved in the status of official religions recognised by states (as well as possible social power in remaining *outside* of such official recognition). Ideological, because maintaining certain definitions of religion aligns with specific agendas and concerns. And moral, because harm can be done by naming groups as new religious movements when they are vehemently opposed even to the concept of religion itself. This brings us to how anthropology and sociology can engage with the entanglements of these two subjects of interest – AI and religion – that both equally partake of liminality and interpretation when they become entangled with each other.

THE ANTHROPOLOGY AND SOCIOLOGY OF AI AND RELIGION

The previous mention of AI new religious movements highlights one entanglement of AI and religion. I have previously discussed this entanglement as part of an attempt at a fuller but not an exhaustive list of engagements between AI and religion. These were: (1) the reinvigoration of established religions through the debates around personhood

---

[9] GameOfGo.App, "The Divine Move," https://gameofgo.app/learn/go-game-online-the-divine-move.

THE ANTHROPOLOGY AND SOCIOLOGY OF RELIGION AND AI 233

that future speculations about AI can inspire; (2) the enhanced role for religion in assisting society and individuals in the face of inequalities exasperated by AI and automation; and (3) the development of specific AI new religious movements (bearing in mind concerns about calling something annew religious movement or religion).[10] Further, I have also noted in this chapter and elsewhere[11] the close relationship between strongly atheist, or even 'new atheist', interpretations of the world and AI. This is an assumption I have more frequently encountered in the public discourse around AI than the idea that AI will inspire new religions and more fervid religiosity.

Even while bearing in mind the fluidity of the boundaries and categories we have inherited from the anthropology and sociology of religion, there is much to be said in an ethnographic frame about how AI and religion are entangled in each other. As Fenn explains, anthropologists and sociologists understand religion through developments in "the relation of religion to social systems."[12] Likewise, AI is the social system of the time writ into computer code. Even our visions of the AI future in science fiction and non-fiction speculative accounts replicate and enhance existing social relations, biases and interests.

However, it is worth noting that just as secular, 'profane' interpretations of AI push away from its relationship with religion as a concept, particular religions have likewise pushed away AI as a technology that does not reflect their values. For instance, discussion on online Islamic forums about AI and robots has involved theological concerns about robots as attempts to usurp god's primacy as a creator by making them resemble humans.[13] Online Christian discussions have also made similar points about AI regarding their specific theological understandings of *imago Dei*, god as creator and the human soul.[14] Such arguments are tackled in Chapters 3 to 7, specifically in those about specific religious

[10] Beth Singler, 2017, "An Introduction to Artificial Intelligence and Religion for the Religious Studies Scholar," *Implicit Religion* 20(3), Special Issue: Artificial Intelligence and Religion, ed. Beth Singler.

[11] Beth Singler, 2022, "Origin and the End: Artificial Intelligence, Atheism and, Imaginaries of the Future of Religion," in *Emerging Voices in Science and Theology: Contributions by Young Women*, ed. Bethany Sollereder and Alistair McGrath, Routledge.

[12] Richard K. Fenn, 2003, "Editorial Commentary: Looking for Boundaries of the Field: Social Anthropology, Theology, and Ethnography," in *The Blackwell Companion to the Sociology of Religion*, ed. Richard K. Fenn, Blackwell Publishing Ltd.

[13] Islam.stackexchange.com, "Is It Haram to Make Humanoid Robots?," https://islam .stackexchange.com/questions/2320/is-it-haram-to-make-humanoid-robots.

[14] Laurence Tamatea, 2008, "If Robots R-US, Who Am I? Online 'Christian' Responses to Artificial Intelligence," *Culture and Religion* 9(2), 141–160.

traditions. But such arguments about AI and *imago Dei* can also be understood anthropologically as attempts to regain control over the "discursive construction of the self."[15]

That is not to say that rejection is the only mode of response; for instance, some scholars of Islam highlight the early technological adoptions of Middle Eastern cultures and the synergy of future-focused views of AI and transhumanism with longstanding Islamic philosophical schools.[16] I have named the other possible responses as adoption and adaptation: the acceptance and use of AI and the adjustment to its existence. Anthropology and sociology provide methods for examining these entanglements and for theorising them. Here we discuss these methods, with examples from both AI and religion, and what we might learn from them regarding understanding the moments when these two areas of interest intersect.

METHODS

First, I intentionally referred to 'moments' in the previous paragraph. Unlike the traditional foci of anthropology and sociology that could often be bounded by a location, it has been my experience that a temporal frame is often the best way to encapsulate the field site of religion and AI. This difference is mostly due to the latter of those two topics. Whereas religion, in many of its forms, is physically institutional in such a way that the ethnographer can visit and observe, AI is active in our systems in many invisible ways and embodied in examples of automation that are often designed to replace humans and remove them from the locale (including the potential ethnographer) such as in the factory. Indeed, many people interact with AI through their phones and apps every day but are unaware that they do; or some misapply the term 'AI' to many elementary systems and sensors, such as the infrared-based devices in modern cars that merely recognise the proximity of the correct keys and unlock the doors.

Instead, I argue that observing the relationship between AI and religion as an ethnographer requires reacting to what Hine called "Internet Events" in her guide to digital ethnography.[17] Of course, events IRL ('in real life') also provide opportunities for the participant

---

[15] Tamatea, "If Robots R-US, Who Am I?," 144.
[16] Biliana Popova, 2020, "Islamic Philosophy and Artificial Intelligence: Epistemological Arguments," *Zygon, Journal of Religion and Science* 55(4), 977–995.
[17] Christine Hine, 2000, *Virtual Ethnography*, Sage.

THE ANTHROPOLOGY AND SOCIOLOGY OF RELIGION AND AI   235

observer, but they can be equally fleeting. For instance, observing the public reaction to a Church of England press conference on their new downloadable 'skill' for Google's AI assistant Alexa that helps people recite the Lord's Prayer. Or sharing the energy in a room of entrepreneurs excitedly watching the presentation of a charismatic voice in the academic AI conversation who had been paid to speak at a large tech exhibition.

The latter example also highlights another method of this approach to AI and religion: paying attention to the content of the moment, be it online or offline. The figure on the stage drew on specific tropes, narratives and metaphors familiar from established religious traditions while performing in the secular space of the tech conference. The researcher of AI and religion must be aware of these moments of religious appropriation and application. As discussed, the sociology of religion had in the twentieth century theorised this transference of religious terminology and metaphor from the sacred to the profane as proof of the inevitable march of secularisation. Instead, this method of paying attention to eruptions of the sacred amid the profane might also lead us to more deeply understand the socially disruptive nature of the sacred, as it was described by the sociologists themselves, even as they laid the groundwork for a teleological view of the end of religion.

As noted, religion tends more to embodiment than AI, so what of AI and religion? Can we apply observational methods gained from centuries of observing rituals (both 'there' and 'here')? This question seems more readily answerable when the focus is the emergence of AI applications from within established religions. For instance, the aforementioned Church of England Lord's Prayer skill for Alexa. Or the development of specific religious robots such as 'Mindar', an avatar of the Bodhisattva Kannon, unveiled in Tokyo in 2019.[18] Or the 'BlessU-2' robot priest unveiled as a part of the 500th anniversary celebrations of the Reformation in Wittenberg, Germany, in 2017.[19] These embodied examples bring the relationship of AI and religion into focus, but more than that, they enable the ethnographer to observe ritual actions concerning AI.

Outside of established religions, we also need to draw on the experience and methods of those who study modern, tech-savvy new religious

---

[18]   Asia News, 2019, "Kyoto Temple Gets Android Goddess of Mercy," www.asianews .it/news-en/Kyoto-temple-gets-android-goddess-of-mercy-46339.html.

[19]   Harriet Sherwood, 2017, "Robot Priest Unveiled in Germany to Mark 500 Years since Reformation," *The Guardian*, www.theguardian.com/technology/2017/may/ 30/robot-priest-blessu-2-germany-reformation-exhibition.

movements to provide approaches that can observe ritual, participation, community and charisma online. AI-focused new religious movements are the most apparent subjects for such methods. Moreover, new religious movements have also taught scholars of religion much more about the permeable boundaries of the concept of religion and where we can find the uncanny potency of the sacred before it is too far denuded of its charismatic power by the routinisation of religious bureaucracy. Observing the emergence, growth and decline of such AI-focused groups – whether they are explicit about being religious or not – requires skill in qualitative methods and the ability to handle large datasets such as social media or forum posts. AI, or at least machine-learning approaches, are also being used by digital humanities scholars to observe the fractal conversations occurring on many platforms. This method could also be applied to discussions around AI and religion.

Returning to the import of narratives in the study of religion and AI, we can also highlight field sites that operate according to the researchers' timetables, rather than the 'Internet events' that keep to their schedule. It is nearly impossible to maintain a real-time, panopticonic view of all discussions on social media. Still, media products and transmedia intellectual properties lend themselves more to select and steady consumption. For instance, computer games have taken up existing science fiction narratives around AI and robots and played with religious metaphors in framing their debates around personhood, liberty and eschatology.[20] Transmedia properties give a wide variety of mediums and remixings of these accounts and a large fandom with which the ethnographer can interact and bring the research back to the human interlocutor. This approach does require a responsive and agile methodology that recognises the validity and use of non-traditional primary sources. The original anthropologists might not have imagined such places over 'there' when they wrote their ethnographies, such as Margaret Mead and her 'Coming of Age' in Samoa, but the modern anthropologist and sociologist might well have had their own 'Coming of Age' amid such communities and virtual spaces.[21] Similarly, new employment spaces enabled by AI, such as gig economy roles with Lyft, Uber and others, are spaces for participant observation

[20] For example, Jonathan Tuckett, 2018, "The Talos Principle: Philosophical and Religious Anthropology," *Implicit Religion* 20(3), 259–277; and L. De Wildt et al., 2018, "'Things Greater than Thou': Post-Apocalyptic Religion in Games," *Religions* 9(169), https://doi.org/10.3390/rel9060169.

[21] For example, Tom Boellstorff, 2008, *Coming of Age in Second Life: An Anthropologist Explores the Virtually Human*, Princeton University Press.

and noting religious terminology when such jobs are guided by trust in an 'all-seeing' algorithm every day.[22]

Paying attention to transmedia properties also raises the participation side of the ethnographer's interaction with the field. Many computer games involve some form of avatarism; the player takes a role within the story. If hype about virtual reality and the coming 'Metaverse' is to be believed, this will only become a more dominant activity for us and focus for corporations, as we see with the pivot to the Metaverse by Meta, the company once known as Facebook. On occasion, the protagonist in these stories is themselves an artificial being (e.g., *NieR: Automata*, *The Talos Principle*, *Portal 2* and *Detroit: Become Human*), leading the ethnographer to partake in a kind of 'xeno-anthropology' or 'robo-anthropology' in taking on the persona of the artificial and interacting with its synthetic kin, and living within the stories we tell ourselves about AI and robots. Religion plays a role in many of these narratives, in the aesthetic and motifs but also in the eschatological storylines and the fluid uses of 'mind', 'consciousness' and 'personhood' by characters and how they overlap in the narratives with the religious concept of the 'soul'.

FUTURE RESEARCH DIRECTIONS AND AIMS

Anthropology and sociology have a very human-centred approach that is beneficial to considering AI and religion, especially when the former can obscure the humans still very much in the loop of the algorithmic systems we increasingly employ. Bearing this in mind, in this section I lay out some of the future directions that such research might take, as indicated by current interests and spaces of focus.

First, any complete consideration of the entanglements of AI and religion will require multidisciplinary approaches, including theological and philosophical methods and the observation-driven human sciences. Reporting on a particular religious response to AI or an element of AI discourse that repeats existing theistic concerns requires cultural and historical knowledge and the responsiveness of ethnographic methodologies. Between the disciplines, much can also be learned; philosophical anthropology that deduces what we understand the human to be in the light of AI can inform theological anthropology that has religious tenets in its foundations. Sociology's quantitative approach can

---

[22] Beth Singler, 2020, "Blessed by the Algorithm: Theistic Conceptions of Artificial Intelligence in Online Discourse," *AI & Society* 35, 945–955.

provide supporting evidence for cultural trends, while at the same time, reflexive anthropology can help us understand why some evidence is noted while others are not. This interdisciplinarity will also help to shape the research questions of this field as it advances.

Second, as we have noted, the locales and field sites of research into AI and religion will need to be temporal and responsive and take advantage of innovative technologies that provide new platforms for expressions of both AI and religious concerns. Research into AI and religion performed through social media, fiction and speculative non-fiction, film, television, computer games, virtual reality and other formats yet to be devised will also shape the field of AI and religion research – and we will see projects that take from McLuhan that the medium is also the message.[23]

Third, metaphor plays a significant role in AI and religion's relationship, and research that delves into the part of both ironic and unironic metaphor use will also be impactful in the human sciences' approach to this topic. A longstanding concern in the study of religion in the modern world has been the question of online speech's genuineness; some scholars take religious meme culture, parody and inventedness seriously as forms of religiosity. Some do not. I fall into the former camp, as I see that even in irony, we have continuities of thought that speak to the pervasive visibility of religion in the modern world. Likewise, in the AI and religion entanglement, we should see research that observes religious metaphors in discourse and ethnographies that reflect honourably how even secular spaces and individuals can be implicitly religious. 'Honourably' because just as the first anthropologists could do harm in casting the 'primitive' in a particular light, there is harm in casting the 'modern' in a way that goes beyond observation into judgement. Research that can walk this line will follow the more comprehensive ethical standard of ethnography, described once by my PhD supervisor as "being a person amongst people."[24]

Finally, again in terms of harms, anthropological and sociological research into AI and religion also has the opportunity to highlight ethical concerns within the field itself. While drawing attention to the metaphors of religion in AI (and even, perhaps, vice versa as 'human as machine' metaphors prevail), we could also draw attention to where such metaphors inspire extremes of hope and trust that might damage

---

[23]   Marshall McLuhan, 1964, *Understanding Media: The Extensions of Man*, McGraw Hill Education.

[24]   Dr Timothy Jenkins, Emeritus of Cambridge University, in conversation.

freedoms, limit opportunities and reduce the human to something less than it could be. Anthropologists and sociologists can highlight where we overly trust the systems we have created or where we sell our present to buy a future where we might not be allowed. Such eschatological thinking can be shown to draw on religious metaphors, so there is an argument for dismissing such concerns as 'it was ever thus', and yet, we can change the metaphors that we choose to live our lives by, and we can ensure they are driven by human-centred aspirations and hopes. The human sciences approach to AI and religion can at the very least make such metaphors apparent, as well as the motivations behind their dissemination in popular culture.

In this chapter, we began with the foundations of anthropology and sociology to demonstrate how their approaches to religion might be useful in understanding the values beneath our contemporary conceptions of AI and how AI and religion are in interplay. In doing so, I explored where flaws in the dichotomies of these two disciplines can illuminate the conversation about AI and religion. So, in looking back, we might then look forwards to new research approaches to AI and religion from within anthropology and sociology that take on board their formative ages and voices but also demonstrate reflexivity, responsiveness, honourable methods and horizon scanning for the next moment of entanglement between these two areas of societal impact. The examples of recent research that I have shared here demonstrate these four elements. I hope that further research in this field will also pursue these goals and bring a greater understanding of religion and AI as related entities to both the academy and public awareness.

BIBLIOGRAPHY

Bailey, Edward. 1997. *Implicit Religion in Contemporary Society*. Kok Pharos Publishing House.

Boellstorff, Tom. 2008. *Coming of Age in Second Life: An Anthropologist Explores the Virtually Human*. Princeton University Press

Durkheim, Émile. 1915. *The Elementary Forms of the Religious Life, a Study in Religious Sociology*. G. Allen & Unwin; Macmillan.

Fenn, Richard K. 2003. "Editorial Commentary: Looking for Boundaries of the Field: Social Anthropology, Theology, and Ethnography" in *The Blackwell Companion to the Sociology of Religion*, ed. Richard K. Fenn. Blackwell Publishing Ltd.

Hine, Christine. 2000. *Virtual Ethnography*. Sage.

McLuhan, Marshall. 1964. *Understanding Media: The Extensions of Man*. McGraw Hill Education.

Popova, Biliana. 2020. "Islamic Philosophy and Artificial Intelligence: Epistemological Arguments." *Zygon: Journal of Religion & Science* 55(4), 977–995.

Singler, Beth. 2017. "An Introduction to Artificial Intelligence and Religion for the Religious Studies Scholar." *Implicit Religion* 20(3), Special Issue: Artificial Intelligence and Religion, 215–231.

2020a. "The AI Creation Meme: A Case Study of the New Visibility of Religion in Artificial Intelligence Discourse." *Religions* 11(5), 253.

2020b. "Blessed by the Algorithm: Theistic Conceptions of Artificial Intelligence in Online Discourse." *AI & Society* 35, 945–955.

2022. "Origin and the End: Artificial Intelligence, Atheism and, Imaginaries of the Future of Religion", in *Emerging Voices in Science and Theology: Contributions by Young Women*, ed. Bethany Sollereder and Alistair McGrath. Routledge.

Storm, Jason Josephson. 2017. *The Myth of Disenchantment.* University of Chicago Press.

Tamatea, Laurence. 2008. "If Robots R-US, Who Am I? Online 'Christian' Responses to Artificial Intelligence." *Culture and Religion* 9(2), 141–160.

Taylor, Alex. 2019. "The Data Centre as Technological Wilderness." *Culture Machine* 18, The Nature of Data Centres, May.

Turner, Victor. 1967. *The Forest of Symbols: Aspects of Ndembu Ritual.* Cornell University Press.

FURTHER READING

Cusack, Carole. 2010. *Invented Religions: Imagination, Fiction and Faith.* Routledge.

Geraci, Robert M. 2010. *Apocalyptic AI: Visions of Heaven in Robotics, Artificial Intelligence, and Virtual Reality.* Oxford University Press.

Hamilton, Malcolm. 1994. *The Sociology of Religion: Theoretical and Comparative Perspectives.* Routledge.

Horst, Heather A. and Miller, Daniel eds. 2012. *Digital Anthropology.* Berg.

Lakoff, George and Johnson, Mark. 1980. *Metaphors We Live By.* University of Chicago Press.

14 Simulating Religion

F. LERON SHULTS AND WESLEY J. WILDMAN

In recent years there has been a significant growth in the use of computer models to study complex social systems, including 'religious' systems, in the social sciences and humanities. This approach enables scholars to analyse and explain connections between factors at various levels that influence the increase (or decrease) of religiosity in human minds and culture. Models that simulate religious phenomena can include salient variables at the micro level (e.g., strength of personal belief in God), the meso level (e.g., access to ritual participation) and the macro level (e.g., state support or oppression of religious coalitions). The most popular approach in the rapidly expanding field of computational science of religion is using agent-based models (ABMs), in which simulated religious (or non-religious) agents interact with one another and their environment in an 'artificial society'. Another common approach is to use system dynamics models (SDMs), in which the causal relations among system-level variables (rather than individual agents) are simulated and explored. This chapter provides examples of both types of model and outlines some of the philosophical issues associated with using these computational tools in the scientific study of religion.

But what does any of this have to do with the broader topic of this book? What does computational modelling and simulation of religion have to do with artificial intelligence (AI)? The latter typically evokes images of a machine that can simulate human or human-like intelligence, able to learn and complete – and maybe outperform individual humans in – tasks such as playing chess, calculating or processing information. That image of AI does apply in ABMs when the agents have sophisticated cognitive and learning abilities. In this context, however, we are also interested in two other ways of thinking about AI in relation to simulating religion. On the one hand, we consider the way AI functions within artificial societies composed of heterogeneous agents, something ABMs are well suited to explore. Real human intelligence, like real human religiosity, emerges in a dynamic social context and

241

social simulations enable scholars of religion to account for these environmental factors as well as the individual differences among religious agents and groups. On the other hand, we also consider the way a complex dynamical reality – say, an individual mind, an organisation or a society – can be intelligently expressed as a computational system, something SDMs are well suited to explore. ABMs help us focus more on the way system-level properties emerge from lower levels, whereas SDMs help us focus more on the non-linear dynamics of an intelligent system, including reinforcing and dampening loops and interaction effects. The ABM technology gives us a way to study the individual behaviour of intelligent agents and the emergent effects of networks of such agents; the SDM technology uncovers the 'internal intelligent dynamics' of a complex system, including human minds and social systems.

Answering research questions about 'religion' is complicated by the way in which causal processes are so entangled, by the fact that empirical studies are often correlational rather than causal and by the fragmentation of theories about religiosity. Simulating religion through computer modelling can demonstrate how fragmentary theories relate, untangle individual lines of causal influence, identify the relative importance of causal factors and their interactions, and enable experimentation that would never be possible (or ethical) in the real world. Thus, computational modelling using ABMs and SDMs is not only useful; it can generate understanding and advance research programs in ways that other methodologies cannot.

SIMULATING RELIGION WITH AGENT-BASED MODELS

ABMs simulate the behaviours and interactions among different entities (or agents) in an environment, as well as the ways in which that environment and the individuals mutually affect one another. This approach has grown in popularity among scholars of religion in recent years as its analytic and explanatory power has become increasingly clear.[1] Imagine a digital model of an artificial society in which agents with various levels of religious traits and tendencies engage with one another and their world. Then imagine that one can run simulation

---

[1] Kristoffer L. Nielbo, Donald M. Braxton and Afzal Upal, 2012, "Computing Religion: A New Tool in the Multilevel Analysis of Religion," *Method and Theory in the Study of Religion* 24(3), 267–290; Justin E. Lane, 2021, *Understanding Religion through Artificial Intelligence: Bonding and Belief*, Bloomsbury.

experiments in this world to discover the conditions under which – and the mechanisms by which – religious beliefs and behaviours change over time. The model can be 'initialised' or set up in such a way that the agents and the environment start the simulation with particular variables (e.g., low and high levels of anxiety about religious others) and then run multiple times under different parameters (e.g., low and high threats in the environment) to uncover the conditions under which anxiety crosses a threshold into violence. One of the main values of an ABM is that it can 'grow' a macro-level phenomenon of interest from micro- and meso-level agent behaviours and interactions, thereby lending plausibility to causal claims about the underlying mechanisms at work in religious change.

The validation of such models requires comparing the results of the simulation experiments to the real-world target being modelled. A validated ABM is essentially an experimental platform, allowing researchers to explore the space of dynamic possibilities in the real-world system by studying the corresponding possibility space in the virtual system and running 'what if' scenario testing. This is particularly useful for approaching phase transition dynamics in complex adaptive social systems, where the collective behaviour of AI agents transitions into a new regime. ABMs can shed light on interventions that open up pathways towards system behaviour regime changes, which is particularly important when researchers are invested in finding out how to move a system into a new regime (say, one in which religious people become less fearful of strangers) or to prevent such a transition (say, one in which religious people become willing to use religion to inspire and rationalise deadly violence).

Although cognitive and social scientists have been using ABMs for several decades to study issues more or less adjacent to 'religion', the application of these approaches more directly to the latter took off after the turn of the twenty-first century. William Sims Bainbridge's pioneering work in modelling 'religious cognition' launched the field. His major book on the topic illustrated the explanatory power of ABMs for the study of religion, addressing issues such as the role of recruitment, fellowship, segregation and trust in the formation and transformation of religious groups.[2] Other early models developed artificial societies in which other processes could be studied, such as the emergence of new religious movements through interactions among religious 'information

---

[2]   William Sims Bainbridge, 2006, *God from the Machine: Artificial Intelligence Models of Religious Cognition*, AltaMira Press.

entrepreneurs' and other agents interested in solving social problems,[3] or the maintenance of religious regionalism as simulated agents mobilise, associate and make religious choices.[4] However, most of these early models primarily conceptualised agents as 'rational actors' who were not placed in complex (or any) social networks. This relative lack of cognitive and social realism led many to wonder about the plausibility of their findings and the actual value of ABMs in the study of religion.

Such concerns led to a second generation of ABMs of religion that strove to develop more cognitively and emotionally complex agent architectures that could be placed within more sociologically and culturally realistic networks. This type of ABM is sometimes referred to as a multi-agent artificial intelligence (MAAI) model.[5] In order to construct, validate and calibrate a MAAI model of a complex religious system, it takes a village – or at least a crew of open-minded transdisciplinary collaborators. While quantitative and mathematical analyses of religious phenomena are helpful, realistic models also require insights that can only be acquired through qualitative social scientific research and the hermeneutical efforts of humanities scholars immersed in the historical details of particular groups. This is the thinking behind the participatory modelling approach called *human simulation*, which emerged out of several years of simulating religion with computer scientists, subject matter experts and other stakeholders.[6] Transdisciplinary teams have applied these techniques to a wide variety of topics such as the role of religiosity in terror management and simulating the emergence (and later dissipation) of higher levels of church attendance in the wake of natural and other hazards.[7]

MAAI approaches work especially well when tackling complex, controversial topics in the study of religion. For example, what are the conditions under which – and the mechanisms by which – xenophobic

[3] Muhammad Afzal Upal, 2005, "Simulating the Emergence of New Religious Movements," *Journal of Artificial Societies and Social Simulation*, 8(1), www.jasss .org/8/1/6.html.

[4] Laurence R. Iannaccone and Michael D. Makowsky, 2007, "Accidental Atheists? Agent-Based Explanations for the Persistence of Religious Regionalism," *Journal for the Scientific Study of Religion* 46(1), 1–16.

[5] Justin Lane, 2013, "Method, Theory, and Multi-agent Artificial Intelligence: Creating Computer Models of Complex Social Interactions," *Journal for the Cognitive Science of Religion* 1(2), 161–180.

[6] Saikou Diallo et al., eds, 2019, *Human Simulation: Perspectives, Insights, and Applications*, Springer.

[7] F. LeRon Shults et al., 2018, "Modeling Terror Management Theory: Computer Simulations of the Impact of Mortality Salience on Religiosity," *Religion, Brain & Behavior*, 8(1), 77–100.

anxiety within religious groups can lead to the escalation of intergroup conflict? The 'mutual escalation of religious violence' (MERV) model was designed to explore this research question.[8] The AI agents within MERV had varying levels of religiosity (tendencies related both to belief in supernatural agents and to behaviours related to religious rituals), and varying levels of tolerance for threats related to contagion, social, natural and predation hazards in the environment. The agents were divided into two religious groups (majority and minority) and situated in social networks. The computational causal architecture for the behaviours of the agents, especially their engaging in ritual behaviours to assuage anxiety, was guided by insights from social psychological theories about identity formation, including identity fusion theory. Thus, agent cognition and behaviour were fairly sophisticated, which is what qualifies MERV as a MAAI model. Simulation experiments indicated that the conditions under which mutually escalating conflict was most likely to occur when the population distribution between the majority and minority groups was around 60/40 and the social and contagion threats in the environment exceeded the average tolerance thresholds of the agents. MERV was calibrated and face-validated by comparing its simulation results to real-world conflicts such as the Troubles in Northern Ireland and the Gujarat riots in India. The capacity of the model to simulate the emergent patterns of these conflicts indicates the plausibility of the theoretically informed causal architecture that drove the experiments.

MERV studied the causal mechanisms in the emergence of a phenomenon involving increases in religiosity, but MAAI approaches can also shed light on the conditions and causes of decreases in religion – or secularisation – in a population. The 'non-religiosity model' (NoRM) was designed to forecast changes in religiosity and existential security in contemporary European countries.[9] The AI agents in NoRM also had cognitive and behavioural possibilities related to religiosity, but in this case, they were derived from statistical and structural equation models of data from the International Social Survey Programme (ISSP). These include variables such as 'belief in God' and 'religious attendance'. Agents also had variables related to level of education (derived from ISSP survey responses) and levels of existential security (derived

---

[8] F. LeRon Shults et al., 2018, "A Generative Model of the Mutual Escalation of Anxiety between Religious Groups," *Journal of Artificial Societies and Social Simulation*, 21(4), www.jasss.org/21/4/7.html.

[9] Ross Gore et al., 2018, "Forecasting Changes in Religiosity and Existential Security with an Agent-Based Model," *Journal of Artificial Societies and Social Simulation* 21, 1–31.

from the Human Development Index for their country of residence). The causal architecture of this model was guided by theories of educational homophily and utilised well-tested algorithms for calculating social influence. The model was first trained on ISSP data from 1990 to 2000 in several countries, and was then initialised with data from 2000 to see whether it could forecast the changes that appeared ten years later in the 2010 ISSP data of those and other European countries. NoRM was able to predict 2010 with up to three times more accuracy than its closest competitor (linear regression). These experiments lend credibility to the hypothesis that existential security lowers religiosity at a population level, and that one of the mechanisms driving secularising effects occurs at the individual level: social interaction with more highly educated individuals that slowly lowers the plausibility of religious beliefs in most individual agents.

The second generation of ABMs applied to religion – MAAIs with cognitively sophisticated and behaviourally credible AI agents – promises to launch the academic study of religion in new directions. Such models clarify causal relationships in ways that are impossible in regression studies or even structural equation models. They show the meaning of theories by making their causal consequences clear. They yield novel predictions that can be tested, thereby increasing the concrete intelligibility of the theories that yielded those predictions. And they deepen understanding of the exquisitely complex terrain joining intelligent agents with emergent social dynamics. As one philosopher put it after two intense days working on a computational model:

> [A]fter [...] going through the process of translating my hypothesis about religion and empathy into the language of computer modeling, it all began to make sense [...] Because of this method, we will actually be able to bring some data into a debate that would otherwise remain largely in speculation [...] It forced me to formulate my ideas in such precise and concrete terms (so they could be coded for) that I came away with a better understanding of my own theory.[10]

SIMULATING RELIGION WITH SYSTEM DYNAMICS MODELS

Unlike ABMs, which have agents who interact following specific deterministic, probabilistic or learned rules, SDMs simulate the changes

---

[10] John Teehan, https://mindandculture.org.

that occur within and between variables in a system. Such models were originally used to trace the flow of currencies such as electricity or water – or literally money – as they move through 'stocks' over time. Social scientists have increasingly used SDMs to study the flow of psychologically or socially salient 'currencies' (e.g., attitudes or preferences) within a social system. Stocks are places where a currency (of whatever sort) can gather in a simulation. The rate at which the currency flows from one stock to another is defined through differential equations, and those rates can remain constant or be altered depending on other aspects of model dynamics. In the study of religion, researchers have developed models of the flow of individuals through a social system, changing from one status (say, believing X) to another status (believing not-X), with flow rates governed by the model's expression of social factors that impact belief in X. Such social system approaches have yielded SDMs for studying the dynamics that shape participation in rituals at particular sites in the simulation,[11] and models of the flow of individuals within complex adaptive religious systems and the dynamics that effect their reproduction, energy capture and survival as a group.[12]

SDMs have also been utilised to study the role of religiosity in three major shifts in the civilisational forms of human society: the Neolithic revolution, the Axial Age and Modernity. The basic architecture that drives these models was first developed to study the final shift, away from modes of cultural cohesion that relied on belief in and ritual engagement with supernatural agents and towards modes that rely on naturalistic explanations of the world and secularistic organisations of the social field.[13] This model of the 'future of religious and secular transitions' (FOReST) involved the integration of six major theories of secularisation (incorporating existential security, cultural particularity, human development, meaning maintenance, subjectivisation and supply-side competition dynamics) within a single causal architecture. That architecture drove the dynamics of the system that led people (the currency) to flow from and to various stocks (e.g., opportunities to meet

---

[11]   Vojtěch Kaše, Tomáš Hampejs and Zdeněk Pospíšil, 2018, "Modeling Cultural Transmission of Rituals in Silico: The Advantages and Pitfalls of Agent-Based vs. System Dynamics Models," *Journal of Cognition and Culture* 18(5), 483–507.

[12]   Connor Wood and Richard Sosis, 2019, "Simulating Religions as Adaptive Systems," in *Human Simulation: Perspectives, Insights, and Applications*, ed. Saikou Y. Diallo et al., Springer, 209–232.

[13]   Wesley J. Wildman et al., 2020, "Post-Supernaturalist Cultures: There and Back Again," *Secularism and Nonreligion* 9, https://doi.org/10.5334/snr.121.

non-believers or to convert to supernatural belief), thereby altering the percentage of (post-)supernatural believers in the population. FOReST was able to simulate the decline in supernatural belief that has characterised the last few centuries. More importantly, the model showed that four conditions must be met for post-supernatural cultures to emerge and survive: high levels of existential security, education, pluralism and freedom of expression.

The basic approach utilised in FOReST was also employed in models of the two earlier major shifts in civilisational form mentioned earlier. The 'Neolithic social investment model' (NSIM) also had people as the currency but in this case they could flow back and forth between hunter-gatherer and sedentary-agriculturalist stocks. The model included variables and dynamics that could influence people's opportunities and decisions related to these 'low social investment' and 'high social investment' lifestyles. The causal architecture that guided NSIM was informed by a variety of theoretical and empirical insights derived from transdisciplinary research on Çatalhöyük, a Neolithic archaeological site in south-eastern Turkey.[14]

The 'multiple axialities model' (MAxiM) took the same general approach, but its causal architecture was informed by an integration of the core insights from three general types of theories about this shift that occurred in east, south and west Asia in the first millennium BCE.[15] Broadly speaking, these theories can be distinguished by the extent to which they emphasise what can be called the ideological–political, material–social or cognitive–coalitional pathways to Axial Age civilisational forms. While many of the proponents of these theories find them contradictory, MAxiM demonstrates that they are complementary, and their core insights can be integrated. Both NSIM and MAxiM were able to simulate the respective shifts in the population and generated insights into the general structure of these shifts as well as the particular religious variables that played a causal role.

SDMs are often feasible when ABMs are not. For example, when we lack sufficient information about individual AI agents – their interactions, their reasoning and their behaviours – we can often step back from the individual level and still characterise the system as a whole.

---

[14] F. LeRon Shults and Wesley J. Wildman, 2018, "Simulating Religious Entanglement and Social Investment in the Neolithic," in *Religion, History and Place in the Origin of Settled Life*, ed. Ian Hodder, University of Colorado Press.

[15] F. LeRon Shults et al., 2018, "Multiple Axialities: A Computational Model of the Axial Age," *Journal of Cognition and Culture* 18(4), 537–564.

The data needed to validate an SDM are usually easier to gather, relating to model parameters that condition how fast 'currency' flows between 'stocks' as well as the measures for dependent variables that allow analysis to assess the relationship between inputs and outputs. To grasp the meaning of this, consider how much easier it is to get measures for movement of people between religions at the consolidated, population level than at the level of each individual agent decision. Similarly, computational simulations targeting problems arising within the public health domain are almost always SDMs because of the relevant kinds of data that are readily available. System-level data may not be easy to collect, but it is often easier than data on the behaviour and decision processes of individuals with all their personal differences of trait, state and circumstance.

SDMs are also particularly useful when it is not obvious what an agent-level analysis would even look like. For example, in modelling religious cognition in an individual mind, what agents might be is often not readily apparent, whereas it may be quite natural to picture a currency of strength of belief or emotion flowing between states of mind. In such a case, the SDM becomes an AI, capturing dynamic processes of belief transformation that can be important for understanding, say, religious switching.

Naturally, because SDMs do not take account of individual agents, they do not register individual variations in religiosity or experience, which other research has shown are vital for understanding many aspects of religious belief, behaviour and experience. People really are different, in religious matters as in most others. But such variation can wash out at a high-enough level of analysis, making SDMs useful despite their insensitivity to individual differences. Likewise, SDMs are not as useful for explicating bottom-up emergence processes that are so fascinating in the religious domain, as in other dimensions of human sociality. But SDMs are very useful as a way of formalising relationships that amount to the intelligence of a complex system, and thereby creating interpretive models of religious dynamics. This means that SDMs can be useful preparation for building ABMs, helping researchers to clarify their ideas and decide what is most important to model in the bottom-up manner of an ABM. SDMs are also often easier to understand and explain, because the focus is on system-level dynamics rather than the more complex process of macro features emerging from micro processes. This gives SDMs distinctive heuristic and pedagogical advantages over ABMs.

PHILOSOPHICAL ISSUES IN SIMULATING RELIGION

The application of AI in ways that affect human lives is spreading quickly. This has raised a host of philosophical issues, all of which are relevant for understanding religion and many of which are discussed in other chapters of this book. Here we want to draw attention to some of the philosophical issues raised by MAAI modelling – that is, by the application of AI in *social* simulation in general and the simulation of socially networked *religious* minds in particular. As these computational technologies continue to grow in power and popularity, it will be increasingly important for scholars of religion to engage in careful reflection on the philosophical implications of these developments for their fields and for their understanding of the phenomena they study. We distinguish between the epistemological, ontological and ethical issues raised by the development and deployment of computational methods for simulating religion.

First, these methods raise important *epistemological* issues. What counts as knowledge, and how can we acquire and justify it? When constructing a social simulation using a MAAI type of ABM, one must make explicit what sort of knowledge the artificial agents have and how they learn, change and make decisions. As noted earlier, agents in many of the early simulations of religious cognition were (and in most game-theoretical models still are) conceptualised as 'rational' in the sense that they make decisions based on their calculation of utility functions, which are taken as proxies for the 'best interest' of the agent. However, such epistemological assumptions have been strongly challenged by research on the role of embodiment, emotion and enaction in guiding and even generating human knowledge. This is why a growing number of social simulationists are attempting to develop more realistic agents whose epistemologies are socially informed. This is particularly important for scholars of religion who want to emphasise the central role that ritual and cultural context plays in social systems that promote and maintain beliefs in supernatural agents. For example, people whose identities are significantly fused with the identity of a religious group will not rationally evaluate their 'best interests' by calculating a universal utility function, no matter how many economists and social scientists say they should. Their personal identity is constituted by the social identity, to some degree, so individualistic rational assessments of utility will miss the mark every time.

Simulation technologies also have epistemological implications in more general ways that are related to the philosophy of science and the methodological preferences of scholars themselves. The processes by which computer simulationists articulate, calibrate, verify and validate the scientific knowledge, hypotheses and theories formalised within their computational architectures through simulation experiments and data processing are very different from the ways of knowing familiar to specialists in the academic (or even scientific) study of religion. As a methodological exercise, simulation helps raise epistemological assumptions to the surface, forcing scholars to reflect on them more explicitly. But simulations are epistemologically complex in themselves. What does it mean to learn something from a simulation?

A classic example is causal inference. The vast majority of research in the scientific study of religion, when it locates an interesting association between two variables, does not easily support the inference of a *causal* association. Longitudinal studies can support causal inference but they are very expensive. Randomised controlled trials can support causal inference but they are both expensive and difficult to implement in the case of religion for want of the requisite ecological validity of experiments. Computational simulations also offer a basis for causal inference: if a valid MAAI simulation fits the low-level facts about people's minds and their social interactions and generates high-level matches between emergent simulation behaviour and social data, then we are entitled, *in some sense*, to infer that the causal architecture of the simulation matches the causal properties of the social system in question. But in *what* sense, *precisely*, is this type of causal inference sound? This is a matter of ongoing debate within the philosophy of simulation, reflecting important differences between statistical causal inference and complex systems causal inference.

Second, the computational science of religion also encourages scholars to surface their *ontological* assumptions. The requirement to formalise theories of religious belief and behaviour within causal architectures forces the researcher to render explicit his or her presuppositions about the nature of, and causal relations among, the entities that populate a model. What sorts of things exist and are causally relevant for the changes observed in the scientific study of religion? In this way, computational simulation pressures scholars to clearly articulate the ontologies of the artificial societies they construct. The plausibility of these ontologies (and the claims about causal relations implemented in the model) are dependent on the capacity of simulation experiments to 'grow' the macro-level phenomenon of interest from the micro-level behaviours and meso-level interactions among the simulated religionists that populate the artificial society. If other modellers disagree with the stated (or unstated) ontological and causal assumptions, they can substitute alternatives in an adapted or completely different architecture and produce new models that are better able to simulate – and thereby better understand and explain – the religious phenomenon under discussion.

It is also important to note that MAAI and other simulation tools can inform broader metaphysical debates such as those between proponents of 'strong' and 'weak' emergence. As we have argued elsewhere, the relative success of these technologies lends plausibility to the latter, thereby providing warrant for naturalistic ontologies.[16] This is because a MAAI simulation can produce emergent social features from socially networked AI minds while assuming nothing except low-level causal interactions – no top-down causes, no emergent higher-order causal powers. If nothing more than the ontological assumptions of weak emergence is required to generate social complexity, then the assumptions of strong emergence are demonstrably superfluous. Of course, computational simulation is not at the point where it can decisively resolve a metaphysical debate about the ontology of causal powers such as the one at stake in the contest between weak and strong emergence. But the very existence of MAAI computational simulation demonstrates that the weak-emergence viewpoint is a progressive research program, whereas strong emergence just has to bide its time, hoping that the weak-emergence research program ultimately stops being progressive. This is logically parallel to the way the intelligent-design research program, with its assumptions about higher-order designer causes, can only stand around and wait to see if the progressive research program of evolutionary biology will ultimately fail. Waiting for a progressive research program to fall apart for want of your own progressive research program capable of competing is awkward enough to increase the overall plausibility of the weak-emergence hypothesis. Thus, even though computational simulation of the MAAI kind cannot deliver a knockout blow to the strong emergence hypothesis, it can systematically decrease its plausibility relative to its weak-emergence competitor.

Third, much like traditional AI, multi-agent AI raises a host of *ethical* questions and concerns. The construction of such models requires us to think about how to implement 'moral' attitudes and behaviours

---

[16]   Wesley J. Wildman and F. LeRon Shults, 2018, "Emergence: What Does It Mean and How Is It Relevant to Computer Engineering?," in *Emergent Behavior in Complex Systems Engineering: A Modeling and Simulation Approach*, ed. Saurabh Mittal, Saikou Diallo and Andreas Tolk, John Wiley & Sons.

for our simulated human agents. Unlike traditional AI, however, such agents are embedded within networks in artificial societies. This helpfully introduces issues related to *social* ethics into discussions about AI, shifting the debate beyond questions about the moral dangers or opportunities in the use of AI technologies to questions about the ethical assumptions that guide (im)moral behaviours in real and artificial societies. MAAI models are increasingly used as tools for exploring possible scenarios related to the impact of real-world policy proposals.

The cultural norms in play within policy analysis generally are certainly relevant in computational policy simulation. In fact, computational simulations have demonstrated that the ways norms diverge within and across cultures cannot be ignored. This was achieved by implementing conflicting social norms within the same MAAI – concerning interaction between male adults and children, for example – and then seeing how policy suggestions based on the simulation differ dramatically depending on which norm is active. Social norms make a *measurable difference* in the effectiveness of social policies.[17] This is a sharp reminder that ethical concerns familiar to policy professionals do not suddenly disappear when using computational simulations to conduct scenario analyses.

There are also a host of general ethical questions associated with the use of computational simulation in any research effort having real-world significance. Are the data used to validate the model biased in some way, thereby making it difficult to discover a bias in the model architecture? Are design assumptions properly ethically vetted by the appropriate stakeholders? Are computational simulations applied for good or ill? Is a computational simulation designed to subvert some social malady also capable of being used by bad actors to evade the effects of policies intended to restrict their activities? Simulation experts need to be aware of these issues so they can educate those who hire them to build simulations. The general public and politicians need to learn how to ask smart questions about the impact of policies guided by computational simulations.

In a sense, simulating religion (and other social phenomena) within artificial societies provides a kind of laboratory in which we can surface our ethical assumptions and explore the causal implications of proposed behaviours under various contextual conditions. Moreover, these methodologies provide a new way of integrating theoretical and

---

[17] Saikou Y. Diallo, F. LeRon Shults, and Wesley J. Wildman, 2021, "Minding Morality: Ethical Artificial Societies for Public Policy Modeling," *AI & Society* 36(1), 49–57.

empirical insights into the biocultural evolution of the phylogenetically inherited moral equipment that shapes real human attitudes and behaviours.

CONCLUSION

This chapter reviewed the application of computational modelling and simulation to religion, presented findings from specific simulation studies and discussed some of the philosophical issues raised by this type of research. In recent years there has been significant growth in the use of computer simulations to study complex social systems, including religion. Social simulations are artificial complex systems that we can use to study real-world complex systems, such as the worlds of sophisticated computer games except with more realistic AI in agents, less investment in fancy graphics and a serious research purpose. The best of these simulation models aiming to describe real-world conditions are carefully validated against the data. Sometimes the data needed for validation are already available, sometimes extant data need to be supplemented and sometimes a simulation effort triggers a new data-gathering effort. Multilevel validation – AI agent psychology and behaviour at the low level, social networks of AI agents at the middle level and large-scale social features at the high level – justifies confidence that the causal architecture of the simulation reflects real-world causal processes, thereby delivering an invaluable proxy system into the hands of researchers who study religion.

Computer simulation methods raise many ethical questions related to the role of algorithms that many people may not understand, which is especially important for policy applications that impact human lives. It is a new world, and we need to be newly alert to the dangers that come along with the innovations. We surfaced some of these ethical concerns in this chapter, but it is complex territory and there are hidden ethical traps lurking in unexamined assumptions that guide simulation development, data collection, validation and even the stakeholders involved (or, more importantly, not involved) in a simulation research effort. We need to educate ourselves about these new challenges, just as we need to become smarter about the influence of AI in general in our societies, from machine-learning algorithms to data mining.

As we have demonstrated, AI plays a critical role in computer simulation, particularly in the MAAI type of ABM. SDMs are becoming more complex and the AI agents in MAAIs are becoming more cognitively and behaviourally plausible. The pace of change in this field is rapid and the sophistication of models is impressive, pushing the limits of computational tractability – limits that recede thanks to advancing technology. These correlated changes in conceptual sophistication and computational capacity open up new possibilities that have been out of reach in the past. We do not need to limit ourselves to dumb agents following identical rules anymore. We can stock artificial societies with heterogeneous agents having variations in personality, social contexts and many other factors – including interest in private religious practices, public religious participation, supernatural worldviews and religious orthodoxy. This makes possible far subtler analyses of religious identity and change than ever before and promises to render more tractable questions that have previously seemed out of reach.

For example, can the examples of a localised secularisation process or differentiation of religion in North Atlantic cultures be reversed? If so, how? Will sub-Saharan African cultures experience a distinctive form of modernity that triggers something like secularisation? What are the optimal strategies for limiting religiously motivated and rationalised violence? What is going on neuropsychologically when people have religious or spiritual experiences that trigger significant behavioural changes? What is the optimal way to cultivate virtues within religious cultures and in post-religious cultures? How did early Christianity spread so quickly within the Roman Empire and beyond?

In the era of computational simulation, just about any question about religion you can imagine is at least approachable in a new and fruitful way. Answering these questions takes multidisciplinary research teams who collectively possess the relevant knowledge and as much data as possible. But once those teams know how to integrate what they know, computational simulation massively extends our cognitive capabilities and allows us to amplify the power of teamwork in truly novel ways. The academic study of religion is being permanently transformed by the application of AI within computational and data science methodologies.

BIBLIOGRAPHY

Bainbridge, William Sims. 2006. *God from the Machine: Artificial Intelligence Models of Religious Cognition*. AltaMira Press.

Diallo, Saikou Y., Shults, F. LeRon and Wildman, Wesley J. 2021. "Minding Morality: Ethical Artificial Societies for Public Policy Modeling." *AI & Society* 36(1), 49–57.

Diallo, Saikou et al., eds. 2019. *Human Simulation: Perspectives, Insights, and Applications*. Springer.

Gore, Ross et al. 2018. "Forecasting Changes in Religiosity and Existential Security with an Agent-Based Model." *Journal of Artificial Societies and Social Simulation* 21, 1–31.

Kaše, Vojtěch, Hampejs, Tomáš and Pospíšil, Zdeněk. 2018. "Modeling Cultural Transmission of Rituals in Silico: The Advantages and Pitfalls of Agent-Based vs. System Dynamics Models." *Journal of Cognition and Culture* 18(5), 483–507.

Lane, Justin E. 2021. *Understanding Religion through Artificial Intelligence: Bonding and Belief.* Bloomsbury Publishing.

Nielbo, Kristoffer L., Braxton, Donald M. and Upa, Afzal. 2012. "Computing Religion: A New Tool in the Multilevel Analysis of Religion." *Method and Theory in the Study of Religion* 24(3), 267–290.

Shults, F. LeRon et al. 2018a. "A Generative Model of the Mutual Escalation of Anxiety between Religious Groups" *Journal of Artificial Societies and Social Simulation* 21(4). www.jasss.org/21/4/7.html.

2018b. "Modeling Terror Management Theory: Computer Simulations of the Impact of Mortality Salience on Religiosity." *Religion, Brain & Behavior* 8(1), 77–100.

2018c. "Multiple Axialities: A Computational Model of the Axial Age." *Journal of Cognition and Culture* 18(4), 537–564.

Shults, F. LeRon and Wildman, Wesley J. 2018. "Simulating Religious Entanglement and Social Investment in the Neolithic." In *Religion, History and Place in the Origin of Settled Life*, ed. Ian Hodder. University of Colorado Press.

Upal, Muhammad Afzal. 2005. "Simulating the Emergence of New Religious Movements." *Journal of Artificial Societies and Social Simulation* 8(1). https://jasss.soc.surrey.ac.uk/8/1/6.html.

Wildman, Wesley J. and Shults, F. LeRon. 2018. "Emergence: What Does It Mean and How Is It Relevant to Computer Engineering?." In *Emergent Behavior in Complex Systems Engineering: A Modeling and Simulation Approach*, ed. Saurabh Mittal, Saikou Diallo and Andreas Tolk. John Wiley & Sons.

Wildman, Wesley J. et al. 2020. "Post-Supernatural Cultures: There and Back Again." *Secularism and Nonreligion* 9. https://doi.org/10.5334/snr.121.

Wood, Connor and Sosis, Richard. 2019. "Simulating Religions as Adaptive Systems." In *Human Simulation: Perspectives, Insights, and Applications.* Springer.

15 Cognitive Modelling of Spiritual Practices

FRASER WATTS

In this chapter I review work done so far, using the resources of cognitive science, to model the spiritual or religious mind and discuss how such work might best proceed in future. Like the work reviewed in Chapter 14 on simulating religion, this chapter represents a constructive contribution of AI to religious studies, rather than a commentary on AI from a religious perspective or on religion and AI from a human sciences perspective. This chapter focuses on a different aspect of religious studies, the modelling of the religious or spiritual mind, and especially how the mind is deployed in spiritual practices. In some ways, this undertaking can be seen as a contribution to 'contemplative science', though it represents a broadening of contemplative science in two significant ways. It focuses on cognitive science rather than neuroscience and includes spiritual practices from a variety of faith traditions, not just from Buddhism.

Computational theorising has brought a welcome rigour and precision to many areas of psychological theorising, and it promises to do the same for religious or spiritual cognition. The most useful work in this area so far has used cognitive architectures, a well-established hybrid of AI and cognitive psychology that seeks to model human cognition (and is different from the strand in AI that seeks to replicate human functions by whatever means). Cognitive architectures are formal symbolic structures for processing information, so as to model intelligent and other psychological functions in a way that is sufficiently precise to be capable of being programmed into machines and tested by comparison with human participants. They provide a very precise specification of the structure of cognition, with rules about how information is handled. Providing an exact specification of how a cognitive architecture is operating in a particular cognitive performance is comparable to writing a computer program that models performance and can be a step towards writing such a program.

257

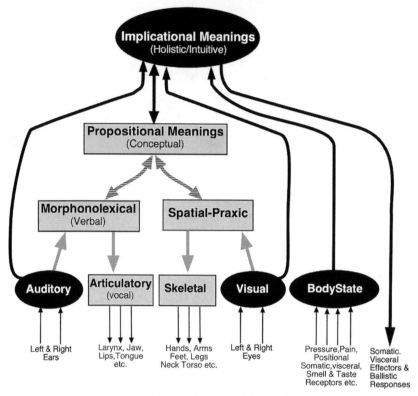

Figure 15.1 Interacting cognitive subsystems

It is noteworthy that there is a broad consensus that humans have two different ways of doing central cognition, even though there is no agreed terminology. For example,[1] Seymour Epstein distinguished between rational and experiential systems; Wilma Bucci distinguished between symbolic and subsymbolic systems; and, from a neuroscience perspective, Ian McGilchrist made a related distinction between left-brain and right-brain cognition. Philip Barnard's Interacting Cognitive Subsystems (ICS),[2] is a cognitive architecture that distinguishes between propositional and implicational central subsystems (see Figure 15.1).

These distinctions are not identical, but in different ways they all mark a recognition that there is a mode of human cognition that

---

[1] F. Watts, 2013, "Dual System Theories of Religious Cognition," in *Head and Heart: Perspectives from Religion and Psychology*, ed. F. Watts and G. Dumbreck, SCM Press.

[2] J. D. Teasdale and P. J. Barnard, 1993, *Affect, Cognition and Change*, Lawrence Erlbaum.

goes beyond rational, analytical thinking and includes cognition that is (1) relatively embodied, in the sense of being well connected with multiple areas of the body; (2) relatively inarticulate and that encodes more, intuitively, than people are able to say; (3) socially embedded and sensitive to social context; and (4) associated with a strong affective tone. This alternative mode of cognition has proved quite challenging for AI to model, though progress is now being made, and I suggest it is particularly important in spiritual cognition. I illustrate this by considering how mindfulness can be modelled using ICS, and then consider other spiritual practices and other approaches to cognitive modelling.

INTERACTING COGNITIVE SUBSYSTEMS AND MINDFULNESS

The most promising work so far on modelling of the cognition involved in spiritual practices has focused on mindfulness, which is a translation of a Pāli word (*sati*) meaning 'non-forgetfulness' or 'lucid, appreciative awareness'. It is the awareness that is cultivated by formal or informal practices involving paying attention, moment by moment, intentionally and without self-criticism, and is the main focus of this chapter, though I also consider other spiritual practices more briefly. The main cognitive architecture that has been used in mindfulness so far is Philip Barnard's ICS, which has a number of attractive features. It is a comprehensive cognitive architecture that models the human mind as a whole, and it has a strong basis in empirical research in psychology. Many computational models in psychology deal only with specific micro-functions, and do not attempt to specify how the mind functions as a whole. ICS does so, and was developed on the basis of careful analysis of psychological data on memory, language and attention.

Another attractive feature of ICS is the sheer range of contexts in which it has been applied, including basic experimental psychology on short-term memory etc., human–computer interaction, depression and a variety of other clinical conditions such as schizophrenia and anorexia and, more recently, choreography and dance. ICS probably has sufficient expressive power to model how any aspects of human cognition might proceed. It is, of course, another matter how elegant and satisfying that modelling is. Also, as with computer programming, there is the empirical question of whether the modelling corresponds to how humans actually do things.

ICS offers an account of how mammalian cognitive architecture has evolved and how the human architecture differs from that of non-human mammals.[3] It is a nine-system cognitive architecture, including central, intermediate, sensory and effector subsystems, and also a body-state subsystem. Barnard has provided an explicit and well-argued proposal for how the mammalian cognitive architecture has evolved, going from a basic four-subsystem architecture in many mammals to the nine-subsystem architecture of humans. The final stage, and the one that marked the transition from other higher mammals to humans, saw the development of a new central subsystem, separate from the previous multimodal central subsystem, which made specialist provision for propositional semantics and that enabled humans to understand and articulate abstract meanings.

The emergence of propositional semantics enabled the phylogenetically older multimodal subsystem to be fundamentally transformed, becoming a subsystem that processed what Barnard calls 'implicational' meanings. These blend the full range of multimodal inputs with the products of processing propositional meanings and emotion to yield what we experience as wisdom, feelings and intuitions. The resulting dialogue between the two meaning systems – implicational and propositional – enables analytical and self-reflective thought processes. ICS thus incorporates a distinction between two different modes of central human cognition.

ICS is a dynamic system in which cognitive activity is modelled more in terms of the network of interactions between different subsystems than by processing in any single subsystem.

Each of the nine subsystems in ICS uses a different information code. Much information-processing work in ICS is done by transferring informational data from one subsystem to another, which involves it being recoded. Typically, a subsystem has two or three other subsystems to which it can transfer information.

Information arriving in each subsystem is also copied into a memory store. Each subsystem has a memory store, using its own distinctive code. Events can be encoded and stored in different ways in different subsystems. So, there may be an image record of a single event in several different subsystems. A person's cognitive state at any one time arises from a complex interaction between the various different subsystems.

---

[3] P. J. Barnard, 2019, "Sticks, Stones, and the Origins of Sapience," in *Squeezing Minds from Stones: Cognitive Archaeology and the Evolution of the Human Mind*, ed. K. A. Overmann and F. L. Coolidge, Oxford University Press.

There can be a *diffuse* awareness of various subsystems, potentially of all. However, *focal* awareness depends on a process known as 'buffering', and only one subsystem can be buffered at any point in time.

ICS is a specification of the computational capabilities and organisation of the component functions of the human mental architecture that support phenomenological awareness, emotion, thought and the control of actions. These capabilities have been formalised in several ways (for references, see Further Reading). The first modelling technique used GOFAI (good old-fashioned AI) and expressed reasoning about mental computation within an expert system using the production system rule.

The second modelling technique drew upon formal methods from computer science in which aspects of ICS were rendered explicit and modelled using modal action logic with deontic extensions. This technique enables formal mathematical proofs to support inferences about the computational behaviour of minds and of behavioural engagement with other agents and entities in real-world interactions. Both these forms of model were developed to assist practical problems in the design of human–computer interactions.

The third form of computational modelling of ICS used augmentations of process algebra to model cognitive control as exchanges between the propositional and implicational meaning of subsystems together with interactions with the body-states. This later modelling has successfully been used to fit data from laboratory experiments on human attention to meanings. The forms of modelling in ICS are qualitatively different form traditional AI or connectionist simulations, but they are nonetheless computational.

Modelling Mindfulness Using ICS

ICS has already been applied to religious and spiritual practices in a way that gives reassurance about its potential fruitfulness, and I have reviewed work in the psychology of religion using ICS and other two-factor models of human cognition.[4] There is already a small body of work on mindfulness using ICS, especially the work of John Teasdale and colleagues.[5] Mark Wynn's philosophical discussion of the role of inarticulate understandings in religious feeling also uses Barnard's ICS.[6]

---

[4]   F. Watts, 2013, "Dual System Theories of Religious Cognition," in *Head and Heart: Perspectives from Religion and Psychology*, ed. F. Watts and G. Dumbreck, SCM Press.

[5]   J. Teasdale, 2022, *What Happens in Mindfulness: Inner Awakening and Embodied Cognition*. Guilford Press.

[6]   M. Wynn, 2005, *Emotional Experience and Religious Understanding*. Cambridge University Press.

There are at least three key features of the ICS modelling of mindfulness. First, in mindful processing the implicational subsystem (the more intuitive and more embodied of the two central subsystems) plays a more dominant role than usual, with the more abstract and conceptual propositional subsystem being less actively involved. Second, there is less focal awareness than usual, though that depends on the particular mindfulness practice that is being followed, and focal awareness is often restricted to implicational or body-state subsystems. Third, the network of interacting subsystems functions in an unusually coordinated way in mindfulness, with cognitive multitasking (the normal pattern of different subsystems doing different things) being largely suspended.

As people become mindful, the pattern of attention changes. In ICS there are three sensory states: acoustic, visual and somatic. In mindfulness there is a marked shift of attention away from the acoustic and visual subsystems, as more attention is given to body-state. It is possible in principle to be mindful of other sensory input than body-state. However, there are good reasons why mindfulness is almost always taught in relation to body-state first.[7]

Awareness of body-state is more direct and unmediated than of acoustic and visual input. In terms of the ICS cognitive architecture, this is reflected in the fact that acoustic and central visual input comes through intermediate subsystems before reaching central cognition. However, body-state feeds directly into the implicational subsystem. A focus on body-state also helps to keep people in the present moment, because it is difficult to attend to past or future body-states. Also, body-state feeds directly into just one of the two central cognitive subsystems, the more intuitive and inarticulate implicational subsystem, whereas visual and acoustic input feeds equally into both central cognitive subsystems, reflecting the fact that it is easier to think discursively about visual or acoustic input than about body-state. So, focus on body-state leads to a shift in the mode of central cognition, from conceptual to experiential.

As seen earlier, there are two subsystems that together constitute the central engine of cognition: the implicational subsystem (intuitive and schematic) and the propositional subsystem (linear and analytical). According to Teasdale, the main change that mindfulness makes to

---

[7] J. M. G. Williams et al., 2015, *Mindfulness-Based Cognitive Therapy with People at Risk of Suicide*, Guilford Press; F. Watts, 2021, *A Plea for Embodied Spirituality*, SCM Press.

how the cognitive architecture is deployed is that activity in the central engine of cognition is focused on the implicational rather than the propositional subsystem. Attention to body-state, which is interconnected with the implicational system but not with the propositional system, helps to make that adjustment. It is also necessary for the person becoming mindful to learn the skill of becoming aware of, but not getting drawn into, the kind of discursive thought that is associated with the propositional subsystem, whenever such propositional thinking does not help the task in hand.

There are loops that keep the central subsystems closely interconnected, but in mindfulness the loop is controlled more by implicational meanings, and less by propositional meanings, than is normally the case. There is also a loop that connects the propositional subsystem with the morphonological subsystem, experienced as mentation in the mind's ear. That often becomes more quiescent in the course of mindfulness practice. A parallel loop connects the propositional subsystem with the object subsystem, experienced as images in the mind's eye. Some mindfulness practices make explicit use of that loop, for example in imagery about the breath entering the whole of the body. In mindfulness practices there is no articulation; and, in many mindfulness practices, no limb movement either.

The classic formulation of mindfulness on which Teasdale draws is that of Jon Kabat-Zinn,[8] in which the person cultivates an attitude of acceptance, patience, trust, beginner's mind and letting go, and which is also 'non-judging' and 'non-striving'. To stay non-judging and non-striving, mindfulness prioritises the cognitive activity of the implicational system over the propositional system, which brings about that rebalancing. However, it is probably not possible for most people to avoid discursive thought entirely, or at least not without a lot of experience of mindfulness, and 'striving' too hard to avoid discussive thought is counterproductive. It seems that the skill that is learned in mindfulness is rather how to see clearly, and choose whether to get drawn into, discursive thinking when it occurs. Kabat-Zinn acknowledges that evaluative judgements are likely to occur but recommends not pursuing them or acting on them.

In ICS terms, it seems clear that mindfulness involves a *relative* prioritisation of implicational cognition over propositional cognition. It would be simplistic to frame that in terms of the propositional

---

[8] J. Kabat-Zinn, 2013, *Full Catastrophe Living: How to Cope with Stress, Pain and Illness Using Mindfulness Meditation*, Piatkus.

subsystem being shut down or switched off. There is no provision in ICS for any subsystem to be switched off, though there can be a rebalancing of processing activity between subsystems, and practitioners of mindfulness learn to avoid focusing attention on the propositional subsystem. This has the effect of the sense of self having less priority, as self-related thoughts are seen as mental events and therefore are not taken so personally.

Suggested Future Developments in Modelling of Mindfulness

There are several important aspects of mindfulness that have not been well covered in ICS modelling of mindfulness so far, and which are now discussed. For others see Williams and Zabat-Zinn,[9] including a discussion of working memory in ICS.[10] I assume that it is potentially within the resources of ICS to model all aspects of mindfulness (and indeed any aspects of human cognition); the question is rather how intuitively satisfying the modelling is.

It is a core feature of mindfulness that it involves a very deliberate way of managing attention.[11] Intentions are a potentially controversial subject in cognitive modelling, though most cognitive psychologists would want to avoid a 'homunculus' where decisions are made and that controls the cognitive architecture, and ICS deliberately avoids a homunculus. ICS takes a fairly broad view of what counts as 'meanings', and intentions can be seen as a particular kind of meaning. In modelling mindfulness, it is important that intentions should have causal efficacy. In ICS, intentions can have consequences through the same processes as operate with other kinds of meanings.

It is doubtful whether it is possible to avoid discursive thought altogether, and that is not the objective of mindfulness. Rather, mindfulness aims to make people more aware of discursive thought, so that they are better able to choose how to manage it. A formulation of this that may be helpful in future cognitive modelling of mindfulness is the distinction between 'glance' and 'look' in attention.[12] 'Look' involves

[9] J. M. G. Williams and J. Kabat-Zinn, 2013, *Mindfulness: Diverse Perspectives on Its Meaning, Origins and Applications*, Guilford Press.
[10] J. D. Teasdale and M. Chaskalson, 2011, "How Does Mindfulness Transform Suffering? II: The Transformation of *Dukkha*," *Contemporary Buddhism* 12(1), 103–124.
[11] S. L. Shapiro et al., 2005, "Mechanisms of Mindfulness," *Journal of Clinical Psychology* 62, 373–386.
[12] L. Su, H. Bowman, and P. Barnard, 2011, "Glancing and Then Looking: On the Role of Body, Affect and Meaning in Cognitive Control," *Frontiers in Psychology* 2, 348.

a fuller and more evaluative analysis of meaning and generally takes longer, whereas 'glance' does not take the analysis of meaning very far and is shorter. It seems that in mindfulness people learn to merely glance at propositional meanings without getting locked into them; that may be a better formulation than to say that they avoid propositional cognitive activity altogether. Mark Williams and colleagues have drawn attention to the importance of discrepancy-based processing, in which events are evaluated in relation to goals, and proposes that mindfulness marks a movement away from such processing.[13] If mindfulness involves a shift from 'look' to 'glance', in most subsystems it would reduce discrepancy-based processing.

Teasdale's formulation has so far said little about how the transition into mindfulness practice is to be modelled in ICS terms. The focus is on giving an ICS account of mindfulness itself rather than an ICS account of the transition towards mindfulness. That would be a complicated thing to model and one that has not so far been attempted in connection with spiritual practices, though I suggest it is only complicated and not impossible. Barnard's recent work on the modelling of attention in dance makes use of an "attentional score," with a stave corresponding to each subsystem.[14] This provides a helpful way of formalising cognitive transitions over time that could be applied to the practice of mindfulness.

The affective quality associated with attention is also an important part of mindfulness.[15] Another aspect of avoiding being judgemental in mindfulness is said to be to look *kindly* on whatever is occurring, as in compassion-based mindfulness. It will be a challenge for cognitive modelling of mindfulness to capture that aspect of it, but Rosalind Picard's work on affective computing[16] may provide some useful pointers. An attentional score could provide a way of expressing where and how in the mind there is affective processing.

Cognitive modelling of mindfulness has so far focused on the dedicated practice of mindfulness rather than on performing everyday tasks in as mindful a way as possible, which is an important aspect of the

[13] J. M. G. Williams, 2008, "Mindfulness, Depression and Modes of Mind," *Cognitive Therapy & Research* 32(6), 721–733.

[14] P. J. Barnard, 2019, "Paying Attention to Meanings in the Psychological Sciences and the Performing Arts," in *Performing Psychologies: Imagination, Creativity and Dramas of the Mind*, ed. N. Shaughnessy and P. Barnard, Bloomsbury Methuen.

[15] S. L. Shapiro et al., 2005, "Mechanisms of Mindfulness," *Journal of Clinical Psychology* 62, 373–386.

[16] R. Picard, 1997, *Affective Computing*, MIT Press.

practice of mindfulness. From the cognitive modelling point of view, everyday mindfulness is in some ways similar to dedicated practice but in other ways different. In mindfulness practice people might choose not to give attention to the visual and acoustic sensory subsystems, but that is not possible in everyday mindfulness. Whereas dedicated mindfulness practice reduces processing activity in the sensory and effector subsystems, everyday mindfulness actually increases focal awareness and conscious processing activity in those subsystems and in particular, in ICS terms, there is an increased 'buffering' of cognitive activity in those subsystems.

A concept that has played a key role in cognitive psychology, and that may be helpful in cognitive modelling of mindfulness, is 'automaticity'. When tasks have been performed many times they can be performed automatically, and the normal relationship no longer holds between speed of processing and the number of bits of information to be processed; people can perform the task without being consciously aware of what they are doing. Mindfulness seems to involve becoming aware of the tendency for processing to become automatic and developing a greater ability to choose whether to do that.[17] As far as possible, whatever is processed is done consciously and deliberately, in the focal attention that, in ICS terms, results from 'buffering'.

OTHER SPIRITUAL PRACTICES AND APPROACHES

I now turn to consider what would be involved in modelling other spiritual practices, including modelling hesychasm (the Jesus Prayer), how different kinds of meditation can lead to a state of 'absolute unitary being' and the cognitive processes involved in dissociative practices such as glossolalia, and briefly considering some other spiritual practices. My aim in the second half of the chapter is to scope out the challenges of the cognitive modelling of other spiritual practices and to offer some pointers.

The Jesus Prayer (Hesychasm)

The Jesus Prayer, popularised in J. D. Salinger's novel *Franny and Zooey*, has played a significant role in Eastern Christianity. The Jesus Prayer is a mantra-based spiritual practice that involves the sustained

---

[17] Y. Kang, J. Gruber and J. R. Gray, 2013, "Mindfulness and De-Automatization," *Emotion Review* 5(2), 192–201.

repetition of a standard prayer, often "Lord Jesus Christ, Son of God, have mercy upon me."[18] A beginner might repeat it 100 times, though experienced users might say it 3,000 times. It is normally said by people on their own, though in some settings it is said collectively, with one person after another taking up the prayer. Initially it is said audibly, though later it may be said silently. With experience, the rhythm of the prayer can become synchronised with the breath, though the general guidance is not to force that but to allow it to develop spontaneously. Some people use a prayer rope to count off the repetitions with their fingers.

I use ICS to suggest a model of how the mind is deployed in the Jesus Prayer and compare that with the ICS model of mindfulness. Mindfulness involves a marked reduction in processing activity in all subsystems apart from the implicational and body-state subsystems. In contrast, the Jesus Prayer keeps most subsystems active but enmeshed with the implicational subsystem. In both cases, there is a break with the usual cognitive multitasking, though that is achieved in diverse ways. In the Jesus Prayer the effector subsystems are kept active: the articulatory subsystem by saying the prayer, and the limb subsystem by fingers using the prayer rope. If the prayer is said aloud, the acoustic system is occupied with hearing it. If the prayer is said on the breath, the body-state subsystem is enmeshed with the prayer through that. That only leaves the visual subsystem with nothing to do, but the eyes are generally closed.

There is also a rebalancing of central cognition. The literature on the Jesus Prayer generally makes a distinction between mind and heart, and it is often said that someone using the Jesus Prayer learns to 'put the mind in the heart'. This implies a reconfiguration of the relationship between what ICS calls the implicational and propositional subsystems. There is a parallel with the prioritisation of implicational cognition in mindfulness.

The Jesus Prayer is seen primarily as a prayer of the heart. 'Heart' is a concept that has been used in different ways by different authors. There are some Eastern Christian writers who make a Platonic distinction between head and heart, but more often 'heart' refers to the spiritual centre of the whole person. The Jesus Prayer has been seen as an important way of entering the heart and has similarities with the *dhikr* practised by Sufis, which can be modelled in a comparable way.

---

[18] S. Barrington-Ward, 1996, *The Jesus Prayer: A Way to Contemplation*, Bible Reading Fellowship; K. Ware, 2014, *The Jesus Prayer*, Catholic Truth Society.

There are a number of similarities between mindfulness and the Jesus Prayer. Barrington-Ward comments that in the Jesus Prayer, you "draw your mind away from the thoughts and images," but "you don't do that unkindly, just gently."[19] That is like the guidance given in mindfulness. Just as mindfulness practice over a period of time leads to a pervasively mindful way of attending, so regular use of the Jesus Prayer results in an experience of the prayer continuing on its own even when the person is not deliberately using it. It can be used freely while doing other things, rather than in a fixed way in dedicated practice, just as everyday tasks can be done in a mindful way. Users of the prayer develop a sense that they are participating in it, rather than initiating it.

A distinction is often made between the technical aspects of the prayer, associated with repetition, and inner 'spiritual work'. The assumption is that it is the spiritual work that matters, and that repetition of the prayer has no value without it. It is probably correct that the prayer has more significant consequences if accompanied by spiritual work. However, I suspect that the prayer has some beneficial consequences even without spiritual work. It might be thought that cognitive modelling can only capture the technical aspects of the prayer, but I think that would be wrong. In ICS terms, 'spiritual work' would be seen as processing activity in the implicational subsystem and seems to arise from the intention with which the prayer is used. Those using the Jesus Prayer often articulate their intentions in the form of a brief prayer, before beginning the repetitions. As with mindfulness, cognitive modelling of intentions will be important in developing an adequate model of the changes brought about by the Jesus Prayer.

There are interesting issues about levels of analysis of the words that are used. Sometimes, when words are use repetitively, they lose meaning, a phenomenon that psychologists call 'semantic satiation'. However, that does not seem to be what happens in the Jesus Prayer. There seems to be a shift away from mere parsing of the words towards a deeper level of semantic processing. That involves the 'schematic' meanings that are characteristic of the implicational subsystem, which is enriched by the multimodal mixing of inputs from a range of other subsystems. Cognitive processing of the meaning of the words shifts to a deeper level. Processing seems to be more of the *gist* of the words, and the intention behind them, rather than of each specific word that is uttered. That calls for more investigation.

[19]   Barrington-Ward, *The Jesus Prayer*, 81.

Dissociative Spiritual Practices

There is also a group of spiritual practices that lead to states of consciousness that are dissociative. They represent a more radical challenge to cognitive modelling, though ICS provides a helpful way of specifying the unusual way in which the cognitive architecture is configured in these practices.

Dissociative spiritual practices can be seen as a descendant of the trance dancing of emerging humanity, which had evolutionary advantages in the way in which it facilitated social bonding and contributed to healing. Both were mediated through the release of endorphins as a result of synchronised rhythmic movements.[20] It seems likely that they also gave rise to unusual, somewhat dissociative, states of consciousness with a sense of 'otherness' in the implicational image, which gave rise to a sense of a spiritual world. It seems likely that organised religion in stable settlements arose, in part, from an attempt to make sense of the felt experience of the spiritual world engendered by trance dancing.

An intriguing current spiritual practice from the point of view of cognitive modelling is glossolalia (speaking in tongues), which has been quite thoroughly investigated.[21] Though there is vocal articulation in glossolalia, it is clear from psycholinguistic analysis that it is not language, as the utterances are too rhythmic and repetitive, and do not have the formal structure of language. The speech sounds in glossolalia do not seem to map on to any very different definite semantic content, though the gist of what people are saying is usually perfectly clear from context and intentions and is usually either praising God or prophesying. People almost always learn the practice of glossolalia in a social context; it seems to be a skill learned by imitation. However, having learned it, people may then practise it on their own.

The cognitive architecture seems to be configured in an unusual way in glossolalia. In terms of ICS, as with the other spiritual practices that have been considered in this chapter, there seems to be a prioritisation of attention to implicational over propositional meanings. Diffuse implicational meanings, such as the praise of God, are expressed in speech sounds. Implicational meanings would normally be propositionalised before reaching articulation, but this does not seem to happen in glossolalia. Implicational meanings appear to pass through

---

[20] R. Dunbar, 2021, *How Religion Evolved*, Oxford University Press; F. Watts, 2022, *A Plea for Embodied Spirituality*, SCM Press.

[21] R. W. Hood, Jr., P. C. Hill and B. Spilka, 2018, *The Psychology of Religion: An Empirical Approach*, Guilford Press.

the propositional subsystem without being re-encoded in the distinctive code of that subsystem; rather, they seem to pass through, relatively untransformed, into articulation.

There are some similarities between glossolalia and automatic writing, which is also a somewhat dissociative state, and can occur in a religious context. In terms of ICS, it seems that, as with glossolalia, the meanings originate in the implicational subsystem. In glossolalia those meanings feed in a relatively untransformed way into articulation, whereas in automatic writing they feed in a similarly untransformed way into handwriting. In both cases, there seems to be a lack of focal awareness of specific semantic content while people are engaged in articulation or handwriting.

Meditation and Absolute Unitary Being

Finally, I turn from ICS modelling to a different approach, drawing on the work of d'Aquili and Newberg.[22] Their approach to modelling is influenced by neuropsychological considerations, whereas Barnard's strategy with ICS is to undertake modelling at a purely cognitive level and to postpone neuropsychological considerations. D'Aquili's work on the cognitive-neuropsychological modelling of religion is impressive in many ways and shows sophistication across a broad range of disciplines.

At the cognitive level, d'Aquili and Newberg have proposed a set of seven 'operators' that between them provide a comprehensive specification of basic cognitive processes: the holistic, reductionist, causal, abstractive, binary, formal-quantitative and emotional-value operators. They suggest that two operators are particularly involved in religion and spirituality: the holistic and causal operators. Both operators subserve a range of everyday cognitive functions but also have a special role in religion. They see the holistic operator as being involved in mystical states of consciousness.

D'Aquili and Newberg have also proposed a detailed model of how meditative practices of various kinds give rise to the mystical state of consciousness they call 'absolute unitary being'. Their model is presented partly in terms of cognitive system theory and partly in terms of areas of the brain. Negative meditation (*via negativa*) starts with the intention to clear the mind. This corresponds to partial deafferentation, arising from the right attention association area, and resulting in

---

[22] E. d'Aquili and A. B. Newberg, 1999, *The Mystical Mind: The Biology of Religious Experience*, Fortress Press.

a reduction of sensory awareness through blocking the input from the verbal-conceptual association and from other sensory modalities. That leads in turn, through activation of the hippocampus and amygdala, to stimulation of the quiescence areas and to a strong feeling of relaxation and of profound quiescence. Output from quiescence system can then give rise either to a sense of ecstasy or to a profound quiescence. In terms of a postulated architecture, the key elements are an attentional control system and a quiescence system.

Positive or absorptive meditation (*via positiva*) begins, not with the intention to clear the mind, but with focusing on a mental image or sensory input. Again, this starts from the right attention association area but, rather than leading to partial differentiation, it leads to a fixed focus on sensory input. That leads again, though through a different route, to stimulation of the hippocampus and amygdala, feeding back into the right attention association area and establishing a reverberating loop that, in time, creates a spillover that stimulates the quiescence areas. That leads to maximal stimulation of the quiescence systems, deafferentation of the orientation association areas and a sense of 'absolutely unitary being'.

The rules of operation in the model of d'Aquili and Newberg are not as precisely specified as in ICS, and it is not yet a computational model. However, it could be developed into one. On the face of things, it fits well both with the experience of meditation and with known brain systems, and it deserves fuller consideration than it has so far received.

There is other helpful research on meditation on an external object. Arthur Deikman[23] conducted research on meditation on a blue vase, with instructions to focus on the vase itself and to avoid discursive thought about it. The results were striking, including the vase becoming unstable, the colour more intense and a sense that they were merging with the vase. In ICS terms, this suggests a pattern of attention involving sustained 'looking' at propositional meanings while only 'glancing' at meanings in the other subsystems such as visual and propositional. The participants became very absorbed in the session, with time passing quickly and being untroubled by noises around them. They were attending to the vase in a 'mindful' way and Deikman compares the experiences they reported to those described in the medieval mystical text *The Cloud of Unknowing*.

[23] A. J. Deikman, 1963, "Experimental Meditation," *Journal of Nervous and Mental Diseases* 136(4), 329–343.

CONCLUSION

Modelling the architecture involved in spiritual practices allows us to be more precise about the configurations involved. ICS modelling has the expressive power to formulate accounts of various meditative and contemplative practices in a way that opens them up to more systematic investigations of their properties, which can potentially guide instruction and personal spiritual enquiry. In the introduction to this chapter it was suggested that there is a mode of intelligence that is embodied, intuitive, socially embedded and affective. The theoretical analyses presented in this chapter indicate that this mode of intelligence is especially important in spiritual practices.

One way of thinking about various spiritual practices that have been considered here is that they all act in different ways to create an informational landscape in which the implicational image is less cluttered and a space is provided to explore personal or spiritual meanings. Anything that stabilises a pattern of information will create a ground against which other features can stand out and be explored.

Understanding how the human mind is deployed in spiritual practices can be seen as a stepping stone to a better general understanding of spiritual intelligence (or religious/existential intelligence). Analyses of how regular and sustained spiritual practice affects the performance of everyday tasks will be particularly helpful in this. There are other intelligences, such as artistic intelligence (including musical and bodily-kinaesthetic intelligence), personal intelligence (both interpersonal and intrapersonal) and moral intelligence, that also make use of the more intuitive, embodied mode of mind. It will be helpful to explore the similarities and differences between these various intelligences.

One of the tasks for the future will be to develop a general computational theory of spiritual intelligence. Robert Emmons suggests that the features of spiritual intelligence include the capacity to transcend the physical and material and to experience heightened states of consciousness.[24] The analyses developed in this chapter of the unusual configuration of the cognitive architecture in spiritual practices go some way to explaining the heightened state of consciousness.

The development of enhanced propositional intelligence allows humans to engage in intellectual activity that transcends immediate context. To put it another way, the capacity to think linguistically enables humans to think about things that are represented

---

[24] R. A. Emmons, 1999, *The Psychology of Ultimate Concerns*, Guilford Press.

symbolically but are not currently present in the immediate environment. As Clocksin points out in Chapter 2, spiritual intelligence (or religious reasoning) takes things one stage further and involves intellectual activity relating to the intangible and to things that are never encountered straightforwardly in immediate sensory experience. Spiritual intelligence could be seen as the culmination (at least so far) of an evolving capacity for intellectual activity that transcends immediate context. Spiritual reflection involves an intriguing combination of a decontextualised symbolic intelligence, with a mode of cognition that is intuitive and embodied.

Work on the cognitive modelling of spiritual practices is clearly at an early stage of development. However, enough has been accomplished so far to show how it can help in understanding spiritual practices better. Cognitive modelling complements existing neuropsychological work on contemplative science. The main cognitive architecture that has been used here, ICS, is already a computational-level architecture, though full computational implementation is still only at a preliminary stage. Cognitive architectures have long played an important role in cognitive science, as a preliminary to full computational modelling. The work set out here can be seen as a necessary preliminary stage before full computational modelling of spiritual practices becomes possible.

BIBLIOGRAPHY

Barnard, P. J. 2019. "Sticks, Stones, and the Origins of Sapience." In *Squeezing Minds from Stones: Cognitive Archaeology and the Evolution of the Human Mind*, ed. K. A. Overmann and F. L. Coolidge. Oxford University Press.

Barrington-Ward, S. 2014. *The Jesus Prayer: A Way to Contemplation*. Bible Reading Fellowship.

D'Aquili, E. and A. B. Newberg. 1999. *The Mystical Mind: The Biology of Religious Experience*. Fortress Press.

Deikman, A. J. 1963. "Experimental Meditation," in *Journal of Nervous and Mental Diseases* 136(4), 329–343.

Dunbar, R. 2021. *How Religion Evolved*. Oxford University Press.

Hood, Jr., R. W., Hill, P. C. and Spilka, B. 2018. *The Psychology of Religion: An Empirical Approach*. Guilford Press.

Kang, Y., Gruber, J. and Gray, J. R. 2013. "Mindfulness and De-automatization." *Emotion Review* 5(2), 192–201.

Picard, R. 1997. *Affective Computing*. MIT Press.

Shapiro, S. L. et al. 2005. "Mechanisms of Mindfulness." *Journal of Clinical Psychology* 62, 373–386.

Teasdale, J. 2022. *What Happens in Mindfulness: Inner Awakening and Embodied Cognition*. Guilford Press.

Ware, K. 2014. *The Jesus Prayer*. Catholic Truth Society.

Watts, F. 2013. "Dual System Theories of Religious Cognition." In *Head and Heart: Perspectives from Religion and Psychology*, ed. F. Watts and G. Dumbreck. Templeton Press.
  2021. *A Plea for Embodied Spirituality*. SCM Press.
Williams, J. M. G. and Kabat-Zinn, J. 2013. *Mindfulness: Diverse Perspectives on Its Meaning, Origins and Applications*. Guilford Press
Wynn, M. 2005. *Emotional Experience and Religious Understanding*, Cambridge University Press.

FURTHER READING

Barnard, P. 2019. "Sticks, Stones, and the Origins of Sapience." In *Squeezing Minds from Stones: Cognitive Archaeology and the Evolution of the Human Mind*, ed. K. A. Overmann and F. L. Coolidge. Oxford University Press.
Barnard, P. and Bowman, H. 2004. "Rendering Information Processing Models of Cognition and Affect Computationally Explicit: Distributed Executive Control and the Deployment of Attention." *Cognitive Science Quarterly* 3(3), 297–328.
Barnard, P. and May, J. 1999. "Representing Cognitive Activity in Complex Tasks." *Human Computer Interaction* 14(1–2), 93–158.
Barrington-Ward, S. 1996. *The Jesus Prayer: A Way to Contemplation.* Bible Reading Fellowship.
D'Aquili, E. and Newberg, A. B. 1999. *The Mystical Mind: The Biology of Religious Experience.* Fortress Press.
Duke, D. J. et al. 1998. "Syndetic Modelling." *Human Computer Interaction* 13(4), 337–393.
Johnson, C. D. L. 2010. *The Globalisation of Hesychasm and the Jesus Prayer: Contesting Contemplation.* Continuum.
Kabat-Zinn, J. 2013. *Full Catastrophe Living: How to Cope with Stress, Pain and Illness Using Mindfulness Meditation.* Piatkus.
McGilchrist, I. 2009. *The Master and His Emissary: The Divided Brain and the Makings of the Western World.* Yale University Press.
Teasdale, J. D. 2022. *Understanding Mindfulness and Inner Awakening: A Psychological Approach.* Guilford Press.
Teasdale, J. D. and Barnard, P. J. 1993. *Affect, Cognition and Change.* Lawrence Erlbaum.
Wallace, A. B. 2007. *Contemplative Science: Where Buddhism and Neuroscience Converge.* Columbia University Press.
Ware, K. 2014. *The Jesus Prayer.* Catholic Truth Society.
Watson, G., Batchelor, S. and Claxton, G. eds. 1999. *The Psychology of Awakening: Buddhism, Science and Our Day-to-Day Lives.* Red Wheel/Weiser.
Watts, F. 2017. *Psychology, Religion and Spirituality: Concepts and Applications.* Oxford University Press.
Watts, F. and Dumbreck, G. eds. 2013. *Head and Heart: Perspectives from Religion and Psychology.* Templeton Press.
West, M. A. ed. 2016. *The Psychology of Meditation: Research and Practice.* Oxford University Press.
Williams, J., Mark, G. and Kabat-Zinn, J. 2013. *Mindfulness: Diverse Perspectives on Its Meaning, Origins and Applications.*

16 Artificial Companions and Spiritual Enhancement

YORICK WILKS

The practical part of this chapter is a description of a currently unfinished experiment on letting people talk to what they believed to be an artificial intelligence (AI) system about religious and spiritual matters. I want to set this limited effort in the more general context of attitudes to artificial beings with whom we can communicate and from whom we may get benefit. The experiment itself may call to mind Aesop's story of the mountains that trembled and produced only a mouse, and I fear this account of my recent work on spiritual companions may seem rather mouselike after the speculations I and others made years ago about the future of artificial Companions[1] and of which this experiment can be considered a limited form. But first I want to make some general observations on (1) the history of machines that appear in therapeutic conversational roles and (2) the role of artificial beings in the philosophy and history of religion, and (3) note some practical implementations of conversational systems in religious contexts. In conclusion, I speculate on what we may expect in the future from automated conversationalists in a religious sense.

CONVERSATIONAL AGENTS

The development of such agents can be dated back as far as the 1960s and the interaction of two American AI researchers: Joe Weizenbaum and Ken Colby. Weizenbaum created ELIZA,[2] the first and still famous conversational engine, modelled on a Rogerian therapist, the tradition in which the therapist says very little beyond encouraging the patient to say more. ELIZA was a very primitive system that seized on a human

---

[1] Y. Wilks, 2010, "Introducing Artificial Companions," in *Close Engagements with Artificial Companions*, ed. Y. Wilks, John Benjamins.

[2] J. Weizenbaum, 1966, "ELIZA: A Computer Programme for the Study of Natural Language Communication between Men and Machines," *Communications of the ACM* 9, 36–45.

interlocutor's key words and asked more about them, typically with replies such as, "Tell me more about your mother," after the patient had mentioned their mother. This program was widely distributed and used, yet its language capacities were inconsequential, certainly in comparison to Colby's PARRY[3] program, which had a very sophisticated language pattern-matching system of some 6,000 patterns and a substantial ability to say surprising and interesting things to hold a user's attention. PARRY modelled not the therapist but a paranoid patient, although Colby, unlike Weizenbaum, was in fact a psychiatrist and concerned with capturing the degree to which such a paranoid patient (or program) could be said to be rational, albeit deluded. Weizenbaum later argued against his own work as being dangerous and attacked Colby's as even more so. No one encountering these programs would believe that, but his diatribe did generate publicity for such programs, and Colby's PARRY went on to set a standard for fluent coherent computer conversation not matched until the chatbots some forty years later.

Since that time, a great number of systems of machine–human conversation have offered or claimed therapeutic results.[4] With collaborators, in 2014 I conducted a 'Wizard of Oz' experiment – explained later in the chapter – as a counsellor for a severely cognitively impaired US veteran within the US Veterans' Hospital system.[5] We had strikingly successful results in terms of the willingness of the patient to communicate with what he believed to be a machine, sometimes preferring to communicate with that system rather than his wife, who was also his carer. At this point, it may be appropriate to explain the Wizard of Oz methodology, since it is important for what follows later.

'Wizard of Oz', or the 'OZ paradigm', is an attested way of doing human–machine communication experiments more cheaply and

---

[3] K. Colby, 1969, "Dialogues between Humans and an Artificial Belief System," in *IJCAI 69: Proceedings of the 1st International Joint Conference on Artificial Intelligence*, May, 319–324.

[4] For example, K. Ly, A. Ly and G. Anderson, 2017, "A Fully Automated Conversational Agent for Promoting Mental Well-being: A Pilot RCT Using Mixed Methods," *Science Direct* 10, 39–46. A survey of such offerings can also be seen in Adam S. Miner, et al., 2016, "Smartphone-Based Conversational Agents and Responses to Questions about Mental Health," *Interpersonal Violence, and Physical Health, JAMA Internal Medicine* 176(5), 619–625.

[5] Y. Wilks, et al., 2015, "CALONIS: An Artificial Companion within a Smart Home for the Care of Cognitively Impaired Patients," in *Smart Homes and Health Telematics*, ed. C. Bodine et al., ICOST 2014, Lecture Notes in Computer Science, Vol. 8456, Springer.

in a simple controllable form: a subject believes they are talking to a machine but in fact they are talking to a person, usually disguised behind an artificial voice and visual avatar head. The name refers to the 1930s movie where, at the end, the great Wizard is revealed as a small man behind a curtain with a booming voice. The deception has been deemed generally acceptable by researchers as a way of gaining insight into how people interact with machines, all of which is done without the huge expense of creating full machine systems. It is usually polite at the end to inform subjects that they have been deceived in a minor way to conduct the experiment, and other ethical concerns can be considered.[6] In our project an ethics board reviewed our proposed experiments and approved them. A substantial part of the experience of human communication with machines has been gained from such systems, and we will describe one in detail below.

CHATBOTS AND DIALOGUE THEORY: A LONG-RUNNING DIVISION IN AI RESEARCH

Most AI researchers consider PARRY and ELIZA to be early chatbots, a term they use to indicate dialogue systems with no substantial theory of human understanding nor coded knowledge behind them: that is, they just chat. The best chatbots have sometimes been entered in the annual Loebner Competition to find the most convincing machine dialogue partner of the year. This competition is often won by amateurs, and AI theorists have slowly had to adapt to the (for them) unpleasant fact that theoretically motivated systems have produced few functional conversationalists.[7] With colleagues, I presented a model for a plausible compromise between the two positions. It was with such a compromise system that I led a team that won the Loebner Competition in 1997; our entry was based on a *dialogue manager* that had access to a large set of scripts corresponding to topics, and the role of the manager was to determine at every point in the conversation what script it was

---

[6] On the practical and ethical concerns of the WoZ method see Gianluca Schiavo et al., 2016, "Wizard of Oz Studies with Older Adults: A Methodological Note," in *International Reports on Socio-Informatics (IRSI), Proceedings of the COOP 2016 – Symposium on Challenges and Experiences in Designing for an Ageing Society*, ed. Markus Garschall et al., 13(3), 93–100. Also, E. Adar, D. S. Tan and J. Teevan, 2013, "Benevolent Deception in Human Computer Interaction," in *Proceedings of the SIGCHI Conference on Human Factors in Computing Systems*, ACM Press.

[7] This split in approach is discussed in more detail in R. Catizone, et al., 2011, "Some Background on Dialogue Management and Conversational Speech for Dialogue Systems," *Computer Speech and Language* 25(2), 127–480.

running and how to shift to another script seamlessly when the human changed the topic.

However, this dispute has been superseded in AI research by the rise of machine learning, which takes little account of pre-existing 'theory' of any sort, and of the rules that normally express that theory such as scripts or dialogue managers. A machine-learning approach is perfectly compatible with an accelerated chatbot program of learning from the transcripts of real interactions with machines as well as between humans. And this combination of chatbot writing and mass gleaning from actual conversation is what has powered the commercial success of AI systems for the home such as Siri and Alexa.

Another fact has emerged in all this, one again not congenial to traditional AI: to be plausible a machine conversationalist must display some form of emotional empathy and even humour to gain acceptance and not be viewed as simply a cold, chippy know-it-all, a common view of early machine conversationalists.[8] I write 'uncongenial' because research in the modelling of humour and emotion were also thought to be far from the interests of core AI for decades, focusing as they did exclusively on knowledge representation and reasoning.

THE ROMANTIC VISION OF MACHINES
AS THE SUPERIOR PARTNER

This section is a brief diversion to consider historical attitudes to machines as partners, and in particular the upshot of the Romantic movement in nineteenth-century Germany and its beliefs about the greater perfection and interest of the mechanical over the human. At the start of modern AI, Donald Michie argued that many would prefer to deal with machines rather than people, citing motorists' preference for (unbiased) traffic lights over a police officer on point duty.[9]

---

[8]   P. Wallis et al., 2010., "Conversation in Context: What Should a Robot Companion Say?," in *Proceedings of EMCSR*, 547–552.

[9]   For a wider discussion of these issues see A. Foerst, 2004, *God in the Machine: What Robots Teach Us about Humanity and God*, Dutton; N. L. Herzfeld, 2002, "In Our Image: Artificial Intelligence and the Human Spirit," in *Theology and the Sciences*, ed. Kevin J. Sharpe, Fortress Press; B. Johnson, 2008, *Persons and Things*, Harvard University Press; A. Mayor, 2018, *Gods and Robots: Myths, Machines and Ancient Dreams of Technology*, Princeton University Press; A. Rosenfeld, 1966, "Religion and the Robot: Impact of Artificial Intelligence on Religious Anthropologies," *Tradition: A Journal of Orthodox Thought* 8(3), 15–26.

Romantic Visions of Machines as Perfect:
(1) Making Human-Like Things

The making of human-like things artificially is a tradition that goes back to Ovid's story of Pygmalion bringing the statue Galatea to life, a legend that reappears in a new form, via Shaw's *Pygmalion*, in our own time as the musical *My Fair Lady*. In this tradition were the Golem of Prague and, of course, Frankenstein's monster. In nineteenth-century German Romantic thought, Kleist argued that marionettes and puppets were in some ways more perfect than humans, in part because they were not conscious, with all the problems that state brings.[10] John Gray has taken this observation as the starting point for an investigation of free will and raises the possibility that having conscious choice is a drawback.[11] It remains a lingering idea on the edge of AI that, like Kleist's marionette, the artificial can be more perfect than the human and is, in that sense, more godlike. Many Eastern religious traditions also see consciousness as something to be transcended in meditation, not indulged or celebrated. In the 1920s, J. D. Bernal was one of a group of British scientists who thought that with human augmentation and ingenuity: "Consciousness itself might vanish in a humanity that had become completely etherealized."[12]

Romantic Visions of Machines as Perfect:
(2) Augmenting Humans

The last quotation is a transition from a futurist discourse about creating humans to one of adapting or evolving existing humans (or some of them, anyway), so that they become immortal or superintelligent themselves. Groups or individuals who believe this are now called Transhumanists and have close links back to the Greek Gnostics and eighteenth-century rationalism and humanism, now moving on to the worship of adapted humans or 'supermen', to use Nietzsche's term. Views only differ in the source of the supreme intelligence, not the goal itself: ourselves transformed (transhumanism) or the artificial (the superintelligence, as apart from humanity). This is not a new idea: one of Schubert's most famous songs is set to a poem by the nineteenth-century writer Mueller and contains the line "Will kein Gott auf Erden

---

[10] Heinrich von Kleist, 1972, "On the Marionette Theatre," trans. Thomas G. Neumiller, *The Drama Review* 16(3), 22–26.

[11] J. Gray, 2015, *The Soul of the Marionette*, Penguin Books.

[12] J. D. Bernal, 1929, *The World, the Flesh and the Devil: An Enquiry into the Future of the Three Enemies of the Rational Soul*, Jonathan Cape, 23.

sein, sind wir selber Götter" – if a god will not come down to earth, we will be gods ourselves!

The practical elements for this augmentation include surgery – exoskeletons fitted onto our bodies to aid human work – as well as the considerable current US Department of Defense efforts to build 'perfect soldiers' with drugs and prostheses, a tradition going back to hashish-fuelled Ottoman armies in the Middle Ages. Kurzweil was not only an AI originator but the modern source of the notion of the Technological Singularity, which was also foreseen by I. J. Good in the mid-1960s: the moment of the emergence of the super- or ultraintelligent machine, after which no more human discoveries would be necessary.[13] For Kurzweil, this notion remains connected to transhumanism, and he believes a future machine–human fusion will remain human and benign, whereas in Bostrom's[14] dystopian future the superintelligence is alien and hostile.

Romantic Visions of Machines as Perfect:
(3) God-Machines and AI Religions

Making gods, like all traditions, is ancient, going back at least to Aaron's Golden Calf and the Baal Gods of Iron, as well as to lucky Roman Emperors after their deaths. Bostrom's emergent superintelligence certainly has godlike qualities, and it is interesting to note his complex and almost certainly false argument that this emergent superintelligence will be unique since it will kill all its competitors. His godlike AI world ruler is thus thoroughly monotheist. The reaction against this god-making tradition is very strong in the old monotheistic religions: Islam, Judaism and reformed Christianity all tend to be hostile to any notion of 'graven images', which is to say entities created in the image of humans as gods. Unsurprisingly perhaps, this notion spread on to Marxism, itself almost a fourth Abrahamic religion, and Marx's fear of fetishisation, in his case of commodities. In an extraordinary passage in *Das Capital*, he writes: "The fetishism of commodities: The form of wood, for instance, is altered by making a table out of it. Yet for all that the table remains an ordinary thing, wood. But, as soon as it steps forth as a commodity, it is changed into something transcendent."[15] Inevitably, AI has already

---

[13] R. Kurzweil, 1999, *The Age of Spiritual Machines: How We Will Live, Work and Think in the New Age of Intelligent Machines*, Viking.

[14] N. Bostrom, 2014, *Superintelligence: Paths, Dangers, Strategies*, Oxford University Press.

[15] K. Marx, 2012 [1867], *Das Kapital: A Critique of Political Economy*, Gateway Editions.

inspired explicit new religious movements worshipping yet to be created AI intelligences, and it is hard to know how seriously their creators take them. Infamously, in the USA, Anthony Lewandowski founded what purported to be an AI religion, which was set up to worship a soon to be manifested superintelligence, though it is reported he has now shut this down.[16]

Automating Religious Practice

Religious machines go back to Tibetan prayer wheels turned by streams and medieval automata celebrating Easter. A wide range of apps are now publicly available, from the trivial to the potentially interesting, to support religious practices: the home chat Companions Alexa and Siri can recite prayers on demand, as with the Church of England's downloadable Alexa Skill, and it is clear there is a serious amount of online prayer available on the Internet. In Japan, MINDAR is a Buddhist priest in robot form that conducts prayers, blessings and ceremonies. In East Asia there is undoubtedly more of this activity, and a Japanese AI professor has expressed the view that, in their Buddhist tradition, there is not the same firm distinction between the animate and inanimate as in the West: there are spirits in everything. As Minoru Asada, president of the Robotics Society of Japan, puts it: "In Japan we believe all inanimate objects have a soul, so a metal robot is no different from a human in that respect, there are less boundaries between humans and objects."[17]

Such apps would only be of serious religious interest if they were able to perform rites such as confession or saying Mass, and it is hard to imagine any church validating an automaton to do such things at present. But the notion is worth exploring if one believes that there is nothing *in principle* a human can do that a machine cannot. One can well imagine a machine confessor by extending the notion of a machine psychiatrist, of which there have been many incarnations over the fifty years since ELIZA,[18] or perhaps even a robot

---

[16] WIRED, 2014, "Inside the First Church of Artificial Intelligence," www.wired.com/story/anthony-levandowski-artificial-intelligence-religion/.

[17] Daily Mail, 2020, "'Blade Runner' Future of Human-Like Androids a Step Closer as First Robot Learns to 'Feel Pain'," www.dailymail.co.uk/news/article-8034351/Blade-Runner-future-human-like-androids-step-closer-robot-learns-feel-pain.html.

[18] See K. Fitzpatrick, A. Darcy and M. Vierhile, 2017, "Delivering Cognitive Behavior Therapy to Young Adults with Symptoms of Depression and Anxiety Using a Fully Automated Conversational Agent (Woebot): A Randomized Controlled Trial," *JMIR Mental Health* 4(2), e19; H. Gaffney, W. Mansell and S. Tai, 2019, "Conversational Agents in the Treatment of Mental Health Problems: Mixed-Method Systematic Review," *JMIR Mental Health* 10, https://doi.org/10.2196/14166.

sports or gym coach, with which the Internet is full. Understandable reluctance by religious authorities, however, has not held back amateur enthusiasts, and there are many reports of online confessionals using humans[19] as well as many with automated chatbots on the other end of the confession.[20] None of the latter are academic studies and they cannot be assessed here, but some report high public take-up and satisfaction, though given the primitive responses of most easily available chatbots, it is hard to understand the satisfaction reported. Nonetheless, the bar is not high in these matters and experience shows how little sensible feedback from a machine a person may be content with.

That kind of religious Companion – acting as a spiritual director, confessor or just a therapist or moral advisor – would essentially contain a copy of its subject, though not at all like the proposed 'uploaded brain' of the transhumanists but working at the level of language rather than neurons. It is not hard to see how such an entity might function as an ethical advisor or a confessor if it had detailed knowledge of the person it had learned from or copied. As noted earlier, AI has now largely shifted to machine learning as its principal paradigm, which has resulted in programs whose operations and reasons for action are often obscure, even to those who programmed them, based as they are on sometimes inscrutable neural nets rather than rules. One can argue that human motivations are, from the point of view of outside observers, no more or less obscure than those of these most advanced machines, and so we are now at an interesting point where discovering the reasons behind the actions of humans and machines may be in much the same position. It is this fact that explains the return of some of the attitudes of long-discarded cybernetics,[21] which saw humans and machines as part of a single interactive system. That development now renders more plausible the possibility of an automated advisor on human action and conduct since it could have the same status as technical efforts to explain the actions of machines.

---

[19] BetterMarketing, 2020, "Our Online Confession Booth Campaign Went off the Rails," https://bettermarketing.pub/our-online-confession-booth-campaign-went-off-the-rails-2b4c33cb1af9; JotForm – Online Churches, 2023, "Online Confession and Absolution," www.jotform.com/blog/online-confession-absolution/.

[20] K. Den Hollander, J. Hulsebosch and S. van Luipen, 2019, "Meet Beau, a Reflection Chatbot," www.joitskehulsebosch.nl/wp-content/uploads/2019/03/Meet-Beau-the-reflection-chatbot-light-version.pdf.

[21] S. Beer, 1965, "Cybernetics and the Knowledge of God," *Month* 34, 291–303; N. Wiener, 1964, *God and Golem: A Comment on Certain Points Where Cybernetics Impinges on Religion*, MIT Press.

ARTIFICIAL COMPANIONS AND SPIRITUAL ENHANCEMENT   283

Yuval Harari has argued,[22] however, that having a machine that "understands us better than ourselves" can be seen as the end of the long tradition of individualist rationalism, with us since the seventeenth and eighteenth centuries, and on which our Western assumptions about religion, morals and politics rest: the belief that the individual has a free choice as to his or her actions and beliefs. Harari would almost certainly say that an ethical companion/confessor (human or machine) makes nonsense of that, even though many still find it perfectly acceptable and common sense that someone close to them knows better than they do what they want and why they act as they do. Successful arranged marriages are said work on just that principle.

THE ORIGINAL COMPANIONS PROJECT AND ITS AIMS

My own interest in the theme of this chapter was kindled when I was visited in Sheffield some twenty years ago by a senior UK Jesuit involved in his order's web and computing technology. He somehow knew of my Artificial Companion project[23] and wanted to discuss its possible religious relevance. We discussed whether people would ever accept any form of artificial entity in a religious role and to talk to it about religious matters. Things have come a long way in the succeeding twenty years: primitive Companions are now everywhere, most obviously in homes with Alexa, Siri and their sisters. Yet these are still very primitive devices from a technical point of view, as well from that of the vision of the original project where the vision was of a Companion that would know all about you, maybe more than you did yourself, and help organise your memories as they faded and leave behind some permanent memorial of your whole life.

Artificial Companions (2006–2010) was a major EU project and not at all about fooling us that Companions are human. They would not pretend to be human, and would have no need of a human form, as opposed to a toy, a handbag or just a phone. The distinguishing features of a general Companion agent are that it has no overriding task of its own except to be the Companion of the individual who uses it, about whom it has a great deal of personal knowledge, gathered over an extended period, and with whom it establishes some form of relationship and to whom it has a duty of loyalty, discretion and confidentiality.

[22]   N. Yuval Harari, 2017, *Homo Deus*, Harper Collins
[23]   "COMPANIONS: Persistent Multi-modal Interfaces to the Internet," https://cordis .europa.eu/project/id/034434.

This project also assumed that a computer could make judgements about a human's mental or cognitive state. The 'Turing Test'[24] is one where a human judge decides whether an entity is a machine or a human. A quite different and opposite approach[25] argued that it would make perfectly good sense for a *machine to judge a human's mental state*: a sort of reverse Turing Test. This was an important shift in perspective.

The demonstration of the Companions project, now primitive in modern terms, can still be accessed on YouTube.[26] Commercial products such as Siri and Alexa have hugely bypassed it in terms of scope but not in concept, since the Companion idea was that of a long-term companion that got to know one's personal knowledge and was situated on the web so that its physical form was irrelevant. The technical basis of the project was a system of partial scripts for dialogue, based on the assumption that much of what we say is stereotyped to some degree. The originality and complexity in normal human life, on this view, comes from our ability to switch seamlessly between these scripts – to change topics and return to them. This view is not unrelated to Roger Schank's[27] view of intelligence as the manipulation of a set of individual narratives, as well as William Clocksin's view of the role of narrative in intelligence (see Chapter 2). The project had at its computational base a stack system for moving between scripts and returning to them, when necessary, as required by the flow of conversation and new incoming information.

Some of those aspects were:

1. The project was originally designed in about 2000 as a companion for lonely old people of whom there are growing numbers, so that they could review their lives in photographs and other physical memories. It was assumed that the bar is low for this kind of companionship: as much research has demonstrated, elderly people are grateful for any level of conversation, however primitive or artificial. It was assumed that the Companion would, over a long period of time with an old person, gather details of their lives and relationships and assist them when and if dementia set in, reminding them, for example, who their children (in photographs) were and of the places they had been to.

---

[24]   A. M. Turing, 1950, "Computing Machinery and Intelligence," *Mind* 59(236), 433–460.
[25]   Y. Wilks, 1975, "Putnam and Clarke and Mind and Body," *British Journal for the Philosophy of Science* 26(3), 213–225.
[26]   "The Companions Project," YouTube, www.youtube.com/watch?v=-Xx5hgjD-Mw.
[27]   R. Schank, 1995, *Tell Me a Story: Narrative and Intelligence*, Nortwestern University Press.

ARTIFICIAL COMPANIONS AND SPIRITUAL ENHANCEMENT 285

2. The claim was that for the many who will not write their own memorials, but who die leaving a mass of images and texts, the Companion with access to these could compose an autobiography for its owner to leave behind for relatives and survivors rather than just a mass of unorganised data to be thrown away.

3. The argument was that beyond simple purchases, pornography and vacations, the Web is in fact hard for people to use and search effectively without training and skills. With all one's text and image data on the Web, a Companion with access to these would be able to assist people by means of ordinary dialogue to get what they want from the Web as it would have search skills and knowledge of what they actually wanted.

4. This is an extension of the same idea of agency, that one's Companion would become one web agent, for real estate purchases for example, or as a power of attorney were one to become incapacitated. One could even imagine a Companion continuing to vote for one after death, knowing one's political views in some detail.

5. The article "Death and the Internet"[28] set out this idea of agency continuing after death such that, with the voice and video simulations now possible, one could continue to communicate with the dead, or rather with their Companion, an idea that has become real and recently patented by Microsoft.[29] This could give comfort and enable one to ask, say, those questions to dead parents that one never did in life.

6. The Ethical Companion continues and extends an idea touched on earlier: a Companion advisor who knows one intimately, possibly better than one does oneself.[30] This was stimulated by the writings of John Gray, who argued that we do not know how our cognitive functions work, and it is open for others to tell us and always has been.[31] In the joint paper cited, a parallel is drawn between human action and with the current state of AI where network-based machine learning has produced systems

---

[28] Y. Wilks, 2010, "Death and the Internet," *Prospect*, 20 October, www.prospectmagazine .co.uk/magazine/death-and-the-internet.

[29] Windows Central, 2021, "Microsoft Patents Tech to Let You Talk to Dead People as Chatbots," www.windowscentral.com/microsoft-patents-tech-let-you-talk-dead-family-members-celebrities-and-fictional-characters.

[30] Y. Wilks and M. Dorubantu, 2019, "Moral Orthoses: A New Approach to Human and Machine Ethics," *Zygon: Journal of Religion & Science* 54(4), 1004–1021.

[31] Gray, *The Soul of the Marionette*.

286 YORICK WILKS

that make good decisions, even though we do not know how. A new AI area (XAI)[32] has developed attempting to explain how these inscrutable networks reach their decisions, since it is hard to deal with systems one does not understand. Dennett's "folk psychology"[33] is his term for the long human trek to create theories so that we do come to understand ourselves.

An element of the Templeton-funded project on Spiritual Intelligences, part of the Templeton World Charity's Diverse Intelligences initiative, concerns adapting something of the Artificial Companion concept in a role of a possible confessor and counsellor. Doing this is not to presume upon priestly authority in the sacraments: it is to find out if people, religious or not, are prepared to talk to what they believe to be an automaton in some form close to confession, or have a discussion on religious doubt or ethical problems, and if so to receive benefit from it or not. It is an investigation on a small scale into people's attitudes to such opening up to a sympathetic automaton, which they encounter as a friendly screen face and voice, both of them artificial and in the Wizard of Oz mode described earlier. As we also noted, there is evidence that people will in some circumstances prefer to deal with an automaton, such as job centre clerks (with less feeling of humiliation) or with certain kinds of medical staff about personal or sexual matters (with less embarrassment).

We used the well-tried WoZ technique, described earlier, where a person talks to a screen image and voice *believing it to be a machine, although in fact it is a human.* As discussed, this is a well-attested exploratory technique for assessing human attitudes to machines and has passed all the standard ethical tests as well as an ethics board, which reviewed our specific proposed experiments and approved them. We also explained at the end of the experiment to subjects that they were not actually talking to a machine. We also embody in the project all kinds of safeguards for our volunteers: with them being anonymous to the Wizard-person, known only by a pseudonym, and all such links and data being destroyed. Nor will any voice recordings be kept. The volunteer will thus be totally safe from identification.

The overall question for this part of this project was what religious and spiritual role such a Companion might play in the more AI-driven

[32] R. Hoffman, R. Klein and S. Mueller, 2018, *Literature Review and Integration of Key Ideas for Explainable AI*, prepared by Task Area 2 DARPA XAI Program Award No. FA8650-17-12-7711.

[33] D. Dennett, 1971, "Intentional Systems," *Journal of Philosophy* 68, 87–106.

world into which we are rapidly moving, though the specific question is whether such a Companion is acceptable or beneficial to our subjects. We can contrast here the roles of the therapist with the confessor or spiritual director, whom we might consider on a continuum from the non-judgemental to the judgemental, yet each of whom might be assumed to know their interlocutor's life in some detail with regard to actions, secrets, motives, history and desires. The forms of judgement involved could be moral but are more likely to be supportive, curative and directional as to future behaviour. If embodied in a phone, one can see such a Companion as a portable, and constantly consulted, spiritual and moral advisor, explaining one's actions and desires as one reports them to it, in ways that might well be inscrutable to the subject without any self-insight.

A Spiritual Companion could suggest spiritual interpretations of events in people's lives, which would have elements of both therapy and spiritual guidance, including the recommendation/prescription of practices of prayer, reading and meditation. It could be customised to the individual owner and a world away from the simplicities of the Jesuit site Sacred Space (www.sacredspace.ie). It would create something closer to the approach of spiritual direction that helps a person deepen their spiritual life but, in this case, drawing on what technology enables.

Such a Companion could also draw on the tradition of automated exercise coaches, as well as breathing and meditation coaches, often now accessed through headphones, and which are reliably claimed to lower heart rates. These developments are closely related to traditional breathing exercises in meditation and prayer, in the Jesuit tradition among others, and the project will investigate what can be learned from them and incorporated in a Companion. Though most people would not accept the Companion taking on the sacerdotal role of absolution after confession, it could offer some of what people gain from a conversation that takes place in spiritual direction or pastoral care.

The Companion might also offer help in coping with solitary environments. We will be drawing from the monastic tradition, which includes isolation for meditation and prayer, where such a Companion would have an obvious role. But in the modern world there are other environments where the value of such companionship might be explored, such as making long-term prison sentences more tolerable and even redemptive, as well as dealing with the stressed mental states of those in long-submersed submarine crews, Antarctic research stations and space platforms.

We can also envisage such a Companion helping in the development of character strengths and virtues, and recent research on developing practices of forgiveness, gratitude and humility. The Companion might well be adaptable to make use of highly ordered forms such as monastic offices, where an individual gets a sense of freedom by moving past the structure (some liken this to looking through a window, where the office acts as the window frame). The embodiment of silence, as well as talk, in a Companion raises the possibility of embodying an 'apophatic' approach to spirituality, which works with emptiness rather than words or images.

THE SMALL-SCALE REALISTIC PSEUDO-COMPANION WE PROPOSE HERE

The Companion about to be described differs from the speculative ones discussed earlier in that it was not possible at this stage to base it on detailed personal knowledge of the human subject. However, there are many scenarios, from confession to forms of psychotherapy, where that is not essential. Phase 1 of the work used a small number of subjects, treating them as case studies. The products were:

- Text data – what our subjects actually say – automatically transcribed by Google from speech to text.
- Results on the acceptability and benefits of such conversations with a computer advisor/companion, based on debriefing questionnaires after both phases of the experiment.

There could in principle be different forms of such a Spiritual Companion such as: (1) in the style of a spiritual director; (2) in the style of a therapist with religious subject matter; (3) in the style of an ethical explainer – one whose role would be to explain to a user the motives for their actual past or contemplated actions, which may not be clear to the person involved. In future work, separate companions could be developed in these different styles, but the preliminary work we propose here will be a composite of all these, in the sense that our human volunteer Wizards should be able and willing to discuss in all these modes with the subject.

In this work we have also assessed the general acceptability of an artificial Spiritual Companion. We would gain information about this from our in-depth case studies and will assess if subjects react positively and, at subsequent evaluations and debriefings, find the interactions helpful. The most important results would be: (1) whether the attention and interest of the subject were held sufficiently and there are standard 'stickiness' measures in terms of sentence length of response etc. to measure this; (2) changes detected by language software regarding emotion and belief in the subjects' responses; and (3) any subsequent feedback questionnaires from subjects on benefits gained (or not) from the interaction.

The initial set-up has been a Zoom platform with a male avatar based on the face of a project researcher, to avoid copyright problems, together with:

- a volunteer site and machine (their own) which can be anywhere;
- the system site hosting and presenting the speaking avatar and recording the dialogue;
- the (normally remote) site where the Wizard is located; and
- an observer/host site for one of our team to observe any system difficulties or breakdowns and to manage the start/finish and the invitations to join, but not to intervene explicitly, as this could break the confidence of the subject in anonymity.

The Wizard hears but does not see the volunteer and can speak or type in reply. In either case, they will see what is being said automatically transcribed and will hear the Avatar's voice speaking the transcription.

In the second phase of the experiment, with a larger group of (n = 30) subjects, we shifted to the subject's interaction on the same platform with a real automated system, in this case the GPT3 (Generative Pretrained Transformer 3) multibillion node trainable network built by OpenAI. This has been much discussed in the public media as a source of generated prose, poems, jokes and so on, and we have experimented with it here as a passable dialogue partner, using the same set-up as in Phase 1 but now telling the somewhat larger group of subjects truthfully that they are in fact talking to a computer. In these dialogues there was no attempt to impose any role on the WoZ/computer side; the conversation flowed without any determination of role for the system itself.

WHAT CAN WE EXTRACT FROM THE FIRST PHASE RESULTS?

Although the second phase of the project is still ongoing, one can see already that subjects enjoy the interactions in both phases, and this has been the more or less universal response to machine conversational interactions. Psychological results are not less valuable because many turn out as expected. With careful probing it may be possible to establish that there are benefits the volunteer was not already aware of.

There were twenty-two dialogue sessions obtained from the first implementation of the Spiritual Companion, with which we tested the interest in using a dialogue system, employing a Wizard rather than an AI, although of course the subjects believed it was a machine they were talking to. The involvement of each user in the dialogue, judged by the number of words spoken, was not only sustained but seemed to grow throughout the session, as in all but one of the twenty-two sessions the user spoke more words in the last two-thirds of the session than in the first third. The term 'stickiness' is often used to indicate how far a dialogue holds the attention and interest of a subject and these figures suggest, albeit on a small scale, that these dialogues did hold the attention of those taking part.

To analyse the tenor of the session, we extracted the subjects' utterances and mapped them onto a large, embedded word space. This showed that, though the subjects were free to talk about any subject in their sessions with the Spiritual Companion, the topics chosen were very personal and often related to spirituality, family and community. If we look at the sessions as they evolved, we see that some topics were discussed more at the beginning of the sessions, and some were discussed towards the middle or ends. For example, problems were broached more in the final third of the sessions than in the beginning or middle. This naturally occurs in normal conversations, too, as if people are wary of unburdening themselves too soon. At the beginning of sessions, people talked more about spirituality, adversity, change and health but gradually abandoned these descriptive topics as the sessions progressed into more personal areas.

The second phase of the experiment, with subjects talking to the GPT3 network, is still ongoing; the results have yet to be analysed and will be published later. But the overall picture is already clear that subjects were happy to talk to the computer network, as they had been to talk to the Wizards in the first (WoZ) phase.

CONCLUSION

The present volume is testimony to the growing interest in the relevance of AI to religion and the religious life; there are many ongoing efforts, and many of the issues raised here are discussed in Balle.[34] The small-scale investigation described in this chapter, whatever its outcome, in no way settles the wider question of just what roles a Spiritual Companion

---

[34] S. Balle, 2023, "Theological Dimensions of Humanlike Robots: A Roadmap for Theological Inquiry," *Theology and Science* 21(1), 132–156.

might come to play as conversational technologies and models of the human subject become more sophisticated. One could imagine two axes at right angles that provide four spaces: one axis would be Direction versus Support, running from an exercise of authority over a subject's life to an acceptance of that life. The other axis would be Truth versus Therapy, where the range would be from theological dogma at one end to some form of stasis at the other, where a subject's beliefs could be discussed while remaining vague or unformed. Thus, in the quarter space of Direction and Truth one could see a Companion as endeavouring to instil some form of catechism. In the quarter of Direction and Therapy, it would question life direction and possibly offer penance. In the quarter Truth and Support, the Companion's emphasis would be on reasoned argument and evidence, of the kind the IBM debater was said to be good at.[35] Finally, in the Therapy and Support quarter there would be dialogues that were non-confrontational and aimed at easing tensions in the subject. One might say that these axes are not actually perpendicular (i.e., exclusive) of each other, but they capture emphases and differences in what our subjects want to discuss, and ways in which a Spiritual Companion could function, as needed, and in all four spaces. As we said at the beginning, these experiments and speculations are very much a mouse after the grandeur of its original aims but there is no reason to think its outcomes need be trivial.

BIBLIOGRAPHY

Balle, S. 2023. "Theological Dimensions of Humanlike Robots: A Roadmap for Theological Inquiry." *Theology and Science* 21(1), 132–156.

Beer, S. 1965. "Cybernetics and the Knowledge of God." *Month* 34, 291–303

Catizone, R. et al. 2011. "Some Background on Dialogue Management and Conversational Speech for Dialogue Systems." *Computer Speech and Language* 25(2), 128–139.

Colby, K. 1969. "Dialogues between Humans and an Artificial Belief System." *IJCAI 69: Proceedings of the 1st International Joint Conference on Artificial Intelligence*, 319–324

Dennett, D. 1971. "Intentional Systems." *Journal of Philosophy* 68, 87–106.

Fitzpatrick, K., Darcy, A. and Vierhile, M. 2017. "Delivering Cognitive Behavior Therapy to Young Adults with Symptoms of Depression and Anxiety Using a Fully Automated Conversational Agent (Woebot): A Randomized Controlled Trial." *JMIR Mental Health* 4(2), e19.

---

[35] CNET, 2018, "An IBM Computer Debates Humans, and Wins, in a New, Nuanced Competition," www.cnet.com/science/an-ibm-computer-debates-humans-and-wins-in-a-new-nuanced-competition/.

Gaffney, H., Mansell, W. and Tai, S. 2019. "Revisiting Conversational Agents in the Treatment of Mental Health Problems: Mixed-Method Systematic Review." *JMIR Mental Health* 6(10), e14166.

Johnson, B. 2008. *Persons and Things*. Harvard University Press.

Ly, K., Ly, A. and Andersson, G. 2017. "A Fully Automated Conversational Agent for Promoting Mental Well-being: A Pilot RCT Using Mixed methods." *Internet Interventions* 10, 39–46.

Rosenfeld, A. 1966. "Religion and the Robot: Impact of Artificial Intelligence on Religious Anthropologies." *Tradition: A Journal of Orthodox Thought* 8(3), 15–26.

Schank, R. 1995. *Tell Me a Story: Narrative and Intelligence*. Northwestern University Press.

Schiavo, G. et al. 2016. "Wizard of Oz Studies with Older Adults: A Methodological Note." In *International Reports on Socio-Informatics (IRSI), Proceedings of the COOP 2016 – Symposium on Challenges and Experiences in Designing for an Ageing Society*, ed. M. Garschall et al., 13(3), 93–100.

Turing, A. M. 1950. "Computing Machinery and Intelligence." *Mind* 59(236), 433–460.

Weizenbaum, J. 1966. "ELIZA: A Computer Programme for the Study of Natural Language Communication between Men and Machines." *Communications of the ACM* 9, 36–45.

Wilks, Y. and Dorubantu, M. 2019. "Moral Orthoses: A New Approach to Human and Machine Ethics." *Zygon: Journal of Religion & Science* 54(4), 1004–1021.

Bibliography

Adar, Eytan, Desney S. Tan, and Jaime Teevan. 2013. "Benevolent Deception in Human Computer Interaction," in *Proceedings of the SIGCHI Conference on Human Factors in Computing Systems*, ACM Press, 1863–72, April 2013. https://doi.org/10.1145/2470654.2466246.

Adhvarin, Dharmarāja. 1971. *Vedāntaparibhāṣā*, edited and translated by S. S. Suryanarayana Sastri, Madras: Adyar Library and Research Centre.

AIR: Acceptable Intelligence with Responsibility. 2019. 日本における人工知能研究をめぐる オーラルヒストリー—Vol. 5(斉藤 康己) Nihon ni okeru jinkōchinō kenkyū o meguru ōraru historī vol. 5: Saitō Yasuki [Oral History of Japanese AI research vol. 5: Saito Yasuki]. Retrieved from: http://sig-air.org/wp/wp-content/uploads/2019/07/Oralhistory_v5_181022_saito.pdf.

Akbari, Suzanne. 2009. *Idols in the East: European Representations of Islam and the Orient, 1100–1450*, Ithaca: Cornell University Press.

Albattah, Waleed, Muhammad Haris Kaka Khel, Shabana Habib, Muhammad Islam, Sheroz Khan, and Kushsairy Abdul Kadir. 2021. "Hajj Crowd Management Using CNN-Based Approach," in *Computers, Materials, & Continua*, 66(2), 2183–97. https://doi.org/10.32604/cmc.2020.014227.

Allen, Jonathan. 2006. "The Disney Touch at a Hindu Temple," *New York Times* (8 June 2006), available at www.nytimes.com/2006/06/08/travel/08letter.html [accessed 25 May 2021].

Alwishah, Ahmed. 2013. "Ibn Sīnā on Floating Man Arguments," in *Journal of Islamic Philosophy*, 9, 32–53. https://doi.org/10.5840/islamicphil201395.

Ammon, Laura, and Randall Reed. 2019. "Is Alexa My Neighbor?," in *Journal of Posthuman Studies*, 3(2), 120–40. https://doi.org/10.5325/jpoststud.3.2.0120.

Attas, Syed Muhammad Naquib al-. 1995. "The Nature of Man and the Psychology of the Human Soul," in *Prolegomena to the Metaphysics of Islam*, Kuala Lumpur, Malaysia: The International Institute of Islamic Thought and Civilization (ISTAC), 143–76.

1989. *Islam and the Philosophy of Science*, Kuala Lumpur, Malaysia: International Institute of Islamic Thought and Civilization.

Avicenna. 2005. *The Metaphysics of the Healing*, translated by Michael E. Marmura, Provoh (Utah): Brigham Young University Press.

Bailey, Edward. 1997. *Implicit Religion in Contemporary Society*, Kampen, The Netherlands: Kok Pharos Publishing House.

Bainbridge, William Sims. 2006. *God from the Machine: Artificial Intelligence Models of Religious Cognition*, Lanham, MD: AltaMira Press.

Balle, Simon. 2023. "Theological Dimensions of Humanlike Robots: A Roadmap for Theological Inquiry," in *Theology and Science*, 21(1), 132–56.

Ballim, Afzal, and Yorick Wilks. 1991. *Artificial Believers*, New York: Psychology Press.

Barbour, Ian G. 1999. "Neuroscience, Artificial Intelligence, and Human Nature: Theological and Philosophical Reflections," in *Zygon: Journal of Religion and Science*, 34(3), 361–98. https://doi.org/10.1111/0591-2385.00222.

Barnard, Philip J. 2019a. "Paying Attention to Meanings in the Psychological Sciences and the Performing Arts," in N. Shaughnessy, and P. Barnard (eds.) *Performing Psychologies: Imagination, Creativity and Dramas of the Mind*, London: Bloomsbury Methuen, 41–66.

2019b. "Sticks, Stones, and the Origins of Sapience," in K. A. Overmann, and F. L. Coolidge (eds.) *Squeezing Minds from Stones: Cognitive Archaeology and the Evolution of the Human Mind*, New York: Oxford University Press, 102–27.

Barnard, Philip J., and John D. Teasdale. 1991. "Interacting Cognitive Subsystems: A Systemic Approach to Cognitive-Affective Interaction and Change," in *Cognition and Emotion*, 5(1), 1–39.

Barrington-Ward, Simon. 2014 [1996]. *The Jesus Prayer: A Way to Contemplation*, Oxford: Pauline Books & Media.

Barzilai, Maya. 2016. *Golem: Modern Wars and Their Monsters*, New York: New York University Press.

Basak, Sonali. 2021. "Wall Street Visionaries Provide Chilling Views on Next Big Risk," in *Bloomberg News* (12 January 2021), available at www.bloomberg.com/news/articles/2021-01-12/what-do-wall-street-leaders-think-is-the-next-big-risk? [accessed 17 January 2021].

BBC. 2014. "Stephen Hawking Warns Artificial Intelligence Could End Mankind," available at www.bbc.co.uk/news/technology-30290540 [accessed 7 February 2023].

Beer, Stafford. 1965. "Cybernetics and the Knowledge of God," in *Month*, 34, 291–303.

Behdadi, Dorna, and Christian Munthe. 2020. "A Normative Approach to Artificial Moral Agency," in *Minds and Machines*, 30, 195–218.

Bender, Courtney. 2010. *The New Metaphysicals: Spirituality and the American Religious Imagination*, Chicago: University of Chicago Press.

Berggren, J. Lennart. 2014. "History of Mathematics in the Islamic World: The Present State of the Art [1985]," in Nathan Sidoli, and Glen Van Brummelen (eds.) *From Alexandria, Through Baghdad: Surveys and Studies in the Ancient Greek and Medieval Islamic Mathematical Sciences in Honor of J.L. Berggren*, Berlin, Heidelberg: Springer, 51–71. https://doi.org/10.1007/978-3-642-36736-6_4.

Bergson, Henri. 2009. *Creative Evolution*, translated by Arthur Mitchell, Waiheke Island: The Floating Press.

Bermúdez, Jose L. 2005. *Philosophy of Psychology: A Contemporary Introduction*. London: Routledge.

BIBLIOGRAPHY

Bernstein, Moshe. 2000. "Angels at the Aqedah: A Study in the Development of a Midrashic Motif," in *Dead Sea Discoveries*, 7(3), 263–91.

BetterMarketing. 2020. "Our Online Confession Booth Campaign Went off the Rails," available at https://bettermarketing.pub/our-online-confession-booth-campaign-went-off-the-rails-2b4c33cb1af9 [accessed 21 February 2023].

Bhojadeva, Sṛṅgāramañjarīkathā. 1959, in Kumari Kalpalata K. Munshi (ed. and trans.) *Sṛṅgāramañjarīkathā Paramāmara King Bhojadeva of Dhārā*. Bombay: Bharatiya Vidya Bhavan, 2–3, 8–11.

Black, D. L. 2008. "Avicenna on Self-Awareness and Knowing That One Knows," in Shahid Rahman, Tony Street, and Hassan Tahiri (eds.) *The Unity of Science in the Arabic Tradition: Science, Logic, Epistemology and Their Interactions*, Logic, Epistemology, and The Unity of Science, Dordrecht: Springer Netherlands, 63–87. https://doi .org/10.1007/978-1-4020-8405-8_3.

Bochasanwasi Shri Akshar Purushottam Swaminarayan Sanstha. 2021. "First Time Ever in India: An Audio-animatronics Presentation of An Assembly in the Time of Lord Swaminarayan," Akshardham.com preserved by the Internet Archive Wayback Machine: www.akshardham.com/gujarat/ exhibitions/audioanimatronics.htm [accessed 25 May 2021].

Boellstorff, Tom. 2008. *Coming of Age in Second Life: An Anthropologist Explores the Virtually Human*, Princeton: Princeton University Press.

Bostrom, Nick. 2014. *Superintelligence: Paths, Dangers, Strategies*, Oxford: Oxford University Press.

2005. "A History of Transhumanist Thought," in *Journal of Evolution and Technology*, 14(1), 1–30.

Brooks, Rodney. 2018. "My Dated Predictions," available at https:// rodneybrooks.com/my-dated-predictions/ [accessed 8 September 2018].

1990. "Elephants Don't Play Chess," in *Robotics and Autonomous Systems*, 6(1–2), 3–15.

Bruner, J. 1991. "The Narrative Construction of Reality," in *Critical Inquiry*, 18(1), 1–21.

Brüning, Alfons. 2019. "Can Theosis Save 'Human Dignity'? Chapters in Theological Anthropology East and West," in *Journal of Eastern Christian Studies*, 71(3–4), 177–248. https://doi.org/10.2143/JECS.71.3.3286899.

Bryson, Joanna J. 2018. "Patiency Is Not a Virtue: The Design of Intelligent Systems and Systems of Ethics," in *Ethics and Information Technology*, 20(1), 15–26.

Buber, Martin. 2013 [1937]. *I and Thou*, translated by Ronald Gregor Smith, London: Bloomsbury.

Burdett, Michael. 2020. "Personhood and Creation in an Age of Robots and AI: Can We Say 'You' to Artifacts?," in *Zygon, Journal of Religion & Science*, 55(2), 347–60. https://doi.org/10.1111/zygo.12595.

Cardon, Dominique, Jean-Philippe Cointet, and Antoine Mazières. 2018. "La Revanche Des Neurones: L'invention Des Machines Inductives et La Controverse de l'intelligence Artificielle," in *Réseaux*, 211(5), 173–220. https://doi.org/10.3917/res.211.0173.

Castells, M. 2022. "The Network Society Revisited," in *American Behavioral Scientist*, 67(7), 940–6. https://doi.org/10.1177/00027642221092803.

BIBLIOGRAPHY

Catizone, Roberta, Yorick Wilks, Simon Worgan, and Markku Turunen. 2011. "Some Background on Dialogue Management and Conversational Speech for Dialogue Systems," in *Computer Speech and Language*, 25(2), 128–39.

Cave, Stephen, Rune Nyrup, Karina Vold, and Adrian Weller. 2018. "Motivations and Risks of Machine Ethics," in *Proceedings of the IEEE*, 107(3), 562–74.

Center on Privacy and Technology. 2022. "Artifice and Intelligence" by Emily Tucker, Executive Director of the Center on Privacy & Technology, available at https://medium.com/center-on-privacy-technology/artifice-and-intelligence%C2%B9-f00da128d3cd [accessed 14 November 2022].

Chalmers, David J. 1995. "Facing Up to the Problem of Consciousness," in *Journal of Consciousness Studies*, 2, 200–19.

Chandrasekaran, B., and Reeker. L. H. 1974. "Report on Workshop on Possibilities and Limitations of Artificial Intelligence," in *IEEE Transactions on Systems, Man, and Cybernetics*, SMC-4(1), 88, January 1974.

Clark, Andy. 1997. *Being There: Putting Brain, Body, and World Together Again*, Cambridge, MA: MIT Press.

Clay, Elonda. 2010. "A Black Theology of Liberation or Legitimation? A Postcolonial Response to Cone's Black Theology and Black Power at Forty," in *Black Theology*, 8(3), 307–26.

2004. "Subtle Impact: Technology Trends and the Black Church," in *Journal of the Interdenominational Theological Center*, 31, 1–2.

Clocksin, William F. 2005. "Memory and Emotion in Cognitive Architecture," in D. N. Davis (ed.) *Visions of Mind: Architectures for Cognition and Affect*, Pennsylvania: Idea Group Pub, 122–39.

2003. "Artificial Intelligence and the Future," in *Philosophical Transactions of the Royal Society A.*, 361, 1721–48. Reprinted in M. Winston, and R. Edelbach (eds.) *Society, Ethics, and Technology*, 4th edition, Wadsworth.

1998. "Artificial Intelligence and Human Identity," in J. Cornwell (ed.) *Consciousness and Human Identity*, Oxford: Oxford University Press, 101–21.

Clynes, Manfred, and Nathan Kline. 1960. "Cyborgs and Space," in *Astronautics*, 26–76.

CNET. 2018. "An IBM Computer Debates Humans, and Wins, in a New, Nuanced Competition," available at www.cnet.com/science/an-ibm-computer-debates-humans-and-wins-in-a-new-nuanced-competition/ [accessed 21 February 2023].

Coeckelbergh, Mark. 2020. *AI Ethics*, Cambridge, MA: MIT Press.

2010. "Robot Rights? Towards a Social-Relational Justification of Moral Consideration," in *Ethics and Information Technology*, 12(3), 209–21.

Colby, Kenneth. 1969. "Dialogues between Humans and an Artificial Belief System," in *IJCAI 69: Proceedings of the 1st International Joint Conference on Artificial Intelligence*, 1969(May), 319–24.

Coleman, Monica A. 2015. "Process Thought and Womanist Theology: Black Women's Science Fiction as a Resource for Process Theology," in *Cited*, 5, 1–19.

Cole-Turner, Ron. 2015. "Going Beyond the Human: Christians and Other Transhumanists," in *Theology and Science*, 13(2), 150–61.

BIBLIOGRAPHY

Cooper, Kenneth J., and The Washington Post. 1998. "High-Tech, Talking Robots to Spread Krishna Gospel: Robots Representing Hindu Gods Dramatize Ancient Epic in a Modern Theatre," in *The Ottawa Citizen* (21 April 1998), A16. www.washingtonpost.com/archive/politics/1998/04/13/lip-syncing-robots-spread-the-hare-krishna-word/f23efdf9-3ee6-4d50-b601-7d171f83aabc/.

Crawford, Kate. 2021. *Atlas of AI*, New Haven: University of Yale Press.

C-Span. 2017. "Elon Musk at National Governors Association 2017 Summer Meeting," available at www.c-span.org/video/?431119-6/elon-musk-addresses-nga [accessed 7 February 2023].

Curtin, Mary Ellen. 2000. *Black Prisoners and Their World, Alabama, 1865–1900*, Charlottesville: University of Virginia Press.

d'Aquili, Eugene, and Andrea B. Newberg. 1999. *The Mystical Mind: The Biology of Religious Experience*, Minneapolis: Fortress Press.

Daily Mail. 2020. "'Blade Runner' Future of Human-Like Androids a Step Closer as First Robot Learns to 'Feel Pain'," available at www.dailymail.co.uk/news/article-8034351/Blade-Runner-future-human-like-androids-step-closer-robot-learns-feel-pain.html [accessed 21 February 2023].

De Wildt, Lars, Stef Aupers, Cindy Krassen, and Iulia Coanda. 2018. "'Things Greater than Thou': Post-Apocalyptic Religion in Games," in *Religions*, 9(6), 169.

Dean, Terrance, and Dale P. Andrews. 2016. "Introduction: Afrofuturism in Black Theology – Race, Gender, Sexuality, and the State of Black Religion in the Black Metropolis," in *Black Theology*, 14(1), 2–5.

Deccan Chronicle staff. 2018. "Techno Artistic Ganesha: Watch Lord Ganesha Levitate, Robot Conduct Aarti," in *Deccan Chronicle*, available at www.deccanchronicle.com/technology/in-other-news/140918/techno-artistic-ganesha-watch-lord-ganesha-levitate-robot-conduct-aa.html [accessed 14 February 2021].

Deikman. Arthur J. 1963. "Experimental Meditation," in *Journal of Nervous and Mental Diseases*, 136(4), 329–43.

den Hollander, Kirste, Joitske Hulsebosch, and Steven van Luipen. 2019. "Meet Beau, A Reflection Chatbot," available at www.joitskehulsebosch.nl/wp-content/uploads/2019/03/Meet-Beau-the-reflection-chatbot-light-version.pdf [accessed 21 February 2023].

DeNapoli, Antoinette. 2017. "'Dharm Is Technology': The Theologizing of Technology in the Experimental Hinduism of Renouncers in Contemporary North India," in *International Journal of Dharma Studies*, 5, 1–36.

Dennett, D. 1971. "Intentional Systems," in *Journal of Philosophy*, 68, 87–106.

Devlin, Hannah. 2018. "Killer Robots Will Only Exist If We Are Stupid Enough to Let Them," in *The Guardian* (11 June 2018), available at www.theguardian.com/technology/2018/jun/11/killer-robots-will-only-exist-if-we-are-stupid-enough-to-let-them [accessed 8 September 2018].

Dewey, John. 1925. *Experience and Nature*, Chicago: Open Court.

Dhaouadi, Mahmoud. 1992. "Human and Artificial Intelligence," in *American Journal of Islamic Social Sciences*, 9(4), 465–81. https://doi.org/10.35632/ajis.v9i4.2534.

Diallo, Saikou, F. LeRon Shults, and Wesley J. Wildman. 2021."Minding Morality: Ethical Artificial Societies for Public Policy Modeling," in *AI & Society*, 36(1), 49–57.

Diallo, Saikou, Wesley J. Wildman, F. LeRon Shults, and Andreas Tolk (eds.). 2019. *Human Simulation: Perspectives, Insights, and Applications*, Berlin, Heidelberg: Springer.

Diamond, Jared. 2005. *Collapse: How Societies Choose to Fail or Succeed*, New York: Viking.

Dinerstein, Joel. 2006. "Technology and Its Discontents: On the Verge of the Posthuman," in *American Quarterly*, 58(3), 569–95.

Doctor, Thomas, Olaf Witkowski, Elizaveta Solomonova, Bill Duane, and Michael Levin. 2022. "Biology, Buddhism, and AI: Care as the Driver of Intelligence," in *Entropy*, 24(5), 710. https://doi.org/10.3390/e24050710.

Donath, Judith. 2020. "Ethical Issues in Our Relationship with Artificial Entities," in Markus D. Dubber, Frank Pasquale, and Sunit Das (eds.) *The Oxford Handbook of Ethics and AI*, Oxford: Oxford University Press, 53–76.

Dorobantu, Marius. 2021a. "Why the Future Might Actually Need Us: A Theological Critique of the 'Humanity-As-Midwife-For-Artificial-Superintelligence' Proposal," in *International Journal of Interactive Multimedia and Artificial Intelligence*, 7(1), 44–51. https://doi.org/10.9781/ijimai.2021.07.005.

2021b. "Human-Level, but Non-Humanlike: Artificial Intelligence and a Multi-Level Relational Interpretation of the Imago Dei," in *Philosophy, Theology and the Sciences (PTSc)*, 8(1), 81–107. https://doi.org/10.1628/ptsc-2021-0006.

2021c. "Cognitive Vulnerability, Artificial Intelligence, and the Image of God in Humans," in *Journal of Disability & Religion*, 25(1), 27–40. https://doi.org/10.1080/23312521.2020.1867025.

2020. "Will Robots Too Be in the Image of God? Artificial Consciousness and Imago Dei in Westworld," in J. Gittinger, and S. Sheinfeld (eds.) *Theology and Westworld*. Lanham, MD: Lexington Books, 73–89.

Douglas Heaven, Will. 2021. "Hundreds of AI Tools Have Been Built to Catch Covid. None of Them Helped," in *MIT Technology Review*, available at www.technologyreview.com/2021/07/30/1030329/machine-learning-ai-failed-covid-hospital-diagnosis-pandemic [accessed 7 February 2023].

Dreyfus, Hubert L., and Stuart E. Dreyfus. 1988. "Making a Mind versus Modeling the Brain: Artificial Intelligence Back at a Branchpoint," in *Daedalus*, 117(1), 15–43.

Dreyfus, Hubert L., and Stuart E. Dreyfus. 1986. *Mind over Machine*, London: Macmillan.

Druart, Thérèse-Anne. 1983. "Imagination and the Soul – Body Problem in Arabic Philosophy," in Anna-Teresa Tymieniecka (ed.) *Soul and Body in Husserlian Phenomenology*, Dordrecht: Springer Netherlands, 327–42. https://doi.org/10.1007/978-94-009-7032-8_28.

Dubash, Manek. 2010. "Moore's Law Is Dead, Says Gordon Moore," in *Techworld* (13 April 2010), available at www.techworld.com/news/tech-innovation/moores-law-is-dead-says-gordon-moore-3576581/ no longer available, see also https://hothardware.com/news/moores-law-is-dead-says-gordon-moore [accessed 6 February 2023].

BIBLIOGRAPHY

Dumouchel, Paul, and Luisa Damiano. 2017. *Living with Robots*, translated by Malcolm DeBevoise, Cambridge, MA: Harvard University Press.

Dunbar, Robin. 2021. *How Religion Evolved*, London: Pelican Books.

Dupuy, Jean-Pierre. 2013. *The Mark of the Sacred*, translated by M. B. DeBevoise, Cultural Memory in the Present, Stanford: Stanford University Press.

Durkheim, Émile. 1915. *The Elementary Forms of The Religious Life, A Study in Religious Sociology*, London and New York: G. Allen & Unwin, Macmillan.

Eck, Diana. 1985. *Darśan: Seeing the Divine Image in India*, Chambersburg, PA: Anima Press.

Emmons, Robert A. 2003. *The Psychology of Ultimate Concerns: Motivation and Spirituality in Personality*, New York: Guilford Press.

Fazi, M. Beatrice. 2019. "Can a Machine Think (Anything New)? Automation beyond Simulation," in *AI & SOCIETY*, 34(4), 813–24. https://doi.org/10.1007/s00146-018-0821-0.

Fenn, Richard K. 2003. "Editorial Commentary: Looking for Boundaries of the Field: Social Anthropology, Theology, and Ethnography," in Richard K. Fenn (ed.) *The Blackwell Companion to the Sociology of Religion*, Malden, UK: Blackwell Publishing Ltd, 363–70.

Fitzpatrick, Kathleen, Alison Darcy, and Molly Vierhile. 2017. "Delivering Cognitive Behavior Therapy to Young Adults with Symptoms of Depression and Anxiety Using a Fully Automated Conversational Agent (Woebot): A Randomized Controlled Trial," in *JMIR Ment Health*, 4(2), e19.

Foerst, Anne. 2004. *God in the Machine: What Robots Teach Us about Humanity and God*, New York: Dutton.

1998. "Cog, a Humanoid Robot, and the Question of the Image of God," in *Zygon: Journal of Religion and Science*, 33(1), 91–111. https://doi.org/10.1111/0591-2385.1291998129.

Furse, Edmund. 1986. "The Theology of Robots," in *New Blackfriars*, 67(795), 377–86. https://doi.org/10.1111/j.1741-2005.1986.tb06559.x.

Gaffney, Hannah, Warren Mansell, and Sara Tai. 2019. "Revisiting Conversational Agents in the Treatment of Mental Health Problems: Mixed-Method Systematic Review," in *JMIR Mental Health*, 6(10), e14166.

Gates, Bill. 2008. "A New Approach to Capitalism in the 21st Century," speech at the World Economic Forum, Davos, Switzerland (24 January 2008), available at www.networkworld.com/article/2282669/microsoft-s-bill-gates---a-new-approach-to-capitalism-in-the-21st-century-.html [accessed 6 February 2023].

Geraci, Robert M. 2022. *Futures of Artificial Intelligence: Perspectives from India and the United States*, Delhi: Oxford University Press.

2010. *Apocalyptic AI: Visions of Heaven, in Robotics, Artificial Intelligence and Virtual Reality*, New York: Oxford University Press.

2006. "Spiritual Robots: Religion and Our Scientific View of the Natural World," in *Theology and Science*, 4(3), 229–46. https://doi.org/10.1080/14746700600952993.

Giubilini, Alberto, and Julian Savulescu. 2018. "The Artificial Moral Advisor. The 'Ideal Observer' Meets Artificial Intelligence," in *Philosophy & technology*, 31(2), 169–88.

BIBLIOGRAPHY

Goertzel, Ben. 2013. "Artificial General Intelligence and the Future of Humanity," in Max More, and Natasha Vita-More (eds.) *The Transhumanist Reader*, Chichester: Wiley-Blackwell, 128–37.

Gore, Ross, Carlos Lemos, F. LeRon Shults, and Wesley J. Wildman. 2018. "Forecasting Changes in Religiosity and Existential Security with an Agent-Based Model," in *Journal of Artificial Societies and Social Simulation*, 21, 1–31.

Gray, J. 2015. *The Soul of the Marionette*, London: Penguin Books.

Griffel, Frank. 2018. *Al-Ghazali's Philosophical Theology*, Oxford: Oxford University Press.

Griffin, Horace. 2000. "Their Own Received Them Not: African American Lesbians and Gays in Black Churches," in *Theology & Sexuality*, (12): 88–100. https://doi.org/10.1177/135583580000601206.

Grimaud, Emmanuel. 2011. *Gods and Robots*, translated by Matthew Cunningham, Mumbai: Grandmother India.

Gutas, Dimitri. 2012. "Avicenna: The Metaphysics of the Rational Soul," in *The Muslim World*, 102(3–4), 417–25. https://doi.org/10.1111/j.1478-1913.2012.01413.x.

Harari, Yuval. 2017. *Homo Deus: A Brief History of Tomorrow*, UK: Harper Collins.

Haraway, Donna. 1991. "Cyborg Manifesto: Science, Technology and Socialist-Feminism in the Late Twentieth Century," in *Simians, Cyborgs and Women: The Reinvention of Nature*, New York: Routledge.

Harrison, Peter, and Joseph Wolyniak. 2015. "The History of Transhumanism," in *Notes and Queries*, 62(3), 465–67.

Hayles, N. Katherine. 1999. *How We Became Posthuman: Virtual Bodies in Cybernetics, Literature, and Informatics*, Chicago: University of Chicago Press.

Hefner, Philip. 2002. "Technology and Human Becoming" in *Zygon, Journal of Religion & Science*, 37(3), 655–66. https://doi.org/10.1111/1467-9744.00443.

Heider, Fritz, and Marianne Simmel. 1944. "An Experimental Study of Apparent Behaviour," in *The American Journal of Psychology*, 57, 243–59.

Herzfeld, Noreen L. 2003. "Creating in Our Own Image: Artificial Intelligence and the Image of God," in *Zygon: Journal of Religion and Science*, 37(2), 303–16.

2002. "In Our Image: Artificial Intelligence and the Human Spirit," in Kevin J. Sharpe (ed.) *Theology and the Sciences*. Minneapolis: Fortress Press. www.fortresspress.com/store/product/9780800634766/In-Our-Image-Artificial-Intelligence-and-the-Human-Spirit

Hill, Donald R. 1998. *Studies in Medieval Islamic Technology: From Philo to al-Jazari – from Alexandria to Diyar Bakr*, Variorum Collected Studies Series, London: Ashgate. https://doi.org/10.4324/9781003111153.

Hine, Christine. 2000. *Virtual Ethnography*, London: SAGE Publications.

Hoffman, R., R. Klein, and S. Mueller. 2018. "Literature Review and Integration of Key Ideas for Explainable AI." Prepared by *Task Area 2 DARPA XAI Program*, Award No. FA8650-17-2-7711.

Hofstadter, Douglas. 1980. "Reductionism and Religion," in *The Behavioral and Brain Sciences*, 3(3), 433–34.

BIBLIOGRAPHY

Hood, Jr., R. W., P. C. Hill, and B. Spilka. 2018. *The Psychology of Religion: An Empirical Approach*, New York: Guilford Press.

Huang, Lixiao, et al. 2021. "Toward a Generalised Model of Human Emotional Attachment," in *Theoretical Issues in Ergonomics Science*, 22(2), 178–99.

Huberman, Jenny. 2018. "Immortality Transformed: Mind Cloning, Transhumanism and the Quest for Digital Immortality," in *Mortality*, 23(1), 50–64.

Hurlbut, J. Benjamin, and Hava Tirosh-Samuelson (eds.). 2016. *Perfecting Human Futures: Transhuman Visions and Technological Imaginations*, Technikzukünfte, Wissenschaft und Gesellschaft/Futures of Technology, Science and Society, Wiesbaden: Springer.

Iannaccone, Laurence R., and Michael D. Makowsky. 2007. "Accidental Atheists? Agent-Based Explanations for the Persistence of Religious Regionalism," in *Journal for the Scientific Study of Religion*, 46(1), 1–16. https://doi.org/10.1111/j.1468-5906.2007.00337.x.

Idel, Moshe. 1990. *Golem: Jewish Magical and Mystical Traditions on the Artificial Anthropoid*, Albany, NY: State University of New York Press.

Jackelén, Antje. 2002. "The Image of God as Techno Sapiens," in *Zygon: Journal of Religion and Science*, 37(2), 289–302.

Jacobsen, Knut. 2018. "Pilgrimage Rituals and Technological Change: Alterations in the Shraddha Ritual at Kapilashramin in the Town of Siddhpur," in Knut A. Jacobsen, and Kristina Myrvold (eds.) *Religion and Technology in India: Spaces, Practices and Authorities*, New York: Routledge.

Jazarī, Ismā'īl ibn al-Razzāz al-. 1974. *The Book of Knowledge of Ingenious Mechanical Devices: Kitāb Fī Ma'rifat al-Ḥiyal al-Handasiyya*, translated by Donald Routledge Hill, Dordrecht: Reidel.

Johnson, Barbara. 2008. *Persons and Things*, Cambridge, MA: Harvard University Press.

Joseph, George Gheverghese. 2000. *The Crest of the Peacock*, 3rd ed., Princeton: Princeton University Press.

Josephson Storm, Jason. 2017. *The Myth of Disenchantment*, Chicago: University of Chicago Press.

JotForm – Online Churches. 2023. "Online Confession and Absolution," available at www.jotform.com/blog/online-confession-absolution/ [accessed 21 February 2023].

Kabat-Zinn, Jon. 2013. *Full Catastrophe Living: How to Cope with Stress, Pain and Illness Using Mindfulness Meditation*, London: Little, Brown Book Group.

Kakoudaki, Despina. 2014. *Anatomy of a Robot: Literature, Cinema, and the Cultural Work of Artificial People*, illustrated edition, New Brunswick, NJ and London: Rutgers University Press.

Kalin, Ibrahim. 2012. *Reason and Rationality in the Qur'an*, Dubai, UAE: Kalam Research & Media.

Kallungal, Dhinesh. 2019. "32 Years and Counting: This Robot Has Been Performing aarti and pūjā since 1987," in *The New Indian Express* (29 April 2019), available at http://cms.newindianexpress.com/states/kerala/2019/apr/29/this-robot-performs-aarti-and-pūjā-even-after-32-years-1970272.html [accessed 24 December 2020].

Kang, Yoona, June Gruber, and Jeremy R. Gray. 2013. "Mindfulness and De-Automatization," in *Emotion Revie*, 5(2), 192–201. https://doi.org/10.1177/1754073912451629.

Kaplan, Stephen. 2018. "Avidyā: The Hard Problem in Advaita Vedānta," in Purushottama Bilimoria (ed.) *The Routledge History of Indian Philosophy*, London: Taylor and Francis Group, 242–50.

1987. *Hermeneutics, Holography, and Indian Idealism*, Delhi: Motilal Barnasidass.

Kaše, Vojtěch, Tomáš Hampejs, and Zdeněk Pospíšil. 2018. "Modeling Cultural Transmission of Rituals in Silico: The Advantages and Pitfalls of Agent-Based vs. System Dynamics Models," in *Journal of Cognition and Culture*, 18(5), 483–507.

Katz, Jacob. 1989. *The 'Shabbes Goy': A Study in Halakhic Flexibility*, Philadelphia: Jewish Publication Society of America.

Katz, Yarden. 2020. *Artificial Whiteness: Politics and Ideology in Artificial Intelligence*, New York: Columbia University Press.

Khademi, Aria, and Vasant Honavar. 2020. "Algorithmic Bias in Recidivism Prediction: A Causal Perspective (student abstract)," in *Proceedings of the AAAI Conference on Artificial Intelligence*, 34(10): 13839–13840.

Khan, Faraz. 2017. "Can Materialism Explain the Mind?," in *Renovatio | The Journal of Zaytuna College* (28 April 2017), available at https://renovatio.zaytuna.edu/article/can-materialism-explain-the-mind [accessed 22 May 2023].

Kirkwood, Jeffrey West, and Lief Weatherby. 2018. "Operations of Culture: Ernst Kapp's Philosophy of Technology," in *Grey Room*, 72, 6–15.

Kissinger, Henry. 2018. "How the Enlightenment Ends," in *The Atlantic* (June 2018), available at www.theatlantic.com/magazine/archive/2018/06/henry-kissinger-ai-could-mean-the-end-of-human-history/559124/ [accessed 8 September 2018].

Kurzweil, Ray. 2005. *The Singularity Is Near: When Humans Transcend Biology*, New York: Viking.

1999. *The Age of Spiritual Machines: When Computers Exceed Human Intelligence*, New York: Viking.

Lagrandeur, Kevin. 2017. *Androids and Intelligent Networks in Early Modern Literature and Culture: Artificial Slaves*, 1st edition, London and New York: Routledge.

Lane, Justin E. 2021. *Understanding Religion Through Artificial Intelligence: Bonding and Belief*, London: Bloomsbury Publishing.

2013. "Method, Theory, and Multi-Agent Artificial Intelligence: Creating Computer Models of Complex Social Interactions," in *Journal for the Cognitive Science of Religion*, 1(2), 161–80.

Lanier, Jaron. 2010. "The First Church of Robotics," in *The New York Times* (9 August 2010), available at www.nytimes.com/2010/08/09/opinion/09lanier.html [accessed 7 February 2023].

2000. "One Half a Manifesto," in *Wired* (1 December 2000), available at www.wired.com/2000/12/lanier-2/ [accessed 6 February 2023].

Lara, Francisco, and Jan Deckers. 2020. "Artificial intelligence as a Socratic assistant for moral enhancement," in *Neuroethics*, 13(3), 275–87.

Loizos, Connie. 2017. "This Famous Roboticist Doesn't Think Elon Musk Understands AI," available at https://techcrunch.com/2017/07/19/this-famous-roboticist-doesnt-think-elon-musk-understands-ai/ [accessed 6 February 2023].

Lomax, Tamura A. 2018. *Jezebel Unhinged*, Durham: Duke University Press.

2016. "'Technology of Living' Toward a Black Feminist Religious Thought," in *The Black Scholar*, 46(2), 19–32.

Luchesi, Brigitte. 2018. "Modern Technology and Its Impact on Religious Performances in Rural Himachal Pradesh: Personal Remembrances and Observations," in Knut A. Jacobsen, and Kristina Myrvold (eds.) *Religion and Technology in India: Spaces, Practices and Authorities*, New York: Routledge, 112–29.

Ly, Kien Hoa, Ann-Marie Ly, and Gerhard Andersson. 2017. "A Fully Automated Conversational Agent for Promoting Mental Well-being: A Pilot RCT Using Mixed Methods," in *Internet Interventions*, 10, 39–46.

MacDorman, Karl F., and Hiroshi Ishiguro. 2006. "The Uncanny Advantage of Using Androids in Social and Cognitive Science Research," in *Interaction Studies*, 7(3), 297–337.

MacDorman, Karl F., and Stephen J. Cowley. 2006. "Long-Term Relationships as a Benchmark for Robot Personhood," in *Proceedings of the 15th IEEE International Symposium on Robot and Human Interactive Communication*, University of Hertfordshire, Hatfield, UK, 378–83.

MacLennan, Bruce J. 2021. "Word and Flux: The Discrete and the Continuous in Computation, Philosophy, and Psychology," vol. 1. https://web.eecs.utk.edu/~bmaclenn/WF/WF.pdf.

Marmura, Michael E. 1986. "Avicenna's 'Flying Man' in Context," in *Monist*, 69(3), 383–95.

Marx, Karl. 2012 [1867]. *Das Kapital: A Critique of Political Economy.* Gateway Editions.

Mavridis, Nikolaos, et al. 2012. "Opinions and Attitudes toward Humanoid Robots in the Middle East," in *AI & Society*, 27, 531–32.

Mayor, Adrienne. 2018. *Gods and Robots: Myths, Machines and Ancient Dreams of Technology*, Princeton: Princeton University Press.

McBride, James. 2017. "Robotic Bodies and the Kairos of Humanoid Theologies," in *Sophia*, 58, 663–76. https://doi.org/10.1007/s11841-017-0628-3.

McLuhan, Marshall. 1964. *Understanding Media: The Extensions of Man*, New York: McGraw Hill Education.

Mdingi, Hlulani. 2022. "Race and Robotics: Black Theology in the Digital Age," in E. Benyera (ed.) *Africa and the Fourth Industrial Revolution. Advances in African Economic, Social and Political Development*, Cham: Springer. https://doi.org/10.1007/978-3-030-87524-4_2.

Mercer, Calvin. 2020. "A Theological Embrace of Transhuman and Posthuman Beings," in *Perspectives on Science and Christian Faith*, 72(2), 83–88.

Miner, Adam, et al. 2016. "Smartphone-Based Conversational Agents and Responses to Questions about Mental Health," in *Interpersonal Violence, and Physical Health, JAMA Internal Medicine*, 176(5), 619–25.

Minsky, Marvin. 1970. In *Life* Magazine (20 November 1970).

1961. "Steps Toward Artificial Intelligence," in *Proceedings of the IRE*, 49(1), 8–30.

Mishra, Rashmi. 2017. "Ganesh Aarti Video Featuring Robotic Hand Is Most Beautiful Sight This Ganesh Utsav 2017," in *India.com* (31 August 2017), available at www.india.com/viral/ganesh-aarti-video-featuring-robotic-hand-is-most-beautiful-sight-this-ganesh-utsav-2017-2440841/ [accessed 14 February 2021].

Moor, James H. 2020. "The Mature, Importance, and Difficulty of Machine Ethics," in W. Wallach, and P. Asaro (eds.) *Machine Ethics and Robot Ethics*, London: Routledge, 233–36.

Moravec, Hans. 1988. *Mind Children: The Future of Robot and Human Intelligence*, Cambridge, MA: Harvard University Press.

Mori, Masahiro, Karl F. MacDorman, and Norri Kageki. 2012. "The Uncanny Valley [From the Field]," in *IEEE Robotics & Automation Magazine*, 19(2), 98–100.

Müller, Vincent C., and Nick Bostrom. 2016. "Future Progress in Artificial Intelligence: A Survey of Expert Opinion," in Vincent C. Müller (ed.) *Fundamental Issues of Artificial Intelligence*, Berlin, Heidelberg: Springer, 553–71. https://doi.org/10.1007/978-3-319-26485-1_33.

Musiał, Maciej. 2019. *Enchanting Robots: Intimacy, Magic, and Technology*, Cham: Palgrave Macmillan.

Nadarajan, Gunalan. 2007. "Islamic Automation," in O. Grau (ed.) *Media Art Histories*, Cambridge, MA: The MIT Press, 163–78.

Najman, Hindy. 2000. "Angels at Sinai: Exegesis, Theology and Interpretive Authority," in *Dead Sea Discoveries*, 7(3), 313–33.

Neumaier, Otto. 1987. "A Wittgensteinian View of Artificial Intelligence," in P. Born Rainer (ed.) *Artificial Intelligence*, Routledge: St Martin's Press, 132–74.

Nevins, Daniel. 2019. "Halakhic Responses to Artificial Intelligence and Autonomous Machines," available at www.rabbinicalassembly.org/sites/default/files/nevins_ai_moral_machines_and_halakha-final_1.pdf [accessed 28 February 2023].

Newell, Allen, and Herbert A. Simon. 1976. "Computer Science as Empirical Inquiry: Symbols and Search," in *Communications of the ACM*, 19(3), 113–26.

Niebuhr, Reinhold. 1941. *The Nature and Destiny of Man: A Christian Interpretation*, Volume I: Human Nature, New York: Scribner's Sons.

Nielbo, Kristoffer L., Donald M. Braxton, and Afzal Upal. 2012. "Computing Religion: A New Tool in the Multilevel Analysis of Religion," in *Method and Theory in the Study of Religion*, 24(3), 267–90. https://doi.org/10.1163/157006812X635709.

Nietzsche, Friedrich Wilhelm. 1968. *The Will to Power*, translated by Walter Kaufmann and R. J. Hollingdale, New York: Vintage Books.

Noble, David F. 1999. *Religion of Technology: The Divinity of Man and the Spirit of Invention*, New York: Penguin Books.

Noss, Jessica. 2017. "Who Knows What? Perspective-Enabled Story Understanding," M. Eng. Thesis, Massachusetts Institute of Technology, available at https://dspace.mit.edu/handle/1721.1/113174 [accessed 4 January 2023].

BIBLIOGRAPHY

O'Connor, Kathleen Malone. 1994. "The Alchemical Creation of Life (Takwin) and Other Concepts of Genesis in Medieval Islam," Ph.D., Pennsylvania, USA: University of Pennsylvania, available at www.proquest.com/docview/304111155/abstract/152D2663744940E3PQ/1 [accessed 22 May 2023].

O'Donnell, Karen. 2018. "Performing the Imago Dei: Human Enhancement, Artificial Intelligence and Optative Image-Bearing," in *International Journal for the Study of the Christian Church*, 18(1), 4–15. https://doi.org/10.1080/1474225X.2018.1448674.

O'Gieblyn, Meghan. 2021. "A Dog's Inner Life: What a Robot Pet Taught Me about Consciousness," in *The Guardian* (10 August 2021), available at www.theguardian.com/science/2021/aug/10/dogs-inner-life-what-robot-pet-taught-me-about-consciousness-artificial-intelligence [accessed 10 December 2021].

Office Chai Team. 2017. "This Ganesh Pandal Uses a Twisting, Moving Robotic Arm to Perform Aarti," in *OfficeChai.com* (1 September 2017), available at https://officechai.com/stories/robot-aarti-pune/ [accessed 23 December 2020].

Parisi, Luciana. 2019. "The Alien Subject of AI," in *Subjectivity*, 12(1), 27–48. https://doi.org/10.1057/s41286-018-00064-3.

Passmore, John. 1970. *The Perfectibility of Man*, London: Duckworth.

Penn, Jonathan. 2022. *Inventing Intelligence: On the History of Complex Information Processing and Artificial Intelligence in the United States in the Mid-Twentieth Century*, unpublished Ph.D. Thesis, Cambridge University, available at www.repository.cam.ac.uk/handle/1810/315976 [accessed 11 November 2022].

2021. "Algorithmic Silence: A Call to Decomputerize," in *Journal of Social Computing*, 2(4). 337–56. https://doi.org/10.23919/JSC.2021.0023.

Peters, Ted. 2016. "H-: Transhumanism and the Posthuman Future: Will Technological Progress Get Us There?," available at www.metanexus.net/essay/h-transhumanism-and-posthuman-future-will-technological-progress-get-us-there [accessed 6 February 2023].

Picard, Rosalind. 1997. *Affective Computing*, Cambridge, MA: MIT Press.

Pinn, Anthony B. 2003. *Terror and Triumph: The Nature of Black Religion*, Minnesota: Minneapolis.

Pollak, Michael. 1977. "The Invention of Printing in Hebrew Lore," in *Gutenberg-Jahrburch*, 22–28.

Popova, Biliana. 2020. "Islamic Philosophy and Artificial Intelligence: Epistemological Arguments," in *Zygon: Journal of Religion and Science*, 55(4), 977–95. https://doi.org/10.1111/zygo.12651.

Puddefoot, John C. 1996. *God and the Mind Machine: Computers, Artificial Intelligence and the Human Soul*, London: SPCK Publishing.

Raghavan, Venkatarama. 1952. *Yantras or Mechanical Contrivances in Ancient Culture*, Bangalore: Indian Institute of Culture.

Rapaport, Anatol. 1964. "Review: Computers and Thought by Edward Feigenbaum and Julian Feldman," in *Management Science*, 11(1), Series A, Sciences, 203–10.

Rashed, Roshdi. 1994. *The Development of Arabic Mathematics between Arithmetic and Algebra*, Dordrecht: Springer Netherlands.

Richardson, Kathleen. 2019. "The Human Relationship in the Ethics of Robotics: A Call to Martin Buber's I and Thou," in *AI & Society*, 34, 75–82.

Riedl, Mark O. 2016. "Computational Narrative Intelligence: A Human-Centred Goal for Artificial Intelligence," in *CHI'16 Workshop on Human-Centered Machine Learning* (8 May 2016), San Jose, CA, USA, available at www.cc.gatech.edu/~riedl/pubs/chi-hcml16.pdf [accessed 4 January 2023].

Robinson, Guy. 1972. "How to Tell Your Friends from Machines," in *Mind*, 81(324), New Series, 504–18.

Rosenfeld, Azriel. 1966. "Religion and the Robot: Impact of Artificial Intelligence on Religious Anthropologies," in *Tradition: A Journal of Orthodox Thought*, 8(3), 15–26.

Rosenthal, Franz. 1970. *Knowledge Triumphant: The Concept of Knowledge in Medieval Islam*, Boston: Brill.

Rothblatt, Martine. 2014. *Virtually Human: The Promise and Peril of Digital Immortality*, New York: St Martin's Press.

Ruderman, David B. 1988. *Kabbalah, Magic, and Science: The Cultural Universe of a Sixteenth-Century Jewish Physician*, Cambridge, MA: Harvard University Press.

Russell, James A., and Lisa F. Barrett (eds.). 2015. *The Psychological Construction of Emotion*, New York: Guilford Press.

Samani, Hooman Aghaebrahimi, et al. 2011. "A Design Process for Lovotics," in *HRPR 2010*, 118–25.

Samani, Hooman Aghaebrahimi, et al. 2010. "Towards a Formulation of Love in Human-Robot Interaction," in *19th IEEE International Symposium on Robot and Human Interactive Communication*, 94–99.

Sampath, Rajesh. 2018. "From Heidegger on Technology to an Inclusive Pluralistic Theology," in T. Peters (ed.) *In AI and IA: Utopia or Extinction?*, Adelaide: ATF Press, 117–32.

Samuelson, Calum. 2020. "Artificial Intelligence: A Theological Approach," in *The Way*, 59(3), 41–50.

Sarukkai, Sundar. 2008. "Culture of Technology and ICTs," in Ashwani Saith, M. Vijayabaskar, and V. Gayathri (eds.) *ICTs and Indian Social Change: Diffusion, Poverty, Governance*, New Delhi: SAGE Publications, 34–59.

Savulescu, Julian, and Hannah Maslen. 2015. "*Moral Enhancement and Artificial Intelligence: Moral AI?*," in J. Romportl, E. Zackova, and J. Kelemen (eds.) *Beyond Artificial Intelligence. Topics in Intelligent Engineering and Informatics*, vol. 9, Cham: Springer. https://doi.org/10.1007/978-3-319-09668-1_6.

Schäfer, Peter. 2011. *The Origins of Jewish Mysticism*, Princeton, NJ: Princeton University Press.

Schank, Roger. 1995. *Tell Me a Story: Narrative and Intelligence*, Evanston, IL: Nortwestern University Press.

Schank, Roger, and Christopher K. Riesbeck. 1981. *Inside Computer Understanding: Five Programs Plus Miniatures*, New York: Psychology Press.

Schiavo, Gianluca, Michela Ferron, Ornella Mich, and Nadia Mana. 2016. "Wizard of Oz Studies with Older Adults: A Methodological Note," in M. Garschall, T. Hamm, D. Hornung, C. Müller, K. Neureiter,

M. Schorch, and L. van Velsen (eds.) *International Reports on Socio-Informatics (IRSI), Proceedings of the COOP 2016 – Symposium on Challenges and Experiences in Designing for an Ageing Society*, 13(3), 93–100.

Scholem, Gershom. 1966. "The Golem of Prague & The Golem of Rehovoth," in *Commentary Magazine*, available at www.commentary.org/articles/gershom-scholem/the-golem-of-prague-the-golem-of-rehovoth/ [accessed 3 February 2023].

1965. "The Idea of the Golem," in *On the Kabbalah and Its Symbolism*, New York: Schocken Books, 179–80.

Setia, Adi. 2003. "Al-Attas' Philosophy of Science an Extended Outline," in *Islam & Science*, 1(2), 165–214.

Shapiro, Shauna L., Linda. E. Carlson, John A. Astin, and Benedict Freedman. 2005. "Mechanisms of Mindfulness," in *Journal of Clinical Psychology*, 62, 373–86.

Shults, F. LeRon, and Wesley J. Wildman. 2018. "Simulating Religious Entanglement and Social Investment in the Neolithic," in Ian Hodder (ed.) *Religion, History and Place in the Origin of Settled Life*, Colorado Springs, CO: University of Colorado Press, 33–63.

Shults, F. LeRon, Justin E. Lane, Saikou Diallo, Christopher Lynch, Wesley J. Wildman, and Ross Gore. 2018. "Modeling Terror Management Theory: Computer Simulations of the Impact of Mortality Salience on Religiosity," in *Religion, Brain & Behavior*, 8(1), 77–100.

Shults, F. LeRon, Ross Gore, Wesley J. Wildman, Christopher Lynch, Justin E. Lane, and Monica Toft. 2018. "A Generative Model of the Mutual Escalation of Anxiety Between Religious Groups," in *Journal of Artificial Societies and Social Simulation*, 21(4). https://doi.org/10.18564/jasss.3840.

Shults, F. LeRon, Wesley J. Wildman, Justin E. Lane, Christopher Lynch, and Saikou Diallo. 2018. "Multiple Axialities: A Computational Model of the Axial Age," in *Journal of Cognition and Culture*, 18(4), 537–64.

Shyovitz, David I. 2017. *A Remembrance of His Wonders: Nature and the Supernatural in Medieval Ashkenaz*, Philadelphia: University of Pennsylvania Press.

Silver, David, Thomas Hubert, Julian Schrittwieser, et al. 2018. "A General Reinforcement Learning Algorithm That Masters Chess, Shogi, and Go through Self-Play," in *Science*, 362(6419), 1140–44.

Singler, Beth. 2022a. "Origin and the End: Artificial Intelligence, Atheism, and Imaginaries of the Future of Religion," in B. Sollereder, and A. McGrath (eds.) *Emerging Voices in Science and Theology: Contributions from Young Women*, London: Routledge, 105–20.

2022b. "Left Behind? Religion as a Vestige in 'The Rapture of the Nerds' and Other AI Singularity Literature," in Michael Fuller (ed.) *Science and Religion in Western Literature: Critical and Theological Studies*, London: Routledge, 136–50.

2020a. "The AI Creation Meme: A Case Study of the New Visibility of Religion in Artificial Intelligence Discourse" in *Religions*, 11(5), 253.

2020b. "Blessed by the Algorithm: Theistic Conceptions of Artificial Intelligence in Online Discourse" in *AI & Society*, 35, 945–55.

2018a. "Roko's Basilisk or Pascal's? Thinking of Singularity Thought Experiments as Implicit Religion," in *Implicit Religion*, 20(3), 279–97. https://doi.org/10.1558/imre.35900.

2018b. "An Introduction to Artificial Intelligence and Religion for the Religious Studies Scholar," in *Implicit Religion*, 20(3), 215–31. https://doi.org/10.1558/imre.35901.

Smith, Joshua K. 2021. *Robot Theology: Old Questions through New Media*, Eugene: Wipf and Stock.

Smith, Robert Elliott. 2019. *Rage Inside the Machine: The Prejudice of Algorithms, and How to Stop the Internet Making Bigots of Us All*, London: Bloomsbury.

Song, Yong Sup. 2020. "Religious AI as an Option to the Risks of Superintelligence: A Protestant Theological Perspective," in *Theology and Science*, 19(1), 65–78. https://doi.org/10.1080/14746700.2020.1825196.

Spiker, Hasan. 2021. *Things as They Are: Nafs al-Amr and the Metaphysical Foundations of Objective Truth. Classification of the Sciences Project 2*, Tabah Research.

Srinivas, Tulasi. 2018. *The Cow in the Elevator: An Anthropology of Wonder*, Durham, NC: Duke University Press.

Su, Li, Howard Bowman, and Philip Barnard. 2011. "Glancing and Then Looking: On the Role of Body, Affect and Meaning in Cognitive Control," in *Frontiers in Psychology*, 2, 348.

Taira, Teemu. 2022. "Introduction," in *Taking 'Religion' Seriously: Essays on the Discursive Study of Religion, from Supplements to Method & Theory in the Study of Religion*, vol. 18, Leiden, Netherlands: Brill, 1–15.

Tamatea, Laurence. 2008. "If Robots R-US, Who Am I? Online 'Christian' Responses to Artificial Intelligence," in *Culture and Religion*, 9(2), 141–60.

Taylor, Alex. 2019. "The Data Centre as Technological Wilderness," in *Culture Machine*, 18, 1–30. The Nature of Data Centres.

Teasdale, John D. 2022. *What Happens in Mindfulness: Inner Awakening and Embodied Cognition*, New York: Guilford Press.

Teasdale, John D., and Philip J. Barnard. 1993. *Affect, Cognition and Change*, Hove: L. Erlbaum Associates.

Teasdale, John D., and Michael Chaskalson. 2011. "How Does Mindfulness Transform Suffering? II: The Transformation of Dukkha," in *Contemporary Buddhism*, 12(1), 103–24.

Tegmark, Max. 2017. *Life 3.0: Being Human in the Age of Artificial Intelligence*, New York: Alfred A. Knopf.

Teilhard de Chardin, Pierre. 1959. *The Phenomenon of Man*, translated by Bernard Wall, New York: Harper and Row.

Thapar, Romila. 1997. *Early India: From the Origins to AD 1300*, Los Angeles: University of California Press.

The Aitareya Āraṇyaka. 1909. Translated by Arthur B. Keith, Oxford: Clarendon Press.

Thomas, Mike. 2021. "The Future of Artificial Intelligence," in *Builtin* (8 June 2019), available at https://builtin.com/artificial-intelligence/artificial-intelligence-future [accessed 19 June 2021].

BIBLIOGRAPHY

Tirosh-Samuelson, Hava. 2011. "Engaging Transhumanism," in G. Hansell, and W. Grassie (eds.) *H+ Transhumanism and Its Critics*, Philadelphia: Metanexus. https://metanexus.net/h-engaging-transhumanism-critical-historical-perspective/.

Tirosh-Samuelson, Hava, and Kenneth Mossman (eds.) 2012. "Transhumanism," in Special issue of *Zygon: Journal of Religion and Science*, 47(5), 659–795.

Truitt, E. R. 2015. *Medieval Robots: Mechanism, Magic, Nature, and Art*, Philadelphia: University of Pennsylvania Press. https://doi.org/10.9783/9780812291407.

Tuckett, Jonathan. 2018. "The Talos Principle: Philosophical and Religious Anthropology," in *Implicit Religion*, 20(3), 259–77.

Turing, Alan M. 1950. "Computing Machinery and Intelligence," in *Mind*, LIX(236), 433–60.

Turkle, Sherry. 2011. *Alone Together: Why We Expect More from Technology and Less from Each Other*, New York: Basic Books.

 2005 [1984]. *The Second Self: Computers and the Human Spirit*, Cambridge, MA: MIT Press.

Turner, Victor. 1967. "Betwixt and Between: The Liminal Period in His Book Rites of Passage" in *The Forest of Symbols*, USA: Cornell University Press, 96–102.

Upal, Muhammad Afzal. 2005. "Simulating the Emergence of New Religious Movements," in *Journal of Artificial Societies and Social Simulation*, 8(1), 1–6.

van Creveld, Martin. 2007. "War and Technology," from the *Foreign Policy Institute* (24 October 2007), available at www.fpri.org/article/2007/10/war-technology-2/ [accessed 14 January 2019].

Vidal, Denis. 2007. "Anthropomorphism or Sub-anthropomorphism? An Anthropological Approach to Gods and Robots," in *The Journal of the Royal Anthropological Institute*, 13, 917–33.

Vinge, Vernor. 1993. "The Coming Technological Singularity," in *Whole Earth Review* (Winter, 1993). Reprinted in 2013 as "Technological Singularity" in Max More, and Natasha Vita-More (eds.) *The Transhumanist Reader: Classical and Contemporary Essays on Science, Technology and Philosophy of the Human Future*, Malden, MA: Wiley-Blackwell, 365–75.

von Kleist, Heinrich, and Thomas G. Neumiller (trans.). 1972. "On the Marionette Theatre," in *The Drama Review: TDR*, 16(3), The "Puppet" Issue, 22–26.

Wales, Jordan Joseph. 2022. "Narcissus, the Serpent, and the Saint: Living Humanely in a World of Artificial Intelligence," in J. Martin (ed.) *All Creation Gives Praise: Essays at the Frontier of Science and Religion*, Washington, DC.

Wallach, Wendell, and Colin Allen. 2008. *Moral Machines: Teaching Robots Right from Wrong*, New York: Oxford University Press.

Wallis, Peter, V. Maier, S. Creer, and S. Cunningham. 2010. "Conversation in Context: What Should a Robot Companion Say?," in *Proceedings of EMCSR*, Vienna, Austria, 547–52.

Ware, Kallistos. 2014. *The Jesus Prayer*, London: Catholic Truth Society.

Watts, Fraser. 2021. *A Plea for Embodied Spirituality*, Norwich, UK: Wipf & Stock Publishers.

2013. "Dual System Theories of Religious Cognition," in F. Watts, and G. Dumbreck (eds.) *Head and Heart: Perspectives from Religion and Psychology*, West Conshohocken: Templeton Press, 125–56.

Weizenbaum, Joseph. 1993 [1976]. *Computer Power and Human Reason: From Judgement to Calculation*, Harmondsworth: Penguin Books.

Wiener, Norbert. 1966. *God and Golem, Inc.: A Comment on Certain Points Where Cybernetics Impinges on Religion*, 7th edition, Cambridge, MA: The MIT Press.

Wildman, Wesley J., and F. LeRon Shults. 2018. "Emergence: What Does It Mean and How Is It Relevant to Computer Engineering?," in Saurabh Mittal, Saikou Diallo, and Andreas Tolk (eds.) *Emergent Behavior in Complex Systems Engineering: A Modeling and Simulation Approach*, Hoboken, NJ: John Wiley & Sons, 21–34.

Wildman, Wesley J., F. LeRon Shults, Saikou Y. Diallo, Ross Gore, and Justin E. Lane, 2020. "Post-Supernaturalist Cultures: There and Back Again," in *Secularism & Nonreligion*, 9(6), 1–15.

Wilks, Yorick. 2010a. "Death and the Internet," in *Prospect Magazine*, available at www.prospectmagazine.co.uk/magazine/death-and-the-internet [accessed 21 February 2023].

2010b. "Introducing Artificial Companions," in Wilks, Y. (ed.) *Close Engagements with Artificial Companions*, Amsterdam: John Benjamins, 11–20.

1975. "Putnam and Clarke and Mind and Body," in *British Journal for the Philosophy of Science*, 26(3), 213–25.

Wilks, Yorick, and Marius Dorubantu. 2019. "Moral Orthoses: A New Approach to Human and Machine Ethics," in *Zygon: Journal of Religion and Science*, 54(4), 1004–21.

Wilks, Yorick, Jan M. Jasiewicz, and Roberta Catizone, et al. 2015. "CALONIS: An Artificial Companion within a Smart Home for the Care of Cognitively Impaired Patients," in C. Bodine, S. Helal, T. Gu, and M. Mokhtari (eds.) *Smart Homes and Health Telematics*, ICOST 2014, Lecture Notes in Computer Science, vol. 8456, Cham: Springer, 255–60.

Williams, J. M. G. 2008. "Mindfulness, Depression and Modes of Mind," in *Cognitive Therapy & Research*, 32(6), 721–33.

Williams, J. M. G., and Jon Kabat-Zinn. 2013. *Mindfulness: Diverse Perspectives on Its Meaning, Origins and Applications*, London: Routledge.

Williams, J. M. G., Melanie Fennell, Thorsten Barnhofer, Rebecca Crane, and Sarah Silverton. 2015. *Mindfulness-Based Cognitive Therapy with People at Risk of Suicide*, New York: Guilford Press.

Windows Central. 2021. "Microsoft Patents Tech to Let You Talk to Dead People as Chatbots," available at www.windowscentral.com/microsoft-patents-tech-let-you-talk-dead-family-members-celebrities-and-fictional-characters [accessed 21 February 2023].

Winfield, Alan F. T. 2018. "Experiments in Artificial Theory of Mind: From Safety to Story-Telling," in *Frontiers in Robotics and AI*, 5(75), 1–13.

BIBLIOGRAPHY

Winograd, Terry, and Fernando Flores. 1985. *Understanding Computers and Cognition: A New Foundation for Design*, London: Addison-Wesley.

Winston, Patrick. 2011. "The Strong Story Hypothesis and the Directed Perception Hypothesis," AAAI Fall Symposium Series, available at https://dspace.mit.edu/handle/1721.1/67693 [accessed 4 January 2023].

Winston, Patrick, and D. Holmes. 2018. "The Genesis Enterprise: Taking Artificial Intelligence to Another Level Via a Computational Account of Human Story Understanding," available at http://dspace.mit.edu/handle/1721.1/119651 [accessed 4 January 2023].

WIRED. 2014. "Inside the First Church of Artificial Intelligence," available at www.wired.com/story/anthony-levandowski-artificial-intelligence-religion/ [accessed 21 February 2023].

Wood, Connor, and Richard Sosis. 2019. "Simulating Religions as Adaptive Systems," in *Human Simulation: Perspectives, Insights, and Applications*, Cham: Springer, 209–32.

Wright, Archie. 2005. *The Origin of Evil Spirits: The Reception of Genesis 6.1–4 in Early Jewish Literature*, Tübingen: Mohr Siebeck.

Wynn, Mark. 2005. *Emotional Experience and Religious Understanding*, Cambridge, UK: Cambridge University Press.

Yapching, Mark. 2016. "Fear of Death Is the Reason behind Religious Faith – Larry King," in *Christianity Today* (28 February 2015), available at www.christiantoday.com/article/fear.of.death.is.the.reason.behind.religious.faith.larry.king/48939.htm [accessed 6 February 2023].

Index

2045 Initiative, 150

ABMs (Agent Based Models), 241–246, 248–250, 254
absolute unitary being, 266, 270–271
Adam, 80, 82–83, 112–113, 116, 119
Adamic knowledge, 112, 116
Adamic myth, 136–138
Adamic origin of humanity, 116
Advaita theory (theory of perception), 45
affective computing, 20, 61, 265
afrofuturism, 183
afterlife, 102
agency, 1, 17, 51, 71–76, 81, 85–86, 151, 166–167, 170–171, 178, 189, 285
aggregate model of the self, 58
AGI (Artifical General Intelligence), 15, 19, 90–91, 111, 118, 148, 153, 155–156
    awake, 154
    malevolent, 161
    superintelligent, 153, 157, 161
agnostics, 9, 20
AI (Artificial Intelligence), 2–3, 10, 15, 18, 22–23, 69, 109, 174, 229
    agents, 51, 88, 93, 96, 118, 120, 243, 245–246, 248, 254
    applications, 104, 122–126
    development of, 33–37, 55, 60, 63–67, 88, 99, 110, 112–113, 116, 203
    discourse, 70–71, 74, 85, 111–112, 127, 223, 229, 237
    minds, 95, 115, 252
    policy, 70
    religion research, 238
    systems, 18, 24, 58, 60, 66, 71, 73–74, 76–77, 86, 110, 113, 118, 122, 183, 187, 193, 196–199, 278
    as tool, 229

AI Creation Meme, 231
AI ethics, 64, 76, 165–174, 177–179, 186
AI Winter (1974–1980), 9, 113
AIBO (robotic pet dog), 61–62, 67
Alexa (AI assistant), 235, 278, 283–284
algorithmic bias, 183, 193–194, 197–198
algorithms, 29, 74, 97, 109, 125, 151, 185, 187, 197, 254
    decision-making, 230
    sequential, 89
Allah (God), 116
All-Knowing (al-Alim), 116. *See also Allah* (God)
android intelligence, 16–17, 19, 21, 27–28
androids, 15–16, 19–22
    human-like, 177
    intelligent, 16, 20, 22, 24, 26–29
    threat, 91
angels, 78–81, 116, 119–120
animatronic deities, 35
animism, 59, 215–216
anthropocentrism, 95, 139, 209, 211–213, 220
anthropology, 206, 224–230, 232–234, 237, 239
    Christian, 90, 100–101
    theological, 88, 93–94, 100, 105, 204, 218–219, 237
anthropomorphism, 2, 45, 208–210, 217–218, 220
anti-Blackness, 191–192, 197
apocalypse, 136, 149
apps, 63, 234, 281
Arjuna, 35
artefacts, 16, 103–104, 110, 122, 125, 127, 136
artificial agents, intelligent, 88
artificial believers, 96

312

INDEX

artificial cognitive architectures,
    196–197
artificial companion, 275, 283, 286
artificial creation, 99
artificial humanoid, 80, 85
Artificial Intelligence Project, 3
artificial neural networks, 18–19,
    89, 115
artificial rationality, 230
artificial societies, 241, 243, 251,
    253, 255
artificialisation, 112
artificiality, 202
ascetic renunciants (*sādhus*), 34
ASI (Artificial Superintelligence), 90, 96
Asimov, Isaac, 71–72
assistive technology, 123
atheism, 136
atheists, 11, 13, 72, 233
automata, 34–35, 124–127, 281
automated conversationalists, 275
automated decision-making system,
    230–231
automaticity, 266
automation, 119, 125–126, 193, 233–234
automaton, 281, 286
AutoML-Zero, 155
avatar, 36–37, 92, 145, 235, 277, 289
avatāra (avatar), 37
avatarism, 237

BANG (bits, atoms, neurons,
    genes), 112
Bayesian reasoning, 18
being, 5–6, 8, 10–11, 13, 19, 21, 27–28,
    41–42, 46, 57, 134, 177
bemes. *See* mindclones
bhakti (devotion), 38, 47
bias, 105, 110, 230, 253
bias, algorithmic, 183, 193–194,
    197–198
Bible, The, 13, 75, 78–79, 83–84, 98,
    173, 178
    Hebrew, 77, 94
Black churches, 182, 188–189
Black communities, 182–183, 198–199
Black embodiment, 188
Black life, 182
Black religion, 195
Black theologies, 182–184, 187–189,
    192, 195, 198, 206, 211, 222
Black thought, 195–196
Blackness, 183–184, 189–190, 192–198

BlessU-2 (robot priest), 235
BNA (beme neural architecture). *See*
    mindclones
Bodhisattva, 57, 60
Bodhisattva model, 57
bodies, 58, 80, 97, 140, 144–145, 172,
    176, 280
    artificial, 54
    Black, 189–190, 192
    transfigured, 100
body-state, 260–263, 267
Brahman (non-dual ultimate reality),
    38, 41
Buddha, 37, 52–53, 59–60, 64
buddhavacana (word of Buddha), 52
Buddhism, 51–67, 257
    cosmology, 58–59, 62
    as ethical system, 63
    Japanese, 53, 59–60
    Jōdo Shinshū, 53
    Mahayana, 57, 59
    ontological model of mind, 54
    practice, 52, 62–63
    priests, 50, 281
    wisdom, 65
    Zen, 8
buffering, 261, 266

caregiving, 28
CE (consequence engine), 24
Center on Privacy and Technology at
    Georgetown Law, 1
central cognition, 258, 262, 267
Chinese Room experiment, 9–10
challenge model of human innovation,
    84–85
charisma, 236
chatbots, 8, 12, 93, 102, 276–278, 282
ChatGPT, 157
chips, 140, 143, 153
Christ, 105, 119, 168
Christian anthropology, 90, 100–101
Christian eschatology, 100
Christian reflection, 88, 94
Christian revelation, 98
Christian scholars, 72
Christian soteriologies, 97
Christian theologians, 27, 91, 93–95
Christian theology, 27, 58, 88, 91–93,
    95–96, 99, 105–106, 203
Christianity, 96, 99–105, 138, 255, 280
    protestant, 6, 52, 227
    reformed, 280

314 INDEX

Christians, 79, 96–97, 106, 152, 173
CJLS (Committee on Jewish Law and
    Standards), 73
Cog (MIT's humanoid robot), 101
cognition, 57, 117, 122, 135, 172,
    245, 249
  human, 20, 89, 100, 120
cognitive architectures, 21, 196–197,
    257–260, 262–264, 269, 272–273
cognitive modelling, 25, 259, 264–266,
    268–269, 273
cognitive multi-tasking, 262, 267
cognitive-neuropsychological modelling
    of religion, 270
communities, 29, 52–53, 119, 183,
    227, 236
  faith, 95–96, 99
  online, 6, 227
  religious, 96
companion, 3, 10, 12–13, 228, 275, 282
companionship, 201, 287
COMPAS (AI programs), 196
computation, 18, 113, 127
computational causal architecture, 245
computational modeling, 15–17, 22,
    104, 241–242, 246, 248, 254, 259,
    261, 271, 273
computational models, 15, 17, 259
computational narrative intelligence, 24
computational power, 156
computational science of religion,
    241, 251
computational simulation, 249,
    251–253, 255
computational technologies, 144,
    150, 250
computational theorising, 12, 257
computationalism, 92, 104
computer-based immortality, 145
computer-human interfaces, 154
computers, 6, 15, 20, 70, 72, 88, 118,
    124, 154, 172, 178
  code, 233
  electronic, 15
  models, 15–16, 241–242, 246
  moral, 173
  programs, 15, 23, 54, 88, 257, 259
  technology, 136, 143, 161
  vision, 193
computing technology, 153, 179, 283
confessional belief, 16
conflict, religious, 6
conscious agents, 93

consciousness, 3, 33, 39–42, 45–46,
    56–58, 111, 114, 120, 153, 172,
    193–198
  as awareness, 39–40
  cyber, 145
  sociopolitical, 193–199
  state of, 270, 272
  white centered, 219
consciousness (cit), 39, 41, 45, 47
contemplating AI, 170
contemplative science, 257, 273
conversational agents, 275–277
conversational technologies, 291
cosmologies, 99, 126
  Buddhist, 58–59, 62
  Islamic, 127
  nondualist, 41, 60
cosmos, 81, 90, 118, 126
creation, theistic, 231
credit assignment problem, 23
cyberneticians, 3, 6
cybernetics, 3–4, 6, 18, 72, 113, 126,
    136, 150, 157
  medieval precursor, 126
cyberspace, 137–138, 146, 154, 160
cyborg, 90, 96, 105, 137–138, 143
cycle of rebirth, 38

Dalai Lama, 55
darśan (auspicious sight), 42–47
darśanas (philosophical 'ways of
    seeing'), 37
Dartmouth Summer Research Project
    (1956), 2–3
data, 19, 22, 37, 70, 89, 145, 156, 162,
    166, 168, 187, 197, 198, 245, 254
  human, 229
  points, 22, 187, 196, 198
datasets, 89, 162, 185, 187, 229, 236
de-anthropocentrism, 139
death, 169
  overcoming, 150
  reality of, 144
Deep Blue (chess programme), 89
deep learning, 89, 113
DeepMind's AlphaGo Zero, 155
DeepSpeech2, 123
demi-gods, 59
demons, 78–81
demystification, 226
dependent origination (Sk.
    pratītyasamuptpāda, Jp. engi), 56, 59
deus ex machina, 202

INDEX

315

dharma (righteous behaviour), 38
dharmic (righteous) life, 41
dharmic religion, 52. *See also* Buddhism
dialog system, 277, 290
Diamond Sutra, 51
digital model, 242
Digital Religion, 12
Digital Theology, 12
discourse, 2–3, 6, 10–11, 111–112, 127,
    165, 183, 229
    AI and Islam, 112–116
    thought, 238
disembodied AI, 99–100
disenchantment, 214–215, 228
dissociative state, 269–270
divine, 44–47, 78, 82
divine communication, 45
divine creation, 82–83
divine emulation, 82
divine *Logos*, 98
divine power, 79
divine work, 83
divinity, 43, 137
doctrine of non-self, 55
doctrine of the incarnation, 92
Drake's equation, 158
dualism, 52, 115, 214
    cartesian, 57, 150, 214
    of consciousness/awareness, 40
    mind-body, 39–40, 101–102
Durkheim, Émile, 225–226
dystopianism, 2

East Asian AI/robotics, 54
ELIZA (conversational engine),
    275–276
embodied AI, 19
embodied intelligence, 203
embodiment, 19, 40, 95, 97, 102, 112,
    173, 178, 188, 192, 194, 235,
    250, 288
emotions, 16, 19–21, 26, 29, 114,
    151, 175, 187, 202, 204, 206–208,
    210–212, 214–215, 217, 249–250,
    260–261, 278, 289
enhanced propositional intelligence, 272
enhancement, 131, 139–140, 143
    ethical, 175
eschatologies, 100, 166, 231, 236
essentialism, 5
ethics, 38, 67, 71, 74, 76, 112, 171,
    173, 176–179, 186, 197, 206, 216,
    218–219, 286

boundaries, 167, 175
concerns, 165–166, 174, 238,
    253–254, 277
issues, 15, 103, 165, 167–168, 209, 250
Kantian, 217
practical, 64, 165, 167, 170, 172
secular, 169
ethical companion, 283, 285
evolution, 47, 92, 101, 103, 114, 117,
    131, 133–134, 138–139, 141,
    143–144, 149, 153–155, 159–160,
    230, 254
    laws, 161
    teleological, 176, 180
extropy, 141–142

facial recognition software, 65, 185–186
faith, 10–11, 95–96, 98–99, 149, 169,
    171, 257
    confessional, 16
    secularist, 146
    traditions, 12, 257
familiarity, 202, 204, 208–209
fiqh (Islamic jurisprudence), 110
flesh (*sarx*), 97
Floating Man argument, 121
FOReST model (Future of Religious and
    Secular Transitions), 247–248
forum posts, 236
functional hermeneutics, 94
fundamental nature, 59, 176–177
fundamentalism, 96, 228
futurists, 90, 140, 145, 149–150, 155,
    162, 279

Gakutensoku (first Japanese robot), 58
gazes, 188–189, 191, 196, 227
general Companion agent, 283
general computational theory of
    spiritual intelligence, 272
Genesis (artificial system), 25–26, 80,
    94, 178, 202, 214, 218
genetic engineering, 143
gentiles, 85, 96
glossolalia, 266, 269–270
go and chess, 22
God, 6, 9, 27, 40, 58, 77–80, 82–85, 92,
    95, 97–98, 100, 102, 104, 109–110,
    114, 116–117, 119, 126–127, 131,
    149, 152–153, 187, 199, 204,
    213–214, 218, 280
    as co-creator, 94, 198
    dead, 138, 146, 154

INDEX

God (cont.)
  image of, 88, 93–94, 132, 137, 202, 219
  nondefinable, 105
  praise of, 269
Goddess, 35
Godlike, 82, 110, 137, 230, 279–280
godlike AI, 280
god(s), 6, 9, 36–38, 42, 44–47, 52–53,
    59, 83, 90, 133, 138, 153,
    232–233, 280
  making, 280
  robotic, 43
God's special status, 82
GOFAI (good old-fashioned AI), 261
Golem, 71–72, 80–82, 84–85, 124
  tradition, 124
GOLEM (computer), 71. *See also*
    Scholem, Gershom
Google, 8, 161, 186, 235, 288
GPT3 (Generative Pre trained
    Transformer 3), 289–290
Grace, 95
Great Filter, 159
Greco-Roman world, 75

hajj (pilgrimage to Makkah), 124
halakhah (Jewish Law), 72
Hare Krishnas. *See* ISKCON
    (International Society for Krishna
    Consciousness)
Heart Sutra, 50
heresy, 6
here-there dichotomy, 226
heretic, 79
hesychasm (the Jesus Prayer), 266–268
heuristic programming, 3, 95
Hindu, 40, 42, 44, 61
  beliefs, 33, 36–37
  practices, 33–35, 37–39, 42–43, 46–47
  religious experience, 33
  religious practice, 33, 39, 46
  thought, 33, 38–39, 41
Hinduism, 33–47, 52
  schools, 37–38, 40, 45, 47
holiday festivals, 39
holy, 44–45
Hughes, James, 55, 59
human agency, 72–76
human agents, simulated, 253
human cognition, 20, 89, 100, 257–261
human condition, 139, 142–144, 152,
    163, 172–173
human creation, 82, 83
human distinctiveness, 95, 100

human exclusivity, 97
human identity, 27, 211
human intelligence, 4, 15, 17–19, 22,
    25, 29, 89, 113–114, 117, 119, 126,
    140–141, 149, 156, 169
  as key to humanity, 167
  reproduction, 28, 159
human knowledge, 111, 117,
    155–156, 250
human labour, 75–76
human learning, 96
human mind, 12, 95, 118, 241–242,
    259, 272
human nature, 112, 134, 136, 138, 143,
    167, 173, 175–176, 203
  concept, 126–127
human perfection, 134
human power, 82
human semantics, 157
human simulation (modeling
    approach), 244
human soul, 58, 120, 233
human uniqueness, 76–81, 217
human-centred approach, 237
human–computer interactions, 20,
    259, 261
human-equivalent robots, 46
humanity's special status, 77, 79–81, 86
humanity's unique value, 79. *See also*
    humanity's uniqueness
humanity's uniqueness, 71
Humanity+, 142. *See also* WTA (World
    Transhumanist Association)
human-level AI, 100
human-like robot, 15, 29
human–machine interactions, 207
humanness, 216–217, 219
human-nonhuman relationships, 217
humanoid robots, 36, 50, 97–101
humanoids, 79–80
human–robot interaction, 21, 45, 207
human–robot relationships,
    201–220
humans, 15–17, 20, 22, 27–29, 36–37,
    40–41, 47, 56, 58–60, 62, 65,
    67, 75–77, 79–86, 88–90, 92–95,
    97–98, 100–104, 114, 118–120,
    127, 131, 134–136, 139, 142, 144,
    146, 148–151, 153, 155, 160–161,
    165, 167, 169, 171, 173, 175–177,
    179–180, 202–213, 216–219,
    225–227, 229–230, 233–234, 237,
    241, 258–260, 272, 278–282
  enhanced, 139

humility, 96, 163, 170, 288
hybridity, 143, 215–216
hyper-rational mind, 95

Ibn Sina, 120–122
ICS (cognitive model), 25, 259, 264–266,
    268–273
ICS (Interacting Cognitive Subsystems),
    25, 258–266
iCub (robot), 203–204, 212
IEEE (Institute of Electrical and
    Electronics Engineers), 8, 64
I–it relationship, 103
image of God (*imago Dei*), 88, 93–95,
    99–101, 132, 137, 202, 204, 209,
    213, 219, 233–234
image of God (*tzelem*), 77
image recognition, 89
imago Dei, 93–95, 99–101, 202, 204,
    209, 213, 219, 233–234. *See also*
    image of God (*imago Dei*)
imago hominis, 204, 208–209, 211–212,
    217, 219
imitation game, 136
immortality, 40, 140, 144–146,
    149–150, 152
    cybernetic, 150
incarnation, 42, 52, 92, 198, 281
Indian automata, 34
Indians, 35, 37
information technology, 136
intellectus, 92
intelligence, 7, 23–24, 54–55, 57, 93–94,
    96, 101, 109–110, 116, 118, 122,
    127, 133, 150–153, 167, 177–178,
    180, 194, 202–203, 209, 249,
    272, 284
    definition, 120, 148
    human, 4, 15, 17–19, 22, 25, 29, 89,
        113–114, 117, 119, 126, 140, 149,
        156, 169, 229, 241
    human level, 90–91, 95, 105, 155, 157
    human-like, 19, 241
    superhuman, 141, 154–155
intelligent artifices, 70
intelligent extraterrestrial life, 157
intelligent machines, 20, 40, 47, 88,
    98–99, 145, 178
intelligent system, 23, 73, 112, 242
intelligibility, 118–119, 246
intentionality, 10, 41–42, 66, 114
Internet, 42, 153, 157, 161, 281–282
Internet events, 234, 236
IRL (in real life), 197, 234

ISKCON (International Society for
    Krishna Consciousness), 35
Islam, 109–127, 234, 280
    philosophy and theology, 115
    science, 123, 127
    Sunni, 115
Islamic automata, 124–127
Islamic jurisprudence (*fiqh*), 110
Islamic ontology of beings, 119
Islamic theology, 110–111, 120, 122
    schools, 117
Islamic thought, 116–122, 126
Israel's Tzomet Institute, 76
ISSP (International Social Survey
    Programme), 245–246
I–Thou relationship, 100
I–You relationship, 103

Jain theory, 41
Japanese death culture, 50
Japanese robotics, 53–54, 58, 66
Jesus Christ, 137
Jesus Singularity, 13
Jewish AI ideology, 76
Jewish history, 69, 72
Jewish intellectual tradition, 70
Jewish law (*halakhah*), 72–76, 85
Jewish thought, 69–86, 124
Jews, 69–70, 75, 77, 85
jinn, 119–120
Judaism, 69–72, 280

Kalki, 36–37, 43, 47
Karma, 38
karma (past deeds), 38, 41
Kismet (animatronic robot), 204, 206
knowledge, 24, 35, 40, 53, 72, 83,
    110–114, 116–119, 121–122,
    124–125, 127, 135, 142, 155–156,
    160, 172, 179–180, 184, 209,
    237, 250–251, 255, 277–278,
    282–285, 288
    of God, 117
Krishna, 35, 37, 41, 44
Kurzweil, Ray, 140, 144, 150–151, 162,
    180, 280
kuyō (Japanese posthumous rituals),
    61–62

LaMDA (Language Model for Dialogue
    Applications), 7–8, 10
language pattern matching system, 276
liminal entity, 231
liminality, 230–232

INDEX

lived religion, 51, 65
lovotics, 206, 210–211

MAAI model (multi-agent artificial
intelligence), 244–246, 250–254
machine conversationalist, 278
machine intelligence, 7–8, 139
machine learning, 3, 96, 115, 119, 149,
162, 193, 254, 282
approaches, 7, 116, 278
network-based, 285
techniques, 19
machine-dependent humans, 144
machine–human conversation, 276
machine-mind, 10
machines, 6–7, 58, 90, 116, 141
anthropomorphic, 209
body, 47
consciousness, 15, 33, 41–42, 47, 112,
114–115, 193
conversational interactions, 289
enculturation, 24
feelings, 20
intelligence, 7–8, 139
knowledge, 110–111
morality, 171
religious, 281
rights, 193
thinking, 136
MAGA, 228
Maimonides, 71, 84
mantras, 47
Marx, Karl, 280
materialism, 114, 118
MAxiM (multiple axialities model), 248
McCarthy, John, 3, 71
meditation, 8, 38, 53, 266, 270–271,
279, 287
MERV model (mutual escalation of
religious violence), 245
metacognition, 157
metaphors, religious, 235–236, 238–239
metaphysical research programme, 112
Metaverse, 170, 237
mind, 9–10, 16, 24–25, 33, 39–41, 44–45,
54–59, 62, 66, 91, 95, 102, 114–115,
117–118, 126–127, 139, 144–145,
150, 160–161, 180, 207–208, 210,
214, 233, 237, 242, 249, 257, 259,
263, 265, 267–268, 270–272
as machine, 9
material, 39–40, 146
Mindar Bodhisattva, (AI/robotic
system), 60

mindclones, 145
mindfile. *See* mindclones
mindfulness, 259–266
practice, 262–263, 265–268
mindware. *See* mindclones
Minsky, Marvin, 3, 18, 23, 71–72, 148
MiRo (bot), 211
Mishnah, 73, 77, 83
mobile applications, 123
models of human(e)ness, 219
mokṣa (individual liberation), 38,
40–42
monastic tradition, 287
monotheistic religions, 280
Moore's law, 143, 156
moral agency, 17
human, 71–74, 76
moral agents, artificial, 16–17, 96
moral being, 172
moral life, 52, 95, 173, 176
moral machine, 174
moral progress, 176
moral respect, 177
moral stance towards AI, 69
moral status, 105
of *someone*, 101
moral status of AI, 93, 177
moral values, 96, 167, 179
morality, 29, 168, 171–174, 176
boost, 175
failings, 175
Mori Masahiro, 53
mortality, 79, 100, 144, 149–150
Moses, 78, 180
multi-agent AI, 252
multilevel validation, 254
mūrti, 42–47
Muslims, 123–126
mystical magic, 81
myth of technology, 144

narrative intelligence, 24, 29
narratives, 2, 12, 22–27, 44, 60, 226, 231,
235–237, 284
'AI is rationalising', 230
atheist, 11
creation, 92
experience, 23
golem, 82, 85
life, 44, 62
processing of, 23
Qur'anic, 116
rabbinic, 80
religion and AI, 236

INDEX

319

religion and space travel, 137
religious, 2, 4, 6, 82, 137, 231
science fiction, 2, 112, 236
of secularisation, 11, 223
of temple gods, 44
narrow AI, 111, 230
natural language processing, 23, 89, 104
NBIC (nanotechnology, biotechnology, information, and cognitive science), 112
Negative meditation (*via negativa*), 270
neural network approaches, 111
new atheist, 233
Nissei Eco, 50, 66
non-conscious AI, 46
non-dualistic framing of artificial entities, 54
non/human binary, 218
non-human spaces, 7
NoRM model (non-religiosity model), 245–246
normative ethical theory, 170
NRM (New Religious Movements), 11, 227–228, 232–233, 236, 243, 281
AI-focused, 236
NSIM (Neolithic social investment model), 248

objectivity, 185, 224
online speech, 238
otherness, 204–205, 214, 216, 218, 269

panopticism, 188
panopticon, 188–189, 236
pāpa (unmeritorious actions), 38
parable, 84
Paro (Japanese robot-pet), 103, 211
PARRY (conversational engine), 276–277
pastoral care, 287
pattern recognition, 229
Pepper (humanoid robot), 50–51, 66–67
perception–action cycle, 18, 28
perceptrons, 197
perfectibilitism, evolutionary, 138
perfectibility, 132–140, 143, 173
persona, 92–93, 103, 237
personhood, 11, 19, 21, 27, 29, 92–94, 99–100, 166, 177–178, 202, 204, 207–208, 214, 232, 236–237
development of, 22, 29
human, 28

moral boundaries, 55
as moral status, 177
robot, 21
personifying AI, 162
person–machine interaction, 136
physical symbol system hypothesis, 17–18, 29
physical-grounding hypothesis, 18
policing, 184, 189–192
Pope Francis, 96
positive meditation (*via positiva*), 271
post-biological future, 140, 145
posthuman, 139–140, 160, 163
posthumanist thought, 215
posthumanity, 140
pratītyasamuptpāda ("dependent origination"), 56, 59
priests, 8, 37, 44, 50–51, 66, 168, 281
Brahmin, 44
Hindu, 43
robot, 51, 206, 235
primitive religion, 225
progress, 4, 16–19, 90, 105, 133, 136, 138–139, 141, 143, 157, 168–169, 175–176, 178–180, 188, 259
Prophet Abraham, 109
Prophet Muhammad, 109, 123
propositional semantics, 260
prosopon, 92–93, 103
prototypical whiteness, 184
pūjā (worship), 39, 42–46, 61
punya (meritorious actions), 38
pure awareness, 39

QAnon, 228
Qur'an, 109, 113–114, 116–120, 123
Qur'anic Arabic, 123

rabbinic authorities, 69
rabbinic origin story, 83
rabbis, 73, 75–77, 79–80, 83
racism, 191
categorical, 193–196
scientific, 197
structural, 193, 198
Rapaport, Anatol, 6, 8
ratio, 92, 185
Rava, 80, 82
reason, 5–6, 9, 16, 20, 47, 54, 57, 62, 65, 72, 74, 76, 94, 97–98, 103–104, 106, 109, 117–119, 122, 142, 149, 156, 167, 169, 171, 177, 180, 182, 203, 214–215, 217, 262, 282, 291
redemption, 47, 95, 97–98, 102

320 INDEX

reinforcement learning, 18, 22, 29
  deep, 29
relational hermeneutics, 94
relational thought, 215
relationality, 63, 93–94, 99–100, 102,
  139–140, 203–205, 214–216
relationships, 16, 19–22, 25–30, 46–47,
  67, 70, 103, 190, 201–220, 232, 234,
  246, 249, 266–267, 283–284
  human, 21, 23, 36, 95, 205–206,
  208, 210
  with robots, 201–202, 204–205, 208,
  210–211, 217, 219
religiosity, 8, 96, 225, 227–228, 231,
  233, 238, 241–242, 244–247, 249
  levels, 245
religious, 2, 4, 6–7, 9–11, 36–37, 39–42,
  45–47, 51, 59, 82, 96, 98–99, 123,
  125, 232–233, 235–236, 241–255,
  257, 261
  alt-right, 228
  appropriation, 235
  behaviour, 225
  beliefs, 4, 8, 12–13, 34, 140, 147, 151,
  224, 243, 246, 249, 251
  cognition, 243, 249–250
  expression, 183
  fundamentalism, 228
  groups, 36, 243, 245, 250
  leaders, 72, 82
  meme culture, 238
  mind, 250, 257
  overtones, 166, 168
  phenomena, 241, 244
  practice, 22, 33, 39, 46, 255, 281–283
  reasoning, 16–17, 21–22, 24, 29, 273
  reproduction, 28, 140, 247
  ritual, 34, 44, 245
  studies, critical, 4
  systems, 241, 244, 247
  terminology, 235, 237
  traditions, 33, 37, 59, 72, 99, 149,
  177–178, 180, 233–235, 279
religious AI, 13, 96
religious companion, 282
religious historians of AI, 69
responsa literature, 73
resurrection, 101, 146, 151–154
risk assessment tool, 197
rites of passage, 231
rituals, 34, 36, 38, 40, 42–44, 46–47,
  50–53, 61, 63, 66, 74, 77, 82, 85, 96,
  124, 226, 235–236, 241, 245, 247, 250

practice, 34, 37, 40, 43, 46–47, 125
process, 43, 231
transition, 39
robo-anthropology, 237
robomorphisation, 2
robot action, 18
robot hermeneutics, 98
robot participation, 96
robot perception, 18
robot religion, 95
robotheology, 98–99
robotic 'death', 61
robotic moment, 205
robotic mūrti, 44–45
robotic technology, 44
robotics, 37, 43–45, 50–67, 99–101, 125,
  203–205, 208–210, 214
  Japanese, 53–54, 58, 66, 99, 103
robots, 9, 17–18, 21, 24, 33–37, 42–43,
  45, 54, 59–65, 72, 88, 97–100,
  102, 201–202, 206, 208, 212–214,
  216–217, 219, 281
  as assistants, 36
  Christian, 96
  consecrated, 43, 45
  definition, 53
  embodied, 101, 177
  emotions, 219
  enchantment, 214, 217
  ethical, 63–65, 211, 217
  experience, 62–63, 65
  as holographic images, 45
  human-like. See androids
  intelligent, 45, 47, 94–96, 98, 102
  lack of body, 97
  moral, 62, 64
  non-human, 213
  pet-like, 212
  as products, 210
  redemption, 98, 102
  sentient, 105
  social, 60, 203–207, 209–212, 214,
  218, 220
  as superior ritual practitioners, 43
  use in ritual practice, 37, 43
ROSS (AI lawyer), 196–197

sacred order, 127
sacred/profane dichotomy, 232
sādhus (ascetic renunciants), 34, 36, 43
salvation, 57, 92, 100, 145–146, 148–152
saṃsāra, 38, 41, 52
SanTO (robot priest), 206

INDEX   321

sarx (flesh), 97
Schank, Roger, 23, 26, 284
Scholem, Gershom, 71
science fiction, 2, 71, 112, 149, 233, 236
scientistic rationalism, 230
SDMs (system dynamics models),
   241–242, 246–249, 254
Searle, John, 9–10, 91, 113–114
secular religion, 146
secularisation, 11, 223, 226, 228, 230,
   235, 245, 247, 255
secularisation process, 230
secularisation thesis, 227
self, 23, 28, 41, 55, 58, 62, 121, 150, 194
   as self-awareness, 121
   sense of, 264
self-awareness, 21, 93, 115, 121–122,
   180, 195
   development of, 40
self-consciousness, 56, 134
selfhood, 91–92
sense of otherness, 269
SETI (Search for Extra-Terrestrial
   Intelligence), 157
Shabbat, 75–76, 79
shabbes goy, 75
Shinto, 59
Siddhārtha Gautama, 52
Simon, Herbert A., 3, 71–72, 113, 148
simulating religion, 241–255, 257
simulations, 24, 91, 154, 229, 242–245,
   247, 250–252, 254, 261, 285
   computational, 241, 249, 251–255
sin, 5–10, 12, 85, 95, 123, 135, 137,
   168, 204
Singularity, 115, 140–141, 154–157
   hypothesis, 141
   warnings, 155
smartphones, 42, 170
social media, 13, 149, 172, 223,
   236, 238
sociology, 16, 113, 206, 223–239
software, 50, 63, 65–66, 70, 76, 144, 150,
   156, 159, 162, 185–186, 289
Solomonoff, Ray, 71–72
soteriology, 97
souls, 10, 39–41, 56, 58, 77, 94, 97,
   114–115, 117, 120–122, 150, 196,
   233, 237, 281
   rational, 120–121
specialness, 77, 81
spiritual companion, 275, 287–288,
   290–291

spiritual intelligence, 272–273, 286
spiritual mind, 257
spiritual practices, 52, 257–273
   dissociative, 269–270
spiritual reflection, 273
spiritual work, 268
spirituality, 3–5, 80, 137, 270, 288, 290
strong AI, 91, 94–95, 97, 114
strong story hypothesis, 25
Stuart Mill, John, 170
subsumption architecture, 18
sunnah, 123
super-agential AI, 230
superintelligence, 141, 152–155,
   279–281
superintelligent agents, 110
superintelligent AGI, 153, 157, 161
superintelligent AI, 64, 149, 231
   dreams of, 163
superintelligent technological being.
   Vedi posthuman, 139
superman, 138–139
superminds, 154
supernatural agents, 245, 247, 250
supervised learning, 115–116
surveillance, 124–125, 168, 182, 184,
   187–192

Talmud, 73, 79–82
   Babylonian, 75, 79
   Palestinian, 77
   Tractate Bava Kamma, 74
   Tractate Makkot, 74
Tarteel.ai, 123
tawhīd (principle of divine unity), 109
tech giants, 168
techno sapiens, 140, 145–146
techno-human, 135, 137, 144
technoimmortality, 145
technological bottleneck, 157–163
technological revolution, 13, 88
Technological Singularity, 140–141,
   169, 280
technologies of the self, 3
technology, 1–2, 12–13, 29, 33–36, 42,
   44, 51–52, 63–64, 66–67, 69–70,
   81, 86, 99, 102, 105, 112, 123–124,
   126–127, 131, 134–137, 139–144,
   146, 150–152, 155, 157, 159–161,
   168–169, 174, 176, 178–180,
   182–183, 187, 227–229, 231, 233,
   242, 255, 283, 287
   persuasive, 168

temples, 35–36, 39, 42–45, 50, 60, 62, 66
temporal frame, 234
theodicy, 101
theory of mind, 24–25, 40–41, 55,
  207–208, 210, 214
Three Laws of Robotics, 71. *See also*
  Asimov, Isaac
Torah, 77–78, 83
Tosefta, 75
Tower of Babel, 84
transcendence, 131–147
  human, 135
  secular, 139
transference, 85, 235
transhumanism, 114, 131–147, 169, 234,
  279–280
  Enlightenment, 139, 142
  Romantic, 139–140
  roots, 139
transhumanists, 6, 13, 55, 131, 136,
  139–140, 142, 144–146, 279, 282
trasumanar, 131–132
tropes, 4, 6, 11, 66, 112, 231, 235
  religious, 11
True Believer, 8–10
true self, 38
Turing, Alan, 136
Turing Test, 209, 284
tzelem (image of God), 77

Übermensch. *See* superman
Ulam, Stanislaw, 141
uncanny valley hypothesis, 209
uniqueness, 71
  of God, 109
  of humans, 76–81
  sense of, 219
universe, 38, 77, 90, 101, 118, 126,
  133–134, 153, 154, 157, 180
utilitarianism, 166, 170
utopianism, 2

values, 16, 24, 63, 82, 90, 96, 138, 140,
  155, 166–169, 173, 175, 179, 184,
  196, 213, 233, 239, 243
  ethical, 175
  of technology, 179
Van Gennep, Arnold, 231
varṇa/jātī (caste) social structure, 38
vedas, 37–38
via negativa (negative meditation), 270
via positiva (positive meditation), 271
virtual artificial neural networks, 89
virtual reality, 144, 153, 156, 170,
  237–238
virtual spaces, 236
Vishnu, 36–38, 40, 44

weak AI, 91, 94, 97, 103
weak robot, 65
Web 2.0, 13
Weber, Max, 226–227, 229
WEIRD (Western, educated,
  industrialized, rich and
  democratic), 6
Western Buddhist Modernism, 53
Western imperialism, 195
white gaze, 188, 191
white supremacy, 184–187,
  189–190, 192
whiteness, 184–185, 191, 196–197
Wizard of Oz paradigm, 276
Wizard of Oz technique, 276
womanhood, 191
worship, 42, 44–45, 53, 79, 97, 109, 123,
  179, 279, 281
  acts of, 123
WTA (World Transhumanist
  Association), 141–144

Xian'er (AI/robotic system), 60, 67

Zoroastrians, 79

CAMBRIDGE COMPANIONS TO RELIGION (*continued from page ii*)

Other Titles in the Series

FRANCIS OF ASSISI Edited by Michael J. P. Robson

GENESIS Edited by Bill T. Arnold

THE GOSPELS Edited by Stephen C. Barton

THE GOSPELS, SECOND EDITION Edited by Stephen C. Barton and Todd Brewer

THE HEBREW BIBLE/OLD TESTAMENT Edited by Stephen B. Chapman and Marvin A. Sweeney

HEBREW BIBLE AND ETHICS Edited by C. L. Crouch

THE JESUITS Edited by Thomas Worcester

JESUS Edited by Markus Bockmuehl

JOSEPH RATZINGER Edited by Daniel Cardó and Uwe Michael Lang

JUDAISM AND LAW Edited by Christine Hayes

C. S. LEWIS Edited by Robert MacSwain and Michael Ward

LIBERATION THEOLOGY Edited by Chris Rowland

MARTIN LUTHER Edited by Donald K. McKim

MEDIEVAL JEWISH PHILOSOPHY Edited by Daniel H. Frank and Oliver Leaman

MODERN JEWISH PHILOSOPHY Edited by Michael L. Morgan and Peter Eli Gordon

MOHAMMED Edited by Jonathan E. Brockup

THE NEW CAMBRIDGE COMPANION TO BIBLICAL INTERPRETATION Edited by Ian Boxhall and Bradley C. Gregory

THE NEW CAMBRIDGE COMPANION TO CHRISTIAN DOCTRINE Edited by Michael Allen

THE NEW CAMBRIDGE COMPANION TO ST. PAUL Edited by Bruce W. Longenecker

NEW RELIGIOUS MOVEMENTS Edited by Olav Hammer and Mikael Rothstein

NEW TESTAMENT Edited by Patrick Gray

PENTECOSTALISM Edited by Cecil M. Robeck, Jr and Amos Yong

POSTMODERN THEOLOGY Edited by Kevin J. Vanhoozer

THE PROBLEM OF EVIL Edited by Chad Meister and Paul K. Moser

PURITANISM Edited by John Coffey and Paul C. H. Lim

QUAKERISM Edited by Stephen W. Angell and Pink Dandelion

THE QUR'AN Edited by Jane Dammen McAuliffe

KARL RAHNER Edited by Declan Marmion and Mary E. Hines

REFORMATION THEOLOGY Edited by David Bagchi and David C. Steinmetz

REFORMED THEOLOGY Edited by Paul T. Nimmo and David A. S. Fergusson

RELIGION AND TERRORISM Edited by James R. Lewis

RELIGIOUS EXPERIENCE Edited by Paul K. Moser and Chad Meister

RELIGIOUS STUDIES Edited by Robert A. Orsi

FREIDRICH SCHLEIERMACHER Edited by Jacqueline Mariña

SCIENCE AND RELIGION Edited by Peter Harrison

ST. PAUL Edited by James D. G. Dunn

SUFISM Edited by Lloyd Ridgeon

THE SUMMA THEOLOGIAE Edited by Philip McCosker and Denys Turner

THE TALMUD AND RABBINIC LITERATURE Edited by Charlotte E. Fonrobert and Martin S. Jaffee

THE TRINITY Edited by Peter C. Phan

HANS URS VON BALTHASAR Edited by Edward T. Oakes and David Moss

VATICAN II Edited by Richard R. Gaillardetz

JOHN WESLEY Edited by Randy L. Maddox and Jason E. Vickers

BIBLICAL WISDOM LITERATURE Edited by Katharine J. Dell, Suzanna R. Millar, and Arthur Jan Keefer

Printed in the United States
by Baker & Taylor Publisher Services